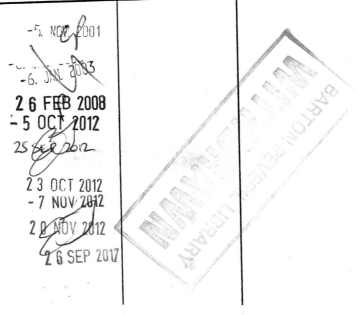

BARTON PEVERIL COLLEGE LIBRARY
EASTLEIGH

This book must be returned on or before the last date stamped below

-5. NOV 2001

-6. JAN 2003

2 6 FEB 2008

- 5 OCT 2012

25 SEP 2012

2 3 OCT 2012

- 7 NOV 2012

2 0 NOV 2012

2 6 SEP 2017

Barton Peveril College Library

171953

Author	Shelf Number
KOLB, E	943. 085 KOL

D1353597

The Weimar Republic

The Weimar Republic

EBERHARD KOLB

Translated from the German by P. S. Falla

London and New York

This translation © Unwin Hyman, 1988

Die Originalansgabe erschien unter dem Titel Eberhard Kolb, *Die Weimarer Republik* im R. Oldenbourg Verlag München, Wien, © 1984 by R. Oldenbourg Verglag GmbH München.

This translation first published in 1988 by Unwin Hyman
Second Impression 1990

Reprinted 1992 by Routledge
11 New Fetter Lane, London EC4P 4EE
29 West 35th Street, New York NY 10001

British Library Cataloguing in Publication Data

Kolb, Eberhard, 1933–
 The Weimar Republic.
1. Germany 1918–1933
I. Title II. Die Weimarer Republik. English
943.085

Library of Congress Cataloguing in Publication Data

Kolb, Eberhard, 1933–
 The Weimar Republik.
 Translation of: Die Weimarer Republik.
 Bibliography: p.
 Includes index.
 1. Germany—History—1918–1933. I. Title.
DD237.K6713 1988 943.085 88–72

ISBN 0–415–09077–6

Typeset in 10 on 12 point Plantin by Grove Graphics
and printed in Great Britain by Mackays of Chatham

Contents

Contents

Preface

Although the Weimar Republic existed only for the relatively short span of about fourteen years, it has proved a difficult task to describe its history and outline the state of research concerning it, within closely prescribed limits of space. The history of these fourteen years is immensely complex and full of events; and the international consequences of the collapse of the Weimar democracy in themselves call for a particularly careful analysis of its causes, which, however, can only be suggested in outline in a brief survey such as the present.

As regards the development and present state of research, it has also been necessary to confine this book to essential aspects. For decades past, German and international research has been so intensively devoted to the Weimar era that it is difficult even for a specialist to give a full account of the relevant literature. A detailed account of the progress and achievement of research on all aspects of the Weimar period would exceed the bounds prescribed for this work; the most that can be done is to indicate the most important results and to throw light on some problem areas that have at times been the subject of controversy. It should be pointed out that the narrative part of this work and the account of research activities are closely interwoven; so that a number of events that are only briefly mentioned in the first part are described and discussed in more detail in the second.

The arrangement of the material and the selection of problems for fuller discussion were governed by the fact that the book is designed for students and teachers as well as general readers who are interested in history.

I extend my warm thanks to those who have helped me in many ways: in particular to Dr Klaus Schönhoven of Würzburg, who not only read the manuscript and furnished expert comment, but to whom I owe many stimulating conversations about the Weimar period. My assistants in Cologne – Dr Peter Alter, Hans-Georg Fleck, Christine Lattek and Georg Mölich – have given me valuable help as the work progressed. I also owe thanks to my secretary, Renate Kolwert, for typing the manuscript. Finally I wish warmly to thank Professor Lothar Gall for his attention and consideration and for subjecting the manuscript to a thorough and fruitful scrutiny.

Eberhard Kolb,
Cologne, April 1983

Part II has been brought up to date for the English edition. The bibliography has been revised to take account of works published until February 1987, and several English-language titles have been added.

Eberhard Kolb,
Cologne, March 1987

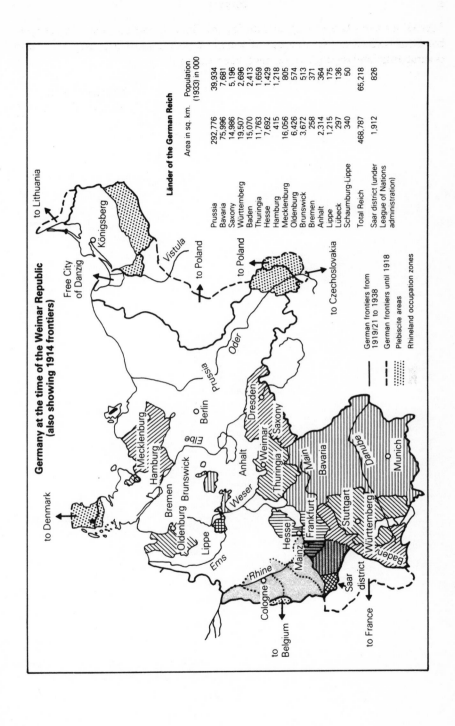

Germany at the time of the Weimar Republic
(also showing 1914 frontiers)

Länder of the German Reich	Area in sq. km.	Population (1933) in 000
Prussia	292,776	39,934
Bavaria	75,996	7,681
Saxony	14,986	5,196
Württemberg	19,507	2,696
Baden	15,070	2,413
Thuringia	11,763	1,659
Hesse	7,692	1,429
Hamburg	415	1,218
Mecklenburg	16,056	805
Oldenburg	6,426	574
Brunswick	3,672	513
Bremen	258	371
Anhalt	2,314	364
Lippe	1,215	175
Lübeck	297	136
Schaumburg-Lippe	340	50
Total Reich	468,787	65,218
Saar district (under League of Nations administration)	1,912	826

to Lithuania

Königsberg

Free City of Danzig

Vistula

to Poland

to Poland

to Czechoslovakia

Oder

Prussia

German frontiers from 1919/21 to 1938
German frontiers until 1918
Plebiscite areas
Rhineland occupation zones

Mecklenburg

Berlin

Dresden

Elbe

Hamburg

Weimar   Saxony

Bremen   Anhalt

Brunswick   Thuringia   Main   Bavaria

Oldenburg   Weser

Lippe   Munich

Ems   Hesse

Danube

Rhine   Mainz   Frankfurt   Stuttgart   Württemberg

Cologne   Baden

Saar district

to Belgium

to France

to Denmark

List of Abbreviations

(a) *In the text*

ADGB	Allgemeiner deutscher Gewerkschaftsbund (General German Trade Union Congress)
BVP	Bayerische Volkspartei (Bavarian People's Party: Catholic)
DDP	Deutsche Demokratische Partei (German Democratic Party: liberal)
DNVP	Deutschnationale Volkspartei (German National People's Party: nationalist)
DVP	Deutsche Volkspartei (German People's Party: national liberal)
KPD	Kommunistische Partei Deutschlands (German Communist Party)
NSDAP	Nationalsozialistische Deutsche Arbeiterpartei (National Socialist German Workers' Party: National Socialists, or Nazis)
OHL	Oberste Heeresleitung (Army High Command)
SA	Sturmabteilung (Nazi storm troopers)
SPD	Sozialdemokratische Partei Deutschlands (Social Democratic Party: Social Democrats)
SS	Schutzstaffel (Nazi élite guard)
USPD	Unabhängige Sozialdemokratische Partei Deutschlands (Independent Social Democratic Party: Independent Socialists)

(b) *Periodicals cited in Part Two and the Bibliography*

AfS	*Archiv für Sozialgeschichte*
GG	*Geschichte und Gesellschaft*
GWU	*Geschichte in Wissenschaft und Unterricht*
HZ	*Historische Zeitschrift*
IWK	*Internationale wissenschaftliche Korrespondenz zur Geschichte der deutschen Arbeiterbewegung*
JMH	*Journal of Modern History*
MGM	*Militärgeschichtliche Mitteilungen*
NPL	*Neue Politische Literatur*
PVS	*Politische Vierteljahresschrift*
VfZg	*Vierteljahrshefte für Zeitgeschichte*

PART ONE

Historical Survey

(A) ORIGIN AND CONSOLIDATION OF THE REPUBLIC, 1918/19–1923

1

The Revolution and the Foundation of the Republic, 1918/19

The Weimar Republic has been called a 'makeshift democracy'. This suggestive phrase is intended to convey that the first German democracy was not the achievement of a strong republican movement with its roots in many sections of the population, which strove systematically over a long period to transform the monarchical, authoritarian state and finally succeeded in doing so by a major effort. Rather, it was improvised as an 'emergency solution' to mitigate, as far as possible, the effects on the German people of defeat in the First World War. When it failed to produce the desired result, and the victorious Allies imposed an oppressive peace despite the establishment of a democratic republic, the new constitution was thereby discredited in the eyes of a great majority of the population: the republic, which many had not wanted anyway, had failed to perform the service expected of it. Thus the foundations of the improvised democracy were shaky from the outset.

The above interpretation of the origin and first beginnings of the Weimar Republic is partly right and partly wrong. Certainly until the last days of the war no major political group contemplated the substitution of a republic for the monarchy. There was no strong republican movement in German politics. The left-wing liberals who had had republican leanings before, during and even after the 1848 Revolution had long since come to terms with the monarchical regime. Even the Social Democrats, whose programme still included the replacement of the monarchy by a republic, did not in practice regard this objective as a primary one to be pursued with their utmost strength.

But the 'improvisation' theory does not do justice to certain important factors. First, even before the military leaders admitted that the war was lost, a majority in the Reichstag (the Majority Socialists, the Centre Party and the Progressives) had intensified their efforts to extend parliamentary government and so strengthen the democratic element in the constitution. Thus the transition from a constitutional to a parliamentary monarchy, at least, was not simply improvised, but deliberately engineered by powerful political forces. Secondly,

though the republic certainly began its life in highly unpropitious circumstances, these did not necessarily determine the degree of solidity or fragility of
the first German democracy; the specific form of the republic was first determined during the months of the revolutionary period. Thirdly, even after the
initial phase was completed, the last word had not yet been spoken on the
longer-term viability of the Weimar democracy. The French Third Republic
had come into being in the 1870s as a result of defeat in war, and in its first
phase had to fight for its life in the face of a massive attack by anti-republican
forces, but in the long run it consolidated itself as a democratic republic. We
should therefore guard against assuming that the fate of the Weimar democracy
was sealed from the outset because it had not been achieved by a democratic
republican people's movement, but was the direct consequence of a defeat and
was saddled with the after-effects of a war that Germany had lost.

Whatever view we may take in general of the stability and flexibility of the
German Empire and its capacity for political development, it had weathered the
difficulties of the war as long as the great majority of Germans were borne up
by the belief in ultimate victory. It was only when this belief faded and military
defeat was in sight that the political and social tensions of the empire, which
were partly latent and partly manifest, rapidly developed into an acute political
crisis that ended in the collapse of the state, the coming of revolution and the
founding of the republic.

Until the summer of 1918 the parties of the Reichstag majority had pursued
their policy of extending the power of Parliament with caution rather than
impetuosity; but from July–August onwards, as the military situation of the
Central Powers grew rapidly worse, drastic changes soon ensued in home
affairs. After the Austro-Hungarian peace note of 14 September and the collapse
of Bulgaria (armistice, 30 September) the Army High Command (Oberste
Heeresleitung, OHL) was obliged to recognize that Germany had lost the war
and that only an immediate armistice could prevent a military disaster.

The OHL made this declaration of bankruptcy at a GHQ conference at Spa
in Belgium on 28–29 September, attended by leading representatives of the
imperial regime. It was decided to address an appeal immediately to President
Wilson for an armistice and peace, and to support this on the home front by
establishing a parliamentary government, a decree to this effect being issued on
30 September. On this basis, with the OHL still pressing for the immediate
dispatch of the request for an armistice, negotiations were conducted for the
formation of a new government. Prince Max of Baden, who was appointed
Chancellor on 3 October, formed this government in full consultation with the
parties of the Reichstag majority, and thus a decisive step was taken on the path
from constitutional to parliamentary monarchy.

However, to present the transition to a parliamentary system in the dying days
of the empire as a 'revolution from above', brought about by the Emperor
William II and the OHL, would be an undue simplification of the extremely

complex process by which the constitutional structure of the country was transformed in the autumn of 1918. As recent research has shown, the majority parties in the Reichstag were far from obediently assuming power as mere instruments of Ludendorff's intentions. They had of their own accord taken the initiative in the constitutional crisis, before the decision was taken at GHQ at the end of September to make way for parliamentary government. On 28 September the inter-party committee which co-ordinated the action of the majority parties in Parliament called for an amendment of the constitution as a 'precondition for the creation of a strong government supported by the confidence of a majority of the Reichstag'. Beyond question this initiative of 28 September had ample force behind it, as the majority parties were determined to make full use of the potential power that the Reichstag had displayed by its peace resolution in July 1917. If, in September 1918, matters did not come to a showdown between the OHL and the Reichstag majority, it was because Ludendorff, seeing that the military situation was hopeless, judged it wiser to let the parties take power, and thus place on them the responsibility for terminating the war effort.

The first parliamentary government of the Reich began to function in the most unfavourable conditions that could be imagined: the first task imposed on it by the OHL was to sue for an armistice. It was not until 2 October, in the midst of negotiations for the formation of a new majority government, that the leaders of the parliamentary party groups were informed by a representative of the OHL that the hopeless military situation made an immediate armistice necessary. Prince Max of Baden fought desperately for at least a few days' delay, but in vain. Ludendorff demanded that the note to Wilson should be sent at once: 'The army cannot wait 48 hours.' The new government bowed to the OHL ultimatum. On the evening of 3 October the German government asked the US President to bring about the 'restoration of peace' on the basis he had laid down, especially his Fourteen Points. Then came the momentous sentence: 'To avoid further bloodshed the German government requests the immediate conclusion of an armistice on land, at sea and in the air.'

This frank acknowledgment of defeat came as a bombshell to the German public, which was completely unprepared for it. To the very last, the great majority had believed the overoptimistic estimates of the war situation that had been systematically put about by official propaganda. The request for an armistice suddenly and dramatically revealed that this propaganda was illusory, and from then on the German people's only desire was to see the war ended, as quickly as possible and at any price. The peace movement gathered momentum like an avalanche in the course of October; it grew increasingly radical in complexion, exposing the government and parties to strong pressure from below. The revolutionary groups had hitherto been few in number and weak in organization, and much hampered in their activities by government police measures, but they now received ever-increasing support and encouragement from the population.

Although popular opinion was not primarily anti-monarchical, wide circles of both the bourgeoisie and the working class increasingly feared that it might be impossible to put a rapid end to hostilities on the strength of the constitutional changes so far introduced. To achieve peace, people were ready to call for more radical political changes, and even the Kaiser's abdication.

This radicalization of the peace movement was triggered off by Wilson's replies to the German offer. Above all, his third note of 23 October contained alarming passages which aroused deep depression in Germany, but also an increasing determination to comply with his terms for the sake of peace. The President declared unmistakably that if the US government had to negotiate with military rulers and autocratic monarchs, 'it must demand, not peace negotiations, but surrender'. The German public construed this, whatever its real intent, as meaning that if the Kaiser abdicated Germany would be offered lenient armistice terms. The demand for abdication was voiced more and more insistently, and openly discussed in the press in spite of censorship.

While the exchange of notes with President Wilson was taking place, and was attracting the principal share of public attention, the new government was planning constitutional reform in consultation with the majority parties. The mass of the people scarcely realized at this time the potential scope of the move towards a parliamentary system that was beginning, and for this unawareness the new government and the parties that supported it were in part to blame. The Reichstag – which, given the critical internal and external situation, ought to have played a key role in articulating the demand for a parliamentary system and pushing for constitutional reform — met far too infrequently during October. Having approved of the government declaration on 5 October, it went into recess until the 22nd at the instance of the majority parties. At that time, however, public opinion was chiefly interested not in constitutional reform but in ending the war and in the Kaiser's abdication as a means of doing so.

On 28 October the two Bills 'for the amendment of the Reich constitution' came into force. Although they affected only a few articles of Bismarck's constitution of 1871, they meant the Reich was now a parliamentary monarchy in terms of constitutional law. The essential provisions were that in future the chancellor had to possess the confidence of the Reichstag, and both he and his deputy were responsible to the Bundesrat and the Reichstag for the performance of their duties; members of the Reichstag could henceforth become ministers without having to resign their seats.

While historians differ greatly in their opionion of the viability and prospects of the October reform, it is hardly in doubt that, despite the constitutional change that was then in progress, the monarchy and the army were not prepared to subordinate themselves to the civil government and take orders from it. This was clearly shown on several occasions, of which two were of particular importance. First, the naval leaders, without the government's knowledge, ordered the High Seas Fleet to sail out into the North Sea; and secondly, against the government's will, the Kaiser betook himself to GHQ at Spa, where he was beyond the control of the civil power. This 'flight' to Spa took place at a moment when the internal crisis was reaching its height. The call for abdication grew louder, and on 28 October for the first time sailors of the fleet at its anchorage in the Schillig Roadstead near Wilhelmshaven refused to obey orders. The sailors feared that the object of their commanders' manoeuvre was to undermine the government's policy by launching a last desperate battle against the British, the prospects of which were at least doubtful, and which appeared to the sailors both senseless and irresponsible. The admirals, on the other hand, faithful to a traditional code of honour, were unwilling to surrender tamely without throwing the fleet into action for the last time. About a thousand naval mutineers were arrested at Wilhelmshaven; five ships of the line were sent to Kiel where more arrests took place. Soldiers and sailors, concerned for the fate of their comrades, rallied at Kiel; mass meetings demanded the release of those arrested; shots were fired, soldiers' councils formed and officers disarmed. The commanders were no longer masters of the situation and declared themselves willing to accept the mutineers' demands. By the evening of 4 November Kiel was in the hands of the mutinying sailors and soldiers.

The next few days made clear the full extent of the 'paralysis of the will to maintain order'. The military and police apparatus of the old regime surrendered everywhere, offering virtually no resistance to the rebellion that spread like a forest fire. The sailors swarmed out from Kiel, and wherever they came they were joined by the local garrison of soldiers and by factory workers. Workers' and soldiers' councils were set up; local officials of the workers' parties and trade unions took charge without waiting for instructions from their central offices. This occurred on 6 November in Hamburg, Bremen, Wilhelmshaven and Lübeck; on 7 November in Hanover; and on 8 November in Cologne, Brunswick, Düsseldorf, Leipzig and Frankfurt. It was not a question of a centrally planned campaign of subversive action by revolutionary elements, but a spontaneous outbreak by the war-weary people, who hoped in this way to force their rulers to make peace. However, the movement stirred up a determination, which had hitherto been more or less latent amid wide sections of the population, in favour of a more thoroughgoing reform of the political and social order; this trend was to become more articulate and forceful in the coming months.

The wave of revolution reached the national capital on 9 November, when several conflicting events took place in Berlin. The Chancellor, Prince Max of Baden, was convinced that the monarchy had a chance of survival only if William II and the crown prince abdicated without delay; he therefore made frantic efforts from early dawn to persuade the Kaiser at Spa to authorize him to issue a proclamation to that effect. Towards noon, as armies of demonstrators marched through the streets of the capital and the soldiers in barracks joined the movement, Prince Max announced the Kaiser's abdication, although he did not yet have the authority to do so; at the same time he transferred the office of chancellor to Friedrich Ebert, leader of the SPD. Ebert, with several of his party colleagues, had appeared at the chancellery and demanded that political power should be handed over to those who possessed the 'full confidence of the people'. He declared himself prepared to take over the chancellorship and undertook to govern according to the Reich constitution. The socialist deputation also agreed to the calling of elections for a national constituent assembly. Ebert's object at this time was to head off the revolutionary movement by reconstructing the government on the basis of the October constitution. He had in mind a coalition in which the Independent Socialists (USPD) – an anti-war group which had broken away from the SPD in 1917 – would join the existing majority parties – Social Democrats (SPD), Catholic Centre and Progressive Party – and a caretaker Cabinet with dictatorial powers, to be appointed pending the immediate convening of a national assembly which would decide on the future constitution of the state. Consequently, Ebert was exasperated to learn that his party colleague Scheidemann had already proclaimed the republic to a crowd assembled outside the Reichstag building. Ebert moved into the chancellery with a few assistants, but his chancellorship lasted only a few hours.

The revolutionary groups in Berlin had not stood idly by on 9 November. The Revolutionary Shop Stewards (*revolutionäre Obleute*), who belonged to the left wing of the USPD and enjoyed considerable support among the Berlin workers, persuaded a soldiers' meeting to adopt a resolution that workers' and soldiers' councils would be elected next morning in the Berlin factories and garrisons, and would proceed on the same day to form an assembly and appoint a provisional government. In this way the Berlin soldiers' councils, who were the real holders of power in the capital from the afternoon of the 9th onwards, laid claim to a decisive voice in the formation of the new government.

In this situation Ebert and his colleagues decided to drop the plan for a coalition Cabinet of socialists and the bourgeois parties, and to seek a direct understanding with the USPD leaders, so as to create a *fait accompli* before the assembly of councils could meet; far-reaching though the USPD conditions were, the SPD accepted them for the sake of this overriding aim. Thus, early in the afternoon of the 10th, the two sets of leaders reached agreement on the formation of a new government on a basis of equality: the Council of People's Representatives (Rat der Volksbeauftragten) consisted of three SPD members (Ebert, Scheidemann and Landsberg) and three from the USPD (Haase, Dittmann and Barth).

The assembly of 3,000 delegates elected by the Berlin workers and soldiers greeted the SPD–USPD agreement with wild applause. The mood of the hour was well expressed by the headline in the socialist newspaper *Vorwärts* on 10 November: 'No war between brothers!' The assembly 'confirmed' the Council of People's Representatives as a provisional government but, in addition, reflecting the intentions of the left-wing radicals, it appointed an Executive Council, the Vollzugsrat. Only after heated debate were the Majority Socialists (the SPD

– so-called to distinguish them from the USPD) and soldiers' representatives able to obtain equal membership of this body despite resistance from the Revolutionary Shop Stewards and their supporters. Owing to this equality, and also to the lack of organizational skill and tactical errors by the left-wing members of the Executive Council, the latter was unable to play the part of a revolutionary 'counter-government' to the Council of People's Representatives, as the radicals had intended. Even during the weeks of transition when the country was without a constitution, there was no 'dual control' at the top level as in Russia. By the end of November the Council of People's Representatives had decisively won the trial of strength with the Executive Council. Above all, the Majority Socialist representatives possessed strong support among the 'expert ministers' (heads of government departments) who were nearly all members of bourgeois parties or could be regarded as such (Solf, Preuss, Schiffer, von Krause, Loeth).

As in the Reich as a whole, the monarchical system in the federal German states was abolished in November 1918. The revolutionary governments that seized power there were in some cases composed equally of SPD and USPD members (Prussia, Saxony); Majority Socialists predominated in some (Württemberg, Hesse), Independents in others (Brunswick, Hamburg, Bremen, some small Thuringian states); in others again, some of the ministers represented the middle classes (Baden, Mecklenburg-Schwerin). In Bavaria the revolutionary government, which included SPD and USPD members, were headed by the Independent, Kurt Eisner, who seized the initiative in Munich at the crucial moment and, as early as 7 November, proclaimed the overthrow of the Wittelsbach dynasty and the establishment of a republic.

The fall of the monarchies and the appointment of revolutionary governments of the Reich and the individual states coincided with the ending of the war. An American note received in Berlin on 6 November gave the green light for armistice negotiations, and on the same day a German delegation left for the West. By agreement with the Army High Command it was headed by Matthias Erzberger of the Centre Party; it would certainly have been better for the chief delegate to be a representative of the General Staff, so as to make clear to the world who was actually responsible for the German surrender. The terms presented to the delegation by Marshal Foch were extremely severe. The Germans were to evacuate all occupied territory in the West and the whole left bank of the Rhine, as well as three bridgeheads at Cologne, Mainz and Koblenz; to surrender a large quantity of war *matériel*, the submarine fleet and the High Seas Fleet, as well as locomotives, rolling stock and motor vehicles. Allied prisoners were to be returned without any reciprocal obligation; the peace treaties of Brest Litovsk and Bucharest were to be abrogated; German troops were to be withdrawn from territories in the east, though not until the Allies should so require; the blockade of Germany was to continue. The Army High Command, consulted on the terms, replied that the delegation should try to secure some concessions, but if this was impossible, they should 'accept them nevertheless'. The delegation were only able to obtain a slight postponement of the date for the withdrawal of German troops. The armistice agreement was signed on 11 November. A few hours later the guns fell silent on all fronts, after more than four years of bitter fighting.

Now that hostilities were over, all energies in Germany were concentrated on issues of internal politics. What were the objectives and political strategy of the groups and parties heading the revolutionary movement, as well as the chief members of the revolutionary government, and how did the middle class react to the change of regime?

None of the political groups possessed a patent recipe – a strategy carefully elaborated over a long period and adequate to the acute political and social crisis that had broken out at the end of October. The course of events took all of them completely by surprise. The total and unexpected collapse of the existing order produced a situation for which no one was prepared: neither the political right, which looked on helplessly as if paralysed, and, in the first few days, accepted the fall of the monarchy without any attempt at resistance; nor the bourgeois parties, whose chief concern was the threat of a radical overthrow of the social order; nor the Social Democrats, who had achieved their main objectives with the October reform and on 9 November crossed the Rubicon only with reluctance; nor even the radical left, who had desired and worked for a revolutionary change and who should have been most likely to possess a clear strategy to cope with it. But, until the last days of October, even the left-wing radicals had not reckoned with such a sudden collapse of the imperial regime.

We may begin with the extreme Left, the Spartacus Union (which was organizationally part of the USPD until the end of December 1918). The objective of Karl Liebkneckt, Rosa Luxemburg and their supporters was clear: they wished to see a Soviet Germany in alliance with Soviet Russia. The position reached by 10 November was to them an unendurable half-way house: 'On with the revolution' was their cry. Accordingly, they called for the abolition of the Council of People's Representatives; the immediate transfer of political power to the workers' and soldiers' councils; cancellation of the decision to convene a national assembly; the disarming of the police, of all officers and 'non-proletarian soldiers'; the creation of a workers' militia; the expropriation of all large and medium-sized agricultural concerns, as well as mines, iron and steel works, and large industrial and commercial firms.

The supporters of Liebknecht and Rosa Luxemburg were certainly not lacking in revolutionary zeal, but they were a small handful: probably at most a thousand when the revolution broke out. The most fervent exponents of the watchword 'All power to the councils' had themselves hardly won a seat on any of those bodies. For that reason they took to the streets, organizing demonstrations in a frenzy of revolutionary impatience and seeking to counterfeit a strength they did not possess. 'Revolutionary gymnastics' was the mocking comment of the Revolutionary Shop Stewards in Berlin, whose programme was similar to that of the Spartacists but who rejected their tactics. The demonstrations were indeed unsuccessful in the days of November and December, but they were not without consequences. To large sections of the people they gave the impression that the plan to convene a national assembly – the common aim of all bourgeois circles, the Social Democrats and most of the workers' and soldiers' councils – was in danger; many, too, saw the demonstrations as a foretaste of Bolshevist anarchy.

The threat from the left provoked a strong defensive reaction, not only from the middle class but from supporters of social democracy and most of the workers' and soldiers' councils. But, above all, it confirmed the belief of the Social Democratic People's Representatives that it was only in co-operation with the corps of officers and the traditional bureaucracy that they could maintain order and solve day-to-day problems. In this way a vicious circle set in from October onwards. The activities of the extreme left drove the Social Democratic Representatives towards the light; but their strong reliance on the old repositories of power became increasingly unacceptable to many supporters of the Majority Socialists, who wished for the abolition of the 'authoritarian state'.

The Independent Social Democratic Party (USPD) was split internally from the outset of the revolutionary period. Widely different views prevailed among its officials and members concerning key questions of revolutionary policy and the re-ordering of the state and society. Hence the party evolved no coherent strategy: from December onwards its left and right wing to a large extent cancelled each other out and impeded action, though party membership was rising rapidly: about 100,000 in October 1918, over 300,000 in January 1919. (In March 1919 the Majority Social Democrats numbered about a million members.)

The left wing of the USPD sympathized with the radical socialist programme of Liebknecht and Luxemburg; it was opposed to calling a national assembly and was in favour of a system of councils (soviets). However, it rejected the Spartacist tactics of using street demonstrations and rallies to whip up the emotions of anonymous masses whose political stability could not be taken for granted. Instead, the USPD left wing preferred to rely on disciplined action by radical workers in their factories.

For the time being, however, it was still the right wing of the USPD that determined the party's policy. Its members sat on the Council of People's Representatives and on many workers' councils. Like the Majority Social Democrats, they favoured the calling of a national assembly. They did not want an election too early, wishing to lay a foundation of social democracy in the interim; on this point they differed from the Majority Socialists. But it was the decisive weakness of the moderate Independents that they only stood a chance of putting their wishes into effect if the Majority Socialists were prepared to take the same line; and from mid-November onwards it was increasingly clear that this was not the case.

The leaders of the Majority Socialists had attained their political objective with the October reform. They regarded the November revolution as both unnecessary and harmful, as it complicated the solution of all the difficult problems arising out of the defeat and the cessation of hostilities: the withdrawal of the armies within the short time-limit imposed by the armistice; food supplies; conversion of the economy from a war to a peace-time footing; reabsorption on to the labour market of soldiers returning from the front and disbanded from their garrisons; preservation of the unity of the Reich; execution of the armistice terms and preparation for peace negotiations. All these tasks had to be tackled at once in the feverish, revolutionary atmosphere of November 1918, and in the Majority Socialists' view they could only be mastered if the civil service was functioning properly, disturbances of public order and economic life were reduced to a minimum, and firm discipline was maintained among the returning troops and in army barracks. Hence the Majority Socialist leaders were vitally interested in obtaining loyal support from the ruling élite of the empire – the bureaucracy, expecially its upper echelons, big business and the officers' corps. As they saw the priorities, it was inopportune to introduce drastic structural reforms at once, as the USPD advocated, or even to take preliminary social and economic measures designed to provide a firmer foundation for eventual parliamentary democracy (cf. below, pages 141 ff.). Instead, from 9 November onwards the Majority Social Democrats did their best to channel the revolutionary movement into the calmer waters of an election campaign. Pending the convocation of the National Assembly they governed on a strictly caretaker basis, leaving to the assembly all important decisions concerning the new political and social order.

During the first weeks after the revolution, in November and December, the decisive political initiative lay with the left-wing parties and groups, while the middle class and its political organizations played a largely passive role. The military defeat and revolutionary events, the uncertain future and the fear of a major social upheaval initially had a paralysing effect on large sections of the middle class. The situation following the collapse of the state called imperatively for organizational reform and political reorientation; only the future could show how much of this reflected a genuine change and how much was merely a concession to the spirit of the time.

On the political right a new party came into existence, the German National People's Party (Deutschnationale Volkspartei – DNVP). It consisted basically of the previous conservative parties (Deutschkonservative and Reichspartei), together with anti-Semites from the old and new middle class, some sections of the working class who voted on denominational lines, and part of the heavy-industrial wing of the old National Liberal Party. The DNVP was loyal to the monarchical constitution, the social basis and values of the Kaiser's Germany; it saw itself as a party of conviction, dedicated to the restoration of the national spirit, but had at the same time close ties with the world of industry and the landowning classes.

The (Catholic) Centre Party attempted at an early stage, but unsuccessfully, to establish itself as a non-denominational group under the name Christian People's Party. It continued to be the main electoral force representing Catholic voters, with a wide social span from aristocratic landowners to Christian trade unionists. While the overthrow of the Protestant dynasty of Hohenzollern might inspire various political hopes, in large sections of the party there could be no question of active allegiance to republicanism; this was especially the case in Bavaria, where the local Centre Party constituted itself as an independent group at the end of 1918 (Bayerische Volkspartei – BVP).

The liberals did not succeed in forming a united party. At the outset the newly founded German Democratic Party (Deutsche Demokratische Partei – DDP) offered a broader political spectrum than its effective predecessor, the Progressive People's Party. But a section of the National Liberals refrained from joining the DDP, and certain individuals were deliberately excluded, as being politically discredited by their annexationist policy during the war years. In December 1918 these members of the former National Liberal Party founded the German People's Party (Deutsche Volkspartei – DVP) under the leadership of Gustav Stresemann, the last chairman of the National Liberals in the Reichstag. Meanwhile, in the months of revolution the DDP served as a focus for the hopes of the non-Catholic bourgeoisie that the party would adapt itself to the new forms of parliamentary democracy and that, by prudently accepting social change, it would achieve political stability and enable the middle class to play a major role in the new society.

Having thus surveyed the forces in the political arena after 9 November 1918, we may cast a glance at the principal events and stages of the internal struggle during the first months after the revolution.

As early as 10 November an agreement was achieved between Ebert and General Groener, who had succeeded Ludendorff as quartermaster-general of the army on 26 October and was the dominant personality at Army Headquarters during the revolutionary months. Both men were anxious to come to terms on a basis that would not shake the foundations of the state; they were both firmly opposed to a leftward development, and wished to restore the 'rule of law' as quickly as possible by convening a national constituent assembly. Consequently Groener gave a promise of loyalty to the new government on behalf of the OHL. In return he expected the Council of People's Representatives to support the attempts of the high command to maintain discipline in the ranks and preserve the authority of the officer corps. To this Ebert consented; it was hard to do otherwise in the confused situation of 10 November. But it did not necessarily follow from this agreement (which has been wrongly presented as an 'offensive alliance' in internal affairs) that Ebert and the Council of People's Representatives were to be permanently dependent on the OHL. The important decisions on military-political affairs were not taken until the following weeks.

From the point of view of damping down agitation on the home front, as the

Majority Socialist leaders desired, an event of at least equal importance was the Central Working Association (Zentralarbeitsgemeinschaft) agreement concluded on 15 November between the employers' associations and the trade unions. Negotiations for the agreement had been instituted by both sides before the revolution. The employers believed that in the stormy period to come they could not rely exclusively on the protection of the state apparatus, and that they should come to a direct understanding with the trade unions to ensure the continuance of a free market economy. The union negotiators put their trust in the partnership of capital and labour and hoped that long-desired reforms could now be put into effect. The agreement of 15 November seemed to justify these hopes. The employers recognized the trade unions as the 'authorized representation of the workers' and as a proper body with which to negotiate collective wage rates; they dropped their support for the more amenable 'yellow' unions (*Werkvereine*); they agreed to the eight-hour day (with full wage adjustment) and the establishment of workers' committees in all concerns with a workforce of at least fifty. By these concessions the employers managed to a large extent to keep the trade union leaders quiet and even to secure their partial support in the debate on basic economic organization. With the idea of 'social partnership' the employers offered a model of how far the demands and interests of the workers could be met without resorting to 'socialization', that is, nationalization. 'Social policy in exchange for renouncing socialization' – such was the employers' strategy during the revolutionary months. The agreement of 15 November 1918 has rightly been described as one of 'mutual benefit between the unions and heavy industry, which in quasi-syndicalist fashion asserted the primacy of the economy over workers' councils, state bureaucracy and a revolutionary government' (Heinrich A. Winkler). In this way, before the party system was constituted and the authorities of the Republic were fully organized, the business world and especially that of heavy industry was able to safeguard and even enlarge its sphere of influence. This success is all the more remarkable since the fighting strength of the unions was appreciably increased by a mass influx of members in the months after the November collapse: for instance, the membership of the 'free trade unions' associated with the workers' parties rose from about 2·8 million at the end of 1918 to 7·3 million at the end of 1919.

The primary aim of the Majority Socialist leaders from 9 November onwards was to convene a national assembly as soon as possible: it was for this body alone, in their view, to take decisions as to the future organization of state and society. Although the left-wing radicals agitated loudly against the plan for a national assembly – their watchword being 'All power to the councils' – a dictatorship of the latter bodies was not on the cards in November 1919. This was clear to anyone whose attention was not fixed exclusively on certain meetings in Berlin. All political forces of importance were in favour of a national assembly: the middle class no less solidly than the SPD and trade unions, even the majority of the USPD, most of the workers' councils and – of especial importance in the initial weeks – practically all the soldiers' councils. On 29 November the Council of People's Representatives passed the law providing for elections to a constituent assembly. Apart from introducing a strict system of proportional representation, probably its most important provision was that, contrary to the state of affairs in imperial Germany, women were henceforth entitled to vote and to stand for election.

The date for the election to the assembly was left to be decided by the first National Congress of Workers' and Soldiers' Councils, which sat in Berlin from 16 to 20 December. Out of about 500 delegates, nearly two-thirds were members of the SPD; less than a dozen were Spartacists; Liebkneckt and Rosa Luxemburg received no mandate. By an overwhelming majority the date for the election was set at 19 January 1919. A proposal to adopt the system of councils as the 'basis of the constitution of the socialist republic', and to invest the councils with supreme legislative and executive power, was rejected by a large majority.

Despite its domination by the Majority Socialists, however, the congress also took decisions which were clearly contrary to the wishes of the party's leaders, and which indicated the direction in which the social democratic workers and soldiers were impatient for the government to move. The congress called on the government to 'put in hand forthwith the socialization of all industries that are ripe for this purpose, especially the mining industry' and to 'take all necessary steps to disarm the counter-revolution'. To symbolize the 'destruction of militarism and the abolition of the doctrine of blind obedience (*Kadavergehorsam*),' all badges of rank and the wearing of uniform off duty were to be prohibited; soldiers were to elect their own officers, and a 'People's militia' (*Volkswehr*) was to be created speedily to replace the standing army.

These demands (the so-called 'Hamburg points') outlined a programme for which there was a broad consensus in the democratic mass movement of those weeks, amounting to the 'democratization' of the army (especially), the civil service and the economy.

> The nationalization of heavy industry was regarded as a matter of course, but not the most urgent priority in view of the acute problems of demobilization and supply. The basic decision in favour of a National Assembly and a parliamentary system did not mean that all decisions concerning the process of democratization were to be left to the assembly. On the contrary, the government was expected to take decisive steps at once to consolidate the power situation brought about by the revolution and to prevent the revival of reactionary forces (R. Rürup).

However, from the end of December the prospects of the government carrying out such a policy of reform in a short time receded from day to day. On 28 December the Independent Socialists withdrew from the Council of People's Representatives. The immediate occasion of their doing so was a difference of opinion as to the justification and advisability of the SPD Representatives' action in using troops to put down the disturbances in Berlin at Christmas time. The underlying cause, however, was the disagreement between the SPD and the USPD on basic policy, especially towards the military and the OHL, together with increasing pressure by the left-wing Independents to persuade the USPD Representatives to withdraw from the goverment and break up the coalition with the SPD. After the resignation of Representatives Haase, Dittmann and Barth, and the accession of the Majority Socialists Noske and Wissell, the Reich government was entirely in the hands of the Majority Socialists, assisted by the imperial bureaucracy and experts from non-socialist parties who were given ministerial posts. On 3 January 1919 the USPD members of the Prussian government also resigned.

While the more moderate elements in the USPD were at this time losing ground – they included the party chairman Haase and the theoreticians Kautsky and Hilferding – the extreme left for the first time organized itself as an independent party: the Spartakusbund (Spartacus Union) and the 'Bremen left-wing radicals' united to form the German Communist Party (Kommunistische Partei Deutschlands – KPD), which held its inaugural congress in Berlin on 1 January 1919. On 5 January the Berlin 'left Radicals' launched the so-called 'January rising' (armed occupation of newspaper offices, appointment of a revolutionary committee, and proclamation of the deposition of the Ebert–Scheidemann government). The rising, conducted by the Revolutionary Shop Stewards and KPD headquarters without a clear strategic plan, was hopelessly mismanaged and to some extent half-hearted. The government used troops to put it down, and for this purpose encouraged the formation of *Freikorps* (anti-Communist volunteer units), which had been developing for some time past and in the ensuing months were used similarly in other parts of the Reich.

The January rising has been called 'the revolution's Battle of the Marne'. Its bloody suppression caused a deep rift within the workers' movement and gave a stimulus to political escalation. The murder of Liebknecht and Rosa Luxemburg on 15 January by members of the Horse Guards Division aroused indignation and horror among many who in no way shared the victims' political views. While the USPD took on a more radical hue, the SPD leaders more and more openly sought close co-operation with the officer corps and higher bureaucracy, and intensified their contacts, which had never been broken off, with the bourgeois parties.

Although from the beginning of January 1919 radicalization made rapid progress not only in Berlin but in other industrial centres, it was not reflected to a great extent in the election to the National Assembly on 19 January (cf. table, pages 194–5). The SPD maintained its dominant position with about 38 per cent of the vote (165 seats out of 423), while the USPD obtained only 7·6 per cent (22 seats). However, a majority in the National Assembly was held by the bourgeois parties who, aided by unrestricted freedom of the press and the right of public assembly, had conducted an intensive electoral campaign. The strongest middle-class party proved to be the Centre (19·7 per cent; 91 seats), closely followed by the DDP (18·5 per cent; 75 seats). The DNVP obtained only 10·3 per cent of votes (44 seats) but, in addition to the traditional conservative strongholds in Germany east of the Elbe, it made some advance among the urban petty bourgeoisie of the west and south. The DVP, which had entered the election campaign relatively late, gained 4·4 per cent of votes (19 seats). Despite visible shifts and changes, the German party system showed remarkable continuity before and after the upheavals of 1918–19. In view of the election result, it was inevitable that the October coalition of Majority Socialists, the Centre and the DDP would develop into the 'Weimar coalition'. This, however, meant that the constitution had to reflect a compromise between the Social Democrats and the bourgeois democratic parties. The way had been prepared for such a compromise in November: on the 15th of that month Hugo Preuss – a respected left-wing liberal, an outspoken opponent of the old authoritarian state, but certainly not a socialist – had been appointed secretary of state in the Ministry of the Interior with the specific task of drafting a constitution.

The National Assembly convened at Weimar on 6 February. The government had chosen that venue under the impact of the January rising in Berlin, intending to protect the assembly from the revolutionary excitement of the capital and demonstrations by the anxious population. As all parties to the right of the USPD were determined to end the transition period as soon as possible, the National Assembly took a very short time to lay the constitutional foundations of the new state. On 8 February a Bill 'Concerning the Provisional Exercise of Political Power' was submitted to the assembly by the Reich government, which had prepared it in consultation with representatives of the state governments, and two days later it was passed, without the assembly having debated its principles or subjected it to a thorough examination.

The interim law, which contained only ten paragraphs, provided for the essential constitutional organs of the republic. (1) The National Assembly was empowered to adopt, in addition to the constitution, 'other urgent national laws', that is, it was vested with the functions of a legislature, the Reichstag; (2) The individual German states were represented by a Committee of States, which had been set up at a conference of representatives of all the states on 25 January and had since then exercised a strong influence on the constitutional discussions; it was to some extent a precursor of the Reichsrat. Laws for the whole Reich were to be passed with the concurrence of the National Assembly and the Committee of States. The states were also given the assurance that their territorial boundaries could not be altered without their consent. (3) The business of the Reich was conducted by a president, to be elected by the National Assembly; he would in turn appoint the Cabinet, whose members must possess the confidence of the National Assembly. While all these arrangements were designated 'provisional', in practice the basic structure of the constitution – with the Reichstag, President and Cabinet – was thus predetermined before the constitutional discussions began.

On 11 February the National Assembly elected Friedrich Ebert to be the first President of the Reich. On the same day Ebert called on Scheidemann, the SPD deputy, to form a government, and on 13 February he appointed the new Reich Cabinet, composed of the Weimar coalition of Majority Socialists, Democrats and the Centre Party.

Some days later the National Assembly began to debate the constitution. The draft prepared by Preuss, now Minister of the Interior, had a complicated history behind it. After full discussion in the ministry, in which the sociologist Max Weber took part, a first version had been prepared at the end of December 1918. This provided for a 'strong president' as a counterweight to the Reichstag, and also made decisive changes in the relationship between the Reich and the individual states. Germany was to be a federal state with markedly unitary features; Prussia was to be split up and other state boundaries altered so as to form sixteen 'Reich districts' (*Gebiete des Reichs*), to which German Austria and Vienna might eventually be added. Preuss's draft was published on 20 January after two important alterations had been made at the direction of the Council of People's Representatives: a short list of basic rights was added, and the specific proposals for changes in territorial boundaries were replaced by a vague indication that such changes might be necessary. The unitary features of the draft aroused the alarm of the individual states, who now became active and secured further modification. The draft submitted to the assembly in February 1919 thus differed in important respects from its author's intention, and Preuss could do no more than hope that the sovereign assembly would set firm bounds to the ambitions of the individual states.

These hopes were to some extent realized. During the discussions, which chiefly took place in the Constitutional Committee of twenty-eight members – and which, from the beginning of May, were overshadowed by the peace terms and the dispute over the signature of the Treaty of Versailles – the tendency was to enlarge the powers of the central government, especially as regards taxation policy and tax administration. The prerogatives of Bavaria and Württemberg in regard to military matters, post and communications were abolished. The states were re-designated as 'lands' (*Länder*). The Reichsrat, representing the *Länder*, had distinctly less power than the Bundesrat before 1918, its functions being confined essentially to advising on legislation.

The 'Weimar constitution', which was adopted by the National Assembly on 31 July and signed by the President on 11 August 1919, established the Reich as a parliamentary republic. Its principal organ was the Reichstag, which enacted legislation and controlled the executive: the Reich government had to possess its confidence. In order to create a strong counterweight to 'parliamentary absolutism', a danger especially feared by the political right, the president was given extensive powers. He was directly elected by the people and thus independent of the parliamentary majority; he held office for seven years and could be re-elected indefinitely; he appointed and dismissed the Reich government; he could dissolve the Reichstag; he could intervene in the legislative process by ordering a referendum; and under Article 48 he could proclaim a state of emergency to preserve public security and order. The parliamentary majority failed to perceive the potential range of this article; it was not a subject of dispute among the coalition parties; and its original version was even strengthened in the course of debate, despite emphatic USPD warnings against giving the president a blank cheque in this way. The USPD deputy Cohn urged the Assembly to consider what might happen under Article 48 'if some henchman of the Hohenzollern, a general perhaps, were to be at the head of the Reich or the Defence Ministry'.

The provisions which made the president a kind of 'ersatz emperor' reflected the mistrust that the fathers of the constitution felt towards a fully parliamentary system on a democratic party basis. The inclusion of plebiscitary elements in the constitution (initiative and referendum) was also primarily designed to set bounds to one-sided parliamentary rule. Thus the founding fathers were not inspired by the doctrine of parliamentary sovereignty as it prevailed, for example, in the British system. This is surprising on the part of the Majority Socialists, conflicting as it did with the constitutional ideas they had previously espoused. In the case of the political centre and right wing, on the other hand, there were specific calculations behind their attitude as well as the force of political tradition. Under an unrestricted parliamentary system the country might one day be governed by a socialist majority – and in January 1919 the two socialist parties already had nearly 50 per cent of the votes between them.

The section of the constitution dealing with fundamental rights became the subject of long and earnest debate when the Liberal leader Friedrich Naumann made a proposal extending the list of basic rights contained in the draft constitution. The discussion threatened to get out of hand as the various political and social groups endeavoured to have their particular ideas and demands written into the constitution. The Centre, for instance, carried through several articles about church and educational affairs, while the workers secured a clause regarding the conversion into public property of 'suitable' private economic concerns; the workers' councils were likewise anchored in the constitution (Articles 156, 165). While some articles sanctioned the economic and social status quo, others offered a handle for its alteration. Thus the section on basic human rights did not reflect any coherent socialist philosophy or programme, but rather the divergences inherent in a modern, pluralistic industrial society. The section exhibited to a special extent the 'undecided' nature (Otto Kirchheimer) of the constitution as a whole, which was a system of political and social compromises between the moderate elements of the workers' movement and the democratic middle class. As such it left many points open, while by the same token leaving room for future development.

Despite the revolutionary circumstances of its origin, the Weimar constitution was strongly influenced by the ideas of bourgeois liberalism, and left-wing liberals played a key part in preparing it: Preuss produced the first draft, Haussmann was the first chairman of the constitutional committee of the National Assembly, while Naumann was the moving spirit in the debate on fundamental rights. The SPD, by contrast, although much the largest party in the Assembly, was able to impart to the document very little of its own constitutional and social programme. There were several reasons for this state of affairs. One was the need for compromise imposed by the conditions of the governmental alliance; another was the fact that the Social Democrats had no clear-cut constitutional theory of their own and consequently had little difficulty in accepting liberal ideas, especially as at this stage it was impossible to forecast clearly how the provisions of the constitution would work out in terms of political and social reality. A further important reason was that in the spring and summer of 1919 the SPD was already in a much weaker position *vis-à-vis* its coalition partners in particular, than it had been in January immediately after the election to the National Assembly.

To explain this we must look briefly at the development of the balance of forces and political climate between January and the early summer of 1919 (cf. also page 142 below). The months from January to April/May were much more turbulent than the previous November/December. In many parts of the Reich major strikes broke out; factories, newspaper offices and public buildings were occupied; some short-lived Republics of Councils (*Räterepubliken*) were set up (for example, Bremen, Munich), and armed clashes took place in many regions. The revolution of 1918–19 came to an end only when the strikes, disturbances and Soviet-type experiments of the spring of 1919 were put down by the massive use of Freikorps formations. The mass movement of these spring months differed greatly in character from that of November/December as regards the radicalization of political aims and forms of action.

While radical forces increasingly took control of the mass movement, making it an instrument of their political aims and activities, at the same time many Majority Socialists and trade unionists withdrew from the movement, which thus forfeited in terms of breadth what it gained by way of radicalism and revolutionary dynamism. Also in these months the USPD was reinforced by many industrial workers who had supported the Majority Socialists during the autumn and winter of 1918. Meanwhile, the leftists in the USPD had decisively gained the upper hand, so that the party now declared itself against parliamentary democracy; workers' councils and shop stewards, with legislative and executive powers, were to 'represent the working population' in political and economic matters, taking the place of parliamentary institutions.

In these months the Majority Socialists paid the price for the political line that their leaders had followed between November and January. An appreciable number of members and supporters left the party, disappointed by its compromise policy of co-operation with the bourgeois parties, the generals and senior bureaucrats. This disappointment and embitterment showed itself in two ways: in the radicalization that caused many SPD supporters to switch to the USPD, and also in increasing resignation and political neutralism on the part of those who did not favour a more radical policy but equally could no longer support the government line, and who therefore, for instance, abstained from voting in the elections. At the Landtag and local elections in the spring of 1919 the SPD suffered considerable, in some cases drastic losses, while the USPD scored important gains and took the lead from the SPD in many places. Thus the radicalization was reflected in election results. Both trends – increasing radicalization and the increasing disinterest of former supporters – caused a decisive weakening of the SPD. Its leaders did little or nothing to check this drift by paying greater attention to the views and demands of their working-class adherents. They reacted to these with irritation, obstinacy and closer contact with their bourgeois partners in the coalition, holding to the strategic concept that had marked their activities since the outbreak of the revolution: namely, a moderate process of political and social change in collaboration with the bourgeois parties, but no radical structural reforms.

If the results of 1918–19 are judged by how far the aims of the revolutionary movement were achieved and how strong a mark they made on the political and social constitution of the Weimar Republic, the verdict can only be that the revolutionary mass movement was essentially a failure, both in its first moderate phase and in its second radical phase. One can speak of a 'revolution that ran aground', and with which none of the chief political groups wished to be identified. Scarcely anyone in Germany had wanted the revolution to develop and come to a stop in the way it did. Some wanted no revolution at all, others a revolution with a quite different result. To this day the revolution of 1918–19 does not rank among the events which, by common consent, represent major positive developments in German history.

It was not exactly democracy that was 'improvised' in Germany in 1918, but the parliamentary republic. The Reich was transformed into a republic in consequence of a total military defeat, involving the heavy burden of an oppressive peace treaty. The first days of the republic were accompanied by bitter conflict, similar in nature to a civil war, between rival views as to the shaping of the new order; more adverse conditions for the foundation of a democracy can hardly be imagined. Thus, when the Weimar state left the hands of its founders in mid-1919, it was undoubtedly a fragile creation, threatened by both left and right. The radical left, frustrated by the failure of the revolution to run its course, denounced it as a bourgeois republic and prepared to overthrow it by force of arms. The right wing, for its part, not only hankered nostalgically for the empire but mustered its forces for an onslaught on parliamentary democracy.

The crucial question for the new order was therefore: would the foundation on which the Weimar Republic was erected prove strong enough in the long run – the alliance, born of expediency, between the moderate wing of the workers' movement and the democratically minded section of the middle class?

Would the leaders of the two groups continue to co-operate loyally on the basis of the political and social compromises entered into in the autumn of 1918 and the revolutionary months, and would their supporters and voters back them in doing so? Only in that case was there any hope that a majority of the population would whole-heartedly accept the new order that had come about so suddenly, or at least come to tolerate it; and this was an indispensable condition of the long-term consolidation and stabilization of the republic.

2

The Paris Peace Conference and the Treaty of Versailles

The statesmen assembled at the Paris conference of 1919 did not succeed in devising a peace settlement in Europe or a world security system that offered any prospect of durability. From the very first, their work was subjected to extensive criticism. The settlement was condemned with particular vehemence by the defeated nations, especially the German people, but it was by no means approved without reservation in the victorious countries: some considered the terms of Versailles and its associated treaties too lenient, others too severe.

At a distance of some decades, and with the sources of information that are now available, the historian is inclined to take a less censorious view of the peacemakers of 1919. The 'irreparable circumstances' (Gerhard Schulz) which brought about the war and conditioned the peace made it extremely difficult, if not impossible, to reach decisions that would endure. In a world war lasting over four years, in which all the great nations of Europe and many non-European states were involved, the propaganda apparatus of both sides had attained unprecedented intensity, whipping up patriotic passions and doing its best to turn the war into a crusade for particular ideals and ideologies, with the inference that the enemy was an incarnation of evil. From this point of view the First World War was already a 'total war', and it also deserved this description inasmuch as each side mobilized its entire economic potential.

As the war was a total one, so was the military collapse of the Central Powers and the victory of the Allies. Since Germany did not surrender until she became completely unable to carry on the fight, she was in no position to negotiate more lenient peace terms as a country might which was prepared, if need be, to go on fighting. Moreover – and this was another aspect of 'total victory' – there was by the end of the war no important neutral state that might have influenced the peace negotiations in favour of the vanquished, either as a mediator or by the threat of intervention. Thus the disputes and conflicts at the peace conference took place not between the Allies and their defeated enemies but within the Allied camp itself.

Given the emotional and expectant mood in the Allied countries, their statesmen could not and would not relinquish the fruits of victory for which their peoples hoped; they were themselves prisoners of the total military victory. In this sense, the course of the peace negotiations was only partly within the Allied statesmen's control.

It was indeed a 'world war' whose consequences they had to deal with. Germany was the central theme of the peace negotiations, but by no means the only one. Recent research has brought into particular prominence the degree to which the Allied statesmen were preoccupied by the anxious, ever-recurring question: 'What is to be done about Russia?' The desire of the Western victors – all capitalist countries – to overthrow or at least 'contain' Soviet power led to Allied intervention in the Russian civil war and also had its affect on discussions of the future of East Central and South-Eastern Europe – the 'lands between', which were intended to form a barrier against Soviet Russia as well as against Germany. France especially hoped to use these countries as a partial substitute for her erstwhile Russian ally and as a *cordon sanitaire* between Germany and the Soviet Union. In the political spectrum of the first half of 1919 the strategy of 'containing' Bolshevik Russia was certainly a factor of the first importance; though it would be an exaggeration to suggest that the Allies' policy towards Germany could be interpreted and evaluated as no more than a function of their policy towards Russia.

But there were also difficult problems to be solved outside Central and Eastern Europe. Complications arose in the Adriatic, where Italy strove for predominance against Serbia, now expanded into the Kingdom of the Serbs, Croats and Slovenes; in the Near East, where the legacy of the Ottoman Empire had to be settled; and in East Asia, where Japanese imperialism had begun its advance. Not the least of the problems was the disposal of the German colonies. All these disputes gave rise to dissension among the victorious powers, which complicated the debate concerning the terms to be imposed on defeated Germany. In view of the worldwide conflicts of interest that were thus coming into prominence, it is not surprising that the Allied representatives in Paris devoted more attention and effort to attempting to compose their own differences and form a common front *vis-à-vis* Germany, than to any real negotiations with their prostrate adversaries.

The peace conference, at which thirty-two states were represented, was opened in Paris by President Poincaré on 18 January 1919. On Wilson's proposal the delegates elected Clemenceau, the French Prime Minister, to be chairman of the conference. The plenary assembly met on only a few occasions – it was scarcely capable of functioning effectively, having over a thousand participants. In the first phase of the conference the Council of Ten acted as the supreme decision-taking body, consisting of the heads of government and foreign ministers of the four great powers – the USA, Britain, France and Italy – and two representatives of Japan. After the first ten weeks its place was taken, on 24 March, by the Council of Four – Wilson, Clemenceau, Lloyd George and Orlando – who debated and decided the knottiest issues without their foreign ministers and without the Japanese, who showed little interest in European disputes and concentrated on securing their Chinese prey. For over three months the Council of Four met almost daily, sometimes several times a day; altogether it held 148 sessions. During that time it exerted weighty authority not only as regards the peace terms to be imposed on Germany and her allies, but in all important matters affecting the pacification of Europe, events in Russia and overseas problems. The compromises on which the overall settlement was based were hammered out in this forum.

Subordinate to the Council of Four and the Council of Foreign Ministers were the committees comprising representatives of the great powers and other allies, assisted by numerous advisers for each country.

President Wilson's chief priority was the creation of the League of Nations. To him this was 'the key to the whole peace', designed to lay the foundation for a world security system based on the rule of law and peaceful compromise among nations. This conception of future peace was by no means confined to Wilson: Smuts, for instance, the South African Prime Minister, contributed a useful study of the idea of a league of nations in a memorandum of December 1918. Wilson was prepared to make many concessions for the sake of bringing the League into existence, believing that any deviations from his principles that might be temporarily necessary could gradually be corrected by the League itself ('The Covenant will put that right'). Despite initial resistance by the European statesmen he succeeded in having the creation of the League placed in the forefront of the conference's work, and the Covenant adopted as an integral part of the peace treaty itself.

The organization of the League was simple and clear. The Assembly, composed of representatives of all member states, was to meet at regular intervals; the Council, on which the great powers were represented as permanent members and some other powers on a non-permanent basis, was to meet once a year or more frequently if necessary; there was a permanent secretariat with headquarters at Geneva, where Assembly and Council sessions also took place.

The Covenant guaranteed the territorial integrity and political independence of member states (Article 10). Thus the possibility of 'reconsideration by Members of the League of treaties which have become inapplicable' (Article 19) was restricted in advance to non-territorial problems. The League thus became the custodian of the territorial status quo created by the peace treaties – a situation welcome to France and the smaller nations, while the defeated countries were unable to work for treaty revision within the framework of the League. Any member state was entitled to request the Council and the Assembly to debate any dispute that arose between it and another member. Various possibilities were envisaged for the settlement of international conflicts: debate by the Council or Assembly, arbitration, reference to the International Court of Justice. In no case was war to be resorted to within three months of an arbitration award or a report by the Council (Article 12). A state which went to war in violation of the Covenant was to be exposed to sanctions by all other members, ranging from the severance of financial and trade relations, that is, an economic boycott, to joint military action (Article 16). The former German colonies and parts of the Ottoman Empire were placed under the administration of particular Allied countries in the form of League of Nations mandates; Article 22 laid down the principle of the mandatories' responsibility and the development of the mandated territories, as far as possible, into self-governing entities. Thus began the process which was gradually to lead to world-wide decolonialization.

The attempt to create a system of collective security by means of the League of Nations is certainly to be regarded as the truly progressive idea of the peace conference. But the new institution soon turned out to be full of weaknesses and beset by problems; it only fulfilled to a small extent the great expectations it had aroused, and came in the end to possess only a shadowy existence. This was not necessarily an inevitable process or one that could have been foreseen when the League was created; it was to a large extent the effect of later developments and decisions.

A particularly grave circumstance was that the idea of the League of Nations was decisively rejected in the USA, so that the very state whose chief representative was the real founder of the League failed to join it. Moreover, the Soviet Union did not become a member until 1934, and the defeated states in 1919 were not at once admitted as Wilson had at first intended. Thus the League began its existence as an association of the victors. France saw it primarily as a means of preserving and consolidating her own power, while the British sought to use it to preserve a balance of power on the Continent. There was no 'revolution in foreign policy' such as had been desired by Wilson and the other supporters of the League idea. International affairs continued to be overwhelmingly a matter of national power politics, buttressed by bilateral and multilateral alliances in the same way as before 1914. The abolition of war as an instrument of policy, for which millions had longed at the end of the First World War, and which was at least attempted by the founders of the League of Nations, did not become a reality.

Wilson's insistence on the priority of the League of Nations was partly due to the fact that from October 1918 onwards he came to perceive that the peace negotiations would lead to difficult debates and severe tension among the victorious powers. Not only the French and British, but also the other Allies showed themselves determined to press their claims and interests to the utmost without regard to Wilson's peace programme as contained in the Fourteen Points and in certain later speeches.

French strategy in the Paris negotiations was based on a doctrine of security based on military, geopolitical and demographic considerations. The French statesmen were conscious that France was momentarily stronger than her eastern neighbour, but weaker in the long run; and they were determined to take advantage of the unique opportunity to reduce German power as far as possible and create a system of French hegemony in Europe. Specifically this meant: larger amputations of territory in eastern and western Germany; drastic restrictions on German armament, and far-reaching reparations demands; a firm French system of alliances especially in Eastern Europe (the *cordon sanitaire*); and generally strengthening France's allies at Germany's expense. A key role was assigned to Poland, which had recovered its independence as a result of the war, and in which France saw a replacement for her former Russian ally. Given the new constellation of power, and also the traditional Polish friendship with France, an enlarged Polish state, amply supplied with armaments, was expected to be a strong bulwark against both Germany and the Soviet Union. The other victorious powers were ready to support Polish claims to a large extent: the thirteenth of Wilson's points had stipulated that Poland should have a frontier based on self-determination and free access to the sea.

The tendency of British policy in the spring of 1919 was to maintain a certain equilibrium on the Continent, limiting French hegemony so as to prevent the undue weakening of Germany and to improve the chances of a lasting peace. The British also feared that if Germany were desperate and deprived of hope she might throw herself into the arms of Bolshevik Russia (Fontainebleau memorandum of 25 March 1919). For this reason Lloyd George opposed French ambitions at several points. But it must not be overlooked that in December 1918 Lloyd George had conducted a campaign of unbridled rhetoric in the ultra-nationalist 'khaki election', leading the British public to expect that their representatives in Paris would insist on widely interpreted demands for reparations. Moreover, as Clemenceau acidly but with some reason pointed out, the British had already achieved their main war aims under the armistice terms — surrender of all U-boats and merchant vessels, interning of the German High Seas Fleet — whereas France's need for security could only be met by appropriate terms of the peace treaty.

None the less, in long and tense discussions Wilson and Lloyd George were able to induce the French to abate their maximum demands as regards Germany's eastern and western frontiers. True, Poland was awarded without a plebiscite the greater part of the provinces of West Prussia and Posen (Poznań). (In the south of East Prussia, and in West Prussia east of the Vistula, a plebiscite on 11 July 1920 resulted in an almost unanimous vote for remaining in Germany.) But Danzig (Gdańsk) was not given to Poland as was originally planned; instead, the town and its surroundings were made into a Free City under the protection of the League of Nations, so that it was able to retain its German character. Again, instead of the original intention to give Poland the whole of Upper Silesia, a plebiscite was held in March 1921 as a result of which the greater part of the area remained German, though Poland gained the central industrial district. Also in the east, Germany ceded the small Hlučín (Hultschin) area to Czechoslovakia and the port and district of Memel to the Allies (French occupation, then Lithuanian sovereignty from 1923/4). Another plebiscite took place in North Schleswig, with the result that the northern part of the area went to Denmark while the southern part remained German.

The question of Germany's western frontier was throughout debated with vehemence in the Council of Four. There was no disagreement about Alsace-Lorraine, however. Wilson had taken up a stand in his Fourteen Points, and the British had recognized the French claim soon after the war began. Hence the territory was returned to France without a plebiscite, while the Eupen-Malmédy area of Prussia was ceded to Belgium. But, in view of Germany's total military defeat, the French government and public opinion perceived a long-awaited opportunity to drive their aggressive neighbour a considerable way further back, perhaps even as far as the Rhine. The French set their sights first on the Saar coal basin and, secondly, if not actually the Rhine frontier, at all events permanent military control of the river and bridgeheads, together with the creation of one or more independent states, detached from the Reich, on the left bank. The principal champion of this plan, supported by President Poincaré, was Marshal Foch ('If we are not on the Rhine, everything is lost').

Wilson firmly rejected the demands of Foch and other French soldiers and politicians, and was supported in principle by Lloyd George; both were opposed to a more or less veiled French annexation of the left bank of the Rhine. Significantly, Clemenceau did not continue to press the French claim at the risk of a split with the Americans and British. In view of their obduracy he withdrew his support from Foch and settled for the demilitarization of the Rhineland and a fifteen-year occupation of the left bank and bridgeheads, which remained German territory. After vehement argument Clemenceau also yielded on the Saar question. The Saar was placed under League of Nations administration for fifteen years, after which a plebiscite was to decide whether the inhabitants wished to belong to France or Germany, or to be independent. Ownership of the Saar coal mines was transferred from Germany to France, with a right of repurchase if the plebiscite turned out in Germany's favour.

Given the strength of French nationalism, these were considerable concessions. Clemenceau agreed to them because he regarded the alliance with Britain and a good understanding with the USA as indispensable conditions of a realistic French security policy. In return for Clemenceau's relative moderation over the Rhine question, Wilson and Lloyd George offered an Anglo-American treaty guaranteeing military support for France if German troops should at any time cross the Rhine without the consent of the League of Nations. This promise, however, was not implemented: after the failure of Wilson's policy with regard to the peace treaty, the US Congress refused to ratify the treaty of guarantee, whereupon the British withdrew also. It was largely for this reason that Clemenceau, who in November 1918 had been acclaimed in France as the 'father of victory', was soon accused of having 'lost the peace'. Large sections of the population, especially leading political circles, regarded the Treaty of Versailles as insufficient and far too moderate, and the right-wing governments that succeeded Clemenceau did their best to revise the peace settlement in the direction of radical nationalist aims.

Apart from the territorial dispositions of the peace (as a result of which Germany lost 15 per cent of her agricultural production, about 20 per cent of her coal, iron and steel industry, and 6–7 per cent of her processing industry), the question of reparations gave rise to acute controversy among the Allies in Paris. After long resistance Wilson finally agrèed to a settlement in complete contrast to his original idea, which had been to confine reparations to two categories: damages on the ground of violations of international law (Belgian neutrality; the illegal treatment of prisoners), and damage suffered by the civilian populations of the states which had been at war with Germany. But the American delegation stood alone in defending this view against a united front of all the other victors, who demanded reparations on a much greater scale, amounting to a complete restitution of all their war costs, particularly as they had incurred large war debts to the USA. (In the Anglo-US agreement of 19 June 1923 the total British funded debt was fixed at 4,600 million dollars; the French debt, by a similar agreement of 29 April 1926, at 4,000 million dollars.) On a strict application of Wilson's principle the British would have come out more or less empty-handed, and accordingly Britain and her Dominions were prominent in pressing for a wider definition of reparations. On this matter Lloyd George was under strong domestic pressure: 233 MPs addressed a telegram to him on 8 April 1919 demanding that Germany be made to acknowledge her debt and to pay a large sum in damages.

It was chiefly Wilson's concern for Lloyd George's internal positions that made him gradually give way over the reparations question, just as he consented to compromise over the Rhineland for the sake of Clemenceau's political survival. If Lloyd George and Clemenceau had been overthrown by their right-wing opponents it might have delayed the peace negotiations or even led to their failure and the collapse of the League of Nations project, and this was something Wilson could not contemplate.

This being the situation at the conference, the reparations dispute was finally settled in April as laid down in Part VIII of the peace treaty. In accordance with the demands of Lloyd George and General Smuts, family allowances and civilian and military pensions were included as war damages. Since France had borne 54·4 per cent of the total material damage suffered by the Allies, but only 38 per cent of the personal damage, adoption of the British proposal meant diminishing France's share. On the other hand, this widening of the definition of reparations imposed a huge burden on Germany. Since the estimates of Allied experts as to Germany's ability to pay differed widely, it was finally agreed not to fix any particular sum for the time being but to set up a Reparations Commission with wide powers to receive, examine and quantify claims against Germany and decide how much she could pay annually in the light of her economic situation.

In order to establish the principle of Germany's total liability for damages, even though these could in practice be only partially exacted, the fateful Article 231 was prefaced to the relevant section of the treaty. This obliged Germany to recognize that she and her allies were responsible for all the damage suffered by the victors as a result of the war imposed upon them. The object of Article 231 was to provide a firm legal basis for the reparations claim by asserting the juridical liability of the Reich for the damage caused. As a result of the exchanges occasioned by Germany's vehement protest against this article, it came to assume, a great deal more strongly than was originally intended, the character of a moral judgement of 'war guilt', which became Germany's trauma for the whole of the Weimar period.

Of the further peace terms imposed on Germany, mention should be made of the disarmament provisions, which were stated to be intended 'to render possible the initiation of a general limitation' of armaments. Germany was to have a professional army limited to 100,000 men, a navy of not more than 15,000 men; the General Staff was to be disbanded, fortresses in the neutral zone dismantled; no submarines, tanks or air force; gas warfare prohibited; supervision by inter-Allied commissions. The penalty clauses included the surrender of war criminals and the indictment of the Kaiser for 'a supreme offence against international morality and the sanctity of treaties'. Finally the union of German Austria with Germany was forbidden (Article 80).

Between January and the beginning of May 1919 no exact information seeped out as to the progress of the discussions among the victors. Consequently neither the German government nor German public opinion had anything like a clear, realistic idea of the scope of the terms to be imposed on Germany. In the 'dreamland of the Armistice period' (Ernst Troeltsch) people still hoped for lenient, 'Wilsonian' peace conditions. Immediately after the armistice the German government began preparing for peace negotiations. Many groups of experts were engaged in collecting material and working up a basis for negotiation. As recent research has shown, the reparations problem occupied a central place in the German preparations.

> All thoughts were concentrated on how Germany's economic potential could be preserved as a power factor and protected from extreme reparations demands; the object was to make the country's defeat inoperative in the economic sphere . . . Thus it was intended to leave the way free for Germany to recover her prewar status as a great power by preserving the social and economic status quo. (Peter Krüger)

However, the intensive German preparations had no effect on the discussions in Paris, as the German delegation was not allowed to take part in them.

The period of illusions ended abruptly on 7 May, when the completed treaty was presented to the German delegation at Versailles. Even the worst pessimists in Germany had not expected such terms. The nation reacted with indignation and alarm; all political parties agreed in rejecting the treaty. At a session of the National Assembly in the great hall of Berlin University on 12 May, Prime Minster Scheidemann declared that in the government's view the treaty was unacceptable: 'What hand would not wither that binds itself and us in these fetters?'

The victorious Allies did not permit any oral discussion of the text; they allowed the German delegation only fourteen days to formulate written observations. The Foreign Minister, Count Brockdorff-Rantzau, who led the German delegation, attacked the basis of the treaty on two main grounds. (1) Wilson's peace programme as expressed in the Fourteen Points, together with the German–American exchange of notes of October 1918. These, the Germans argued, constituted a preliminary treaty binding on both sides, a *pactum de contrahendo*, and the Allies could therefore not rely on any absolute right conferred by victory. A comparison of the Paris terms with Wilson's programme as interpreted by the Germans showed that the two were completely incompatible. (2) The German delegation concentrated its attack on the 'war guilt' thesis. By rebutting the assertion of Germany's guilt for the war they attempted to destroy the moral basis of the Allied terms in general and especially as regards reparations. The German delegation handed over its counter-proposals on 29 May; it was Brockdorff-Rantzau's intention, unless the victors accepted them *in toto*, to refuse to sign the treaty in order, as he hoped, to divide the Allies from one another. At the beginning of June he systematically prepared the German government for this eventuality, which he already regarded as probable. However, the effect of his open resistance was to strengthen Allied solidarity. There can no longer be any doubt that the Allies were determined to take military action if Germany refused to sign the treaty. Foch's plan was to advance along the Main river, disarming south Germany and separating it from the Reich, and to pursue operations in north Germany as far as the Weser. The marshal and those about him actually hoped for a German refusal so that the peace terms could be revised in accordance with their wishes.

The final text of the treaty was presented to the Germans on 16 June. Their counter-proposals had achieved a degree of success on only one point, the question of Upper Silesia, where there was to be a plebiscite instead of an immediate cession of territory. In a covering note the 'war guilt' thesis was expressed much more sharply in the form of a moral judgement upon Germany. The Germans were required to accept the terms within five days, this ultimatum being subsequently amended to seven days.

No party in Germany would of its own accord have been willing to accept the terms; but, given the prevailing constraints, the forces for rejection were not so resolute as the first reactions in May suggested, either in the government or among the population. Brockdorff-Rantzau's plan of action was, rightly, thought by many to be too risky; Hindenburg and Groener declared that there was no hope of resisting an Allied advance by force of arms. At a decisive Cabinet meeting on the night of 18/19 June seven ministers voted for signing the treaty, and seven against. On the 20th, Scheidemann's Cabinet resigned. A new government, which included no DDP members, was formed next day by the Social Democrat Gustav Bauer, with Hermann Müller of the same party as Foreign Minister; the strongest political force in the Cabinet, however, was Erzberger of the Centre Party, who was already recognized as Brockdorff-Rantzau's real opponent and who now, undeterred by the nationalist agitation, was in favour of a conditional acceptance of the peace terms.

On 22 June, a day before the ultimatum was due to expire, the new government declared itself willing to accept the terms with the proviso that it did not acknowledge Germany's responsibility for the war or agree to the condemnation of the Kaiser and the surrender of other individuals for trial. This declaration was approved in the National Assembly by 237 votes to 138. However, the Allied representatives rejected the German conditions and demanded that the treaty be signed without reservation. This brought about fresh confusion in Weimar. With the ultimatum about to expire, and under the threat of a resumption of military operations, the National Assembly passed a resolution on 23 June to the effect that the government, despite the altered circumstances, was still authorized to sign the treaty. Representatives of the DNVP, DVP and DDP had previously stated that they acknowledged the sincerity of the motives of those who voted for signature. The government thereupon informed the Allies on 23 June that they were prepared to accept the peace terms. On 28 June the Foreign Minister, Hermann Müller (SPD), and the Minister of Communications, Johannes Bell (Centre Party), signed the treaty in the Hall of Mirrors at Versailles.

During the ensuing months peace treaties with the other defeated states were signed by the Allies at different localities near Paris: with Austria at St Germain on 10 September 1919, with Bulgaria at Neuilly on 27 November 1919, with Hungary at Trianon on 4 June 1920, and with Turkey at Sèvres on 10 August 1920. Germany's former allies were obliged to limit their armed forces, to pay reparations and to cede large amounts of territory. Austria had to recognize the independence of Hungary, Czechoslovakia, Poland and Yugoslavia, and to cede Eastern Galicia, the Tyrol south of the Brenner Pass, Trieste, Istria and Dalmatia, as well as parts of Carinthia and Carniola. Bulgaria lost parts of Thrace to Greece. After the former Ottoman Empire, Hungary lost the greatest proportion of her territory, namely: Slovakia to the new Czechoslovak republic; Croatia, Slavonia and part of the Banat to Yugoslavia; the rest of the Banat and the whole of Transylvania to Romania. Turkey – whose Parliament did not ratify the Sèvres treaty – was to cede Eastern Thrace, the Aegean Islands, and Smyrna with its hinterland to Greece; Syria and Cilicia to France; Rhodes and the other islands of the Dodecanese to Italy; Mesopotamia (Iraq) and Palestine to Britain, which also exercised a protectorate over Egypt and Arabia. Turkish Armenia, for a short time, became independent.

The states thus deprived of territory were not prepared to acquiesce in the position, and it became the declared object of their policy to bring about a revision of the peace treaties. This was true of Hungary, Bulgaria and, above all, Germany, which throughout the interwar period was the revisionist state *par excellence*.

It has rightly been said that the Treaty of Versailles, depending on one's point of view, was either too severe or too lenient. 'Too severe, since Germany could do no other, from the first moment onwards, than try to shake it off; too lenient, because Germany was not so far weakened as to be deprived of the hope and possibility of either extricating herself from the treaty or tearing it up' (Karl Dietrich Erdmann). In forming a historical judgement today it is important to recognize two points which were insufficiently observed in Germany between the wars, to her own grave disadvantage, owing to the almost unanimous emotional rejection of the 'dictated peace'. On the one hand, the treaty was a heavy encumbrance for a young democracy, and it may be doubted whether the victors acted wisely in visiting the consequences of defeat on those German politicians and parties which shared Wilson's ideas concerning international understanding. But, severe though the terms were, in some respects they were less so than might have been expected from the course of the negotiations. The treaty did have the nature of a compromise: it was not the generous 'Wilsonian peace' that the Germans had fondly hoped for (but that Wilson himself had never intended in such a form), yet neither was it a 'Carthaginian peace' such as had been demanded by influential statesmen and large parts of public opinion in the victorious countries. Secondly, despite the Treaty of Versailles, Germany continued to be a great power with the longer-term prospect of again playing an active part in European affairs, and with greater freedom of movement than she had had in 1914. For Russia had been dislodged from Central Europe and for a long time was absorbed in her internal problems, while, provided Germany pursued a steady and cautious policy towards South-Eastern Europe, that area might in time be turned into an economic and political sphere of German influence. From this point of view we may fully agree with Gerhard Ritter's statement at the end of the Second World War that:

The long-term future offered the best opportunities for a patient, prudent and rational German policy, devoted wholly to making our country an effective peace-keeping agent in Central Europe. The fact that we missed this chance and, in boundless impatience and blind hatred of the so-called 'Versailles system', threw ourselves into the arms of a violent adventurer is the greatest misfortune and the most fatal mistake in modern German history.

3

The Years of Crisis, 1919–23

The conclusion of the peace treaty and the adoption of the Weimar constitution did not usher in a period of internal consolidation. On the contrary, during the first few years the very existence of the political system created in 1918–19 was more than once threatened. Successive governments were confronted by a multitude of political, economic and social problems that seemed almost insoluble; they had to resist fierce attacks from the opponents of parliamentary democracy, and were under massive pressure from outside. In particular, France, where the 1919 elections had returned a conservative-nationalist majority, insisted relentlessly on the precise execution of the peace terms. Further, having failed to obtain their full security demands at the peace conference, the French sought to achieve them in the post-war years and thus 'revise' the Treaty of Versailles at Germany's expense. It is almost a miracle that the Weimar democracy succeeded in maintaining its existence during these years of extreme tribulation in home and foreign affairs. Only after the succession of crises reached and passed its peak in 1923 did a phase begin which seemed to be one of order and stability in home affairs and *détente* in foreign relations.

By 1919 party politics had already formed the pattern they were to display throughout the republic's existence, with fatal results: organized opponents of parliamentary democracy combined from left and right to attack the 'system'. It was already becoming clear that neither the extreme left nor the extreme right saw itself as a loyal opposition whose proper purpose was to take over from the governmental coalition as an alternative government within the framework of the constitution. On the contrary, they were opposed in principle to the system of parliamentary democracy and did their best to destroy it. The extreme right aimed either at a restoration of the pre-democratic monarchy or at a post-democratic dictatorship of a nationalist and plebiscitary character. On the extreme left, a continuous radicalization developed from the beginning of 1919 and culminated in the autumn of that year in an attitude of complete hostility to the parliamentary regime.

The USPD, who had more than 750,000 members by the end of 1919, adopted a programme of action at its congress in Leipzig (30 November–6 December 1919) which concluded: 'The dictatorship of the proletariat is a revolutionary means of abolishing all classes and class domination in order to achieve socialist democracy . . . Socialist society is to be organized according to the system of councils (soviets).' Thus the USPD took an ideological stand which excluded political co-operation with the SPD, let alone a reuniting of the two wings of the socialist workers' movement. Compared to the USPD with its numerous members and increasingly firm organization, the KPD was no more than a splinter party. Its sphere of action was, in any case, small and was further reduced by violent doctrinal disputes: in October 1919 its leaders expelled the ultra-left groups from the party, which in this way lost about half its membership of approximately 100,000.

The second half of 1919 saw no major activity by the left, and even the strike movement became less serious. In January 1920, however, fresh unrest threatened with a rail strike and miners' demands for a six-hour shift, as well as a mass demonstration by the USPD in Berlin followed by an attack on the Reichstag building (13 January 1920). The government declared a state of emergency and quickly brought the situation under control. It continued to regard the left as the chief danger to the political system, and to prepare for further putsches and strikes, while underrating the increasing danger of an upsurge from the right. A close observer, Ernst Troeltsch, noted in December 1919 that the chief supporters of the right-wing assault were the Protestant churches and 'urban and academic elements'. There was, according to Troeltsch, a dramatic change of mood among the student body. 'A year ago, when one spoke of students one had to imagine wildly contradictory strains of pacifism, revolution, and idealistic Bolshevism; today one has to expect protests of an anti-Semitic, nationalist, anti-revolutionary kind. In many law faculties the students scrape the ground with their feet when they hear the words "national constitution".' Apart from the circles mentioned by Troeltsch, however, the 'rightist wave' (*Welle von rechts*) now included many white-collar employees and members of the petty bourgeoisie, who had previously tended to occupy the central ground.

Right-wing publications and rallies combined agitation against the 'shameful peace' (*Schmachfrieden*) with the 'stab in the back' legend: the civilians had betrayed the men at the front, and the political left was therefore responsible for the military defeat and the crushing terms of the peace treaty. Hindenburg lent the authority of his name to this interpretation of the German collapse, in a statement to the Investigation Committee of the National Assembly on 18 November 1919. For the conservative-nationalist right the 'stab in the back' legend, supplemented by the denial of Germany's war guilt, performed a very useful double function. On the one hand, it relieved the old regime of responsibility by covering up the failure of the political and military leaders of imperial Germany; on the other, it laid the blame for defeat, and hence for the unbearable hardships of the present, on the forces of revolution and, directly or indirectly, on the leading figures of the Weimar Republic. Within a few months the legend became a mainstay of the conservative-nationalist ideology of self-justification and aggression. It was effective far beyond the circle of uncompromising opponents of the Republic, since large sections of the population were also loath to admit that Germany had been defeated. It has aptly been said (by Albert Schwarz) that the legend itself operated as a 'stab in the back' of the new-born state.

Erzberger, the Centre Party statesman, was exposed to especially virulent attacks by the rightist opposition. They hated him as the mover of the peace resolution of 1917, the head of the Armistice delegation, the advocate of signing the peace treaty, and as the Finance Minister who, by a major reform, had carried out the intentions of the constitution by asserting the financial authority of the central government over the *Länder*. A blow at Erzberger, the 'Chancellor in secret', would also hit at the 'key point of the system' (Ernst Troeltsch), since it was he who held the Centre–SPD coalition together. A libel action brought by Erzberger against the DNVP leader Helfferich, who had accused him of 'dishonestly combining political activity with his own financial interests', ended after weeks of excitement on 12 March 1920 with a judgement that Helfferich's accusations were partly founded in fact. However, Helfferich was merely fined a derisory sum for technical libel. On the same day, Erzberger resigned his office to the jubilation of the nationalist right. The verdict in the Erzberger case was not the first, but a particularly striking example of a long series of judgements that have made the 'political justice' of the Weimar Republic distressingly famous. Many judges, whose political and social attitudes were stamped by the values and conservative ideology of imperial times, questioned the legitimacy of the new order. Protected by the privilege of irremovability, which the revolutionary government left unchallenged and which was then enshrined in the new constitution, they handed down many judgments which openly expressed their aversion to the republic and its loyal supporters. In this way the judiciary bears a large share of responsibility for the collapse of the republic, 'contributing to its overthrow by authoritarian and totalitarian movements' (Karl Dietrich Bracher).

On 13 March 1920, a day after the verdict in the Erzberger case was announced, right-wing military circles tried to seize power from the government in the Kapp-Lüttwitz putsch. Since the beginning of July 1919 a group of extremists headed by General Ludendorff and Wolfgang Kapp, a rural official from East Prussia and former founding member of the Vaterlandspartei (Patriotic Party), had formed the intention of forcibly overthrowing the government; in October 1919 they established the Nationale Vereinigung (National Association) as their organizational nucleus. The conspirators were active in seeking to recruit officers and politicians for their plan, and were in close contact with General von Lüttwitz, the 'father of the Freikorps', who from the spring of 1919 onwards was in command of all troops east of the Elbe and units in Saxony, Thuringia and Hanover. The reduction of the regular army in accordance with the peace treaty began in the autumn of 1919; many Freikorps members feared for their livelihood and were prepared to take part in anti-government activities.

Kapp, Lüttwitz and their circle planned to take advantage of this mood among the rank and file. At the beginning of March 1920 the government ordered the disbandment of, *inter alia*, the Ehrhardt Marine Brigade which was quartered near Berlin. Thereupon, on 10 March, Lüttwitz called on President Ebert to put a stop to all further disbandment; he also demanded the resignation of the President and government, and fresh elections to the Reichstag. The government responded by dismissing him, whereupon he made his way to the Ehrhardt Brigade, and early on the morning of 13 March the brigade, under his command, occupied the government district of Berlin and proclaimed Kapp as the new Chancellor. Among the army leaders only the commander in chief, General Reinhardt, was prepared to resist the putsch by force of arms; General von Seeckt, head of the camouflaged General Staff (known as the Truppenamt or Troop Bureau), declared that it was impossible to send in troops. Consequently Noske, the Defence Minister, had no force at his disposal to put down the rebellious soldiers in Berlin. Left in the lurch by the military, the President and government fled first to Dresden and then to Stuttgart.

Although the rebels had occupied Berlin without striking a blow, and many army commanders in various parts of Germany were ready to support them, the putsch rapidly collapsed. The trade unions called a general strike, which was spontaneously joined by workers throughout the country, and the national and Prussian bureaucracy adopted a wait-and-see attitude, refusing for the time being to carry out Kapp's orders. On 18 March, Kapp, Lüttwitz and their closest supporters fled to Sweden.

However, the inglorious end of the putsch and the return of the government to Berlin was not followed by drastic action against the militant opponents of the system, as many of the striking workers and democratic elements of the middle class expected and hoped. No practical effect was given to the unions' demands for the expulsion of unreliable elements from the civil service and the military establishment, the punishment of the guilty, the socialization of suitable branches of industry, and a reconstitution of the government in consultation with the union leaders. Noske, however, was obliged to resign: he was anathema not only to radicals but to many working-class socialists. In 1919, on his responsibility Freikorps units had been used ruthlessly against striking or rebellious workers; and it was attributed to his blind trust in the officers' corps that the counter-revolutionaries had organized their putsch under the government's very nose. The new Defence Minister was Otto Gessler (DDP), and the new head of the Army Command (*Chef der Heeresleitung*) was Hans von Seeckt, despite his refusal to allow the army to be used to defeat the putsch.

The failure of the Kapp putsch offered an opportunity for a thorough stabilization of the democratic order. One reason why this opportunity was left largely unused, however, was that in several parts of Germany the reactions of the striking workers had assumed violent dimensions. In Saxony and Thuringia the workers' self-defence units carried out armed attacks on Freikorps and regular troops; in the Ruhr district a 'Red Army' was formed by socialist workers of various tendencies. Supporters of the USPD and syndicalist groups were especially active. The communists gradually gained influence, though their leaders had adopted an ambiguous standpoint and had not at first supported the call for a strike. For several weeks the 'Red Army' controlled large parts of the Ruhr and fought bitterly against the Freikorps troops whom the government sent into action against them; these battles were conducted with great ferocity on both sides. As the government troops penetrated into the demilitarized zone to carry out their operations, the French as a counter-measure temporarily occupied Frankfurt and Darmstadt and the surrounding countryside.

Thus, in order to suppress the rebellions in the Ruhr district and central Germany in particular, the government used the very troops who had displayed at best a highly ambiguous loyalty to the government and state during the Kapp–Lüttwitz putsch. This use of the army constituted, as it were, the bridge over which the Reichswehr marched, with colours flying, into the post-Kapp era. Seeckt turned the Reichswehr into a 'state within the state', largely insulated against parliamentary control. The insistence on its 'non-political' character meant that all demands for a more republican and democratic attitude on the part of the Reichswehr could be repulsed on the ground that they were inadmissible attempts to politicize the army. Thus in the 'Seeckt era' the Reichswehr became a reliable instrument in the hands of its commanders, but it considered itself as owing loyalty only to an abstract idea of the state and not primarily to the parliamentary republic as such. The officers as a body regarded the Reichswehr as an independent factor of power in home affairs; they lived in an ideological world 'in which monarchistic, authoritarian survivals blended with a sense of humiliation due to the lost war and the Versailles system; borne up by an élitist sense of mission; custodians of the "state as a whole", as opposed to the democratic state of political parties, which they regarded in principle as something inferior' (Hagen Schulze). Accordingly, the political left for its part viewed the Reichswehr with pronounced mistrust.

In Bavaria the Kapp putsch can be said to have been successful. The Reichswehr commanders in that state, who were in sympathy with the putsch, obliged the coalition government formed by the Social Democrat Hoffmann to resign; it was replaced by a sharply right-wing government whose object was to make Bavaria a 'focus of order' in the Reich. From 1920 onwards Bavaria was an Eldorado for extreme right organizations and leading personalities of militant right-wing radicalism.

Before the Kapp–Lüttwitz putsch the government had intended to hold elections to the Reichstag in the autumn of 1920 at the earliest. After the defeat of the putsch and of the rebellions in the Ruhr and Central Germany, however, they advanced the date to 6 June. The election was a débâcle for the parties of the 'Weimar coalition'. The SPD and DDP suffered heavy losses, while the opposition parties (DNVP, DVP and USPD) scored huge gains (see table, pages 194–5). The coalition thus lost its parliamentary majority at Reich level, and was destined never to recover it. In the National Assembly the coalition had commanded over 78 per cent of the seats (331 out of 423), whereas now the SPD, Centre and DDP together had only 44.6 per cent (205 seats out of 459). As a result, supporters of the Weimar constitution were confronted in the Reichstag by two compact blocs, the 'red' and the 'red, white and black' (the imperial colours). The normal alternation of government and opposition was thus excluded; the possibility of forming a stable democratic government was in doubt at the outset, and was to remain so throughout the republican period (see pages 66 ff. below). The process of forming a Cabinet in the summer of 1920 was extremely difficult. The SPD, after its drastic losses at the election, showed no desire to take up the reins again, and after long negotiations a minority Cabinet was finally formed by the Centre politician Konstantin Fehrenbach. The DVP was associated with the government, having made a formal declaration of support for the republican system; in addition the government was tolerated by the SPD, which was henceforth 'a kind of cross between a government party and an opposition one' (Alfred Kastning).

The USPD was unable to convert its considerable success at the polls into political influence, as in 1920 it was entirely preoccupied by an internal conflict. Its left wing wanted to join the Communist International (Comintern), which had been set up in March 1919, and was prepared to accept Moscow's terms, namely, that national Communist parties should be completely subordinated to the Executive Committee of the Comintern. The right wing of the USPD firmly rejected this. At the congress in Halle on 12–17 October 1920 the dispute split the party more or less equally (its membership was then about 900,000). The left wing united with the KPD, which for the first time gained a strong base in the working class: on 1 October, before the merger, it had only 78,000 members. The right wing or 'residual USPD' with rather less than half the membership of October 1920, gradually moved closer to the Majority Socialists and merged with them in September 1922.

Soon after the formation of the Fehrenbach Cabinet the question of reparations became the main problem of German foreign policy, and of internal affairs as well. It was to remain a dominant theme, indeed perhaps *the* dominant theme, for years to come. As explained above (page 29), the Treaty of Versailles had laid down the principle of Germany's obligation to pay reparations but had not specified any particular sum. A Reparations Commission, vested with extensive powers, was instructed to report by 1 May 1921 as to the total amount to be paid by Germany, and to work out a plan of payments. By that date Germany, as an advance against the total, was to pay 20,000 million gold marks in the form of money and material assets. However, before the figures were presented it was already clear that they would be extremely high and that the whole problem of reparations would lead to irreconcilable disagreements between Germany and the victorious powers.

The production and transfer of sums of money and goods on a completely un-precedented scale meant advancing into a *terra incognita* of international financial, economic and monetary policy for which all the participants were ill equipped. Above all, the problem was not seen as one that affected the world economy and that could only be solved by a joint effort of all the countries con-cerned; instead, each state was guided solely by its own interest. The Germans tried to get the claim scaled down as much as possible and, if they could, to con-fine it to deliveries in kind. The Allies, on the other hand, took the view that in determining the amount of reparations and mode of payment the main factor must be the creditors' needs, which Germany was bound to satisfy regardless of whether she was actually able to do so. Thus the victors showed no will-ingness to accept increased German exports, though it was only in this way that Germany could compensate for the value of the outgoing reparations payment. National tariff policies, collective prejudices and well-organized interest groups, such as French and British heavy industry, all stood in the way of Germany marketing her goods abroad. Moreover, the transfer of money and goods from Germany scarcely increased the purchasing power of the receiving states, because all of them owed large sums to the USA. Thus a large share of German payments finished up in the USA, whence it returned temporarily to Germany in the form of loans after the stabilization of the mark.

While the economic policy of the victorious powers prevented a rational implementation of the reparations programme, Germany's monetary policy was anything but well designed to facilitate the meeting of her obligations. The legacy of the bankrupt empire to the republican government included a cur-rency that was already gravely undermined. Between 1913 and 1919 the national debt had risen from 5,000 million to 144,000 million marks, as the imperial government had not financed the war by rigorous taxation but chiefly by long-term borrowing (war loans) and by increasing the floating debt; paper money in circulation, including Reichsbank notes, rose from 2,000 million in 1913 to 45,000 million in 1919. The policy of reckless borrowing was continued after 1918: given the very critical internal situation this was the most convenient way, for the time being at least, of coping with the economic and social burdens resulting from the defeat (cost-of-living bonuses, family benefits, unemployment relief, compensation to industries in ceded or occupied areas, compensation to shipowners, interest on war loans). The government and the Reichsbank real-ized, of course, that the currency would not be stabilized as long as the gap between receipts and expenditure, which was only to a minor extent the result of the Versailles obligation, was bridged with paper money instead of by taking firm measures to balance the budget. After 1921 at the latest the only possible remedy was a drastic currency reform; there was no longer any way of balancing the budget by conventional means. By December 1922 the Reich's internal deficit reached 469,000 million marks.

The government's passiveness in the matter of currency stabilization is no doubt to be interpreted as part of its strategy over reparations. The inflation could be turned to account in foreign policy so as to undermine the reparations programme and thus the execution of the peace treaty: for, as long as inflation lasted, there was no means of calculating Germany's ability to pay and to carry out deliveries. The German negotiators did not cease to point this out to their Allied opposite numbers, adding that any cash payment of reparations would only make the situation worse.

The Allies, for their part, firmly refused to agree to a reduction of the sums due or to an extension of the timetable on account of Germany's dire financial situation. They demanded that the German government should immediately create a basis for a realistic calculation of reparations by ceasing to print money and balancing the budget, if necessary by drastically increased taxation.

By their strategy in regard to currency and reparations the German governments down to 1923 were unintentionally playing into the hands of the political forces in France which were interested in politicizing the reparations question. From 1920 onwards, and especially after Poincaré became both Prime Minister and Foreign Minister (17 January 1922), the French government sought to make use of the reparations question to make up for their failure at the Paris peace conference to gain control of the Ruhr district and the left bank of the Rhine. For a time at least they seemed close to success, not least owing to the weaknesses of German policy. Only after 1923, when Germany surrendered for the second time by stabilizing her currency and putting an end to passive resistance in the Ruhr, were the French obliged gradually to abandon their revisionist designs.

Such is an outline of the basic attitudes in the reparations dispute down to 1923. It may be completed by a few details of the negotiations.

In a series of conferences – no fewer than twenty-three in all – the Allied representatives dealt with the amount of the total claim, and the rate and modalities of annual payments. In July 1920 a distribution was agreed according to which France would receive 52 per cent of the total sum, Britain 22 per cent, Italy 10 per cent and Belgium 8 per cent. In January 1921 an inter-Allied conference in Paris agreed on a figure of 226,000 million gold marks for the total debt, to be paid off over forty-two years. At the beginning of March the German government was summoned to accept this decision within four days or make satisfactory counter-proposals, otherwise sanctions would follow. The German government rejected the terms, and on 8 March 1921 French troops occupied Düsseldorf, Duisburg and Ruhrort; the boundary between the occupied area and the rest of Germany became a customs frontier.

The German protests were not entirely without effect, however. In April the Reparations Commission fixed the total claim at 132,000 million gold marks and drew up a schedule known as the London payments plan. The effect of this complex scheme was that Germany would make annual payments of 2,000 million gold marks plus 26 per cent of the value of her exports (about another

1,000 million), the first 1,000 million in gold marks to be paid by 31 August 1921.

The London plan was received in Berlin on 6 May 1921 with a six-day ultimatum from the Allied Supreme Council, threatening immediate occupation of the Ruhr if it was not accepted. Influential circles in Paris were anxious to see the Ruhr occupied and would not have been displeased by a German refusal, but this did not occur. After the resignation of the Fehrenbach government and the formation of a 'Weimar coalition' Cabinet by Wirth (10 May 1921), the Reichstag voted by 220 to 172 to comply with the London ultimatum.

An important factor in this decision was the fear of losing British support in regard to Upper Silesia. The plebiscite provided for by the Treaty of Versailles and held on 20 March 1921 had resulted in Germany's favour: nearly 60 per cent of the votes were cast in favour of remaining in the Reich, while a good 40 per cent were for union with Poland. Thereupon, at the beginning of May 1921 the Poles launched a rising in which they were aided by the French occupying troops, whereas the British, who wished the industrial area to go to Germany, allowed the Germans to organize a defensive force. Despite successes by the Freikorps (storming of the Annaberg, 23 May), the result of the conflict was a bitter disappointment to Germany. On a recommendation by the Council of the League of Nations, the Allied Supreme Council decided on 20 October 1921 to partition the plebiscite area (a possibility for which the Treaty of Versailles had allowed), in a manner unfavourable to German interests. The industrial area in the eastern part of Upper Silesia was given almost entirely to Poland (1,240 square miles with about a million inhabitants, about 56 per cent of whom had voted for Poland), while Germany retained the Western part of the territory, which was larger but industrially less valuable.

The acceptance of the London payments plan by the German government marked the beginning of the 'policy of fulfilment' which was tenaciously opposed by German nationalists. The intention of the policy, which its opponents failed to perceive or regard as valid, was to demonstrate, by complying with the reparations demands to the utmost of Germany's ability, that they were impossible to execute, and thus compel a revision. It was also hoped to improve Germany's position by gaining time in the 'cold war' with France. In the view of Germany's creditors, however, a German policy of fulfilment without a prior stabilization of the currency, that is, a radical curtailment of expenditure and the raising of drastic new taxes, could not be regarded as a serious attempt to meet the country's obligations. Their opinion was reinforced when Germany, after paying the first 1,000 million gold marks, immediately asked her creditors for a moratorium.

On 12 July 1922 the German government requested the Reparations Commission to agree to the suspension of the remaining payments due in that year, and also declared that Germany could make no cash payments in 1923 or 1924. In November 1922 the government went some steps further. As the precondition of a stabilization of the currency it asked to be freed from all obligations under the Treaty of Versailles for three or four years and to be granted an international bank credit of 500 million gold marks; scarcely any reference was made to special efforts on Germany's part, except perhaps in return for further Allied concessions. The 'fulfilment' phase was for the time being at an end.

The 'fulfilment policy' of 1921–2 is connected with the names of Chancellor Wirth and Walther Rathenau (Minister of Reconstruction, then Foreign Minister from January 1922). These two statesmen are also associated with the first manifestation of an independent German foreign policy after 1918: namely, the German–Soviet Treaty of Rapallo, signed on 16 April 1922. By this treaty the powers mutually renounced any claims to compensation for war costs and damage, including civilian damage; Germany, in addition, waived her claims in respect of the nationalization of German property in Russia by the Soviet regime. To Germany the treaty had the advantage of countering Article 116 of the Treaty of Versailles, which had given Russia a vague assurance of reparations from Germany. It was also agreed that German–Soviet trade would be stepped up on a most-favoured-nation basis, and the two countries would enter into full diplomatic relations.

The Rapallo treaty had been preceded by a phase of close economic contact (commercial treaty of 6 May 1921) and limited co-operation between the Reichswehr and the Red Army (exchange of officers for advanced training courses, co-operation in the armaments industry from 1920 onwards). The treaty itself was concluded on the occasion of the Genoa conference, at which no fewer than twenty-eight states assembled in April 1922 to discuss the economic recovery of Central and Eastern Europe. The French government (headed by Poincaré since January) favoured an international financial and economic consortium to raise and allocate the resources necessary for reconstruction in Russia and to exercise some kind of economic supervision over the Soviet government. Behind this was the intention to create a united front, *vis-à-vis* the Soviets, of all European states that had granted credits to pre-revolutionary Russia, or whose nationals had suffered losses due to socialization since the Bolsheviks assumed power. The Russians, seeing the plan for a consortium as designed merely to exploit Russia and infringe her sovereignty, naturally sought to defeat it and instead to make separate agreements with individual powers on the best terms they could. For this purpose Soviet diplomacy endeavoured to exploit Anglo-French tensions and to cultivate closer relations with Germany. In view of the unfriendly attitude of the Western powers at Genoa, the German delegation responded to the Soviet advances as a means of breaking Germany's isolation. The signature of the treaty in fact created a sensation: France and Britain took offence at Germany's action, and the plan for an international consortium was torpedoed.

The Rapallo policy gave rise to controversy in its time, and opinons are still divided as to its significance, scope and consequences. What did Rapallo really mean in the context of German foreign policy? Some advocates of the policy attached far-reaching expectations to it, such as an early German–Soviet assault on Poland or a complete overthrow of the Versailles system. Seeckt, in particular, dreamt of concerted action by the two powers to erase Poland from the map and restore the frontier of 1914 (memorandum of 11 September 1922). But Rapallo did not necessarily portend an eastward orientation of German policy, although many of its supporters would have liked it to: it was also a strategic move towards a policy of normalizing relations with the Western powers (Karl Dietrich Erdmann). The German delegation at Genoa did not use the treaty as a means of playing off the West and East against each other; on the contrary, they even sought to bring about a kind of accommodation between Soviet Russia and the Western powers. Thus the importance of the Rapallo treaty on the international stage should not be overestimated.

It soon became clear how limited the effect of the treaty was. It did not produce a breathing-space for Germany in foreign affairs, or do anything to remove the massive threat on the home front from militant radicalism of the right and left.

In the spring of 1921 the KPD leaders – influenced to a large extent by emissaries of the Comintern, and overestimating the increase of their strength resulting from the accession of the left wing of the USPD – launched a rebellion in the central industrial area of Merseburg, Halle and Mansfeld: the 'March operation' (*Märzaktion*), intended to herald a revolutionary frontal attack on the parliamentary system. The rebellion was suppressed in a few days by the Prussian police, after fierce fighting in some places. The severe defeat and the resulting dissension within the party (leading officials left the KPD or were expelled, the parliamentary section of the party split in two) reduced its ability and desire for action in the ensuing months. But the strength of the Communist movement was by no means broken: it was able to maintain control of most of its organizations, and from the summer of 1921 onwards its 'united front' tactics made inroads on the membership of the SPD and the residual USPD.

The years 1921–2 saw a regrouping and intensified mobilization of the militant right. The right-wing radicals formed patriotic leagues (*Vaterländische Verbände*) and numerous secret organizations, mostly illegal successors to the Freikorps which had by this time been officially disbanded; one of these was the 'Consul' organization, headed by Captain Ehrhardt. Members of these groups increasingly resorted to the weapon of political murder, which had previously been uncommon in Germany. In addition to actual or supposed deserters from their ranks, or individuals suspected of giving away the location of illegal stores of arms (the *Feme* or *Vehmgericht* murders), victims of these crimes included leading representatives of democratic Germany. On 9 June 1921 the USPD leader Karl Gareis was shot dead in Munich; Matthias Erzberger met the same fate in the Black Forest on 26 August 1921; Scheidemann and the journalist

Max Harden were attacked and narrowly escaped death. The most eminent victim of extreme right terrorists was Rathenau, the Foreign Minister, who was shot by members of the Consul organization on 24 June 1922. His murder caused great indignation among the public, including the middle class, by whom he was much respected. 'The enemy is on the right!' Chancellor Wirth exclaimed in the Reichstag, addressing the DNVP and Helfferich in particular, and thus proclaiming that the whole right wing, in their boundless hatred of the democratic republic and its representatives, were to blame for the unheard-of brutalization of the political conflict.

On 21 July 1921, as a direct result of Rathenau's murder, the Reichstag passed a Law for the Protection of the Republic, valid for five years, which imposed severe penalties for conspiracy to murder and provided a means of prohibiting extremist organizations. The DNVP, BVP and KPD voted against the Bill, and Bavaria refused to recognize the new measure: in this state there was by now a decided swing to the right, giving a clear field to extremist organizations including the NSDAP (National Socialist German Workers' Party, that is, the Nazis), who were already growing in importance. If, contrary to republican hopes and expectations, the law of 21 July did not prove an effective weapon against enemies of the democratic state, this was above all because its application was in the hands of a judiciary that made no secret of its dislike for democracy and its sympathy with the political right. 'The communists were made to feel the full rigour of the law, but their right-wing opponents were all too often treated with marked indulgence. The failing of many judges and lawyers to perform their duty in this respect cannot be argued away and will always be a distressing chapter in the annals of German justice' (Gotthard Jasper).

In the furore caused by Rathenau's murder, the government parties thought it inopportune to hold a plebiscite for the election of a new President as required by the constitution. Accordingly, on 24 October 1922 the Reichstag passed an amending resolution prolonging Ebert's period of office until June 1925. Three weeks later the Wirth Cabinet fell because the Social Democrats in the Reichstag would not agree to enlarge the 'Weimar coalition' to a 'grand coalition' by taking in the DVP, but preferred to go back into opposition. (On the general problem of coalition politics see pages 66 ff. below.) A Cabinet of decidedly right-wing complexion took office on 22 November 1922, led by Wilhelm Cuno, the head of the Hamburg–America shipping line, who was officially non-party but regarded as a member of the DVP.

While Germany during these weeks was moving away from the 'fulfilment policy', the French government under Poincaré was determined to assert all its rights under the peace treaty, including sanctions against Germany. Poincaré's slogan was 'no moratorium without pledges'; his objective was to secure pledges, and the insistent German request for a moratorium therefore suited him admirably. Britain was opposed to demanding 'productive pledges' (*gages productifs*), but was increasingly impatient with German efforts to 'present the German currency crisis as a crisis of Germany's ability to pay' (Hermann Graml). The British were therefore not prepared to take Germany's side unreservedly and, by so doing, to prevent Poincaré from advancing into the Ruhr.

To Poincaré it appeared that the time and opportunity to realize his long-standing objective had come when, at the end of December 1922, the Reparations Commission declared Germany to be in default on deliveries of timber and coal and – against the vote of the British delegate – pronounced this to be a basic violation of her obligations. On this flimsy juridical pretext Poincaré, with Belgian and Italian support, initiated the occupation of the Ruhr on 9 January 1923. A group of engineers were sent with instructions to take charge of the coal syndicate and ensure strict compliance with the delivery programme laid down by the Reparations Commission. The engineers were 'protected' by five French and one Belgian division, 60,000 men in all, who occupied the whole area of the Ruhr. In the course of 1923 their numbers were increased to 100,000. While Poincaré was interested in reparations as such, he also wished to create a political basis for pushing Germany's frontier back to the Rhine and thus achieving the permanent weakening of Germany which, in his view, ought to have been effected in 1919. In this sense the occupation of the Ruhr was a deliberate act of revisionism on the part of France.

Germany reacted to the occupation of the Ruhr with an almost unanimous outcry of national indignation. The spirit of August 1914 seemed to return; class antagonisms receded for the time being, giving place to a sense of shared national destiny. The central government, powerless to take military action, at once suspended all reparations payments to France and Belgium and called on the population of the Ruhr district to offer 'passive resistance': all officials, including those of the railway, were forbidden to take orders from the occupation authorities. The French and Belgians replied to the 'general strike' of the German government and population by the expulsion of officials, especially those of the railways and administration, by confiscations and by completely severing economic links between the Ruhr and the rest of Germany. An open state of conflict existed between Germany and the victorious powers, especially France.

The object of the German government was to demonstrate to the French and Belgians, by means of passive resistance, that the policy of 'pledges', which in practice were the reverse of productive, was not worth their while. It was hoped that the French and Belgians would see this and withdraw their troops, so that negotiations could take place concerning the level of reparations and the provision of German material assets as a guarantee of performance. In the first six months of the occupation less coal and coke was delivered to France and Belgium than in the last ten days preceding it. But time was on France's side, as passive resistance could only be kept up for a limited period.

Germany, whose currency was already in a precarious state, had to pay out thousands of millions of marks in currency or in kind to the people of the Ruhr district, who were forfeiting their pay on government orders; tax revenue ceased to flow from the Ruhr, as did coal deliveries to the rest of the country, so that the government's entire supply of foreign currency had to be spent on coal from abroad. The government chose not to impose on the unoccupied part of the country, which was already suffering great hardship, a burden of taxation adequate to redress the emergency situation. By April 1923 the government's financial needs had shot up to seven times the normal revenue level: the gap was filled by the printing press. In December 1922 the mark stood at 8,000 to the dollar; in April 1923 the figure was about 20,000, and at the beginning of August one million. The mark continued to plunge downwards. Assets expressed in money terms, such as government loans, mortgages, bonds and savings bank accounts, became valueless. In August 1923 the quantity of notes in circulation reached 663 billion marks (a billion = a million million), while the floating debt of the Reich was over a trillion (a million billion) marks; there was no German currency any more. (For the economic and social consequences of the inflation see below, pages 161 ff.)

From the spring of 1923 onwards the government endeavoured without success to put an end to the Ruhr conflict without total surrender. Poincaré insisted on the unconditional abandonment of passive resistance before consenting to fresh negotiations. The German government therefore had to give in. After the fall of the Cuno Cabinet a 'grand coalition' government was formed, representing the SPD, DDP, Centre and DVP; as the new Chancellor Gustav Stresemann put it, the object was to include 'all elements loyal to the constitutional idea of the state'. Stresemann was himself the leader of a markedly right-wing party, the DVP; yet it was he who abandoned the bankrupt policy of obstruction and, by a calculated act of surrender, opened the way to a German foreign policy that took account of international realities. On 26 September 1923 he revoked the policy of passive resistance and resumed the payment of reparations and occupation costs in France and Belgium; on 24 October the German government requested the Reparations Commission to carry out an investigation into Germany's economic situation.

The first act of surrender was followed by a second, which was also compelled by circumstances but, after the undue hesitation of previous governments, was at last whole-heartedly undertaken by Stresemann's government: the creation of the *Rentenmark* in November 1923 laid the basis for a stable currency, and also made it possible to embark on constructive negotiations for a settlement of the reparations question.

Before this, however, the German government had to cope with a period of acute difficulty in internal affairs. In October–November 1923 separatist groups became active in western Germany, the Rhineland and the Palatinate: partly with the tacit approval and partly with the open support of the occupying powers, these groups invaded official premises and proclaimed 'autonomous republics'. However, their attempts to seize power were frustrated by popular resistance, and the French authorities finally withdrew their support.

More dangerous attempts at subversion came from extremists of the right and left. On 1 October a putsch in Küstrin by temporary volunteers (the 'Black Reichswehr') was put down by regular troops. Also in October, the KPD made preparations for revolutionary action based on Central Germany. In Saxony and also in Thuringia, where the SPD and KPD together commanded a majority in the *Landtage* (state assemblies), these two parties combined to form a government and began to organize proletarian defence units (hundreds). The KPD entered these governments as a tactical manoeuvre under the slogan of a 'united front', to gain a basis for a revolutionary uprising. Overestimating their own strength and the readiness of the workers to engage in combat, and also under pressure from the Comintern in Moscow, the Communists set about actively creating a military organization in preparation for a rising. But the central government, by rapid and determined action, foiled the plan to unleash an 'October Revolution' in Saxony and Thuringia. On 26 September, as the political crisis became acute, the government had proclaimed a state of emergency throughout Germany, whereby executive power was transferred to regional military commanders as representatives of the Ministry of Defence. When the Saxon Prime Minister, Erich Zeigner (SPD), refused to carry out the orders of the regional commander and disband the proletarian defence units, the central government sent Reichswehr troops into Saxony on 23 October and, a few days later, categorically ordered Zeigner to drop the communists from his Cabinet. However, whereas in Thuringia the KPD ministers resigned and the proletarian defence units were disbanded, Zeigner refused to reform his government. Thereupon, on 29 October, the central government dismissed him from office and appointed Heinze of the DVP as Reich Commissar. However, a right-wing dictatorship did not install itself in Saxony as middle-class elements had hoped, as the Landtag at once elected a new prime minister who formed an all-SPD Cabinet.

By this time the KPD leaders were already beating a retreat. A congress of factory councils at Chemnitz on 21 October produced no majority for a general strike and the election of political workers' councils; the KPD leaders shrank from an all-out struggle for power, and called off the proposed local uprisings. Only in Hamburg, owing to a hitch in communications, did an isolated uprising occur: on 24–26 October a few hundred communists carried on a hopeless battle against the police. The 'German October' planned by the Comintern and the KPD leadership failed to materialize.

The central government and the Reichstag acted much less energetically against right-wing insurgence in Bavaria in November 1923 than they had done against left-wing Saxony and Thuringia in the previous month, with the result that the SPD seceded from the 'grand coalition' on 3 November. In the autumn of 1923 the nationalist right was looking towards Bavaria more hopefully than ever. The state government, itself firmly right wing, was under pressure from still more rightist forces – patriotic, nationalist and paramilitary organizations, acting under Ludendorff's patronage as United Patriotic Associations, who, inspired by the Fascist March on Rome (October 1922), were planning a 'march on Berlin' for the purpose of setting up a nationalist dictatorship.

After the cessation of passive resistance in the Ruhr, the Bavarian government declared a state of emergency and appointed Ritter von Kahr, a member of the Patriotic Associations, as state commissioner-general. The rebellion took on a new dimension in October, when the 7th Reichswehr Division under General von Lossow, stationed in Bavaria, refused to obey the orders of the Reich government. At the beginning of November – by which time the central government had regained control of the situation in Saxony and Thuringia – the conflict with Bavaria became still more acute. The attitude of General von Seeckt, the head of the Reichswehr, was ambiguous at this time. When Ebert on 3 November proposed government intervention in Bavaria, Seeckt declared that this was impossible, as men of the Reichswehr would not march against their comrades; instead he demanded dictatorial powers for himself, which Ebert refused. At the same time, Seeckt emphatically warned Kahr and Lossow not to be carried away by nationalist extremists, and this warning had some effect. The extremist leaders, above all Ludendorff and Hitler, perceived that Kahr and Lossow were lukewarm towards the idea of launching an independent attack. They therefore resolved to take advantage of a rally which Kahr had organized for 8 November in the Bürgerbräu cellar in Munich, to transform it into the opening move in a *coup d'état* and thus after all to bring about a nationalist uprising. Escorted by armed SA (brownshirt) troopers, Hitler burst into the hall, declared that the Bavarian government and the Reich government were deposed, and forced Kahr, Lossow and Seisser (the Bavarian police chief) to agree to proclaim a provisional Reich government composed of Ludendorff, Hitler, Lossow and Seisser. But within a few hours the tables were turned: Kahr, Lossow and Seisser, who had regained their freedom of action during the night, withdrew their agreement to the plan and resolved to defeat the National Socialist putsch. On the morning of 9 November Hitler and Ludendorff found they had been outmanoeuvred, but did not give up their plan. They organized a march through the centre of Munich, which was held up and fired on by a police cordon at the Feldherrnhalle; the demonstrators fled, and the 'national revolution' collapsed. With the failure of the Munich putsch, the worst of the internal crisis was over. Seeckt, to whom Ebert had transferred the executive power of the Reich and supreme command of the army on the night of 8/9 November, was not prepared to cross the Rubicon and become dictator. The NSDAP and other organizations of the extreme right were proscribed throughout Germany, as was the KPD.

In the crucial test of the autumn weeks of 1923, the republic had maintained itself against challenges from both right and left. Putsches by both sets of extremists had been defeated, a currency reform had put a stop to inflation, the conflict in foreign policy had begun to lose its intensity, and internal affairs were slowly beginning to quieten down. The crises of 1923 had, above all, weakened the extreme left for some years to come. With the collapse of the 'German October' the danger of a Communist attempt at revolution could be regarded as finally averted. There was no longer a 'revolutionary situation', and the KPD had lost much of its offensive force; many of its members and supporters fell away, and the energies of its leaders were to a large extent absorbed by internal dissension during the 'Stalinization' of the party. In 1924–30 the KPD was not a truly significant force within the workers' movement or on the stage of national politics: though conspicuous, it had little real power. On the other hand, the right-wing challenge to the republic was thwarted for the time being only. In particular sections of the population and in élite professional groups there was still a massive reservoir of anti-republican and anti-democratic feeling, which could at a suitable opportunity be mobilized for a new frontal attack on the Weimar state. Large sections, particularly of the Protestant clergy and their congregations, were sceptical and hostile towards the new constitutional order. Thus at the end of 1923 it was impossible to foretell whether the republic's success in weathering its postwar crises would lead to a lasting consolidation of the parliamentary democratic system. The omens were at best uncertain. The different degree of determination shown in putting down revolutionary threats from the right and left respectively; the ambiguous attitude of the Reichswehr leaders at moments of crisis; the agitation against the 'November republic', which continued with unabated violence – all these signs indicated how precarious was the position of those who were working for a stabilization of the republic.

(B) THE PHASE OF RELATIVE STABILIZATION, 1924–9

1

German Foreign Policy within the European System

Within a surprisingly short time after the dramatic events of 1923, Germany's internal situation began to stabilize, and she was able by degrees to break out of the diplomatic isolation of the early postwar years. This was due to a fortunate combination of circumstances at home and abroad. German politicians began to take a more realistic view of the possibilities and limitations of their country's foreign policy, and for a variety of reasons Allied statesmen gradually altered their attitude towards defeated Germany and the problems of Europe. The climate of international relations underwent a change. Not only Germany but the other European states had emerged from the immediate postwar period, which had presented a very different character as between the various states, their internal conditions and constitutional structures.

If France was still able in the first years after the war to play the part of a European great power it was because the other powers, with greater or less good will, allowed her to exercise hegemony on the Continent. The USA for the time being withdrew from European affairs; Germany and the Soviet Union were in no position as yet to pursue an active foreign policy, and Britain was absorbed by her colonial, economic and social problems. The British government believed it could only cope with those problems if the wartime coalition remained in being. Hence, immediately after the armistice with Germany, Lloyd George's wing of the Liberal Party concluded an electoral alliance with the Conservatives. In the 'khaki election' on 14 December 1918 (at which, for the first time, the vote was extended to all men over 20 and all women over 30) the alliance scored a triumphant victory, with over 5 million votes and 478 seats; Labour, with 2·89 million votes, obtained 63 seats. The Liberals led by Asquith (Prime Minister from 1908 to 1916), who refused to join the coalition, received 1·3 million votes and only 28 seats. The result was a triumph for Lloyd George but even more for the Conservatives, who numbered no fewer than 339 in the new House of Commons. They thus predominated in the coalition, although Lloyd George, who remained premier until 1922, was the decisive factor in

British policy by virtue of his personal authority, style of leadership and mastery of political tactics.

Admittedly the policy in question was, over long periods, one of 'muddling through'. To keep the coalition together the government had to make constant compromises and adopt contradictory attitudes, especially in regard to economic and social problems, which became acute after the collapse of the postwar boom in the winter of 1920–1. The number of unemployed doubled between December and March, and rose finally to 16 per cent of the working population; *The Economist* called 1921 'one of the worst years of depression since the industrial revolution'. However, despite unemployment and major strikes the government managed to uphold its authority and preserve public order. Moreover, in 1921, it achieved a partial solution of the Irish question, which amounted to granting independence to the South. Thus 1922 was Britain's first 'normal' year since 1914, and the dissolution of the coalition signified a return to normality in party politics also. The Conservative leaders decided on 19 October 1922 to fight the next election independently, whereupon Lloyd George resigned without awaiting the result; the new Prime Minister was Bonar Law. In the November election the Conservatives gained a massive majority (345 seats), while the Liberals, with 116 seats, were well behind Labour with 142. Baldwin, who succeeded Law in May 1923, dissolved parliament prematurely in the same year but was unable to repeat the Conservative success. At the election in December, although the parties secured practically the same number of votes as in 1922, the Conservative victory was not repeated in parliamentary terms: the Liberals gained 40 seats and Labour 50, while the Conservatives lost over 90 seats and had only a relative majority in the new Parliament. During the 1920s the traditional British two-party system underwent a radical change: the Labour Party, with its strongholds in the industrial cities and areas such as Scotland and Wales, began to replace the Liberals as the principal opposition party; this had the immediate effect of destabilizing the old equilibrium, and eventually led to the alternation of Conservatives and Labour as the two main parties.

When the Conservative government was defeated in a Commons vote in January 1924 the Labour statesman James Ramsay MacDonald, as leader of the second largest party in the House, was called on to form the new government. The fact that his minority government was tolerated by the other two main parties, and was able to perform its functions without obstruction by the bureaucracy or business circles, is a striking tribute to British parliamentarianism and, at the same time, an indication of how far the working class and its political representatives had become integrated into the political system. During 1924, a crucial year in European affairs, MacDonald pursued an active foreign policy: he endeavoured to reconcile France and Germany and to strengthen the League of Nations (the Geneva Protocol for the settlement of disputes), and established diplomatic relations with the Soviet Union.

MacDonald's basic policy in European affairs outlasted his short term of office. A Labour defeat in the House of Commons on a relatively minor issue led to fresh elections at the end of October 1924, at which the Conservatives again gained a clear majority. Labour lost a few seats, but the Liberals continued their decline by forfeiting about 100, so that they were no longer of decisive political significance. The five years of Baldwin's second government were marked by a *modus vivendi* between the ruling Conservatives and the Labour Opposition, as well as a gradual economic improvement broken only for a short time by the general strike of 1926. In these years the British government steadily pursued its efforts for a lasting peace in Europe.

Unlike the position in Britain, French politics, plans and activities were dominated by the German problem and by the endeavour to achieve and maintain maximum security *vis-à-vis* the country's eastern neighbour. Certainly on the morrow of the First World War, France was indisputably superior to Germany, politically and militarily. But French statesmen were alarmed by the prospect that, despite Germany's losses of territory and population, in the long run 40 million Frenchmen would again be in an inferior position to 62 million Germans, whose huge economic potential had not been seriously impaired by the war and its consequences. France, for her part, had not only lost 1·4 million men on the battlefields, but had suffered the devastation of her northern and eastern provinces; 2 million hectares (4·94 million acres) of agricultural land was laid waste, over 220,000 houses destroyed and over 120,000 damaged; 60,000 kilometres (37,000 miles) of roads and 5,600 kilometres (3,500 miles) of railroad track were in need of repair. Huge economic and social problems loomed ahead.

None the less, despite massive strikes and frequent rioting in 1919–20, no revolutionary movement developed in France after the war; the nation as a whole was proud of the way it had stood the test of war. The parliamentary election of November 1919 was a triumph for the Bloc National, an alliance of right wing and centre parties which, like the coalition in Britain, sought to prolong the *union sacrée* into the years of peace. The Bloc gained over two-thirds of all seats; the only significant opposition group were the Socialists with 72 seats. Clemenceau remained premier until January 1920, when he was defeated in the presidential election and retired from the political scene, on which he had played a major part for the past fifty years. The premier from January 1921 to January 1922 was Aristide Briand, who after 1924 became the advocate of a policy of reconciliation with Germany. In 1921, however, he held out for the strict execution of the Versailles terms, including sanctions if necessary. Even so he was not radical enough for a majority of the Bloc, and in January 1922 he was forced to resign in favour of their chosen leader, Poincaré. We have already described the latter's intransigence over reparations and his attempt, culminating in the occupation of the Ruhr, to 'revise' the Treaty of Versailles in France's favour. Although the trial of strength in the Ruhr was a technical victory for France, Poincaré did not succeed in converting it into a lasting success for his objectives.

Several factors obliged France to draw in her horns in the course of 1924. The crisis of the franc from the end of 1923 onwards could only be overcome with British and US help, so that France was forced to make some concession to Anglo-American ideas of a reasonable reparations settlement. The Americans and British were also not prepared to allow France to exercise economic hegemony in Central Europe by controlling the industry of the Ruhr. Moreover, after the Ruhr occupation France was no longer seen as an innocent victim of foreign aggression, deserving sympathy and support, but rather as a militarist and imperialist power using force ruthlessly to achieve expansionist aims. This change in world public opinion threatened to damage France's position and perhaps even isolate her in foreign affairs; fear of this gradually inclined the French to show some willingness to seek a solution for the political issues between them and Germany. The elections to the Chamber on 11 May 1924 brought a spectacular defeat for the Bloc National and a victory for the left-wing *Cartel des Gauches*. Poincaré yielded the premiership to the Radical Socialist Edouard Herriot who, with tacit Socialist support, and in the conviction that France needed a period of quiet, co-operated with the British in seeking a *modus vivendi* with Germany. In October 1924 France also entered into diplomatic relations with the Soviet Union. The following years were marked by close co-operation between France and Britain in foreign affairs; the German chargé d'affaires in London reported that this extended to 'all world questions'. This 'intimate relationship between the Foreign Office and the Quai d'Orsay' should not be overlooked in a study of the background to Stresemann's foreign policy.

In Italy the tide of revolution after the end of the war rose considerably higher than in Britain or France. The parliamentary system was much less stable and much less accepted by the country at large than in the Western democracies; the economic and social problems were more acute, and national feelings were exacerbated by Italy's failure to secure all of her extensive postwar demands (Fiume, Dalmatia, Albania, the eastern Mediterranean). These factors constituted a highly explosive mixture. The successive Cabinets of 1919–22 (Nitti, Giolitti, Bonomi, Facta), though they commanded parliamentary support, were unable to cope with unemployment, inflation and the spread of violence. This came first from the left wing, which stirred up unrest by means of strikes and the occupation of factories (Turin and Milan, 1920), but the initiative soon passed to the militant right. Benito Mussolini, who increasingly came to the fore as its organizer and agitator, had parted company with the Socialists in 1914, when he advocated Italy's entry into the war on the side of the Entente. He now became a vociferous spokesman for nationalist emotions and social fears, and set out to organize nationalist, anti-socialist and anti-liberal forces. The *Fasci di combattimento* (fighting squads) were created in 1919, the Partito Nazionale Fascista in 1921. 'Appealing to all classes by a combination of conservative and progressive, anti-communist and state socialist, reactionary and revolutionary aims' (Karl Dietrich Bracher), and making increasing use of 'direct action', Mussolini went to war against liberal democracy. Large sections of the army and the business world sympathized with the Fascists for fear of communism, and government circles were increasingly disposed to 'tame' the movement by associating it with office. Thus it was due not so much to the spectacular March on Rome, which set out from Naples on 27 October 1922, as to defeatism in the political establishment that the king, three days later, invited Mussolini to form a government, while on 25 November Parliament granted him dictatorial powers to restore order and carry out reforms.

The Fascist dictatorship in Italy was not created overnight but was a gradual process, culminating in the election of 1929 in which the party's single list received 99 per cent of the votes cast. This is not the place to describe the development and organization of the dictatorship; from our present point of view the important fact is that in the 1920s the new regime concentrated on strengthening its position at home and showed moderation in foreign affairs. Except for the brief interlude of the occupation of Corfu in 1923, which was swiftly terminated under pressure from the League of Nations and especially Britain, Mussolini refrained from expansionism and co-operated in efforts to organize European security after 1923, so that European statesmen in those years did not see Fascist Italy as a significant threat to the existing order. After concluding a series of treaties of friendship (with Spain in 1926, Hungary in 1927, and Greece, Abyssinia and Turkey in 1928) Mussolini signed the Lateran treaties with the Vatican in 1929, thus putting an end to the conflict between the Church and the Italian state which had existed since 1870. These treaties were not only of great importance for the internal stabilization of the regime but also did much to enhance its international prestige.

The principal crisis area between the wars was east Central Europe, which had undergone a wholesale political reorganization at the end of the First World War owing to the forcing back of Russia and the break-up of Austria-Hungary. The principle invoked was the self-determination of peoples, but it soon proved that, given the medley of races in the area and the chauvinism of the ruling nationalities, self-determination was not a reliable basis for a stable international system. None of the new states succeeded in solving its minority problems, as might have been done by means of a federal constitution or a wide degree of cultural autonomy. The instability that resulted was increased by deep-seated economic and social problems. Both republics and monarchies in the area sought a remedy to the 'crisis of postwar democracy', which set in soon after the war, by turning to authoritarian or semi-authoritarian forms of government: Poland (Pilsudski's *coup d'état*) and Lithuania in 1926, Yugoslavia in 1929, Bulgaria, Estonia and Latvia in 1934, Greece in 1936. In Hungary, after the overthrow in 1919 of the short-lived Soviet republic headed by Béla Kun, an authoritarian regime was established under the Regent, Admiral Miklós

Horthy; in Austria the Christian-Socialist Chancellor, Engelbert Dollfuss, set up a conservative dictatorship in 1933–4. In Czechoslovakia the parliamentary system remained intact, but the rigorously centralized regime and domination by the Czech ethnic group led to permanent internal conflict and eventually furnished a pretext to the neighbouring countries – Germany, Hungary and Poland – to seize those areas inhabited by their own peoples.

Poland received or gained its postwar boundaries thanks to the fact that the geopolitical preponderance of its German and Russian neighbours was eliminated for a brief moment in history, while French protection of the Poles encouraged an adventurous policy on their part. Anticipating what were believed to be aggressive Soviet intentions, on 25 April 1920 Poland invaded the Russian republic, weakened as it was by Entente intervention and civil war. After reverses during which the Red Army threatened Warsaw itself, the Poles won a military victory owing above all to Pilsudski's strategy. As a result, Poland advanced her eastern frontier beyond the demarcation line proposed by the Allies (the Curzon line), so as to take in large areas inhabited chiefly by Ukrainians and Belorussians (preliminary treaty signed on 12 October 1920, final treaty of Riga on 18 March 1921). The Soviet Union was in no way disposed to accept this settlement in the long run, just as Germany refused to resign itself to the German-Polish frontier as fixed by the Treaty of Versailles and by the Allied award in the dispute over Upper Silesia. The dangers inherent in this situation were not lessened by the tendency of Polish statesmen to overestimate their country's strength.

After the October Revolution in Russia, the Bolshevik leaders' approach to the nations of Europe was based on ideas of revolutionary strategy and propaganda, to the exclusion of foreign policy in the sense of international relations. However, after the first attempts to bring about world revolution proved a failure, the Soviet leaders were forced to realize that their country had to behave as a state among others. The change of attitude took place in 1920, after the Russian civil war, the Entente intervention and the war with Poland. Revolutionary internationalism was not given up, but the 'primacy of survival' (Dietrich Geyer) meant absolute priority for internal stabilization and much-needed economic development. After long years of civil war and war communism the desperate economic situation was in itself a compelling reason for giving the Soviet state a period of rest, opening it up to trade with the capitalist world, and encouraging the latter to contribute to Russia's economic recovery. A first step was taken with the decree of 13 November 1920 on economic concessions, designed to attract foreign capital to Soviet Russia. At the Tenth Party Congress in March 1921 the New Economic Policy (NEP) was proclaimed, creating a private capitalist sector alongside the state economy. Private capitalist activity in trade and crafts was again permitted, and many small or medium industrial concerns that had been nationalized in 1918 were reprivatized. Along with this went intensive efforts for international recognition, diplomatic relations and livelier trade contacts. These efforts were not wholly unsuccessful. Commercial treaties with Britain and Germany were concluded in 1921; the Rapallo treaty of 1922 provided for diplomatic relations with Germany, and diplomatic ties with Britain, France and Italy were re-established in 1924. However, despite these treaties and the German–Soviet common front against Poland, the Soviet Union in these years remained isolated on the international scene, 'normal' relations being precluded by deep distrust on both sides. The states of Central and Western Europe saw their internal security endangered by Soviet influence over a section of the working class and by subversive activities inspired by the Comintern. The Soviet leaders, for their part, felt permanently threatened with 'encirclement' by the capitalist powers, and pursued a largely defensive foreign policy designed, first and foremost, to protect the building of 'socialism in one country'.

The USA, which during the war had become the world's leading economic power, was not prepared after 1919 to enter into treaty relations with its war-time allies; but, despite this limitation, there were strong transatlantic bonds of interest and continuous contacts. If only because the USA was the principal creditor of the former belligerents, it had an important say in determining the final amount of reparations and the regulation of German payments. The idea of US isolationism in the 1920s is still widely believed in, but it is a cliché in need of correction. Recent research has shown that US policy at the time was basically governed by economic expansionism and the 'open door' principle. It was thanks to the strong American interest both in Europe as a whole and in a financially 'reasonable' reparations settlement that Stresemann was able to work actively to rescue Germany from the political isolation in which she found himself in the first years after the war.

The hundred days of Stresemann's chancellorship, from 13 August to 23 November 1923, set the course for many important developments in German foreign and domestic policy. Stresemann resigned when defeated in a vote of confidence on the latter date, but was Foreign Minister in all succeeding Cabinets until his death on 3 October 1929. In those years he impressed his personality so strongly on German policy, not only foreign policy, that it is right to speak of a 'Stresemann era'.

Stresemann's career, more than that of any other German statesman since Bismarck, has been caught in a cross-fire of opinions, and for a long time historians held sharply conflicting views of his character and policies. Some regarded him as a good democrat and a European by conviction, others as a doctrinaire nationalist, an unscrupulous power-politician and even a forerunner of Hitler; to communists he is an exponent of imperialist monopoly capitalism. Only in later research do we find a growing consensus as regards his political motives, aims and ambitions (cf. pages 174 ff. below).

Stresemann, the 'republican by conviction' (*Vernunftrepublikaner*), accepted and identified with the Weimar state from 1921–2 onwards. Like all European statesmen of his time he pursued a nationalist foreign policy, which in German terms after 1919 meant a revisionist policy. He desired to see Germany restored to her former greatness and once more asserting her position between East and West. Thus Stresemann was certainly a nationalist and a power-politician. What distinguished him from most German nationalists after 1923 was his realization that a nationalist foreign policy could not be successful if it directly challenged the governments of the victorious powers. With a keen sense of reality he based his policy on an objective appreciation of the constellation of forces in Europe, and 'pursued his revisionist policy as an international policy of reconciliation' (Karl Dietrich Erdmann). In the spring of 1927 he declared: 'In the course of my life I have come to believe that nothing great and permanent has ever been done in the world without give and take, compensation and compromise.' It was this method, far more than his actual objectives, that divided Stresemann from his nationalist opponents, who fought him tooth and nail and whose hatred pursued him beyond the grave.

Given his political realism, Stresemann saw the recovery of German power as an aim to be secured by degrees and in the long term, by negotiation and conciliation. Two points seemed to him axiomatic. First, as Germany was militarily powerless, her recovery could only be set in motion by the judicious use of her economic potential. On 22 November 1925 he told the executive of his party, the DVP: 'I believe the task for any foreign minister today is to take advantage of the world economic situation so as to conduct foreign policy by economic means, as this is the only respect in which we are still a great power.' Thus the motto was 'Back to world politics by way of world economics' (Werner Link). As a corollary to this view, Stresemann was prepared, on occasion, to pay an economic price for the attainment of political ends. Secondly, Germany could only hope to secure a revision of the peace treaty if France's desire for security was first met; consequently German–French co-operation must be welcomed and intensified, France must be Germany-oriented. If France could then be induced to content herself with a solution of the security problem in Western Europe alone, so that her ties with Poland were gradually loosened, a revision of the German–Polish frontier might enter the realm of possibility.

However, in Stresemann's view such an eventuality still lay far ahead, while the burning question of 1923–4 was that of reparations. In the brief period of his chancellorship in 1923, German inflation had been checked and the currency reformed. This provided a basis on which the reparations problem could once again be tackled. A realistic calculation of Germany's ability to pay was not possible; technical ways and means of transferring payments to the victorious countries could be devised; a basis of confidence was created for an international loan to Germany. Thus in 1924 the Dawes Plan came into being. The politicization of the reparations question gave place to an economic and technical approach. The plan also led to the rapid strengthening of links between the American business world and German interests concerned with revisionism and

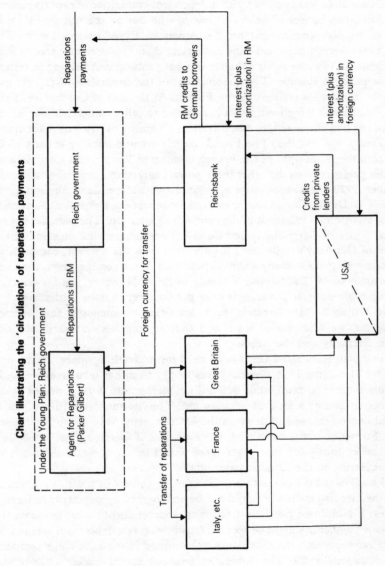

Chart illustrating the 'circulation' of reparations payments

Under the Young Plan: Reich government

Reich government

Reparations payments

Reparations in RM

Agent for Reparations (Parker Gilbert)

Foreign currency for transfer

RM credits to German borrowers

Interest (plus amortization) in RM

Reichsbank

Interest (plus amortization) in foreign currency

Credits from private lenders

USA

Transfer of reparations

Great Britain

France

Italy, etc.

Source: J. Bergmann, K. Megerle and P. Steinbach (eds), *Geschichte als politische Wissenschaft* (Stuttgart, 1979), p. 120.

financial policy; for Germany's need for capital corresponded admirably to the expansionism of the American economy and its interest in the massive export of capital.

The Dawes Plan was evolved by an independent committee of experts chaired by the American banker Charles G. Dawes, who during the war had been in charge of supply procurement for the American Expeditionary Force. The leading part taken by the Americans made clear that they were prepared to lend every assistance towards solving the reparations problem and helping to restore economic peace in Europe. The appointment of the committee of experts had initially been strongly resisted by the French. At the end of October 1923 the British, Italian and US governments had agreed to call a conference, for which the Germans had also asked, to assess Germany's ability to pay within the terms of the Treaty of Versailles. The French merely wanted talks by experts to be held within the framework of the French-dominated Reparations Commission, but under pressure from the other three powers agreed to a compromise: on 30 November 1923 the Commission appointed two independent committees of experts. The Dawes Committee presented its report on 9 April 1924, recommending an interim settlement of the reparations question. The plan did not set any total figure of German payments and left unanswered the question of the duration of Germany's obligation; it only dealt with the amount, composition and guaranteeing of Germany's annual payments in the coming years, the London decisions of 1921 remaining formally in force. However, the Dawes Plan possessed some decisive advantages over previous reparations settlements:

(1) It replaced the extremely high annuities by amounts that seemed tolerable for the first year at least, and thus to some extent eased relations between Germany and the Allies.

(2) The plan recognized Germany's need for a breathing space. In the first period, by 31 August 1925 Germany was to pay from her own resources only 200 million marks in cash, while 800 million marks were to be provided by an international loan as a kind of priming aid. The 'normal' annuities of about 2,500 million marks, as laid down in the London plan, were not to begin until 1928–9. Stresemann was convinced, however, that if Germany met her obligations conscientiously for four years there would be no question thereafter of simply reverting to the London payments.

(3) The Dawes Plan not only provided for the control of transfer operations so that the German currency would not be endangered by payments to foreign countries; it laid down precisely from what sources and to what amounts the reparations payments should be secured (customs, taxes, debentures secured on the state railways, etc.; the latter were to be turned into a joint stock company and 'internationalized'). The American financial expert Parker Gilbert was made Agent for Reparations Payments with headquarters in Berlin, and had responsibility for operating transfers with due regard to the stability of German currency; he was also to report regularly to the Reparations Commission on

Germany's economic and financial situation and, in particular, the pledged sources of revenue.

On 14 April 1924 the German government agreed to negotiate on the basis of the experts' report. At a conference in London from 16 July to 16 August the Dawes Plan was accepted by all the governments concerned, and the German delegation secured a formal assurance that the Ruhr would be evacuated within a year; the last French troops duly withdrew in July 1925. It was uncertain at first whether the legislation for the Dawes Plan would command a majority in the Reichstag. The DDP, Centre, DVP and SPD were certain to vote for it, but the law on the state railways meant an amendment to the constitution and therefore required a two-thirds majority. It thus needed the votes of the DNVP, but during the past months that party had fought the Dawes Plan bitterly with the slogan 'No new Versailles!' However, massive pressure was exerted by industrial and agricultural organizations which expected the plan to be of decided benefit to their interests. Unexpectedly, on 29 August 1924 about half the DNVP votes in the Reichstag were cast for the plan (cf. page 71 below), and the agreement could thus come into force.

It was a feature of the new international climate in and after 1924 that each side took the other's interests seriously: the Germans showed understanding for France's claim to reparations and security, and the Allies respected Germany's desire for sovereignty and equal rights. How greatly the atmosphere had changed was clear as early as February 1925, when Stresemann took the initiative of addressing a memorandum to the French government on the security question. Apart from motives of commercial policy, which have been emphasized by recent research, this was primarily a defensive move. There were indications that Great Britain and Belgium might conclude a pact with France to satisfy the latter's demand for security, and Germany would have had to accept this in accordance with Article 31 of the Treaty of Versailles. Meanwhile, the Allies had given notice at the beginning of 1925 that they would not evacuate the first occupation zone of the Rhineland (Cologne) by the due date of 10 January, because Germany had not complied with the disarmament provisions of Versailles and the security problem was not yet solved. Thus the object of Stresemann's initiative was to blunt the edge of French policy and strengthen the German position by bringing about a Franco-German solution to the security problem. His offer of a pact was accepted with much hesitation by the French government; but it now became clear that the European situation had changed greatly since 1923, as Britain and America both pressed the French to agree to the German proposals. After intensive diplomatic exchanges the leading European statesmen met at Locarno on 5–6 October 1925 and initialled the Locarno treaties, consisting of a pact of guarantee and several arbitration agreements. In the former treaty Germany, on the one hand, and France and Belgium on the other, agreed to refrain from using force to alter their existing frontiers, which were guaranteed by Britain and Italy. Germany concluded arbitration treaties with France, Belgium, Poland and Czechoslovakia, while France concluded treaties of mutual assistance with the last two countries. Germany's treaties with Poland and Czechoslovakia were guaranteed by no one; they did not provide for binding arbitration, and were thus of no practical significance. However, the Locarno system as a whole was 'the most important and significant development based on the European order of 1919' (Theodor Schieder). By means of Locarno, Germany finally broke out of her moral and political isolation of the early postwar years and rejoined the circle of leading European powers. It was a natural further development that Germany became a member of the League of Nations on 10 September 1926, after difficulties had been overcome concerning her non-participation in sanctions and her permanent seat on the League Council.

By the Locarno treaty Germany recognized her western frontier as fixed by the Treaty of Versailles, but she expressly reserved her claim for a revision of the eastern frontier. It was the core of Stresemann's political strategy to clear up outstanding western questions before tackling those of the east; all that was necessary meanwhile, in his opinion, was to present the crystallization of the status quo. Hence he firmly refused to supplement Locarno by an 'eastern Locarno', that is, a voluntary recognition of the German–Polish frontier as determined by Versailles. He did, however, conclude a treaty of friendship with Russia – the Treaty of Berlin, 24 April 1924 – so that the western orientation of Locarno should not have an adverse effect on German–Soviet relations. By this treaty Germany assured the Soviet Union of her neutrality if Russia should be at war with any third power; this meant in practice that in the event of a Russo-Polish war, France would be unable to come to Poland's aid through German territory.

The Locarno treaties had in themselves gravely worsened Poland's position. The Franco-Polish alliance was henceforth of use to Poland only if Germany was unmistakably the aggressor in a German–Polish conflict. Moreover, the general effect of the Franco-German *détente* was to weaken France's interest in her Eastern European allies and hence to encourage German revisionist designs. Accordingly, Stresemann was able to inform the German Cabinet, with truth, that 'Poland saw these treaties as a total defeat'. Thus the western orientation effected under Stresemann had a significant eastern aspect.

Apart from this, an important motive in concluding the Locarno treaties and initiating a policy of reconciliation with France was undoubtedly Stresemann's expectation that it would have such favourable effects as an early evacuation of the Rhineland, a chance to recover Eupen-Malmédy from Belgium, possibly an earlier date for the Saar plebiscite, a further easing of reparations, and an earlier liquidation of Allied military control in Germany. Combined with Poland's political isolation, a vigorous policy of weakening her economically might bring in sight the possibility of altering Germany's eastern frontier without military conflict. To Stresemann himself, these were not merely arguments with which to overcome domestic opposition to his policy of conciliation in the west; in the mood of general euphoria after Locarno he hoped and expected that such 'repercussions' would follow in a fairly short time. They did not in fact occur to so great an extent, and above all not so soon, as he would have desired. But the significance of Locarno and the merit of the policy that it represented are not to be measured solely by the degree to which it brought satisfaction to optimistic German expectations of early advantages in other fields.

Some successes were nevertheless to be recorded. The first Rhineland zone was evacuated before the end of 1925, and the Inter-Allied Military Commission supervising German disarmament was withdrawn in January 1927; Franco-German economic relations improved steadily. In 1926 an agreement on potash was signed and an aluminium cartel set up, while representatives of heavy industry from France, Germany, Belgium and Luxemburg signed an agreement for an international raw-materials consortium. A Franco-German commercial treaty was signed on 17 August 1927. In the negotiations which led to the Briand–Kellogg Pact outlawing war (27 August 1928) German diplomacy played a confident and important part as an intermediary between the Americans and French.

It proved much more difficult, however, to achieve progress on the central issue of German policy, the complete evacuation of the Rhineland before the scheduled date. Stresemann and his French opposite number, Briand, explored the possibility of a general Franco-German settlement at Thoiry on 17 September 1926. This tête-à-tête meeting, which aroused lively interest at the time, was not a spur-of-the-moment event on the occasion of Germany's entry into the League of Nations. It had been prepared by months of negotiations, aimed at an 'overall solution' which would balance Germany's desire for immediate evacuation of the Rhineland against France's interest in the early settlement of the German reparations debt by 'mobilizing' the Dawes Plan obligations, that is, by selling to the public the rail and industrial debentures deposited with the trustees of the Reparations Commission – a possibility foreseen in the Dawes Plan itself. France's share of the profit derived from the conversion of the Dawes obligations would be used to stabilize the franc, to provide financial assistance for Belgium, and to pay the first annuities of France's war debts to the USA and Britain. (The Franco-American war debt agreement had been signed on 29 April 1926, but was not ratified by the French Parliament until July 1929.)

Both sides could have profited from this politico-economic trade-off, but it failed to come about. There was resistance in France to the premature evacuation of the Rhineland; above all, the American banks were not willing to co-operate, and the conversion of the Dawes obligations was impossible without a financial commitment from them. Nevertheless, it is a striking fact that, only three years after the peak of the Ruhr crisis, the German and French foreign ministers could hold serious discussions for a generously conceived settlement of outstanding issues between the two countries.

The Rhineland question remained on the international agenda after Thoiry, and the problem of reparations became acute once more, since the phase of high 'normal' annuities which, under the Dawes Plan, was to begin in 1928-9 was bound to place a heavy burden on the German economy. At the League of Nations meeting in September 1928 the German delegation asked for an early evacuation of the Rhineland without any quid pro quo; France and Britain, however, insisted on linking the Rhineland question with a final reparations settlement. Gilbert, the reparations agent, also thought it time to arrive at a final solution of the problem. Accordingly, an independent committee of experts set to work in January 1929 and, after negotiations which threatened more than once to break down, produced the Young Plan in May; this was adopted by the governments concerned at a conference at The Hague on 6-31 August 1929.

The Young Plan set the reparations total at a revised figure of 112,000 million Reichsmarks, and for the first time set a time-limit on Germany's obligation to pay. Instead of an annuity of 2,500 million Reichsmarks, Germany was to pay an average annual sum of about 2,000 million Reichsmarks for the next fifty-nine years. The great advantage of the Young Plan for Germany was that in the first three years, from 1 April 1929 to 31 March 1932, she would have to pay about 1,700 million Reichsmarks less than under the Dawes Plan. Moreover, the arrangements for foreign supervision (reparations agent, transfer committee, and so on) were now abolished. Above all, the Allies undertook that if Germany accepted the Young Plan they would evacuate the whole Rhineland, including the third zone, by 30 June 1930, five years earlier than the date laid down in the Treaty of Versailles, thus satisfying Stresemann's revisionist programme on a key point. Stresemann thus regarded the plan – which was ratified by the Reichstag after his death, on 12 March 1930 – as a definite step forward. Recent historians are also coming to the view that the Young Plan gave the Weimar Republic a further chance: as Werner Link puts it, 'If the amount of treaty revision achieved at the conferences in Paris and The Hague is compared with the previous situation, it is clear that the direct, indirect and potential advantages were all on Germany's side.'

In Germany, however, the merits of the Young Plan were not appreciated in all quarters. The nationalist right mounted a campaign against it, which will be discussed in more detail elsewhere (cf. page 104 below). It can be said, however, that towards the end of the Stresemann era, and before the onset of the world depression, storm clouds already darkened the sky in Germany: the unbridled agitation of the political right stirred up a wave of aggressive revisionism which threw doubt on the possibility of continuing a foreign policy based on conciliation. Even if it had been Stresemann's lot to conduct Germany's foreign affairs for a longer period, his policy of compromise and cautious steps towards the restoration of German power would have involved violent battles against increasing resistance on the home front.

If Stresemann's performance as Foreign Minister is judged not by the yardstick of European idealism but by that of traditional European diplomacy, which is more appropriate to him and to his time, it must be acknowledged that his six years in office were astonishingly successful. He achieved the liberation of the Ruhr and the early evacuation of the Rhineland, a far-reaching settlement of the reparations question together with the stabilization of the German economy, the ending of Allied military supervision, and the admission of Germany to the League of Nations. All in all, he managed to a great extent to normalize Germany's relations with the victorious powers while adhering in principle to revisionist aims which, he maintained, were to be achieved by peaceful means and a policy of conciliation. In this way, and in a very short time, Stresemann's Germany built up a fund of confidence on both sides of the Atlantic which did much, in Britain and the USA particularly, to improve the opportunities for a policy of 'peaceful change'.

What did it signify for the Weimar Republic that a 'pragmatic conservative' (Henry A. Turner) such as Stresemann was in charge of its foreign policy from 1923 to 1929? Bearing in mind that, as a result of the incomplete revolution of 1918–19, the Weimar regime took the form of a 'conservative republic', it seems natural enough that in foreign policy, too, there was no decisive breach with the mental habits and methods of the past; there was, for instance, no basic renunciation of attempts to alter the peace treaty as early as possible, come what might. Given that the domestic power structure made it natural that a representative of the old Germany should be in charge of foreign policy, Stresemann's personality and attitude to foreign affairs made him virtually the best imaginable statesman for those years. His long-term approach to the achievement of revisionist aims, and his relatively moderate use of the means available, allowed Germany to keep open her options for the future. In 1929 these options still included a policy of increased readiness for peaceful compromise.

2

Structural Problems and Domestic Politics

The years from 1924 to 1929–30 are commonly described as a period of 'relative stabilization' of the Weimar Republic. This is true if stress is laid on the word 'relative'. During those years unquestionable successes were scored in foreign affairs (though many Germans did not recognize them as such), and progress was made in establishing law and order and consolidating the regime; the economy also revived to some degree. But this stabilization was fragile and superficial, and appears increasingly in doubt as historians devote their attention to the middle period of the Weimar Republic. The impression, on the contrary, is one of a 'republic of instability' (Rudolf Morsey) or a 'history of failure' (Michael Stürmer) in respect of this very period. During these years, when the pressure of foreign affairs grew easier and internal quarrels were less acute than in the first stormy period after 1918, the republic did not succeed in con-solidating its political and socio-economic system so as to be capable of facing a serious crisis. Although the parliamentary and party system functioned more or less adequately for some years, no stable government emerged; and in economic and social affairs this was the very period during which relations became increasingly embittered, so that tension between hostile camps accumulated to the point of near-explosion.

This is not to say, with hindsight, that political and social developments from 1923 onwards were a one-way street, leading inevitably to political crisis and the collapse of democracy. The undeniable structural weaknesses of the republic did not necessarily lead to the crisis strategy of 1930–2 and the political events of 1932–3; to the very last there was room for alternative methods and decisions, though the choice became steadily narrower. But an analysis of the structural and political defects of the middle period will indicate the conditions and con-straints which were to affect the actions and reactions of statesmen and large sections of the public when the republic once more entered a phase of acute crisis in 1929–30.

Considering first the development of the parliamentary and party system, it is to be noted that the republic in the middle period did not succeed in evolving an effective parliamentary form of central government in accordance with its constitution. This serious defect was due to several factors.

First, the coalition policy was hampered by a perpetual dilemma. Since there could be no question of a coalition embracing both the SPD and the DNVP, from 1920 onwards the possibilities were limited to three: (a) a bloc consisting of the Centre, DVP and DNVP, who agreed on many domestic issues but disagreed sharply on foreign affairs; (b) the 'great coalition' extending from the SPD to the DVP, who could speak with one voice on foreign affairs but were constantly at odds on economic and social matters; and (c) minority governments formed by middle-of-the-road parties and dependent on support, or at least forbearance, by the right wing or the left. In other words, from 1920 onwards there was no parliamentary majority in the Reichstag prepared to work together and steer a consistent long-term political course in both domestic and foreign affairs. As a result, governments had to cope with the home and foreign issues that arose by means of differently composed majorities — a procedure that was far from calculated to bring about a lasting stabilization of the parliamentary system.

Secondly, the difficulties of coalition policy were increased by the fact that not only the opposition but even the parliamentary parties supporting the government were in a state of tension *vis-à-vis* the latter. Their attitude to the government was determined by complicated, ever-changing shifts of power within the parties themselves, and was thus unstable, unreliable and incalculable. In 1929 Gustav Stolper, an economist and member of the DDP, declared: 'What we have today is a coalition of ministers, not a coalition of parties. There are no government parties, only opposition parties. This state of things is a greater danger to the democratic system than ministers and parliamentarians realize.' To a certain extent this verdict applies to the previous years also.

The instability of the parliamentary and party system afforded opportunities for such intervention by the Reich President, and increasingly called for such intervention. The decline of parliamentary power was not only a phenomenon of the last phase of the republic. During the phase of 'relative stabilization' the Reichstag as the embodiment of parliamentary democracy did not exert its powers as fully as it should have done, with the result that it became perceptibly weaker during those years. Discontent with party and parliamentary government became widespread, already foreshadowing the transformation into an authoritarian presidential regime.

The inability of the parties to play their parliamentary role by forming stable majority coalitions was to some extent a legacy of imperial Germany. Excluded from power under the monarchical system, the parties had never been obliged to compromise in order to form viable governments. After 1918 they held largely to the conception of their role and to the parliamentary habits that had obtained in the past, although their function in a parliamentary democracy was fundamentally different. They were now independent organizations of power and a key element in the political system, 'irrespective of whether they were exercising state power at any given time or were challenging the government in their capacity as an opposition ready to take over from it' (Ernst Rudolf Huber). However, the parties' acceptance of this new role was hesitant and at times reluctant. They shrank from governmental responsibility, fearful of making compromises that might disappoint their own supporters; this feeling generally outweighed their readiness to form stable majorities at the cost of some modification of the party line.

This was particularly the case with the SPD which – except for a few months in 1924 – was the largest party in the Reichstag until 1932 and, if only on that account, bore special responsibility for the functioning of the parliamentary system. The part it actually played at Reich level reflected neither its organizational strength nor its parliamentary weight. In the revolutionary months of 1918–19 the Majority Social Democrats had forgone the opportunity to exercise power alone and had chosen to establish the republic on a basis of compromise and collaboration between the workers and the bourgeoisie. On the same principle it would have been logical for them to claim the leading role in the government alliance and make it their chief objective to exercise an active influence over domestic and foreign policy. But, just as they had not followed the revolutionary-socialist course to the end, so they failed to tread the liberal-democratic path consistently between 1918 and 1930. Restraining tendencies set in at an early stage. Participation in government was increasingly felt to be an encumbrance; the leaders feared that they would lose the confidence of their own supporters because the points in their programme that went beyond the notion of a liberal republic would have to be sacrificed to a coalition with the non-socialist parties. Consequently, the SPD left the government after the electoral defeat of 1920. When, in 1922, the merger with the remnant of the USPD led to a strengthening of the left wing in the party as a whole and among its Reichstag deputies, aversion to forming a coalition with the bourgeois parties grew stronger. At the same time, the SPD failed in its attempt, embodied in the reformist Görlitz programme of 1921, to break through the limitations of a 'strictly proletarian party' and become a broadly based 'left-wing people's party' (Heinrich August Winkler), as it once again adopted essentially Marxist positions in the Heidelberg programme of 1925. This sharpened the contradiction between theoretical statement and reformist practice; the party, in Parliament and outside, found increasing difficulty in compromising between power and principle. Hence the SPD in the Reichstag was in a defensive position during the middle period of the republic. It supported the bourgeois parties on individual issues, especially in important matters of foreign policy, without sharing in the government, thus taking up the curious stance of being 'half in government, half in opposition' (Klaus Schönhoven), with no clear conception of its role in either case.

In Prussia, on the other hand, under the Social Democratic Minister-President, Otto Braun, the regime based on the coalition of SPD, Centre, DDP and for a time DVP showed, during the same period, that stable government could be achieved with a clearly defined and consistently pursued coalition policy. It also showed that the assumption of governmental responsibility by a coalition Cabinet did not necessarily lead to defeat at the polls, but to successes and a strengthening of the democratic process. If Germany achieved relative stabilization after 1923 it was largely because in much the largest of its component states – Prussia comprised about three-fifths of the total area and population of the Reich – the government coalition remained stable and effective until 1932.

Different, but no less difficult, problems affected the DNVP, the party at the opposite wing to the SPD within the spectrum of parties that might combine to form a government coalition. The DNVP considered itself as an anti-parliamentarian party of 'integration'; however, it had to accept the rules of the despised parliamentary game if it were not to forfeit all influence and hence all hope of promoting the economic interests of its supporters. This inner contradiction made it oscillate between opposition to the Weimar 'system' in principle and readiness to co-operate to a limited extent in the governmental and parliamentary sphere. Dissension within the party as regards participation in government flared up violently in 1924 (cf. page 71 below): for, with the consolidation of the republic, the interest groups of landowners, industrialists and business men exercised increasing pressure on the party leaders to form a coalition with the middle-ground parties so that they could gain a bigger share of the economic cake. On this account the DNVP twice joined a government coalition, in 1925 and 1927. The *rapprochement* between the conservatives and the republic reached its peak in these years but came to an abrupt end in 1928, when the party elected the right-wing Hugenberg as its leader. Hugenberg reverted to a course of strict opposition to the system, drove the moderates out of the party and extended a hand to the NSDAP. In this way the DNVP disappeared from the spectrum of parties eligible to join a coalition under the Weimar democracy.

The role of a 'state party' of the Weimar Republic devolved on the Centre, which formed part of all Reich governments, and also all Prussian governments, from 1919 to 1932. Primarily a party of Catholics loyal to their Church, it comprised the most varied social classes. Hence it was intransigent in confessional, educational and cultural matters, but was capable of compromising with either the right or the moderate left on political, economic, or social affairs. This flexibility lent the Centre importance, and it played a key role in the formation of all governments from 1920 to 1931. However, after Erzberger's death and Wirth's resignation in 1922 the party's centre of gravity moved increasingly to the right. This was made clear when Kaas became its leader in 1928 and also during Brüning's chancellorship. Thus the availability of the Centre for a coalition with the SPD gradually diminished during the later 1920s.

The coalition possibilities of the middle-ground liberals were limited, first, by the strong objections of the DVP, especially, to a coalition with the SPD, and secondly by the rapid decline of organized liberalism in the second half of the decade. Neither the DDP nor the DVP succeeded in creating a stable party organization and securing broad, permanent electoral support. In the first years of the republic these parties obtained over 20 per cent of the votes, but in the Reichstag election of 1924 this figure had already diminished, and in 1932 they registered only 2 per cent between them. The mass defection of middle-class voters to the right not only weakened political liberalism but radically modified the Weimar party system: its ability to function was more doubtful than ever, the formation of parliamentary majorities was still more difficult. True, the DVP remained influential until 1932 despite its dwindling membership, chiefly because of the industrial interests behind it. But, as after Stresemann's death the party's right wing had gained the upper hand and was bent on uncompromising economic liberalism, the DVP's influence served not to support parliamentary government but was exercised in favour of an authoritarian transformation of the regime.

Having thus outlined the general development and structural problems of the Weimar parliamentary system, we may give an account of the Reichstag elections and successive governments, together with the causes and outcome of government crises.

At the turn of 1923–4 there was little sign that the Reich would, in a relatively short time, achieve consolidation on the basis of the Weimar constitution. On the contrary, it seemed in those weeks as though the parliamentary system was 'radically called in question' (Michael Stürmer). The Catholic–liberal coalition formed by Wilhelm Marx of the Centre Party after the fall of Stresemann's government (23 November 1923) carried on business under an emergency law of limited duration, and executive power rested with the head of the Army Command (*Chef der Heeresleitung*), backed by the President's emergency powers under Article 48 of the constitution.

This state of emergency did not end until the spring of 1924. In February Seeckt, the army commander, relinquished his special powers, and in March a majority of the Reichstag refused the government's request for a prolongation of the enabling law. Thereupon the President empowered the Chancellor to dissolve the Reichstag.

The Reichstag election of 4 May 1924 (table, pages 194–5) showed to a significant extent the effects of the political and economic convulsions of 1923. Apart from the Centre, which gained one additional seat, all parties that had been connected with the government in the previous year suffered heavy losses in terms of both votes and seats. The DDP lost 11 seats and the DVP 20. The SPD declined from 171 to 100 seats. Here it is to be noted that, after the merger of the SPD with the USPD rump at the end of 1922, sixty-eight USPD deputies had joined the SPD; however, as the election showed, most of their voters did not follow their example. Equally, the voters were clearly not in sympathy with the SPD's vacillation between sharing in government and acting as an opposition. The clear victors in the election were the extreme parties of right and left. The Deutschvölkische Freiheitspartei, a combination of extreme right groups, obtained 32 seats; the DNVP, together with the Landbund (Agricultural League), with 105 seats, became the largest group in the new Reichstag. At the opposite end of the political spectrum, the KPD (Communists) increased their strength from 17 to 62 seats.

The parties responsible for government being thus gravely weakened in comparison with the extreme right and left, the problem of forming a sufficient majority was, if anything, ever more difficult after the May election. A majority coalition could scarcely be formed without the Nationalists, and in the DVP especially, after their heavy defeat at the polls, those elements became active which desired, at almost any price, a right-wing coalition including the DNVP. In these circumstances the decisive factor was the DNVP's attitude to the Dawes Plan, which was to be debated in Parliament in the summer of 1924. Thus the plan became the key not only to Germany's foreign policy but to her domestic situation in that year. During the election the DNVP had opposed it vehemently. The question now was whether the party would be prepared, in return for a share in government, to waive its rooted opposition to the foreign policy pursued by the middle-ground parties and especially Stresemann. This dilemma provoked acute controversy within the DNVP in the summer of 1924. At first its leaders temporized, setting exaggerated conditions for their participation in government so that the negotiations came to nothing. At the beginning of June the former minority Cabinet was formally reconstituted. No secret was made of the endeavour to extend the coalition (of the Centre, DDP and DVP) to the right. In addition, the minority government relied on unconditional support from the SPD on the main foreign issue, the Dawes Plan legislation. The SPD had taken no part in the efforts to form a new government. Under the impact of their heavy electoral defeat they withdrew into complete passivity and left the task of coalition-forming to the middle-ground parties.

The final Reichstag vote on the Dawes Plan took place on 29 August 1924. As the law on the state railways was a constitutional matter it required a two-thirds majority, which could only be obtained if some DNVP deputies voted for it. Hence in the days and weeks beforehand the party's parliamentary group was exposed to massive pressure not only from the government but, above all, from the economic circles that it represented (the Landbund, the Reich Association of German Industry, the Chamber of Industry and Commerce), who had an interest in the adoption of the plan. The crisis within the DNVP thus came to the surface. After a dramatic dispute the leaders of the parliamentary party were obliged, just before the vote was held, to permit their members to vote as individuals. On the railway Bill about half of them voted each way, and the Bill was passed with the aid of the rebel group.

After the passage of the Dawes legislation the problem of foreign policy began to recede behind domestic issues, in particular the incidence of reparation burdens. This seemed to leave open the way for the formation of a 'bourgeois bloc' or middle-ground coalition, but at first matters remained in suspense.

Although the DNVP showed much more readiness to compromise than in early summer, the DDP now refused to combine with the Nationalists, and there were also strong elements in the Centre Party who did not want an alliance with the DNVP. Thus the weeks of complicated negotiation ended not with a re-formed government including the DNVP, but with a second dissolution of the Reichstag.

The election of 7 December 1924 (table, pages 194–5) showed that the gradual consolidation in political and economic affairs was having its effect on the parliamentary system. This time the extreme right and left were the losers: the KPD lost 17 seats, the right extremists 18. The DNVP gained a few seats, bringing its total to 111 including the Landbund. However, this increase was less than the losses of the extreme right. It can therefore be assumed that many who had voted for the DNVP in May had now switched to one of the middle parties, all of whom gained some seats: the Centre and DDP 4 each, the DVP 6. The chief victor was the SPD, whose total rose from 100 seats in May to 131 in December, no doubt at the expense of the KPD. The SPD was again the largest party in the Reichstag, but did not manage to convert its success into political power.

Arithmetically speaking, there were two possibilities of a majority: a 'great coalition' extending from the SPD to the DVP, or a 'bourgeois bloc' from the Centre to the Nationalists. The DVP held the balance, and on the day following the election announced that it would only join a coalition of the bourgeois right. Stresemann now also wanted a government including the Nationalists, so as to make them share responsibility for impending decisions in home and foreign affairs. Weeks of tough negotiation were still needed before the new Cabinet could embark on its functions in January 1925. The Chancellor was Hans Luther, previously Finance Minister, non-party but close to the DVP; the government was a coalition of the Centre, BVP, DVP and DNVP – the first Reich government in the history of the Weimar period in which the Nationalists were represented. (The DDP as a party did not join the coalition, but Gessler, who still belonged to it, continued to be Defence Minister.)

The government parties in Parliament were exposed to much conflicting pressure from powerful economic interests, and the Luther Cabinet had a difficult time with the main domestic issues of 1925, such as tariff policy and the revaluation of the mark. However, foreign policy was crucial from the outset, and led to the collapse of the 'bourgeois bloc' at the end of the year. The Nationalists, under right-wing leadership, mobilized all their forces against Stresemann's Locarno policy; under heavy pressure from the party organizations, the DNVP ministers resigned at the end of October 1925 before the Reichstag voted on the treaties on 27 November. The motion to approve the treaties was carried by the votes of the SPD, Centre, DVP, DDP and BVP, against the DNVP, Völkische Partei, KPD and Wirtschaftspartei (business men's party), and they were signed in London on 1 December. On 5 December the remnant of the Luther Cabinet resigned. Again the problem was to form a majority capable of governing, and again the crisis dragged on for weeks. It would have been logical to form a new majority from the parties that had voted for the Locarno treaties, the more so as only a government with a solid majority could hope to deal with the country's economic difficulties and rising unemployment. The middle parties, especially the DDP and Centre, were prepared to join in a 'great coalition', as were some members of the SPD; notably Otto Braun, the Prussian Minister-President, besought his party comrades to overcome their distaste for power, to show 'confidence in their own strength' and 'the courage to accept responsibility'.

However, the 'great coalition' did not come about; in January 1926 Luther formed a minority Cabinet of the Centre, DVP and DDP. Several factors contributed to this outcome. In the first place, the DVP was still deeply adverse to co-operating with the SPD, chiefly on account of sharp disagreements on social policy; this attitude governed the tactics of the DVP leaders in the exploratory discussions. Secondly, the SPD made it comparatively easy for their opponents to outmanoeuvre them, as their reluctance to join in government was still stronger than any willingness to do so at the price of what were thought to be damaging compromises. Furthermore, the situation was already affected by the new incumbent of the presidency: Field Marshal von Hindenburg, elected in April 1925. Hindenburg, advised by his state secretary Otto Meissner, made it clear from the beginning of the crisis that he would not welcome SPD participation in government; in his view the best solution was to reinstate the bourgeois bloc, and if that was impossible he would prefer a minority government under Luther. The President's office sought to influence the outcome of the government crisis accordingly, with no true intention of allowing a 'great coalition' to be formed. In any case, 'it was the self-exclusion of the Social Democrats that virtually opened the way to the new minority government' (Michael Stürmer).

The course and outcome of the government crisis at the end of 1925 already illustrates the effect that the change of presidency was to have on German politics and the eventual fate of the republic. Friedrich Ebert died at the age of 54 on 28 February 1925, a few months before his term as President was due to expire. His last weeks were overshadowed by the judgment in the Magdeburg libel case, a particularly shocking instance among many cases of one-sided political justice in the Weimar Republic. A nationalist editor had abused Ebert and accused him of high treason in wartime on the ground that he had allowed himself to be elected to the action committee in the strike of January 1918. The Magdeburg court declared in its judgment that this was indeed 'objective treason', and the editor was therefore found guilty not of libel but merely of formal insult. The judgment was quashed on appeal by the public prosecutor, but Ebert was deeply wounded by the trial and its accompanying circumstances. He died of the effects of an appendicitis operation, delayed during the trial and carried out too late.

According to law, the first ballot in the presidential election required an absolute majority, the second ballot a simple one only. As expected, no decision was reached in the first ballot on 29 March 1925. Among seven candidates, the highest number of votes (10·4 million) was obtained by Karl Jarres, mayor of Duisburg, the joint candidate of the DVP and DNVP; then came Otto Braun (SPD) with 7·8 million votes and Wilhelm Marx (Centre) with 3·9 million. A long way behind were Thälmann (KPD), Hellpach (DDP), Held (BVP) and Ludendorff (Völkische Partei). For the second ballot the parties of the 'Weimar coalition' agreed on Marx as the candidate of the 'people's bloc'; he seemed almost certain to win if the Centre, SPD and DDP voters showed a reasonable degree of unanimity. Alarmed by this, the political right sought a candidate of the strongest popular appeal, and found him in Hindenburg. The revered victor of Tannenberg, who was 78 years old and had taken no part in postwar political life, now came forward as the candidate of the right-wing parties united in the 'Reich bloc'. The BVP supported Hindenburg, the north German Protestant, in preference to Marx, the Rhineland Catholic, and was thus instrumental in giving Hindenburg a narrow majority on 26 April: he received 14·6 million votes to Marx's 13·7 million and Thälmann's 1·9 million. 'Hindenburg's victory was due to the splitting of the workers' movement and also the splitting of political Catholicism' (Karl Dietrich Erdmann).

Contrary to a widespread view, the election of the imperial field marshal to the presidency must be regarded as a serious setback for the republic. True, at the outset Hindenburg disappointed those of his supporters who hoped and expected that his presidency would begin with a sharp swing to the right. This would have been beyond his official powers, and was ruled out by the general political situation. Moreover, Hindenburg felt bound by his constitutional oath and was at pains to discharge his office faithfully according to law. Nevertheless, there began with his presidency a 'silent change in the constitution', whereby – gradually and at first barely perceptibly – the balance shifted in favour of presidential power. Given the precariousness of parliamentary majorities, the President was able to bring his personal and political preferences to bear on the formation of governments to an extent greater than the founders of the constitution had dreamt of. Hindenburg's preferences were clear from 1925 onwards: if at all possible the DNVP should be included in government, if at all possible the SPD should be kept out of it; this was a matter of principle, independent of parliamentary constellations and concrete political requirements. That 'government should move to the right' was Hindenburg's idea not only in 1929–30; it was his basic attitude from the time he took office, as is shown by his behaviour in the government crises at the end of 1925 and the end of 1926. It also became clear very soon that he attached cardinal importance to Article 48 of the constitution, which he construed as granting, in effect, unlimited dictatorial powers. When, in 1926, the Ministry of the Interior produced the draft of an implementing statute based on Article 48, Hindenburg declared that he thought it an unsuitable time for such a law; at the same time he made it clear that he thought the law unnecessary anyway. In his words, 'A strictly formalistic definition of the manner of exercising the President's rights, or even a limitation of those rights, would weaken his authority and gravely endanger the security of the state.' Thus in the very first years of his presidency Hindenburg displayed tendencies which were to take full effect in the changed situation after 1929.

Luther's second Cabinet, appointed in January 1926, lasted only four months. It broke up as a result of the 'flag decree' of May 1926, allowing German missions abroad to use the imperial tricolour of black, white and red. The Reichstag passed a vote of no confidence, supported by the left-wing parties and the DDP members of the coalition, whereupon the Cabinet resigned. However, a few days later it was re-formed with almost the same composition, except that the Chancellor was now Marx of the Centre Party instead of Luther.

This new version of the bourgeois minority coalition was from the start regarded on all sides as a mere stop-gap. Count Westarp, chairman of the DNVP deputies, stated on 21 June 1926 that he was continuously in touch with Hindenburg and with Scholz, the DVP chairman in the Reichstag, with a view to 'forming a right-wing government at the earliest possible date'. The Centre and the DDP, on the other hand, wanted to enlarge the minority Cabinet to a 'great coalition' immediately after the referendum concerning the expropriation, without compensation, of the former German princes – an issue which divided the SPD from the non-socialist parties. (This referendum took place on 20 June 1926. The proposal was rejected, but the vote showed a significant trend: the number who supported the left-wing parties exceeded by 3·5 million the total of votes cast for the SPD and KPD at the last Reichstag election.)

For the time being, however, the coalition was not broadened in either a leftward or a rightward direction. The minority government manoeuvred its way through the summer, faced with awkward economic and social problems and growing unemployment. But towards the end of the year it became clear that the balancing act could not last; the minority coalition was not viable without any firm support on the left or right. The crisis came to a head at the beginning of December 1926, when Scholz of the DVP declared in a dramatic speech that his party's ideal was 'co-operation among all bourgeois (*bürgerlich*, middle-of-the-road) parties and forces'. The SPD understood this as terminating the loose co-operation that had existed between the minority coalition and the SPD, and thus rejecting the idea of a 'great coalition'. The Social Democrats reacted with fierce attacks on the government's defence policy (demand for Gessler's resignation; Scheidemann's Reichstag speech on co-operation between the Reichswehr and the Red Army). On 17 December 1926 the (third) Marx government was brought down by a vote of no confidence moved by the SPD.

The Nationalists also voted against the Cabinet, being determined to obtain a share in government. Their manoeuvre succeeded: the fourth Marx government, formed in January 1927, consisted of a bloc representing the Centre, BVP, DVP, and DNVP.

This was preceded by two weeks of hard struggle, as the Centre Party, mindful of its working-class members, had little enthusiasm for an alliance with the DNVP. Its misgivings were at last overcome by steady pressure from the President, who worked for a right-wing coalition throughout the crisis. General Kurt von Schleicher also took a hand in the political negotiations for the first time: since the beginning of 1926 he had been head of the newly created Armed Forces Department of the Defence Ministry, and after Seeckt's dismissal in October 1926 he had become 'in fact if not in name . . . the military-political head of the Reichswehr' (Andreas Hillgruber). Schleicher increasingly gained Hindenburg's confidence and became his trusted adviser. At the turn of the year 1926/7 he suggested to Hindenburg that if it proved impossible to form a right-wing coalition with the DNVP, the President should 'appoint a government in which he had confidence, without consulting the parties or paying attention to their wishes', and then, 'with the order for dissolution ready to hand, give the government every constitutional opportunity to get a majority in Parliament'. Here we already find the conception of an authoritarian presidential government, which was to become a reality a few years later. As Michael Stürmer puts it, 'the new government crisis provided Hindenburg's entourage with a long-sought opportunity to rule out both the "great coalition" and the centre coalition, and to bring the Nationalists to the helm once more. If there was a parliamentary way of doing this, well and good; but if the Centre made difficulties, it might be necessary to govern "against" the Reichstag.'

The 'second bourgeois bloc' was by its very nature a fragile alliance. Foreign affairs were quiescent during its first year, but its inner cohesion was constantly threatened by economic, social and educational problems. To prevent the government collapsing prematurely the DNVP was obliged to make fairly large concessions to the centre parties: for example, the prolongation of the law for the protection of the republic, and the introduction of unemployment insurance. But towards the end of 1927 the will and ability to reconcile divergent interests became increasingly weaker in all the parties concerned. This was the basic reason for the break-up of the coalition, which took place over the schools question in February 1928. The Bill introduced by the Centre Party and supported by the DNVP provided *inter alia* that Catholic schools should be permitted in Länder (such as Baden) where the system was non-denominational; the effect would have been to reintroduce denominational elementary schools. The DVP prevented the Bill becoming law, whereupon the Centre declared the coalition at an end and demanded the immediate dissolution of the Reichstag, pending which it would carry on urgent government business only.

The election of 20 May 1928 (table, pages 194–5) was a clear success for the left wing, and reflected considerable shifts among the non-socialist parties. The SPD won 22 seats, bringing its total to 153 in the new Reichstag, or nearly a third of the total of 491. The KPD rose from 45 to 54 seats. The greatest losses were sustained by the middle-ground parties and the DNVP. The DVP lost 6 seats, the DDP 7, and even the Centre and the BVP, whose following had hitherto been so staunch, lost 7 and 3 seats respectively. The DNVP suffered much more in terms of both votes and seats; its strength in the Reichstag fell from 103 to 73. The extreme right, the NSDAP, lost some votes and returned 12 members to the new Reichstag. The losses of the middle-ground parties and the DNVP accrued to the benefit of small splinter groups representing private or class interests, such as the Wirtschaftspartei ('business men's party'), the Landvolkpartei and the Bauernpartei (large and small farmers respectively).

Despite the weakening of the right wing, however, it would be very superficial to interpret the election of May 1928 as a victory for democratic and republican forces. In the first place, the drift away from middle-ground parties to splinter groups with narrow interests showed to what an extent the former's integrative power had diminished – a process which involved appreciable danger to the existing party system. For many voters who moved away from the middle ground in 1928, the splinter parties were only a temporary situation: some of them were to vote for the Nazis at the next Reichstag election in 1930, and a great many more in 1932. Secondly, the defeat of the DNVP and the Centre set in motion changes within those parties which were anything but favourable to the long-term stabilization of the republic. The right wing of the DNVP, which had only reluctantly gone along with the coalition policy of the past few years, now went over to the offensive and gained the upper hand within the party. In October 1928 Alfred Hugenberg, the leading figure on the nationalist Pan-German wing, was elected party chairman. This put a decisive end to the *rapprochement*, such as it had been, between the DNVP and the republican regime. Under Hugenberg's leadership the party pursued a course of unremitting opposition and obstruction, its anti-democratic sentiments attaining a hitherto unknown pitch of ferocity. The Centre, too, underwent a swing to the right, symbolized by the election of the conservative Monsignor Ludwig Kaas as party chairman at the congress in Cologne in December 1928. Kaas, whose ideal of the state was not parliamentary democracy but a plebiscitary dictatorship, scored an easy victory over the workers' representatives, Joos and Stegerwald.

After the election of May 1928 it was practically impossible to form a government without the SPD, and the latter was at last prepared to come out of opposition: '*Victoire oblige*', as the SPD newspaper *Vorwärts* put it on 25 May. On 12 June, Hermann Müller, chairman of the parliamentary SPD, was charged by the President to form a government 'on the broadest possible basis'. The arithmetic of the situation pointed clearly to the 'great coalition', as no other combination could form a parliamentary majority. But the negotiations proved unexpectedly difficult, as some members of the DVP and the Centre objected to an alliance with the SPD; the DVP put forward conditions that were hard to meet. However, the coalition was at last formed at the end of June; this was due to a powerful intervention by Stresemann from his sick-bed, when the negotiations had reached a deadlock. The government was formed as a 'Cabinet of personalities' irrespective of party, including members of the SPD, DDP, DVP, BVP and Centre, together with General Groener (non-party) as Defence Minister; the parliamentary parties as such were not formally obliged to support the government. Only at the beginning of 1929 was the government transformed into a 'great coalition' backed by the parliamentary parties.

The coalition rested on shaky foundations from the beginning. In foreign affairs there were no essential differences among the parties, but in domestic matters the government's freedom of movement was extremely limited; the divergent interests of its supporting parties blocked one another, and cautious manoeuvring was necessary at all times. The first issue that came up – the dispute over 'Armoured Cruiser "A" ' – could not have been more unfortunate, and led to the first split in the coalition. The building of this warship had been approved by the previous government but had not yet begun owing to shortage of finances. The SPD had campaigned in May with the slogan 'Not armoured cruisers but food for children!', and a storm of indignation broke out in August when the party learnt that the ship was to be built, and that the Social Democratic ministers in the Cabinet had raised no objection. In November the SPD members of the Reichstag moved that the construction should be stopped, and forced the Chancellor and the Social Democratic ministers to support this in spite of the Cabinet decision. The SPD motion was defeated with the aid of votes of the centre and right, but the spectacular conflict did nothing to improve the government's credibility or, above all, that of the largest government party.

Towards the end of 1928 problems of foreign policy came into the foreground; 1929 was dominated by the reparations battle (cf. page 64 above). It became the primary task of the 'great coalition', and its main achievement, to steer the Young Plan safely through the Reichstag despite unrestrained agitation and many diversionary manoeuvres by the 'national opposition'. With the passage of the relevant laws in March 1930 the coalition's stock of common purpose was exhausted. Economic and social problems called for a solution, but it was more and more difficult to achieve a minimum of consensus between, especially, the SPD and the DVP: the latter, since Stresemann's death in October 1929, had become more and more obviously a party of right-wing industrialists. Meanwhile the world depression had set in, and economic and social problems were looming larger from day to day. The coalition broke up in March 1930 owing to the unbridgeable contradictions between the SPD and the DVP over social policies: this was no accident, as the profound division between them on this score was a constant element in the Weimar political situation.

This leads to consideration of a further field in which the phase of 'stabilization' shows a distinct deficit: that of labour relations, the interplay of the organized interests of employers and workers. The constant exacerbation of social conflicts during the 1920s undoubtedly had a destabilizing effect on the social and political system.

In the initial phase of the republic the concept of social partnership expressed in the *Arbeitsgemeinschaft* of employers and trade unions (cf. page 14 above) was a key component of the 'Weimar compromise'. It became clear in the ensuing years, however, that this compact rested on shaky foundations. The employers regarded the agreement of 15 November 1918 as a tactical alliance for the purpose of safeguarding free enterprise against socialization and the move towards a planned economy. Once this aim was achieved, industrial circles quickly lost interest in a continuation of the alliance. From 1923 at the latest, the main question from their point of view was whether the costs entailed by the social achievements of the revolutionary months, which industry had borne with relative ease during the inflation, would be tolerable in the long run; and they answered this question in the negative. Accordingly the employers now sought

to correct the material results of the social, financial and wages policy of the preceding years so as, for instance, to lengthen the working day without increasing nominal wages, or at least resist pressure for higher wages if working hours remained unchanged. But this was more than a purely economic question. The employers' attempt to go back on what they themselves had offered during the crisis of revolution inevitably appeared to the workers, and especially to the trade unions, as a betrayal of the political basis of the Weimar system (Knut Borchardt).

This is a concise expression of the conflict. From a purely economic point of view – as appears from recent studies, cf. page 164 below – the employers' criticism of the level of wages and social benefits was not unjustified. The increase in real wages from 1924 onwards exceeded the increase in productivity and reduced the possibility of financing investment from profits or capital. The unions, on the other hand, insisted that human interests should take precedence over purely economic ones, and they regarded the employers' offensive on the welfare front from 1923 onwards as an attack on the basic principles of the republic. It can hardly be disputed that the initiative and responsibility for the destabilization of labour relations in the Weimar Republic rested primarily with the employers. On the other hand, there are many indications that during the period in question they genuinely felt themselves to be on the defensive. Their statements make it clear that influential business circles still took as their point of reference the state of labour relations before 1914; they measured the social and economic realities of Weimar by the yardstick of prewar conditions, which they wanted to see revived. In other words, the social basis of the republic which they had accepted in 1918–19 was not regarded by the employers as henceforth binding on industry and irreversible, but was increasingly challenged on grounds of economic efficiency. Influential business circles pressed more and more strongly for a 'general rethinking of social policy' (Hans Mommsen).

Central to the social disputes of 1923–9 were the questions of the eight-hour day and the right to collective bargaining. As regards working hours the employers scored an important success when the eight-hour day sanctioned by law, and regarded by the workers as a symbol of the gains of 1918, was partially nullified by an order of 21 December 1923. This provided that, while eight hours continued to be the norm, a ten-hour day could legally be operated as an administrative exception or in accordance with a collective agreement. The matter continued to be a bone of contention in subsequent years, with neither side able to obtain a substantial change in the 1923 regulation.

After 1923 the state's power of arbitration was increasingly exercised in industrial relations. This was contrary to the intention of the order of 30 October 1923, according to which negotiated agreements were to be the norm and state arbitration the exception. Arbitration boards, or an arbitrator appointed by the central government, were empowered to intervene if employers and workers were unable to reach agreement. If an award was designated as binding, the parties were obliged to accept it.

Nothing shows more clearly the hardening of employer–worker relations than the fact that in the disputes after 1923 it was nearly always necessary to invoke the state arbitration procedure, originally envisaged for exceptional cases only. Between 1924 and 1932 the procedure was used 76,000 times, resulting in 4,000 compulsory awards. Initially the decisions tended to favour the employers, while after 1924 they generally took a middle line: at a time when the unions were already losing ground and were hardly capable of offering battle on a large scale, only the intervention of the state could guarantee a degree of social stability. Hence state arbitration was increasingly regarded as a grievance by key industrial organizations.

The resistance of big business to the arbitration procedure reached its peak in November–December 1928 in the 'Ruhr ironworks dispute', which became the most bitter industrial conflict of the Weimar era. The Ruhr industrialists refused to accept the arbitration award, although it was designated as binding. To compel the adoption of new wage rates they declared a lockout for the whole work force of the Ruhr iron and steel industry; about 220,000 workers were deprived of their jobs. A compromise solution was finally adopted, but the conflict dramatically showed how serious the confrontation between the employers and workers had become, well before the world depression with all its economic and social consequences.

The industrialists now openly challenged the state authority and prepared for a frontal attack on the socio-political compromise of Weimar. 'Important business circles, especially in heavy industry, from 1928 onwards increasingly took the view that the German economy could not be put on a sound basis unless the influence of the workers' movement was curbed; they called for an authoritarian revision of the constitution and an acknowledgement of the primacy of economic interests' (Gerhard A. Ritter).

In 1929, in connection with the budget compromise (see below), unemployment insurance became the focus of conflict in social policy. The German system of social insurance, which was already highly developed, was enlarged by a law of 16 July 1927 which replaced unemployment relief by a system of compulsory insurance to be administered by a new body, the Reich Institution for Labour Exchanges and Unemployment Insurance. Those insured were henceforth legally entitled to relief if they were able and willing to work and were unemployed through no fault of their own. Insurance contributions were limited to 3 per cent of wages and were to be paid in equal amounts by the employer and the employee. The resources of the Reich institution were calculated to provide relief for an average of 800,000 unemployed, plus a further 600,000 from an emergency fund to be drawn on in times of crisis. If total contributions together with the institution's reserves were insufficient, the state was to meet the deficit by an interest-free loan or non-repayable grant.

At the time when the law was passed (with the support of the right-wing government coalition and the Social Democratic opposition) the Weimar Republic was in the most prosperous economic phase of its history. The proportion of unemployed, which had been relatively high during the 'stabilization period', was now fairly low (1·3 million or 6·2 per cent compared with 2 million or 10 per cent in 1926); provided the economic boom continued, the scheme appeared financially viable. But already in 1928 there were signs of recession, and in the winter of 1928–9 the number of unemployed rose to nearly 3 million. As the level of relief was fixed by law and the Reich Institution had not sufficient funds, the central government had to help out with loans: by December 1929 the institution's debt to the state was 342 million Reichsmarks. Since the Reich's finances were already in a precarious state, unemployment insurance became a highly charged political issue.

In December 1929 the National Association of German Industry produced a memorandum entitled 'Progress or Decline?' embodying the views and proposals of the business world on financial and social matters. It called for a reduction of taxes on capital and means of production, an increase in capitation and consumption taxes, and a curtailment of social benefits. The memorandum launched a frontal attack on the principle of social welfare by demanding that the 'advantages of the law on social insurance' should 'be confined to those in real need'. In conclusion the memorandum sharply condemned what it termed the 'wrong direction taken by economic, financial and social policies'.

The Müller government succeeded only with great difficulty in securing a vote of confidence in December 1929 for the emergency covering of the budget deficit: 14 DVP deputies voted against, 24 SPD members absented themselves, and the BVP abstained from voting. All political groups were aware that the conflict within the coalition had only been postponed and would break out vehemently as soon as the Reichstag had approved the Young Plan (which it did, by 270 votes to 192, on 11–12 March 1930).

It seemed that the unemployment insurance system could only be saved by increasing contributions or lowering benefits. The unions and employers took up diametrically opposed positions, and their conflicting views were reflected by the parliamentary parties. The SPD argued for maintaining the social obligations of the central government, the *Länder* and local authorities, increasing regular contributions by 4 per cent, and exacting an emergency contribution from those on fixed salaries. The DVP rejected the idea of increased contributions and called for an 'internal reform' of the insurance system by reducing benefits. The SPD members, however, believed that the DVP and the indusialists were not out to remedy abuses and defects in the system, which certainly existed, but to destroy it altogether; they therefore insisted that there should be no reduction of benefits and that the contribution rate should be fixed at 3·75 per cent. Under the influence of its trade-union wing the SPD rejected a last-minute compromise proposal put forward by Brüning, the chairman of the Centre group in the Reichstag, and accepted by the DVP, for an interim solution which would have postponed a final decision on the reform of the system until the autumn. Faced with the SPD refusal, the Cabinet decided on 27 March 1930 to resign as a body.

The 'great coalition' did not break up on account of a fractional alteration in the rate of unemployment insurance contributions; it foundered on a basic issue of social policy, in which all the potential for domestic conflict was concentrated in 1930. But, while disagreement on this issue between the right and left wings of the coalition seemed virtually unbridgeable, the behaviour of the SPD in the Reichstag in the second half of March was highly unskilful tactically and showed great political short-sightedness. For its rigid attitude was not backed by any strategic idea of how the party, after bringing down the government to which it belonged, could hope to influence policy to an extent commensurate with its own importance, or put across its views to other parties or to the Reichstag. By relinquishing power the SPD made it easier for the parties of the opposite persuasion to pursue a course for which guidelines were already set. For some time past the Reich President – and with him the increasingly influential extra-parliamentary opposition, representing military, industrial and big landowning interests – had favoured the creation, at almost any price, of a government of the right, independent of Parliament and if necessary opposed to it. The fall of the Müller Cabinet gave the signal for the realization of this ambition and for the transition to an authoritarian presidential regime. In this sense, the break-up of the 'great coalition' was indeed the decisive turning-point in the republic's history.

3

The Artistic Avant-Garde and Mass Culture in the 'Golden Twenties'

When the Weimar years are referred to nostalgically as the 'golden twenties', those who do so are not thinking of the long-drawn-out political and economic distress but of the eruption of a new vitality, the liberation of creative forces in a short decade of unbounded intellectual and artistic freedom. The multi-faceted picture of the 'golden twenties' includes Thomas Mann's *The Magic Mountain*, Döblin's *Berlin Alexanderplatz*, Zuckmayer's *Der fröhliche Weinberg* and Brecht's *Threepenny Opera*, as well as Piscator's political stage productions, the theatre work of Max Reinhardt and Leopold Jessner, Gropius's Bauhaus and the Weissenhof settlement in Stuttgart; the cartoon cycles of George Grosz and the sculpture of Ernst Barlach; films such as *The Cabinet of Dr Caligari* and *The Blue Angel*, and political cabaret with the sparkling satire of Otto Reutter, Walter Mehring, and others. It would be easy to add to this list. The sharp contrast between the gloomy political and economic conditions, on the one hand, and the unique wealth of artistic and intellectual achievement on the other, is in itself typical of the Weimar era.

What we today call 'Weimar culture' is by no means the result of a posthumous glorification or a selective treatment of cultural history, nor is it a myth forged by émigrés and others after 1933. Certainly, the 1920s – not only, but especially in Germany – were a remarkably fruitful decade in intellectual and artistic matters. The achievements to which we apply the general term 'Weimar culture' were admired and intensively discussed in their own day, they were representative of their time and place and were also internationally famous. There really was such a phenomenon as 'Weimar culture'; but the term needs to be defined more closely and restrictively, in two respects.

In the first place, the cultural and the political life of Weimar Germany were to an unusual extent independent and irrelevant to each other. The liveliness and creativity of the cultural scene did little to win respect for the republic as a political system or to stabilize it as a democracy. It was not sufficiently realized at the time that the conditions for a free development of artistic and intellectual energies were in no small degree ensured by the political system itself. Many representatives of 'Weimar culture' were caustically critical of specific institutions and were far from identifying with the republic as such. To that extent

'Weimar culture' signifies not so much a culture of the Weimar republic, but rather stands for 'German culture at the time of the republic'.

Secondly, the culture of the Weimar period was not confined to the artistic avant-garde and the development of a mass culture. The names, titles and achievements associated with the terms 'Weimar culture' and 'golden twenties' are not fully representative of the cultural and intellectual life of the time. 'Modernity' was not the only factor on the cultural scene; the new art was by no means universally popular and accepted, traditional directions and forms were still influential, and modernism was opposed by strong trends of pessimism and anti-modernism. Thus German culture at the time of the Weimar Republic was a deeply divided culture – we may even say that there were two cultures which had scarcely anything to say to each other and were mutually alien and hostile, each denying (though with very different degrees of justification) that the other was a culture at all.

It does not follow, however, that the phenomena that we label as 'Weimar culture' represent a culture of outsiders or simply of a minority. This would not give a true picture of the cultural scene between 1918 and 1933. For it was indeed from representatives of 'Weimar culture' that the main impulses went out. It was they who determined the themes of discussion; their works occupied public attention, dominated the art market and the literary scene, became widely known and gained an international reputation. In that sense the 'Weimar culture' can certainly be called the 'dominant culture' of the Weimar period. But this prevalence of modern trends in literature, painting, architecture and stagecraft, along with manifestations of a freer attitude towards morals and life-style, was fiercely combated by strong conservative, anti-modernist forces that were rooted in broad sections of the population. Their hour was to come in 1933.

Having thus attempted to define our terms more closely, a few words should be said about the periods into which art and culture in Weimar Germany divide. It is not in dispute that the roots of what is referred to historically as 'Weimar culture' are to be found in imperial Germany. The year 1918 did not mark a watershed in literature and drama, painting and design, music and architecture. The decisive change – not only the search for new artistic styles and forms of expression, but also the profession of a new attitude to life – took place in the first decade of this century. Expressionism, the most important artistic expression of the change, originated soon after 1900; noteworthy Expressionist works of painting, lyric poetry and drama were in existence by 1914. In the first years of the republic, art and culture were entirely under the influence of Expressionism and other avant-garde stylistic movements. These sought to distinguish themselves from Expressionism, but shared with it a mood of revolutionary discontent, radical rejection of bourgeois values, a utopian view of man and society, and love of experimentation. They often took on neo-Expressionist forms, which, in Dadaism, constituted the most provoking challenge so far addressed to all conventional ideas of 'higher' culture.

The avant-garde movements that had begun before 1918 came to an end in about 1922–3, with a fairly abrupt abandonment of the utopian claims of Expressionism. Seething unrest and apocalyptic dreams of salvation were replaced by the search for authenticity, a more sober and practical approach to everyday reality. Technology was no longer, as with the Expressionists, represented as evil and made a scapegoat for all social ills, but was accepted as a necessary part of history. An unsentimental pragmatism came to pervade all artistic styles. Remarkably enough, these tendencies were evinced by the same artists who had, shortly before, been committed to Expressionism. It was the Expressionist playwright Paul Kornfeld who exclaimed in 1924, in his comedy *Palme oder der Gekränkte*: 'Let us hear no more of war and revolution and the salvation of the world! Let us be modest and turn to other, smaller things.'

A term was soon found for the new style: *Neue Sachlichkeit* (new objectivity or matter-of-factness). First applied to the latest style of painting by the art historian Georg Friedrich Hartlaub in 1923, it fitted the mood of the time so closely that it was at once extended to other forms of art. It was also used as a general description of the attitude to life that was dominant in those years: a popular song of 1928 ran: '*Es liegt in der Luft eine Sachlichkeit*' ('There's a matter-of-factness in the air'). There is a strong case for arguing that not Expressionism but *Neue Sachlichkeit* is the 'true' or typical Weimar style. To that extent we would take issue with Peter Gay's judgement: 'The Weimar style was born before the Weimar republic . . . The republic created little; it liberated what was already there.'

Cultural developments after 1929–30 are distinguished by a twofold trend: a certain weakening of artistic creativity, and increasing polarization. While some artists turned away from *Neue Sachlichkeit*, which was now decried as bourgeois and prosaic, and while the extreme left treated art as no more than a weapon in the political battle, the traditionalist forces intensified their attacks on modern literature, painting, architecture and stagecraft. The Nazis and their sympathizers branded the whole of modern art as degenerate 'cultural Bolshevism'. In the last days of the republic, as in politics, so in matters of art and culture, the hostile camps confronted each other irreconcilably.

Studying the succession of dominant stylistic trends between 1918 and 1933, we find a considerable parallelism between political and cultural developments. While the first, agitated years of the republic are dominated by the continuing effects of Expressionism, in the phase of relative stabilization we find the republic-oriented mood of *Neue Sachlichkeit*; finally the extreme polarization of politics in the last phase of Weimar corresponds to the radicalization of art and culture from 1929 to 1930.

We may complete this broad outline with a few details. It is probably not an accident that the terms Expressionism and *Neue Sachlichkeit* were first applied to painting and then to the other arts, for it is in painting that stylistic tendencies and changes are most tangibly expressed. The great break in artistic tradition took place in Germany between 1905 and 1914; in painting, French influences (Cézanne, Gauguin, Van Gogh) played an important part, as did such groups as Die Brücke (Dresden, 1905) and Der blaue Reiter (Munich, 1911). The young Expressionist artists – Ernst Ludwig Kirchner, Erich Heckel, Karl Schmidt-Rottluff, Max Pechstein, Oskar Kokoschka, Max Beckmann, August Macke, Franz Marc, to name only some – regarded themselves as rebels against the self-satisfied, sated world of the bourgeoisie, which they wished to shock and defy. Many Expressionist works were painted before the First World War, and all the typical features of Expressionism were clearly visible before 1914: rejection of existing aesthetic standards and conventional modes of expression, avoidance of 'picturesqueness' and decoration. Expressionist painting is distinguished by aggressive coloration, the impassioned treatment of line, a compact stylization of forms; the gap between this artistic avant-garde and the public taste of the time was probably the widest that had ever existed.

After the war and revolution, Expressionism had reached its peak of creativity but its influence began to broaden. The years after 1918 were a great time of experimentation in the fine arts, under the influence not only of fully developed Expressionism but also of several other avant-garde movements: Cubism and Futurism, Dadaism and Purism, Verism and Constructivism. These all sought to outbid Expressionism in the rejection of the existing social order and bourgeois practices in art, in aggressive anti-aestheticism and in pushing abstraction to its utmost limits. For this reason they considered themselves anti-Expressionist movements; but they are closely related to Expressionism, as they originated in the same intellectual, artistic and, to some extent, political radicalism. In other European countries the artistic and cultural scene during these years was similarly marked by a radical approach; the numerous avant-garde movements were thoroughly international in character.

Political stabilization was accompanied by a decline of revolutionary unrest in the fine arts. In about 1923–4 Expressionism receded into the background along with the other avant-garde movements of the postwar years; objectivity was now the cry. In contrast to the dynamic and ecstatic tendencies of Expressionism the 'new objective' art was distinguished by coolness, soberness and respect for reality, but also a leaning towards abstraction and stylization; still lifes and portraits were among its favourite genres. Similar tendencies can be seen in the painting of other European countries.

During the 1920s the avant-garde gained in public esteem: the works of modern artists were shown at exhibitions and bought by museums, and leading modernists were appointed to art professorships. But this did not close the gap between modern art and the taste of the masses; in fact hostility to modern trends increased as they gained partial recognition. Peter Gay's remark that 'while not all Expressionists loved Weimar, the enemies of Weimar hated all Expressionists' could also be applied to all the other modernist movements of the Weimar period.

German literature of the 1920s presents such an abundance and variety of subjects and styles that it is almost impossible, and hardly seems desirable, to attempt a general description. Only with considerable reservations can we indicate a few dominant trends and relate them to such concepts as Expressionism or *Neue Sachlichkeit*. In literature after 1910 Expressionism was confined to lyric poetry and drama; there were practically no Expressionist novels. Several prominent authors of the years 1910–24 are *not* to be classified as Expressionists: Thomas Mann (*Der Zauberberg – The Magic Mountain –* 1924), Gerhard Hauptmann, Heinrich Mann, Rainer Maria Rilke, Hermann Hesse, and others. If, none the less, Expressionism was, and is, regarded as the prevailing trend of the first postwar years, it is probably because the German theatre in those years was dominated by Expressionist plays and new, unconventional, 'revolutionary' techniques. The theatre, at that time, was indeed something of a national institution. The educated public followed big theatrical events with an intensity of interest that can scarcely be imagined today. Expressionist plays by Ernst Toller, Walter Hasenclever, Fritz von Unruh, George Kaiser and Reinhard Goering were discussed as passionately as the modernistic productions of the classics by Max Reinhardt and Leopold Jessner (such as Jessner's spectacular production of Schiller's *Wilhelm Tell* at the end of 1919, in a bare, symbolic setting, with Albert Bassermann as Tell and Fritz Kortner as Gessler). Berlin, especially, developed in these years into a world theatrical metropolis: it had the most important producers, the finest actors and actresses, the most famous critics, and devoted, sensitive and critical audiences.

The reign of Expressionism on the stage ended in 1922–3: idealist rhetoric had had its day, the prospect of changing the world no longer fascinated. Dramatists like Kaiser and Hasenclever, who had previously produced Expressionist plays, renounced visions and utopias and turned to writing comedies. Next to comedy it was the down-to-earth realistic folk-play that drove Expressionism from the stage in the mid-twenties. Carl Zuckmayer's *Der fröhliche Weinberg* was a sensational popular success: after its first night in December 1925 Alfred Kerr commented drily '*Sic transit gloria expressionismi*', which was an exact statement of the change of mood.

As in painting and architecture, the new realism and sobriety were now dominant in the theatre and in prose literature. In the second half of the twenties the stage was largely given over to topical drama, with Erwin Piscator as a major producer. Such authors as Peter Martin Lampel, Friedrich Wolf, Ferdinand Bruckner and Hans José Rehfisch pilloried social abuses and made the theatre once again a forum in which important questions of the day were discussed: bias in the law courts, abortion, juvenile problems and social distress. The most striking and influential of such plays was *Revolte im Erziehungshaus* (1928) by P. M. Lampel, which led to a wide-ranging public debate on the reform of correctional education. These dramas were not intended to last long or to impress by their literary quality; the criteria were 'topical content, clear definition of social issues, a vigorous approach, a sense of publicity, a desire for justice and a power of conviction' (Günther Rühle).

The great days of the Weimar theatre came to an end in about 1930. The 'crisis in the theatre' was due not only to the world depression (curtailment of public grants) but also to increasing competition from talking films (cf. page 92 below). Several theatres had to close in 1930 and many more in 1931; opera houses and symphony orchestras were also hit by the depression. The economic decline was accompanied by a crisis in the theatre world itself. On the one hand, war plays were presented with considerable success, in the first instance as topical pieces and 'crystallizations of right-wing theatre' (Jost Hermand and Frank Trommler); on the other, around 1930, authors who belonged or were close to the KPD, such as Bertolt Brecht, wrote topical dramas by way of party polemics and propaganda. However, these works did not find favour with the mostly middle-class public; the theatres closed, and the 'political' plays were put on only by independent groups of actors. The polarization and radicalization of the cultural scene in the last days of the republic was particularly evident in this sphere.

Topical novels became popular at about the same time as topical drama: we may mention such authors as Lion Feuchtwanger, Arnold Zweig, Hans Fallada, Ernst Glaeser and Erik Reger. As with the drama, the aim was to feed the 'hunger for immediacy' (Siegfried Kracauer), and the reader was introduced to new themes such as the world of white-collar workers or the misery of the great cities and unemployment in the late Weimar period. This type of novel was characterized by sobriety of language and an interest in factual authenticity and social analysis – all features of *Neue Sachlichkeit*.

Besides the principal trends mentioned above, the literature of this period also reflects 'the increasing tendency to actualize myths and mythical themes as a means of coming to grips with the present' (Jost Hermand and Frank Trommler): either by a rational treatment of the myth as in Thomas Mann, or, as in nationalist and 'populist' (*völkisch*) writers, by turning to the myth as an escape from rationalism. Relevant here are the big sales of writers like Löns, Flex, Carossa, Frenssen, Hans Grimm, and many others; also the revival of *Heimatkunst* (nostalgic literature devoted to regional topics) and the great popularity of novels about the 1914–18 war. After the huge success of anti-war books like Erich Maria Remarque's *Im Westen nichts Neues* (*All Quiet on the Western Front*) (1929) and Ludwig Renn's *Krieg* (1928), there appeared from 1930 onwards a spate of works glorifying the war experience and decrying democracy, by nationalist authors such as Franz Schauwecker, Werner Beumelburg, Josef Magnus Wehner and Hans Zöberlein. The mass popularity of these books is a phenomenon that cannot be left out of account in judging the literary scene in Weimar Germany.

Of all the manifestations of Weimar culture, it was no doubt architecture which made the strongest and most lasting impression outside Germany. Many names and achievements deserve mention, but it can hardly be contested that the spirit of Weimar architecture was most strongly embodied in the Bauhaus. This was indeed more than a school of modern building freed from the clutter of decoration: its members were also active in other fields such as industrial design, photography and commercial art. They were also concerned – in line with ideas already evolved in the Deutscher Werkbund (founded in 1907) – to make everyday objects in a way that combined simplicity, severity of form, functionality and beauty. The renown of the Bauhaus, in its own day and subsequently, is closely connected with the name of Walter Gropius. Appointed to a post at Weimar at the beginning of 1919 for the purpose of merging an academy of art and a school of applied arts, Gropius set out to train artists and craftsmen together in a single school directed by an architect, formulating his programme thus: 'Architects, sculptors, painters – we must all return to craftsmanship. For there is no such thing as an "artist by calling". There is no essential difference between artist and craftsman. The artist is the craftsman raised to a higher power.'

In accordance with this concept of a double training the first, Expressionist period of the Bauhaus's activity was strongly marked by a cult of craftsmanship. But from 1922 onwards there was a progressive change of orientation: the machine age was now finally accepted. The theme of the first Bauhaus exhibition organized by Gropius in 1923, entitled 'Art and Techique – A New Unity', indicated clearly the principle that was to govern its activity in the following years, namely, accommodation to industrial and technical requirements. In 1925, owing to political difficulties with the Thuringian government, the Bauhaus moved from Weimar to Dessau; thereafter, in the second half of the decade, it concentrated on practical experiments in the construction and furnishing of houses and the development of prototypes for crafts and industrial mass production.

The movement for the reform of architecture was dominated from 1923 onwards by *Neue Sachlichkeit*: a greater sense of reality, attention to functional elements of style, simplicity of form, and the use of new materials such as steel, glass and concrete. The modern dwelling or factory was to be an expression of the time: practical and functional, free of superfluous ornament, effective only through its cubic composition. This was precisely expressed by the motto of the Stuttgart Werkbund exhibition of 1924: 'Form without Ornament'. Building and modern town planning were also seen as a great political challenge: it was hoped, purely by altering the public's sense of form, to give German society a more humane and more social structure.

The middle years of the republic were indeed a period of socially significant building. As practically no dwellings were built between 1914 and 1923, at the end of the period of inflation there was an acute shortage of about a million homes. This could only be remedied with government aid. The 15 per cent rent tax introduced in 1924 was used mainly to finance building societies, which were responsible for most of the wave of construction that now began: in Berlin, between 1925 and 1929 about 64,000 homes were built by societies and only 37,000 by private concerns. By means of planned state support for house-building (81 per cent of the 2·8 million homes built between 1919 and 1932 were in part publicly financed) it was possible by the end of the 1920s to mitigate the shortage and improve quality appreciably. However, with the onset of the depression in 1929–30 the period of a liberal housing policy came to an end. The building trade languished, especially as a stop was put to the financing of building societies from the rent tax proceeds. None the less, housing may be regarded as the sector in which Weimar social policy brought lasting results for large sectors of the population, which were visible to all and also served as a model in foreign countries.

During the building boom from 1924 to 1929 it was chiefly modern architects and town-planners who were called on to design apartment blocks and entire settlements and satellite towns, especially in the two great centres of Berlin (Bruno Taut, Martin Wagner) and Frankfurt-on-Main (Ernst May). Then, in 1927, came the great showpiece of modern building, the Weissenhof settlement in Stutt-gart. Commissioned by the Deutscher Werkbund and under the artistic direction of Ludwig Mies van der Rohe, sixteen leading European architects designed about sixty buildings, either single-family houses or apartment blocks, and, although they were not bound by particular directives, the result was a harmonious ensemble. The Weissenhof settlement seemed to introduce a victorious epoch of modern-ism, and attracted much attention both in Germany and abroad. But the building of this model settlement antagonized those who abhorred the new style as 'cultural Bolshevism'. As in other areas of cultural life, the opponents of modernity also made themselves increasingly felt in the field of architecture and design from the late twenties onwards.

It will be clear even from this cursory sketch of some essential aspects of Weimar culture – and would be still clearer if we were able to go into more detail – how the enthusiasm for experimenting with new ideas and new forms produced important creative results and set in motion innovative artistic pro-cesses, all in the short space of twenty years. It says much for Weimar culture and its search for fresh horizons that in the period from 1945 to the present day few artistic ideas and forms have made their appearance that could not be traced back to the 1920s.

As is often and rightly emphasized, the whole structure of the arts in Weimar Germany was 'overwhelmingly urban' (John Willett), with Berlin as the unrivalled, all-dominating centre. Weimar culture is unimaginable without the vibrant intellectual, cultural and social life of the Reich capital, which in those years became the cultural metropolis of Europe – and also a pleasure metropolis, which made it still more attractive. Certainly other big cities such as London, Paris, New York and Moscow witnessed an upsurge of artistic and intellectual life between the end of the First World War and the onset of the depression. But the twenties were 'eminently Berlin's decade', where 'the new ideas and new forces of the whole world were fused in a special, characteristic synthesis. It was not only the Berliners who thought this – the whole world felt it. Berlin, the youngest of the great capitals, had the greatest impetus, because it had the least ballast' (Peter de Mendelssohn). Berlin during those years was a magnet to all talents; its cultural and intellectual life was especially indebted to the Jewish section of the population, 'its international connections, its sensitive restlessness, and above all its infallible instinct for quality' (Gottfried Benn).

The German capital at that time was, after London and New York, the third largest city in the world: in 1929 it had 4·3 million inhabitants, or 1·5 million more than Paris. It was a city of superlatives in several ways, with the most numerous and varied newspapers in the world, great publishing empires, theatres and concert halls, the home of political cabaret; it had the fastest underground railway and the highest ratio of telephones to population – nearly 500,000 lines, carrying 1,250,000 conversations a day. It is not surprising that life in Berlin in those years is celebrated with lyrical enthusiasm in countless memoirs. It was there, in the capital, that the swift development of new attitudes to life and new values took place most clearly. But for that very reason it aroused strong emotions and antagonisms. Those who wished to preserve the old values and who abhorred the spirit of the metropolis saw the new Berlin, which was rapidly becoming Americanized, as a modern Babylon that must be 'cleansed'.

Weimar culture received its particular stamp not only from the multitude of avant-garde movements but also from the rapid development of a 'mass culture'. This term stands for the 'totality of cultural communication values that can be made available to a wide public with the help of mass media under the conditions of technological civilization' (George Friedemann). What is true of the artistic avant-garde is also true of the mass culture, namely, that a continuous development can be traced from before the war to the republican period; but it was only after 1918 that a 'modern mass culture', in the true sense, arose in Germany. Certainly, the press had long been an influential mass medium, and there were numerous cinemas showing silent films before 1914. But after 1918 the press expanded tremendously and produced journals of a new type, the cinema developed meteorically (especially with the talking film); a quite new medium, the radio, began its triumphant career, and the new spectator sports – football, boxing, cycle-racing – conquered a mass public. Thus in the Weimar years there arose a popular culture of a special kind, distinguished by the development of those modern media which have since dominated political, cultural and everyday life in Germany as in the other industrialized countries. As a corollary to this new, rapidly developing mass culture the publisher Samuel Fischer diagnosed a 'reading crisis': in 1926 he lamented that 'books are nowadays the most dispensable objects of everyday life. People go in for sport, they dance, they spend the evenings listening to the wireless or watching a film . . . Our defeat in the war, and the wave of Americanism, have transformed our taste and our approach to life.'

Among the mass media, the press remained in first place. Its chief feature, before and after 1918, was its decentralization: in 1928 there were 3,356 daily papers in Germany, and 147 in Berlin alone. Most of these had a very small circulation, however: only 26 papers, or 0·7 per cent of the total, ran to over 100,000 copies. At the head of the list was the *Berliner Morgenpost*, published by the firm of Ullstein, with over 400,000 copies a day in April 1930 (623,000 on Sundays). In contrast to this, such influential and famous papers as the *Vossische Zeitung* and the *Deutsche Allgemeine Zeitung* had a daily circulation of less than 100,000.

Despite the decentralized structure, there was also a concentration of economic power in the German press world. Before 1914 the Berlin firms of Mosse, Ullstein and Scherl had been in the lead. After 1918, while Mosse and Ullstein were well disposed towards the new regime, the Scherl papers were a bastion of anti-republican forces. Control over this firm had passed to Alfred Hugenberg in 1916 (when he was also a Krupp director); a sworn enemy of the republic and of democracy, in the 1920s he built up Scherl into a large, influential concern. The provincial press was liberally supplied with material in matrix form and with reportage from the Telegraphen-Union, which served 1,600 newspapers in 1926. The nationalist and anti-democratic propaganda thus administered by the Hugenberg concern – sometimes on a massive scale and sometimes in calculated doses – reached far into the German population, over and above those who read the Scherl newspapers.

The press took on a new lease of life after the inflation period. Traditional organizations increased their circulation, tabloids like the *BZ am Mittag* became more and more popular, and many news journals made their appearance, for example, Rowohlt's lively *Die literarische Welt* or Ullstein's *Die grüne Post* (a weekend paper for town and country, with a circulation of over 1,250,000 in July 1931) and *Die Koralle*. The latter's pictorial material from all parts of the world, with its technically first-class reproduction, set new standards for the dissemination of knowledge about the march of science and the natural world. Above all, the illustrated magazine of the 1920s progressed from the illustration of texts to photojournalism and became the 'typical' form of publication of its period: like the cinema, this form of journalism in these years catered for the ever-increasing demand for visual experience and instruction.

In Germany as elsewhere, the cinema had begun its advance a few years before 1914, but the first silent films could satisfy only the simplest tastes. After 1918 the cinema soon became an influential mass medium, and from at least the mid-twenties onwards it was accepted as an art form. At that time, according to contemporary estimates, 2 million people went to the films daily (in Berlin alone, over 40 million tickets were sold in 1924); the number of film theatres rose from about 2,300 in 1918, with 800,000 seats, to over 5,000 in 1930, with 2 million seats. At the end of the 1920s Germany had the most cinemas of any European country; in the 1920s and early 1930s it produced more films than all other European countries put together.

Yet the German film industry was relatively young. It began with the foundation of UFA – the largest film company – in 1917; previously the German
market had been dominated by American, French and Danish productions. But
after 1918 the German industry soon blossomed into a flourishing sector of the
economy and an important earner of foreign currency. Between 1919 and 1924
a number of films of high artistic quality were made; in terms of quantity they
were only a small part of the country's output, but they made German films
instantly famous. Besides historical spectaculars and small, intimate productions, Germany became celebrated for Expressionist films of fantasy. Robert
Wiene's *Cabinet of Dr Caligari* (1920) was the prototype of these films,
characterized by the flight from reality into fantastic dreams or nightmares, a
mystical transfiguration of the world as a scene of cruel tyranny and
superhuman beings. Further outstanding works in this genre were Fritz Lang's
Dr Mabuse der Spieler (The Gambler) and Friedrich Wilhelm Murnau's
Nosferatu – eine Symphonie des Grauens (Dracula) (both 1922).

After 1923 the favourable production conditions of the period of inflation no
longer prevailed; export opportunities diminished, and foreign films once more
invaded the German market. In the ensuing crisis several producers went
bankrupt. Even UFA was threatened; it was temporarily rescued by American
film interests in 1926 and taken over by Hugenberg's concern in 1927. In the
second half of the twenties Charlie Chaplin's films (for example, *The Gold Rush*,
1926) became very popular in Germany, and Russian films were received with
enthusiasm by many (Eisenstein's *Battleship Potemkin* was shown in Berlin in
1926 after various difficulties had been overcome). As in literature and painting,
the German artistic film of these years was characterized by *Neue Sachlichkeit*
– an unsentimental, rational and practical sense of responsibility, together with
realistic social criticism: for instance, G. W. Pabst's *Die freudlose Gasse* (1925)
and W. R. Ruttmann's *Berlin, die Symphonie einer Grossstadt* (1927).

Towards the end of the twenties there was much talk of a 'crisis in the film
industry'. It was rescued by the advent of the talking film, which in 1929 ended
a whole epoch of German film production, while at once making possible
impressive new achievements. The first great German sound film, *The Blue Angel*
(directed by Josef von Sternberg, with Emil Jannings and Marlene Dietrich in
the main roles) was shown on 1 April 1930, and at a stroke anticipated all the
artistic and technical possibilities of the new medium. The amazing success of
the talking film, which threatened the live theatre and put thousands of professional musicians out of work can be seen in the following figures. In 1929
Germany produced 183 feature films of which all but 8 were silent; in 1930 sound
films numbered 101 out of 146; in 1931, 142 out of 144; in 1932, all 127 were
sound films. By October 1930 out of the 5,000-odd German film theatres with
a total of 2 million seats, 900 totalling 600,000 seats were adapted for sound films.
The capital-intensive process led to increased concentration in the film industry,
so that in 1932–3 only three big German concerns existed: UFA, Tobis and Terra.

Public broadcasting, which began at the end of 1923, registered the same triumphant progress as the sound film was to do a few years later. Since 1918 the radio industry had been pressing for a service available to the public, and in 1920 the Reich government granted permission for the use of radio for economic bulletins. The decisive step towards the establishment of radio as a mass medium came in 1923 with the grant of concessions for the erection of transmitters and the manufacture of receiving sets; the Radio-Stunde Company in Berlin sent out its first programme on 29 October 1923. A radio network came into existence in 1924; nine companies were created in different parts of the Reich between March and October of that year, and in 1926 an umbrella organization, the Reichs-Rundfunk-Gesellschaft, was set up. The Post Office held 51 per cent of its shares and controlled programmes through a Broad-casting Commissioner, Hans Bredow, with an advisory board.

The number of listeners rose dramatically from barely 10,000 on 1 April 1924 to 780,000 on 1 April 1925, 1·6 million on 1 April 1927, 2·8 million on 1 April 1929, and 3·7 million on 1 April 1931. In spite of the depression, the number went above 4 million in February 1932; the German listening public was by then the second largest in Europe, Britain being in first place. On 1 April 1932 about every fourth home in Germany possessed a radio.

The directive from the Reich government directed that the broadcasting system should be non-political and devoted to instruction and entertainment. Hence, in addition to music, literary programmes played a great part from the beginning: radio plays, authors' readings and recitations. While pro-republican forces thus abstained from using the radio as an instrument for furthering democratic ideas and consolidating the regime, it is significant that in 1932 Papen's presidential Cabinet reorganized the system and introduced state con-trol, so that after 30 January 1933 the National Socialists were able in a few days to enlist the full power of the medium for their own purposes.

As the above outline shows, the mass media developed during the 1920s to an unprecedented extent. The new technology had a lasting and direct effect on the life and mentality of broad sections of the population, as did the fact that holidays and leisure were ceasing, though gradually, to be the privilege of a small upper class. After 1918 the comprehensive change of life-style and the approach to life which had set in at the turn of the century began to extend to the masses: the abandonment of many ancient taboos, a 'new way of life' in the widest sense, sport, hiking, bathing, a rediscovery of the body, a new attitude to children, young people and the opposite sex, and to sexual matters generally. But what some regarded as progress and the expansion of horizons, the breaking of outworn ties and liberation from irksome constraints, was seen as decadence and libertinism by others, who put the blame on the political and social system of the Weimar democracy. This provided ammunition to the prophets of doom, and increased the deeply rooted enmity which conservative and nationalist circles already felt towards the republic.

A similar observation may be made as regards the connection between Weimar culture and the political development of the republic. The instability which beset the Weimar Republic as a political and social order corresponded to an element of free choice in matters of art and culture; a superfluity of talent as well as of material for conflict, combined with political freedom, made possible unlimited experimentation and an explosion of novelty that can still be felt in our own day. But there was a scarcely bridgeable gap between the artistic achievement of the avant-garde and the taste and mentality of a large part of the population, middle-class and otherwise. The popularity of sentimental literature on regional themes indicates that it touched on problems, fears and desires that occupied the minds and hearts of many. Thus the development of art and culture in the Weimar period, by which later generations are so rightly impressed, did not bring any relief to the republic in its political and social tribulations, or confer on it any higher 'legitimacy'; on the contrary, confrontation in cultural matters still further exacerbated the basic political discord among Germans in the Weimar period. On closer investigation of the 'golden twenties', therefore, the typical feature of the period is seen to be the split between modernism and the fear of modernity, between radicalism and resignation, between sober, factual rationality and the attraction of a profound irrationalism of a mystical, contemplative, or chiliastic kind.

(C) THE DISINTEGRATION AND DESTRUCTION OF THE REPUBLIC, 1930–3

1

The Rise of National Socialism in the Shadow of the World Economic Crisis

The short phase of the relative stabilization of the Weimar Republic came to an abrupt end in 1929–30. Two fatal developments coincided in time and reinforced each other. In the first place, the transformation of the political system which began with the appointment of the first presidential Cabinet in March 1930 led in a short time to an overt political crisis. Secondly, soon after the world depression set in the German economy went into a steep decline, and conflicts over the distribution of wealth were dramatically intensified. The fragility of the political system and the increased potential for social conflict combined to produce fertile conditions for radicalism of the left and right. In particular, the nationalist and anti-democratic forces gathered for an assault on the republic in 1929–30. Their spearhead was the NSDAP, which succeeded in becoming a mass movement in the very months in which the political and economic crisis began to loom, and thus became an essential factor in the political contest.

There is no single explanation for the rise of the Nazi party. Two groups of reasons should be noticed in particular. For a splinter party to gain a mass following in a relatively short time and to become a power on the electoral scene, an essential prerequisite is the existence of an explosive situation in domestic and social affairs. Unquestionably, from the beginning of 1930 onwards Germany was in a state of acute political, social, economic and psychological crisis. But there is a further point. The Nazi party, which had until then been in a completely isolated position, was able to take advantage of the crisis to launch a frontal attack on the political and social foundations of the state because it possessed a firm yet elastic organizational structure which made it possible rapidly to enlarge the cadre party into a comprehensive movement – a refuge for all opponents of the democratic system, all fanatics and all who were embittered or disappointed. It was in this guise that the NSDAP presented itself at the turn of the year 1929–30.

The Nazis themselves always laid great stress on the continuity of the party's development from its modest beginnings in 1919 to the triumphant mass movement of ten years later. Certainly there were elements of such continuity. To begin with, Hitler was the dominant figure in the party, from 1921 at the latest, and his immediate circle of associates remained more or less unchanged over the years. The party's propaganda slogans during the last phase of the republic were essentially the same as those of its early days. On the other hand, as far as party organization and political strategy were concerned, the NSDAP after 1925 differed so markedly from the NSDAP of 1923 and earlier that, in the view of most historians today, what appeared on the scene in 1925 was indeed a 'new party' – and this not only in the superficial sense that it was formally re-founded by Hitler after his release from the Landsberg fortress.

Before the November putsch of 1923 the NSDAP had been, from a geographical point of view, largely confined to Bavaria; politically it was one of many organizations of the extreme nationalist right, working closely with 'patriotic' (*völkisch*) groups and paramilitary associations. Its propaganda and organizing activities in those years, especially in 1923, were entirely related to the idea of a putsch; significantly, it did not compete in a single election before 1924. There is a good deal of evidence that Hitler, dominant though he was in the party before 1923, did not yet regard himself as a charismatic leader in the same way as after 1924, but rather as the 'drum-major' (*Trommler*) beating up support – which was how his allies in the other nationalist groups thought of him and how they intended to make use of him.

After the fiasco of the November putsch the NSDAP was in a parlous condition. Its organization was falling apart, and rivalries among the remaining leaders made it impossible to think of political activity on any considerable scale. Hitler himself, in his fortress detention, maintained an enigmatic silence concerning quarrels in the patriotic and National Socialist camp. But the putsch, though a disastrous failure, had not done any harm to his personal prestige in rightist circles. On the contrary, as the trial for high treason was conducted by the Munich court with the utmost indulgence towards the accused, Hitler was provided with a first-class propaganda platform of which he made effective use; and his period of arrest, while it was made as comfortable as possible, conferred on him a martyr's halo. After his early release in December 1924, he set about reconstituting the party in the first months of 1925, and was helped in doing so by the disruption and leaderless condition of the patriotic and National Socialist movement. As Gerhard Schulz has rightly pointed out, if he had been kept under arrest for longer – for instance, if he had served his full sentence and not been released until November 1928 – it would have been much more difficult, perhaps even impossible, to regenerate a Hitler party.

The failure of the putsch taught Hitler three lessons, which he kept well in mind as he proceeded to rebuild the party. First, he abandoned the idea of a putsch for that of remaining 'within the law' – not excluding the possible use of force, but concentrating for the present on mobilizing the masses. Consequently, the party had to be strictly organized on a basis of larger numbers and a wider geographical area, and clearly marked off from the other patriotic and nationalist groups. The paramilitary SA must be firmly subordinated to the political leadership, and the party must be forged into an instrument of complete obedience to the Führer's will. Hitler was determined to ensure for himself the role of an absolute dictator in the reconstituted party, and this he had no great difficulty in doing.

When Hitler's position in the party is described as that of a 'charismatic leader' (Joseph Nyomarkay), the epithet is not merely a general one for Hitler's demagogic personality; in line with Max Weber's typology of leadership, it denotes very precisely a type of personal authority which gave its special stamp to the internal structure of the NSDAP. Its subservience to a charismatic leader distinguished the NSDAP from both the socialist and the bourgeois parties of the Weimar period, and enabled it to maintain cohesion despite its heterogeneous social composition and the vagueness of its programme. Any dissentient groups within the NSDAP did not organize against Hitler – as charismatic leader he was the source of authority and not to be challenged – but rather competed for his favour. He himself not only tolerated such groups but encouraged them from time to time, as in this way his position as arbiter was strengthened. Only if his supreme authority was called in question did he intervene in disputes within the party, and when he did so the dispute was settled. As soon as he took up a clear position against an internal group, its apparently powerful leaders quickly lost influence. This was partly because, in the relatively few conflicts of this kind, Hitler focused on matters of tactics rather than policy, so that he was able to adopt a conciliatory attitude towards both sides. As the matter at issue was not, or was not thought to be, one of principle, and as it was a question of disavowing particular leaders and not a specific policy, there was no need for a 'purge' within the ranks. The objectors disappeared, the party remained substantially intact, and Hitler's authority was not diminished.

Hitler was able to perform the role of a charismatic leader by virtue of his exceptional gifts as a rhetorician and propagandist. He became aware of these gifts soon after his first public speeches and perfected his oratorical talent into a weapon which he used with masterly skill. The style and inspiration of his rhetoric is effectively described by Martin Broszat:

Given the impression of resoluteness which he conveyed, Hitler knew how to articulate and, as it were, to celebrate what his listeners half consciously desired and felt. He voiced what they secretly thought and wanted, reinforced their still unsure longings and prejudices, and thereby created for them deeply satisfying self-awareness and the feeling of being privy to a new truth and certainty. Such leadership and oratory did not require a refined intellectual discrimination or a calm, mature individuality and

personality, but . . . a psychological and mental disposition which was itself
so infected by the mood of crisis and panic of the time that it instinctively
sounded the correct note.

Just as there were different views among Hitler's contemporaries as to what his
and his party's objectives really were, so it was long debated by historians
whether he had a 'programme' at all, or was merely an unprincipled opportunist, obsessed with power. Nowadays it is almost universally held that he did
have a programme, which took shape in 1923–4 at the latest and was outlined
in *Mein Kampf* (1925–7). It was far from identical with the party's 25-point programme of 1920, but was rather a development of Hitler's *Weltanschauung*
(Eberhard Jäckel), in which various ideas were combined in an internally consistent outlook. Its two main points were both the product of popularized social
Darwinism: the racial theory and that of *Lebensraum* (living space), leading
respectively to anti-Semitism and military conquest. 'These basic elements were
synthesized in the historical picture of a permanent, ruthless battle of
nations for a *Lebensraum* adequate to their growing strength, which could only
be maintained as long as their blood was pure' (Andreas Hillgruber). Specifically, Germany must conquer new living space, especially in the east, and must
get rid of the Jews; all aspects of public life were to be organized as means to
these two ends.

It is certainly of great importance that historians have identified this 'hard
core' of Hitler's philosophy, proof against opportunism or manipulation of any
kind, and have shown that it was the mainspring of his activity, the basis of his
programme, and the supreme objective of his policy. But this does not suffice
to explain the success of National Socialist propaganda. For, important though
Hitler's programme is as a key to his motivation, the philosophy that can be
deduced from his writings and statements was not the staple of National
Socialist propaganda before 1933, which it inspired only to a limited degree or
in a veiled form. The question therefore remains of why and how Hitler and
Nazi propaganda had such a powerful effect on large sections of the German
people from the late 1920s onwards.

The first point to note is that Hitler and the other Nazi propagandists, with
their shrewd understanding of mass psychology, worked on a crude mixture of
discontent composed of nationalist, racialist, anti-Semitic, anti-Marxist and anti-
liberal prejudices, together with the sense of 'awaiting a leader' which was
widespread in Germany in the 1920s. Many individuals in all sections of the
population, especially young people and the middle class, were politically
disoriented, socially isolated and economically insecure. They looked about
them for scapegoats and saviours; radical denunciations fell on greedy ears,
there was a demand for tried remedies. Hitler's propaganda had its strongest
effect on people of this kind, especially as – unlike other 'patriotic' (*völkisch*)
leaders – he steered clear of dogmatic precision and confined himself to a few

key points of racial biology and racial nationalism. At the same time he attacked the state and party system with the utmost vehemence, contrasting it with the utopia of a heroic, warlike 'racial community' (*Volksgemeinschaft*), free of social tensions and political conflict.

These remarks on the effect of National Socialist propaganda on the masses before 1933 anticipate subsequent developments. This propaganda did not in fact achieve any results worth mentioning until the time when domestic conflicts were inflamed and Germany fell a victim to the world depression with all its economic and social consequences.

The NSDAP was re-founded on 27 February 1925, a crowded ceremony in the Bürgerbräu cellar in Munich, at which Hitler was rapturously received. From some time thereafter the party developed quite independently of the problems that were exercising the nation; the press at first took no notice of this splinter group of the extreme right. Its first stages were marked by limited resources and a narrow sphere of action, with the leaders concentrating entirely on party organization. In this respect, Hitler had reason to be pleased with what was achieved in the first eighteen months: the NSDAP was strictly fenced off from other organizations of the populist type, from which it absorbed many members. Further, the creation of a central index of members and financial system laid the foundation for a centralized, bureaucratic administration; the party was run by 'bureaucrats loyal to Hitler, with no political ambitions' (Wolfgang Horn). By the end of 1925 the membership was no larger than 27,000, but the network now extended over large parts of Germany: in 1923 there were only 71 local groups outside Bavaria, while in 1925 there were 262.

While the state of organization and leadership in most of the party districts (*Gaue*) during the initial period of 1925–6 was still precarious, from the end of 1925 onwards the leaders in Munich were gradually able to assert their authority over centrifugal tendencies. A milestone in this respect was the party conference at Bamberg on 14 February 1926. This was held because the Association of North and West German *Gaue* formed by Gregor Strasser, originally with Hitler's approval, had put forward policy ideas ('German socialism', eastward orientation) and concrete proposals (such as National Socialist participation in the referendum on the expropriation of the former princes) that did not meet with the approval of the Munich leaders: Hitler had no desire for a discussion of first principles. At Bamberg he forced the northern and western *Gauleiters* to conform, which they did (including Strasser himself) without resistance. Faced with the choice of either accepting Hitler's viewpoint or sticking to their own ideas and risking a conflict with him, they acknowledged his leadership without hesitation. Thus the north and west German party authorities, which had until then shown a certain amount of independence, recognized Hitler's absolute authority and accepted the autocratic structure of the new party.

The initial period concluded with the first Reich party congress at Weimar in July 1926 and the appointment, late that summer, of the former Freikorps leader Franz Pfeffer von Salomon as commander of the SA. The Weimar congress featured a march-past or military parade of several thousand supporters, designed to show the German people that the NSDAP was back in business and was solidly organised, and to give its members the sense of belonging to a rising political movement. Pfeffer von Salomon's appointment once more defined the relationship between the party and its paramilitary organization. This was governed by Hitler's view that, in accordance with the policy of 'legality', the political leadership must be unmistakably in control of the paramilitary element. The SA was placed under the authority of the party and was forbidden to enter into association with other paramilitary bodies; its function was to consist in matters of training, education and administration, and in providing stewards for meetings. In practice it did not prove possible to make the SA a mere passive instrument of the party. There were repeated conflicts between self-confident SA leaders and middle-rank party officials, but no longer any threat to Hitler's dictatorial power.

The further stages of development of the party cannot be detailed here. However, two aspects of its organization and propaganda should be described, since in the years when the NSDAP was still by no means in the limelight of public attention, certain conditions were created which enabled it, in the time of general crisis, to provide a home for all malcontents and opponents of the system.

In the years after its re-foundation, the party was distinguished by its elaborate efforts to create a 'socio-moral environment' (Rainer M. Lepsius). To develop the movement into a microcosm of society, to incorporate its members and supporters in respect of the particular interests and ambitions of their profession or age-group, a large number of auxiliary bodies or party 'formations' (*Gliederungen*) were created. In some cases the party, as such, took the initiative, but more often it came from individual activists, who founded the organizations first and then sought the blessing of the party leaders.

As early as 1926 two party youth organizations were created, the National Socialist German Students' Association and the Hitler Youth. In both of these, social revolutionary tendencies existed at the beginning but were gradually eliminated. The National Socialist Union of School Pupils, founded in 1929, comprised mostly upper-middle-class children attending grammar schools (*Oberschulen* and *Gymnasien*). Much the most popular of the youth organizations was the Students' Association, which obtained a wide following at an early date, before the party's first electoral successes; at the election in the winter term of 1928–9 for the Allgemeiner Studenten-Ausschuss (General Students' Union) it received 15 per cent of the votes countrywide. At the universities of Erlangen and Greifswald the Nazis attained an absolute majority in 1929; in 1930 they did so at seven more universities, while at others they were only just short of 50 per cent. These results show how gravely the Weimar democracy was threatened, even before 1930, by the alienation of a high percentage of university youth.

Besides youth organizations, the party had associations for particular professions and occupations. The first of these, formed in October 1928, was the Association of National Socialist Jurists, which advocated a 'renewal of the system of law' in a patriotic (*völkisch*) and National Socialist sense. In 1929 some more bodies of this type were formed, such as the National Socialist Association of German Physicians, the National Socialist Teachers' Association and a League of Struggle (*Kampfbund*) for German Culture, whose task was to attract 'culturally active persons' to the NSDAP and to 'rally all defensive forces against the powers of corruption that at present dominate German culture'.

Of much greater importance were the organizations formed to regiment manual workers and farmers. The Agrarpolitischer Apparat (Office for Agriculture) was not created until 1930, but was then built up rapidly. It did much to win over the peasant masses to the NSDAP, and in a relatively short time succeeded in penetrating the independent agricultural associations. At the same time, the NSDAP sought to establish itself among the working class by means of a National Socialist Factory Cell Organization (NSBO) modelled on similar shop-floor organizations of the KPD. The first Nazi cells were formed in 1927–8 in Berlin, the Ruhr and Saxony; the members were chiefly foremen, skilled workers and clerks who were opposed to workers' parties and trade unions. While the factory cells only attracted a small minority of the workers as compared with the millions who belonged to the various unions, the NSBO was nevertheless quite a large part of the National Socialist movement. A figure of 40,000 members is given for 1931, and 100,000 for mid-1932; in October 1932 Gregor Strasser claimed, no doubt with exaggeration, that the membership was nearly 300,000. However, the NSBO had no determining influence on party policy.

For craftsmen and small tradesmen there was a Kampfbund für den Gewerblichen Mittelstand (Militant Association of Retailers), whose chief purpose was to agitate against chain-stores. The existence of organizations for particular occupations and also for such heterogeneous economic interests is one more indication of the peculiar structure of the National Socialist movement which, as we have pointed out, was essentially vague in matters of policy and derived its unity from Hitler's absolute authority.

A second objective of National Socialist organization was to create links with some of the major existing economic associations, so as to gain influence with wider sections of the electorate. This related especially to the white-collar workers' and farmers' organizations.

As regards the former, the NSDAP established contact with leading officials of the Deutschnationaler Handlungsgehilfenverband (Nationalist League of Commercial Employees), a body with numerous members and a long tradition, strongly right-wing and anti-Semitic, and closely connected with the DNVP up to 1929–30. A large number of its officials found their way into the NSDAP from 1929 onwards; they added to the party's strength in the Reichstag and helped it to recruit among their former members. The Nazis also managed to penetrate local and regional associations of craftsmen and small tradesmen and thus exert pressure from the lower ranks upwards.

Still more striking was the success of the NSDAP in infiltrating the association of German farmers. The party capitalized on the discontent among the peasantry, which increased rapidly as the economic situation deteriorated. The price of all agrarian products fell owing to world-wide overproduction, and German agricultural sales in 1932–3 fetched only 62 per cent of the figure for 1928–9. Farmers fell into debt and the annual figure of compulsory auctions grew rapidly. With the help of a close network of local agents, the NSDAP was able in a remarkably short time to acquire influence over the policy of the farmers' associations, which were for the most part Protestant. By the spring of 1932 the Reichslandbund (Reich Agrarian League), the largest and most influential organization and pressure group, was so strongly infiltrated, both ideologically and personally, that at the second ballot in the presidential elections its governing body instructed members to vote for Hitler against Hindenburg. The Reichslandbund also placed itself at the head of the extra-parliamentary agrarian opposition which, in the winter of 1932–3, urged Hindenburg to dismiss Schleicher and appoint Hitler to the chancellorship.

Such possibilities were still far ahead in May 1928, when a new Reichstag was elected for the first time since the re-foundation of the NSDAP. At this election, despite the development of its organization and despite its violent agitation against the democratic parties and republican institutions, the NSDAP did not rise above the rank of a splinter party, securing about 800,000 votes or 2·6 per cent of the votes cast (cf. table, pages 194–5). Only in 4 of the 35 constituencies did the NSDAP receive more than 5 per cent of the votes, and in none of them over 10 per cent; while in 22 constituencies, or two-thirds of the whole Reich territory, its share of the votes was lower than its Reich average of 2·6 per cent. With only 12 seats out of 491 in the Reichstag, the NSDAP in 1928 was practically insignificant in parliamentary terms. None the less, it should not be overlooked that this splinter party already possessed a fairly large and increasing membership and was organized on a strict yet elastic basis – a cadre party, it may be said, that was awaiting its opportunity to expand.

Sooner than anyone could have expected, in 1928 political and economic circumstances combined with the public mood to create a situation especially favourable to National Socialist agitation and action. In two quite different areas the year 1929 furnished the NSDAP with opportunities to break out of its isolation and make a breach in the apparently stabilized structure of the republic. The first of these was the plebiscite over the Young Plan; the second, the world economic depression.

The Young Plan was at the centre of controversy in 1929, both in domestic and in foreign affairs. As we have seen (page 64 above) the economic advantages of the plan lay clearly on the German side; this is the judgement of historians today, and was that of the German government and its supporting parties at the time. Moreover, by accepting the new proposals Germany was to secure the early evacuation of the still-occupied parts of the Rhineland. Nevertheless, the plan gave rise to an outburst of controversy over reparations, more intense than at any previous time. The substantial though reduced annuities, and the prospect of another sixty years of payments, were a convenient target for the right-wing opposition, whose aim was to discredit the republic by mobilizing every form of nationalist resentment. In order to mount a propaganda campaign on the largest scale, the nationalists adopted the course of petitioning for a referendum under Article 73 of the Weimar constitution.

Soon after the Young Plan was published the DNVP, which was pursuing an increasingly radical policy under Hugenberg's chairmanship, together with the Stahlhelm (the ex-servicemen's association), formed a Reich Committee for a German Referendum to oppose the Young Plan; this committee was immediately joined by the National Socialists. By thus allying himself on equal terms with Hugenberg and Seldte, the Stahlhelm leader, Hitler was able to pay an active part in a key question of German politics for the first time since 1923, and to make his name politically with large sections of the nationalist middle class. 'The unscrupulousness of the Nazis' propaganda methods and their aggressive brutality were thus made respectable in bourgeois circles and, as it were, legitimized' (Karl Dietrich Erdmann).

The measure proposed by the Reich Committee for submission to a referendum was known as the 'Freedom law' (Law against the Enslavement of the German People). Sections 1 and 2 of the draft attacked the 'war guilt lie', calling on the government to repudiate the relevant article of the Treaty of Versailles and to demand the immediate evacuation of occupied territory regardless of the Young Plan. Section 3 forbade the government to accept new burdens and obligations *vis-à-vis* foreign powers. The height of demagogy was reached in Section 4, which declared that any Reich chancellor, minister or plenipotentiary who signed treaties of this kind, such as the Young Plan, would be liable to imprisonment for high treason.

As far as the referendum was concerned, the campaign was a complete failure. The minimum number of signatures required by the constitution was just reached, but in the popular vote on 22 December 1929 only 13·8 per cent of the electorate voted for the Freedom law. To the NSDAP, however, their participation in the campaign brought rich rewards. The spectacular propaganda roused the public to a high pitch of emotion which accrued to the Nazis' benefit. Aided by the Reich Committee's funds, they were able to conduct a large-scale campaign of their own, and received free publicity from Hugenberg's newspaper empire. At the Nuremberg congress in 1929, the party's largest so far, they were able, with financial help from the Reich Committee, to muster 200,000 supporters; Hitler took the salute from 20,000 SA men in uniform and in full marching order.

Among the right-wing parties, the NSDAP was in fact the sole gainer from the campaign against the Young Plan, as became clear in the autumn and winter of 1929. In those weeks when the propaganda against the Young Plan, the government and the republic was at its height, the National Socialists scored the first considerable success at the polls, partly at the expense of the DNVP. In the Landtag election in Baden on 27 October 1929 the Nazis obtained 7 per cent of the votes; in Lübeck on 10 November, 8·1 per cent; and in Thuringia on 8 December, 11·3 per cent. In Thuringia, moreover, thanks to a stalemate between the bourgeois and socialist parties and the former's readiness to enter into a coalition, the Nazis for the first time achieved membership of a *Land* government. The NSDAP registered similar gains in the municipal elections in November 1929, and was represented as a result on many local councils, in some cases with an increased number of seats.

Having broken out of its isolation thanks to the campaign for the Freedom law, the NSDAP could no longer be dismissed as a splinter party with a negligible membership and share of the popular vote. By September 1930 the number of members had risen to over 130,000, and that of local branches to 1,378. The NSDAP was decidedly a 'young' party, not only in the sense of being new to the political scene, but because most of its members had been born in 1890 or later. In 1930 nearly 70 per cent of its members were under 40 years old, and 37 per cent under 30; among party officials, these figures were about 65 per cent and 26 per cent respectively. The politicization of quite young people was a characteristic of the time, and in the young generation the pull of National Socialism was clearly felt at all social levels, whereas the other parties – except for the KPD, which was also a 'young' party – had no great attraction for youth. This was especially true of the SPD, whose appeals to reason and argument lacked emotional force, and whose members and officials were elderly compared with those of the NSDAP and the KPD.

As to the classification of NSDAP membership by occupation and social status, the party's statistics for September 1930 give the following figures: manual workers 26·3 per cent, employees 24 per cent, independent (professional) 18·9 per cent, civil servants 7·7 per cent, farmers 13·2 per cent, others 9 per cent. Two conclusions may be drawn from this. In the first place, certain occupational or social groups were clearly over-represented in proportion to the percentage of such groups among all those gainfully employed. This applied to the middle class or petty bourgeoisie, including professionals, small business men, employees and officials. Secondly, in purely numerical terms the manual workers were the largest group in the party membership. There is still disagreement as to how this relatively high proportion of workers is to be evaluated in determining the social structure of the Nazi movement, especially as it is not clear how the term 'worker' was defined by the party statisticians. But recent research tends to the view that the NSDAP cannot simply be described as a party of the petty bourgeoisie, but was developing into a party integrating all the social strata, a nationalist 'people's party'. On this view, it certainly had its main support in the lower middle classes but was able to attract others, particularly manual workers who did not belong to an urban industrial milieu but were employed in small or medium-sized businesses (cf. below, pages 187 ff.).

In the winter of 1929–30 Germany was stricken by the effects of the world economic crisis, which reached its first peak after the collapse of the New York stock exchange at the end of October 1929. The consequences hit Germany especially hard, as her economic development was based largely on short-term foreign credits which were now called in. The German national income in 1932 was 39 per cent less than in 1929 (USA 40 per cent, Britain 15 per cent, France 16 per cent); industrial production, private incomes and living standards had dropped correspondingly. Above all, the political situation was dominated from 1929 onwards by the growth of unemployment. As we have seen (page 81 above), even during the few years of relative stability the unemployment figure was fairly high, a pointer to the structural weakness and fragility of the German economy. From the end of 1929 onwards it rose dramatically, from 1·3 million in September 1929 to over 3 million in September 1930, 4·3 million in September 1931 and 5·1 million in September 1932. At the beginning of 1933 the figure reached over 6 million, as against 12 million in work; in other words, 1 worker in 3 was unemployed (in the USA 1 in 4, in Britain 1 in 5, in France 1 in 7). The German figures, moreover, are based on official statistics which did not include those who, owing to long unemployment, had exhausted their claim to benefit. In addition, the numerous part-time workers had suffered considerable cuts in wages. Virtually every other German family was hit by the depression, the lower middle class and employees as well as manual workers.

The direct economic consequences of the slump, which are only cursorily indicated by these figures, were devastating enough, and the psychological effects no less disastrous. The sense of insecurity spread far beyond the circle of those whose livelihood was directly affected at any given time; the whole population lived in a mood of expecting catastrophe. Fear of the further effects of the crisis was a psychological factor no less potent than its actual effects, and this enabled the radicals to gain a following among those who were less hard hit economically, for example, some sections of the middle class. The atmosphere of catastrophe encouraged right- and left-wing opponents of the republic to carry on unbridled propaganda against the republic and democracy. It was no doubt inevitable that the public should lose confidence in existing institutions and parties; but the propagandists took every advantage of this to represent the crisis as a consequence of the 'system', and ruthlessly mobilized open and latent resentment of parliamentary democracy. As the crisis continued it was soon clear how weak were the foundations of Weimar democracy, in terms of the solidity of its institutions or the loyalty of influential social and political groups and large sections of the population. Thus the world depression with its economic and psychological consequences plunged Germany, from the outset, into a grave political crisis. This was unlike the situation in most other countries, which suffered from the depression almost as much as Germany but were better able to stand its consequences because of the greater stability of their political and social order.

The *Landtag* and municipal elections at the end of 1929 showed a clear, though still limited, trend in favour of the NSDAP. This continued in the first half of 1930, as was evident from the election in Saxony on 22 June, necessitated by a premature dissolution of the *Landtag*. At the previous *Landtag* election, on 12 May 1929 – before the campaign against the Young Plan had got under way – the Nazis had obtained 5 per cent of the votes, already a considerable advance on the 2·7 per cent they had received in Saxony at the Reichstag election of 1928. Now, in June 1930, they increased the figure to 14·4 per cent, that is, they trebled their share of the votes in the space of a year, and became the strongest party after the SPD.

These figures are eloquent, and any analysis of the regional election results must have led to the conclusion that the NSDAP would score appreciable gains if there should be a dissolution of the Reichstag before the end of its current term (which expired in mid-1932). It is symptomatic of the way in which politics were conducted after the collapse of the 'great coalition' – as we shall discuss more fully, see pages 112–13 below – that in the summer of 1930 Brüning obtained a dissolution of the Reichstag in order to carry out without modification his authoritarian programme for dealing with the crisis, and in so doing culpably neglected all prognoses that might have been derived from an analysis of voting trends and regional election figures.

The Reichstag election of 14 September 1930 brought a landslide exceeding even the Nazi leaders' expectations: they increased their number of seats from 12 to 107, becoming at a stroke the second largest party. A victory on this scale was unprecedented in German parliamentary history.

In analysing the result attention should be paid not only to percentages but to absolute numbers of votes, as in September 1930 about 4 million more valid votes were cast than in the Reichstag election of 1928. The total number elected thus rose from 491 to 577 (see table, pages 194–5). The NSDAP increased its votes from 800,000 to about 6·4 million and its share of the poll from 2·6 to 18·2 per cent; the KPD received 4·6 million votes, or 13·1 per cent (in 1928 these figures were 3·3 million and 10·6 per cent). The SPD, on the other hand, lost about half a million votes and 10 seats as compared with its record success of 1928; this brought it to 24·5 per cent and 143 seats. The Centre and the BVP gained a small number of votes and a few additional seats; the Wirtschaftspartei, a lower-middle-class interest group, lost a few thousand votes and no seats. The DVP and the DDP (the latter now called Deutsche Staatspartei) lost hundreds of thousands of votes and a larger number of seats, but were not wiped out.

Some additional seats were gained by smaller parties such as the Christlich-Sozialer Volksdienst and the Deutsche Landvolkpartei. The greatest losses in the election were sustained by the DNVP, whose votes fell from about 4·4 million to 2·46 million. This was 7 per cent of the votes cast, as compared with 14·2 per cent in 1928; this time the party secured only 41 seats, compared with 73 in 1928 and over 100 in December 1924.

The election of September 1930 is certainly a fateful date in German history, marking the breakthrough of the National Socialist movement as a political force that could not be ignored. Two questions call for a brief discussion here. What was the source of the 6·4 million votes obtained by the NSDAP, especially the 5·6 million additional to the 1928 result; and was its success largely due to financial help from business circles, especially heavy industry?

The question as to who voted for the NSDAP in 1930 and where they came from is harder to answer than is often supposed. There were no opinion polls that would enable us to make direct statements concerning the electoral behaviour of particular social groups and the extent to which they shifted their allegiance; all we have are official statistics with the results classified geographically. Hence many assertions about the source of the NSDAP vote are insufficiently founded. For a long time two completely contrary hypotheses prevailed. The first (held by Reinhard Bendix and others) was that the National Socialist success in 1930 was due to the mobilization of first-time voters, the advent to politics of new sections of the population, and the switch of former DNVP supporters to the NSDAP. The opposite view, advanced by Seymour M. Lipset, attributed the result to radicalized white-collar voters who had previously supported the liberal parties. Neither hypothesis is fully borne out by recent investigations (cf. pages 188–9 below); these indicate that the NSDAP gained by the increased turnout at the polls as well as by the losses of the middle-ground parties and the DNVP. In other words, the NSDAP landslide was not purely a victory for the lower middle class but was due to voters of various social classes and from different political parties. Only in 1932, when the NSDAP was already the second strongest party, did it almost completely absorb the Protestant middle-class portion of the electorate.

The relationship of big business to the Nazi Party has been a subject of intensive controversy in recent research. However, despite very different overall assessments some aspects are broadly agreed upon by all but Marxist–Leninist historians (cf. pages 190 ff. below). Two stages are to be distinguished here: the years from 1925 to 1930, and the period from September 1930 onwards. As the sources clearly show, from 1931 onwards several prominent industrialists and bankers sought contact with the NSDAP, though they were a very small proportion of the whole. These men, who acted from a wide variety of motives, also made financial contributions to the party, but even in 1931–2 the total subvention was not large enough to be decisive. More important was the moral and political support that these circles afforded Hitler and his party and, above all, the fact that in 1932–3 they used their influence with Hindenburg and others in favour of Hitler's appointment as Chancellor.

Before 1930, on the other hand, the business world's interest in Hitler and his party remained within very narrow bounds. During that time the financial needs of the NSDAP were met, to a much greater extent than was long supposed, by an elaborate system of self-financing (membership dues, charges for attendance at functions, sale of publications), together with private contributions of which a considerable proportion came from abroad. Germans in foreign countries, and some magnates such as Ford, Deterding and Kreuger, provided the NSDAP with large sums, partly from ideological motives (anti-Semitism) and partly from political and economic calculation. As far as German industry was concerned, a large number of small capitalists contributed much more than a small number of large ones. The big business men, such as Flick and Thyssen, who favoured the NSDAP from an early date and gave it financial aid attracted attention because they were exceptional. All in all, therefore, the Nazi breakthrough of 1929–30 does not appear to have been due to active support by influential business men and financial contributions from heavy industry – just as the large contributions of the business world to the DNVP did not save it from losing nearly half its votes in September 1930. The reasons why the NSDAP became a mass movement in 1929–30 must be sought elsewhere than in a manipulation of the movement by interested business circles. Some of these reasons have already been suggested.

The evidence that the business world's direct financial support for Hitler and his party was relatively small does not, however, exhaust the question. From the outset, German employers were sceptical or openly hostile towards the parliamentary system and the pluralistic Weimar democracy. Even in the years of relative consolidation they could not bring themselves whole-heartedly to accept the political basis of the republic; and after the turn of the year 1929–30 it became the primary object of the industrial leaders to deprive the Reichstag of power and establish an authoritarian system of government. Like other leading groups in society, the manager class in general, and the captains of heavy industry in particular, waged what was often a ruthless fight against parliamentarianism and the 'party state', social democracy and the trade unions. By so doing they were instrumental in opening the breach in the structure of the republic through which the National Socialists were to effect their entry.

2

Disintegration of the Political System: the Period of Presidential Cabinets

Great as were the successes of the NSDAP in mobilizing the potential of a socially heterogeneous membership and electorate from 1930 onwards, it was not through election that Hitler came to power. Even at the height of its mobilization, the party was far from commanding a majority in Parliament. Hitler's appointment as head of a presidential Cabinet, unsupported by a parliamentary majority, became thinkable and finally possible only because the disintegration of the political system had gone so far by the turn of the year 1932–3 that the President believed he had no choice other than to declare a state of emergency or to appoint Hitler to the chancellorship.

This disintegration is the main point to bear in mind in elucidating the causes and conditions of the conquest of state power by the Nazi Party. It must further be emphasized that the disintegration which set in in 1930 was by no means predestined. On the contrary, it was consciously set in motion in 1929–30, before the collapse of the 'great coalition' and the break-through of the NSDAP as a mass movement, and was energetically pursued from 1930 onwards. The express object of its authors was to deprive Parliament of power and exclude the Social Democrats from politics, so as to transform the parliamentary democracy into an authoritarian state governed by the political right. This process was, first and foremost, the work of Hindenburg with his personal entourage and the Reichswehr leaders under General von Schleicher; it was willingly supported, however, by bourgeois elements from the right wing to a large part of the centre, and by powerful interest groups representing industry and agriculture. The press empire of the DNVP leader Hugenberg poured out anti-republican and anti-democratic propaganda. Important help was provided in the journalistic field by the ideologists of the 'conservative revolution', who combined vehement attacks on liberalism, democracy and the parliamentary system with the call for a strong leader and an authoritarian state.

When Karl Dietrich Bracher wrote his pioneering work on the break-up of the Weimar Republic (*Die Auflösung der Weimarer Republik*, 1955), which for the first time subjected the period of presidential Cabinets to a thorough analysis, he distinguished three phases: the 'loss of power' (Brüning), the 'power vacuum' (Papen and Schleicher), and the seizure of power by the National

Socialists. It is appropriate to speak of a 'loss' or 'vacuum' if one has in mind
the rapid demolition of the democratic and parliamentary system. On the other
hand, the instruments of authoritarian power – the Reichswehr, the police and
the bureaucracy – were very much intact during the presidential period, while
the President's own powers, especially the power to issue emergency decrees,
were being more and more extended. In that sense there was no real 'power
vacuum'. What happened in those years was rather a shift of power away from
Parliament and the parties, in favour of the President's ever-expanding authority
and of extra-parliamentary elements, chiefly the Reichswehr and the bureaucracy.

This 'gradual undermining of the constitutional system' (Klaus H. Rever-
mann) from 1930 onwards led to an increasing concentration of power in the
hands of the President and a Cabinet that depended on enjoying his confidence.
As the Reichstag and parties were eased out of the process of political decision-
making, the true centre of power contracted to a small circle of men who
possessed influence over the aged President and knew how to convey to him,
or force upon him, their ideas and proposals. This group was dominated by anti-
liberal and anti-democratic emotions, conceptions and interests. Thus it was
finally possible, as the result of a foolhardy intrigue in January 1933, for Hitler
to be appointed Chancellor, although by that time it was far from inevitable that
he should be.

Such, in very general terms, were the origin, course and outcome of the
disintegration of the political system during the final phase of the republic. We
shall now describe the process in more detail, in three stages: (1) the formation
of the first presidential Cabinet – a precedent of enormous importance; (2)
the development of the presidential regime under Brüning; and (3) the Papen
and Schleicher Cabinets, which no longer enjoyed the 'toleration' of the
Reichstag.

In the light of the sources it can now be firmly stated that the fateful transition
from parliamentary government to the presidential regime was well and carefully planned in advance. The protagonists, and Schleicher in particular, were
not compelled by circumstances or by the hopelessness of the political situation;
they acted with cool deliberation and with the intention of drastically altering
the constitutional system and the balance of social forces in favour of the old
élites of the army, bureaucracy and big business.

The first initiatives were taken in 1929 at Easter. Men in the President's confidence sounded Brüning (who was then *de facto*, though not yet officially, chairman of the parliamentary Centre Party) as to his willingness to head a Cabinet
of more rightward inclination which would 'put an end to the impotence
(*Marasmus*) of politics'. The idea of a 'Hindenburg Cabinet' took on firmer shape
in December 1929, when Schleicher and Meissner, Hindenburg's state
secretary, told Brüning that the President had no intention of allowing the
Müller Cabinet to remain in office after the Young Plan legislation had been
passed, and expected that he, Brüning, would not refuse a call to take its place.

In January 1930 the proposed 'Hindenburg Cabinet' was referred to in the President's palace as 'anti-parliamentarian' and 'anti-Marxist'. It was to be formed without regard to any majority in the Reichstag and without any negotiation with parties in or outside Parliament; the President's powers under Article 48 and the power of dissolution would be placed at the new Chancellor's disposal. The exclusion of the Social Democrats was already decided on. Thus, when the 'great coalition' was facing its supreme trial in March 1930, the new government was already largely decided on. Rumours of a projected Hindenberg Cabinet no doubt did much to weaken the parties' readiness to uphold the coalition, at the same time paralysing the Chancellor's resolution to hold on; a sense of discouragement and apathy was gaining ground.

The coalition Cabinet decided to resign on 27 March 1930 after Hindenberg refused its request for the use of Article 48. No further attempt was made to form a government based on a parliamentary majority. On the 28th, on Schleicher's proposal, Hindenburg commissioned Brüning to form a Cabinet, specifying that it must have a rightward orientation and not include the SPD – though this was by far the strongest party in the Reichstag and the largest and most stable of the republican parties.

Brüning, who accepted these conditions, was able to form the new government on 30 March. The Hindenburg Cabinet was a minority government drawn from the middle-ground parties, but the intention was to extend it further to the right as soon as possible; accordingly, in agreement with Hindenburg, Brüning endeavoured to co-operate in Parliament with the DNVP. From the outset he left it in no doubt that the Reichstag would be dissolved and the country governed by emergency decrees if the Reichstag rejected the government's Bills or passed a vote of no confidence. For the time being, however, a dissolution was avoided. The SPD and KPD moved votes of no confidence, but they did not command a majority and the Reichstag passed the government's fiscal laws and agrarian programme with the tiny majority of 4 votes, thanks to some DNVP members voting in their favour.

The miracle did not repeat itself at the next trial of strength in July 1930. The government introduced a new covering Bill for a reform of the state finances by means of rigorous deflation: cuts in public expenditure, increased taxes and levies, especially on higher incomes, and a so-called 'emergency contribution' by those on fixed salaries. To obtain the support of the DNVP, Brüning, in conversation with Hugenberg, actually offered to break up the Prussian coalition and persuade the Centre Party in Prussia to enter into a coalition with the DNVP. Although Hugenberg rebuffed these advances, Brüning hoped that, as in April, some DNVP deputies would deviate from the Hugenberg line so that the government proposals could be passed by a bare majority. For this reason he did not explore the possibility, which undoubtedly existed, of a compromise with the SPD.

As a result of these doubtful tactics the government was defeated in the

Reichstag on 16 July; despite Brüning's threat to use Article 48, part of the financial Bill was rejected by 256 votes to 193. Thereupon the Cabinet decided to promulgate the entire Bill at once by emergency decree. This was the first time that a Bill rejected by the Reichstag had been made law in this way – a procedure which current legal opinion held to be inadmissible. The SPD deputies at once demanded that the decree be withdrawn, and the Reichstag passed a motion to this effect by 236 votes to 221, the majority consisting of the SPD, KPD, NSDAP and most of the DNVP. Brüning thereupon announced the dissolution of the Reichstag, and the abrogated decree was reissued a few days later in a more drastic form. These decisions in July 1930 showed clearly, if it had not been clear before, that Brüning's presidential Cabinet was a new departure in constitutional terms. Because the Reichstag had made use of its right to demand the withdrawal of an emergency decree issued under Article 48(2) of the constitution, it was punished, so to speak, by the presidential dissolution. As Gerhard Schulz observes: 'With this act and on this day there began the permanent violation of the constitutional system by the dictatorial power of the Reich President, the first exercise of which was immediately directed against the restrictions imposed on that power by the constitution.'

The dissolution of the Reichstag in July 1930 led to the disastrous election of September, the results of which we have already discussed (pages 107–8 above). In the new Reichstag, with 107 members of the NSDAP and 77 of the KPD, there was no possibility of a positive majority for any purpose. The DNVP treated Brüning's assiduous wooing with contumely and refused to support the government. Brüning's attempts to win over the NSDAP for a 'constructive opposition' were also unsuccessful, although in conversation with Hitler, Strasser and Frick on 6 October 1930 he even offered 'to ensure that in all *Land* parliaments where it was arithmetically possible, the NSDAP and the Centre might combine to form a government'.

If the Brüning Cabinet was, nevertheless, not faced by a negative majority in the new Reichstag, this was due to the attitude of the SPD. The latter's opposition in July was understandable and justified after the events of the preceding months, but it had not paid off. The presidential Cabinet was still in being, and the September election had tremendously weakened the democratic, pro-republican forces. Accordingly, the parliamentary SPD – against strong opposition in its own ranks – now took the decision, for 'reasons of state' and as a rational political calculation, to 'tolerate' the Brüning Cabinet. That is to say, it refused to support votes of no confidence, which therefore failed, and by its abstention prevented the Reichstag from voting to invalidate emergency decrees under Article 48.

The SPD's decision in the autumn of 1930 to practise 'toleration' as the lesser evil was based on solid reasons connected with the Prussian coalition composed of the SPD, Centre and Deutsche Staatspartei (formerly DDP), and headed by Otto Braun of the SPD. If the Centre were to pull out of this coalition, which might occur if the Brüning Cabinet fell in consequence of action by the SPD, the latter would have lost its principal remaining bastion of power.

If the way in which the Brüning Cabinet was conceived and appointed was a first stage in the 'silent constitutional changeover' from parliamentary democracy to the presidential system, we may date the second stage from the autumn of 1930, when Brüning started to govern with the 'toleration' of the Reichstag. True, he acted more independently than the advocates of a 'Hindenburg Cabinet' had envisaged at the beginning of 1930; and his mode of government with a 'great coalition of tolerance' (Werner Conze) that included the SPD was a substantial modification of the original idea of a right-wing regime in uncompromising opposition to that party. But Brüning from start to finish regarded himself as holding office solely by virtue of the President's authority and in order to fulfil the mission assigned to him.

During Brüning's chancellorship, which lasted just over two years, the erosion of the parliamentary system proceeded rapidly. The Reichstag sat on 94 days in 1930 (including 67 after the resignation of the 'great coalition'), 42 in 1931 and only 13 in 1932. Ninety-eight laws were passed in 1930; 34 in 1931, only 5 in 1932. On the other hand, the number of emergency decrees rose from 5 in 1930 to 44 in 1931 and 66 in 1932. As the Reichstag lost its power, influence and prestige, so the executive became more independent. The bureaucratic administration pushed forward in all directions, and the relative autonomy of the civil service increased. One consequence was that the executive was able to put through important decisions even against the declared wishes of powerful business circles. Hence the decision-making processes under the presidential system have rightly been described as characterized by 'aloofness' (Reinhard Neebe).

At the top of Brüning's priorities was the liberation of Germany from the burden of reparations. His domestic economic policy was subordinated to that end. Punctual execution of the reparation payments was to demonstrate Germany's good faith but also prove that she could no longer meet her obligations and that the reparation debt must be cancelled. In order to convince the Allies of Germany's condition, Brüning was prepared to contemplate years of mass unemployment and the impoverishment of large sections of the population owing to the world depression. Once he had got rid of reparations and the worst of the economic crisis was over, his intention – as revealed in his memoirs (1970) – was to carry out a radical reform of the constitution, restore the Hohenzollern monarchy and entrust the government to a right-wing Cabinet. When the memoirs were published, his intention concerning the monarchy created a sensation in Germany and was calculated to confirm the critical judgement of his policy and motives that had largely prevailed during the 1960s (cf. below, pages 179 ff.).

However, in the most recent literature it is disputed whether the whole of Brüning's foreign and domestic policy was really based, as he claims in his memoirs, on a comprehensive strategy, or whether he in fact worked from day to day, reacting with tactical expedients to the unforeseeable effects of the economic and political crisis, 'in many ways a prisoner of events rather than directing them' (Hans Mommsen). There has also recently been intensive discussion as to how much freedom of action the Brüning Cabinet possessed in economic policy. Knut Borchardt is strongly of the opinion that until the spring of 1932 Brüning could get no support from any of the politically relevant groups for a policy of increased public expenditure financed by the Reichsbank. His deflationary policy was

the policy to which no basic alternative was offered, either by any of the parties supporting or tolerating his government, by any association of employers, or by the trade unions. This was precisely the consensus that still existed among the different elements of society, which had otherwise become in many ways violently at odds. The SPD leaders, in particular, were opposed to any experiment with the currency, and constantly pointed out the danger of inflation that was bound to result from increased government expenditure.

Probably the last word has not yet been said about Brüning's economic and social policy (cf. also pages 180 f. below). But even if earlier oversimplified judgements stand in need of qualification, there can be no doubt of one central point: Brüning's chief priority was not to cure unemployment and overcome the economic crisis, but to get rid of the reparations burden. He was determined to use the crisis as a means of cancelling reparations once and for all. Consequently, he was not primarily concerned to combat the effects of the slump as promptly as possible and with all available means. For instance, in the summer of 1931 he did not take the opportunity of using foreign credits to help solve the most urgent financial problems, because by doing so he would have forfeited the government's freedom of action in foreign affairs.

During that summer the German crisis reached an acute phase, with two coinciding events. In the first place, the government issued a new batch of emergency decrees coupled with an announcement that reparations payments would soon be suspended; this caused a massive flight of capital from Germany, both foreign and German. Secondly, the failure of the Austrian Creditanstalt also led to a severe banking crisis in Germany. The German banks, which since the inflation had only a narrow capital basis, were besieged by creditors and customers and were obliged daily for weeks on end to repay debts and deposits. On 13 July 1931 the second largest German bank, the Danatbank, stopped payment; on the 14th and 15th all German banks were closed, and even when business resumed customers could only draw out a small fraction of their assets. The government, already burdened with a budget deficit of 600 million Reichsmarks, had to make available 1,000 million Reichsmarks to support the banking system.

The financial crisis caused the US President to intervene. President Herbert Hoover had reluctantly to acknowledge that a financial and economic collapse of Germany would have disastrous consequences not only for the private US creditors and branches of industry that were directly affected, but for the USA as a whole. Accordingly, on 20 June Hoover proposed an international moratorium for one year, during which German reparations payments and the service of Allied war debts were to be suspended. He overcame French resistance by threatening that the USA would act without France if necessary, and in this way the moratorium was put into effect.

The Hoover moratorium was the beginning of the end of reparations. After a body of German experts had certified in August 1931 that Germany would be unable to resume payments, the government asked for a special committee to be convened, as provided for in the Young Plan, to examine Germany's ability to pay. At the end of December this committee reported that Germany would not be in a position to make further payments after the expiry of the moratorium; it therefore proposed the radical solution that both German reparations and the inter-Allied debts should be cancelled.

This proposal was adopted at the Lausanne conference, which met from 16 June to 9 July 1932 and at which all the states concerned with reparations were represented. Germany's creditors renounced further reparations except for a small, more or less symbolic final amount (which was not in fact paid), and terminated their own payments to the USA. The latter accepted this in practice, while not formally abandoning her claims.

When this dearly bought triumph of Brüning's revisionist efforts came about, he was no longer in office. His government fell on 29 May, a fortnight before the Lausanne conference opened. Over a period of several months, the Chancellor had gradually ceased to enjoy the President's confidence.

Hindenburg's confidence in Brüning was still unshaken in the autumn of 1931, when the cabinet had a dangerous period to steer through. The devastating effects of the economic crisis from the summer onwards caused the government to lose more and more of its popular support; sections of the business world began to turn away from Brüning, and the nationalist opposition tried every means to bring him down. On 11 October, on the eve of a short session of the Reichstag – the first for some months – the nationalists mobilized all their forces. A huge demonstration of the DNVP, Stahlhelm and NSDAP was held at Bad Harzburg, accompanied by massive parades of the paramilitary associations (the 'Harzburg front'). There was less harmony behind the scenes, where the leaders were divided by strong personal antipathies and disagreement over tactics; but all were resolved to overthrow the government, come what might. A few days later Brüning was almost unseated by a combined attack from the rightist opposition and the KPD. To meet the increasing criticism of his regime he had reshuffled the Cabinet before the Reichstag session; he himself took on the Foreign Ministry as well as the chancellorship, while Groener, the

Defence Minister, also became Minister of the Interior; Wirth, who had represented the republican wing of the Centre Party in the Cabinet, was discarded. The new Cabinet contained few party representatives of any complexion, and was thus still less in tune with Parliament than Brüning's first government. The votes of no confidence were defeated on 16 October by 295 votes to 270, with 3 abstentions; Brüning's escape was due to the fact that the SPD voted on his side.

If the Chancellor and Cabinet began to lose the President's confidence from the beginning of 1932, the origins of the process may be sought in events prior to the renewal of Hindenburg's presidency. While Hindenburg himself clearly wished to be confirmed in office by a plebiscitary vote, without rival candidates of any significance and without an election campaign, Brüning at first aimed for a prolongation of Hindenburg's term by means of a constitutional amendment, requiring a two-thirds majority of the Reichstag; this, however, foundered through the opposition of Hitler and Hugenberg. In the election, Hindenburg was opposed by the DNVP and Stahlhelm but supported by the SPD; to the aged President this was a violation of the natural order of things, and he laid the blame for it on Brüning. In the first ballot on 13 March 1932 Hindenburg almost secured the necessary absolute majority: he received 49·6 per cent of the votes, Hitler 30·1 per cent, Thälmann (KPD) 13·2 per cent, and Düsterberg (Stahlhelm) 6·8 per cent. The second ballot on 10 April took the form of a plebiscite between Hindenberg and Hitler; Hindenburg obtained 53 per cent of the votes and was thus re-elected for seven years, but Hitler's vote increased by over 6 per cent to 36·8 per cent, while Thälmann lost 3 per cent compared with the first ballot. Despite Hitler's respectable result it is to be noted that nearly two-thirds of the German electorate voted against him on this occasion, though he had thrown all his strength into the election campaign and apparently had hopes of gaining a majority, in which event the SA and SS were ready for action.

After Hindenburg's re-election it was quite logical that the government, by an emergency decree of 13 April 1932, banned the Nazi paramilitary organizations, the SA and SS, which now had a membership of about half a million. Groener had long hesitated over this step, and only made up his mind to it under pressure from the *Land* ministers of the interior. Hindenburg agreed reluctantly; his entourage took it amiss that the loyal republican organization, the Reichsbanner, was not banned along with the SA and SS. Undoubtedly the ban was the principal milestone on the way to Brüning's dismissal, as the NSDAP, backed by the other rightist forces, stepped up its agitation against the government. The deciding factor, however, was that Schleicher now began to intrigue against Groener, his own minister, who had in addition been a fatherly friend and patron of his for many years. From the beginning of May 1932, as we shall see in more detail, Schleicher conspired with the NSDAP against Groener and Brüning with the object of bringing down the latter's government and replacing it by a presidential regime further to the right and tolerated by the NSDAP.

Groener was the first victim of this intrigue. In the Reichstag on 10 May he explained and defended the ban on the SA, whereupon the NSDAP deputies created an uproar and Groener had the utmost difficulty in holding his ground. Schleicher then coolly informed the Defence Minister that he had become finally unacceptable to the chief officers of the Reichswehr. For some time past Groener had himself felt that the officer corps was losing confidence in him; on 12 May he tendered his resignation which, significantly, Hindenburg at once accepted. The President also firmly refused to appoint Groener to the post of Minister of the Interior which he had been filling on a provisional basis since October 1931.

This conflict formed the background to differences in the second half of May between Hindenburg and the Cabinet over an emergency decree, the purpose of which was that large estates in eastern Germany that could no longer pay their way should be broken up for settlement by small farmers. Under the influence of the big landowners whose class interests he shared, Hindenburg refused his assent. Many earlier historians have taken an exaggerated view of this matter as the real cause of Brüning's downfall. In reality it was merely a convenient occasion for his dismissal, which the camarilla of the President's associates had been preparing for weeks, and which took place on 29 May. In a short conversation Hindenburg coldly and brusquely demanded that the Chancellor resign, and on the following day Brüning announced the resignation of his Cabinet. A few days later Hermann Dietrich, who was Vice-Chancellor and Finance Minister in Brüning's government, gave an accurate description of the course of events and the motives of those who had brought about Brüning's fall:

> The deeper reasons for Brüning's removal lie in the fact that a class of people who had ceased to exercise any decisive influence in the state, namely the old Prussian element, decided that they would like to rule once more . . . This element made its first attempts to seize power at the time of the formation of Brüning's government. Brüning was supposed to give the helm a turn to the right. He tried to, but events were too strong for him, and so he was dismissed because he did not fulfil the gentlemen's expectations.

Brüning himself has spared no effort to depict his fall, 'a hundred yards short of the goal', as a sinister intrigue by unauthorized advisers of the President's. But while it is true that his chancellorship was not brought to an end by a vote of no confidence in the Reichstag (where he enjoyed to the last a 'tolerated' majority), but because Hindenburg withdrew his confidence from the government, Brüning was the last person to have any justified complaint on that score. For it was only the establishment of a presidential regime which enabled the President to dismiss the Chancellor, regardless of the parliamentary situation, simply because the latter no longer enjoyed his political and personal confidence; and, in the oligarchic-authoritarian system which Brüning had accepted, intrigue in the President's entourage was a political factor with a recognized weight of its own. In this sense, Brüning's fall was the consequence of his absolute dependence on the President.

Certainly Brüning's moderately authoritarian policy strictly respected the rule of law. But even under Brüning the President's powers were pushed to an extreme limit as compared with all the other elements of the constitution. Parliament was largely excluded from political decisions and confined to purely negative functions; the Reichswehr leaders occupied a key position; the powers of bureaucratic institutions were consolidated, and the public became more and more used to the idea of dictatorial measures. Brüning having cleared the ground, it was easy after his fall for the authoritarian presidential regime to develop still further.

, Even if we do not take a narrowly personalized view of far-reaching historical events and decisions, it cannot be denied that personalities played a major part in the history of Papen's and Schleicher's presidential Cabinets and the events immediately preceding Hitler's appointment as Chancellor. In those months, even more than in the Brüning period, the decisions that were so fateful for the German people and state were prepared and taken by a small circle of individuals surrounding the President. Research has placed beyond doubt the key position of Schleicher in the intrigues and in-fighting of the months before 30 January 1933. As head of the Ministeramt (political bureau) of the Defence Ministry from 1929, and Minister of Defence from June 1932, Schleicher was able to throw the decisive weight of the Reichswehr into the balance. The advocate of a presidential government since long before 1930, champion of the authoritarian dictatorship in Brüning's time, the architect of Brüning's downfall, the ruling spirit of Papen's presidential Cabinet, Schleicher was also the chief exponent of the idea of 'taming' Hitler. His general purpose was to establish a permanent authoritarian, anti-parliamentarian, presidential regime with the Reichswehr as its chief support; the National Socialist movement was to play a part in this system, but a more or less passive one, to be determined by Schleicher himself.

After Schleicher had become Chancellor and when this concept had failed, at the last minute so to speak, he tried to keep Hitler out of power. But his plans for a *coup d'état* in January 1933 did not gain the approval of Hindenburg, who preferred what seemed the less risky course of appointing a Cabinet consisting of Hitler, Papen and Hugenberg. To quote a pithy observation by Volker Hentschel, it was a tragic irony of history that 'Schleicher was finally deprived of the chance of averting a danger that, without his own active assistance, would quite possibly not have existed'.

Schleicher's idea of taming and exploiting the NSDAP by involving it in government was no doubt partly inspired by considerations of army policy. The (supposedly) 'valuable elements' in the National Socialist movement were to be embodied in the 'state' (a nationalist, authoritarian state, not the liberal-democratic one of the Weimar constitution); in practical terms, the SA should be part of the national defence force and should supply cadres for the expansion of the Reichswehr when Germany rearmed according to plan. For this reason Schleicher was opposed to the ban on the SA, though at first he had half-heartedly approved it. On 8 May 1932 he held discussions with Hitler and arrived at what he called an 'agreement': Schleicher undertook that the Brüning government would be dismissed, the ban on the SA lifted, the Reichstag dissolved and a new one elected, while Hitler promised that he would not oppose a nationalist presidential government. Schleicher promptly performed his part of the bargain. A few weeks later Brüning fell, the 'barons' Cabinet' (recruited by Schleicher) was appointed with Papen as Chancellor, the SA ban was lifted, the Reichstag dissolved and the election set for 31 July.

Schleicher did even more than he had promised. He persuaded the President to agree to an 'act of state' against Prussia, planned jointly by himself, Papen and the Reich Minister of the interior, Freiherr von Gayl. On 20 July 1932, ten days before the Reichstag election, a *coup d'état* was carried out whereby the (SPD) Prussian government of Braun and Severing was deposed (it had been functioning on a caretaker basis since the *Landtag* election in April). The Reich chancellor took over the office of Prussian minister-president, while a Reich commissioner was appointed Minister of the Interior. The SPD leader could not summon up the courage to offer open resistance to this action which deprived them of their last bastion, especially control over the Prussian police (cf. below, pages 185 ff.). It seemed to them useless to call on the Prussian police to offer armed resistance, as the Reichswehr was ready and determined to step in if necessary; and, with nearly 6 million unemployed, there was little enthusiasm for a general strike. Moreover, the working class was deeply divided between the SPD and the KPD, and a united front between them was out of the question. For years the Communists had been blackguarding the Social Democrats as 'social fascists' and as the 'chief enemy' against whom the 'main blow' must be delivered. In the summer of 1931 the KPD, on Comintern instructions, had even joined in the popular vote initiated by the right-wing parties against the Prussian government, under the slogan 'All party forces must be thrown into the battle against social democracy'. On 20 July 1932 the SPD ceased to be a decisive element in German domestic politics; in the following months it was in complete political isolation.

In the Reichstag election of 31 July 1932 (see table, pages 194–5) the NSDAP scored a remarkable success but did not gain an absolute majority. The turnout (83·4 per cent) was unusually high; the NSDAP received 13·8 million votes and 230 seats out of 608 in the new Reichstag. While the Centre and BVP gained a few seats, the other middle-of-the-road parties and those representing special interests were almost completely wiped out. The SPD did fairly well, with 133 seats compared with a previous 143, while the KPD rose from 77 seats to 89. Together the NSDAP and the KPD held more than half the seats and could completely paralyse the new Reichstag.

Immediately after the Reichstag election Hitler approached Schleicher and made it clear to him that in view of the results there could be no further question of the NSDAP 'tolerating' the Papen government. Hitler rejected Schleicher's suggestion that he should himself enter the Papen Cabinet or place his nominees in it; instead, he demanded a completely reformed government with himself at its head. Hitler repeated this demand to Hindenburg in an interview on 13 August, but received a flat refusal. An official communiqué was issued directly afterwards, representing the interview as a humiliating defeat for Hitler; Hindenburg, it was indicated, had put him in his place once and for all. Thus for the time being Hitler's bid for power failed as completely as Schleicher's hope of enrolling the NSDAP in the Papen Cabinet, controlled by himself.

The following weeks were a time of extreme confusion and uncertainty. In the short term it even seemed as if the Reichstag might recover its influence. Hitler's dramatic rebuff on 13 August had given the Centre renewed political importance, as the Centre and NSDAP together held a majority in the new Parliament. Contacts took place between the leaders of the two parties; there were rumours of a coalition between them, and on 30 August Göring, with support from the Centre, was elected president of the Reichstag.

Hindenburg, however, was determined to stand by the Papen Cabinet, although Papen and his Minister of the Interior, von Gayl, were working towards a *coup d'état* (dissolution of the Reichstag without provision for a new election). On 12 September the Reichstag inflicted a defeat on Papen's Cabinet such as had never been known in German parliamentary history, the vote of no confidence being carried by 512 votes to 42 (only the DNVP and DVP voting against). The immediate response of Hindenburg and Papen was to dissolve the Reichstag, elected only in the previous July. The original intention was not to set a date for a fresh election, but this was dropped when it became known that the Centre and NSDAP were thinking of indicting the President for violation of the constitution as provided by Article 59, unless a new election was held within the prescribed period.

In the Reichstag election on 6 November 1932 (see table, pages 194–5), the NSDAP vote fell by about 2 million or 4 per cent. This was a severe blow to the myth of its unstoppable advance, but with 196 deputies it was still by far the largest party in the Reichstag. The SPD also lost votes and seats, as did the Centre, BVP and Deutsche Staatspartei. The DNVP, DVP and KPD registered gains. The composition of the Reichstag offered no new coalition possibilities, and the rest of November was spent in feverish efforts to form a viable government.

Papen, who still possessed Hindenburg's confidence, was bent on a presidential solution, and the DNVP was prepared to support him. Hitler, however, wanted the chancellorship for himself, and a group of industrial leaders headed by Schacht, the former Reichsbank president, petitioned Hindenburg to give him the appointment. Hindenburg, however, refused to do so unless Hitler could form a parliamentary majority, and Hitler would not accept this condition; he wished to be Chancellor of a presidential government.

Hitler's 'all or nothing' policy aroused increasing anxiety in some Nazi circles: Gregor Strasser, for instance, thought that after the November election it would be well for the NSDAP to take part in a government even if Hitler were not Chancellor. Hitler was indeed in a dangerous dilemma owing to pressure of time. On top of its losses in the November election, the party suffered a severe setback in the Thuringian municipal elections on 4 December 1932. These setbacks, and the signs of discord in the party and SA at the end of the year, were warnings that could not be ignored. The socially heterogeneous members of the NSDAP and its supporters at the polls were clearly not disposed to wait indefinitely for the 'seizure of power'. *Vorwärts* was not so unrealistic when it proudly proclaimed on 6 December: 'It will be the everlasting historical merit of social democracy to have kept German fascism away from power until it began to decline in popular favour. The decline will hardly be less rapid than its rise has been.' It was indeed only the prospect of an early comprehensive success that ensured the continuation of mass support for the National Socialist movement. Hitler consequently had to show within measurable time that his strategy had paid off.

His hope of reaching the goal could only be based on the fact that Hindenburg was also in a dilemma. Since July 1932 the NSDAP and the KPD had possessed a blocking majority in the Reichstag, so that at any time they could carry a vote of no confidence in a presidential government or annul emergency decrees. Hence any government that wished to remain in power while ignoring the Reichstag could only adopt the course of declaring a state of emergency, that is, dissolving the Reichstag without calling a new election. Article 25 of the constitution laid down that an election must be held within sixty days of a dissolution; hence an indefinite postponement or failure to call an election would have been a clear breach of the constitution, and Hindenburg wished to avoid this if at all possible.

Hindenburg's dilemma became acute at the end of November. Papen, once more commissioned to form a government, wanted to carry through his 'fighting programme' if necessary by force, even at the risk of civil war. This involved eliminating a hostile Reichstag, using the Reichswehr and police to suppress all parties and quasi-political organizations, and forcing through a radical constitutional reform, to be subsequently endorsed by a plebiscite or a specially convened National Assembly. The Defence Minister, Schleicher, did not support this plan, however; in the previous weeks he had been gradually moving away from Papen and devising new combinations, such as enlisting support for the government from the trade unions and sections of the NSDAP close to Gregor Strasser (the so-called 'diagonal front'). Schleicher now declared himself emphatically opposed to proclaiming a military state of emergency, on the ground that it would probably lead to a civil war situation with which the Reichswehr would be unable to cope if at the same time there was trouble on Germany's eastern frontier. Thereupon Hindenburg, most unwillingly, decided to dismiss Papen, and on 3 December Schleicher was appointed Chancellor. On the following day Schleicher offered the vice-chancellorship to Gregor Strasser, the 'second in command' of the NSDAP, who was at first inclined to accept it. But after fierce argument among the Nazi leaders, with Hitler insisting on his 'all or nothing' policy, Strasser gave in, resigned all his party offices and departed on holiday. Thus, on 8 December, the last variant of Schleicher's policy of 'taming' the NSDAP was defeated.

Contrary to the expectations of the political right, Schleicher in his declaration of policy announced a programme of balancing interests and criticized both capitalism and socialism. He offended industry by his plans for job creation and concessions to the trade unions, and upset the big landowners by his policy in regard to tariffs and land settlement. All these unexpected and ill-prepared initiatives aroused mistrust. The bogy of an alliance between the military and the working class against the capitalist bosses appeared on the horizon, and the big industrialists and landowners feared that Schleicher might turn out to be a socialist in general's uniform. In the middle of January 1933 the parliamentary DNVP put forward a resolution calling for a 'complete re-forming of the Cabinet'; Schleicher's economic policy was described as a 'new, further lapse into socialist-international ways of thought'. The resolution spoke of the 'danger of agrarian Bolshevism' and declared that Schleicher was watering down the idea of authority and trying to steer German politics back into channels 'that we thought had been abandoned thanks to the strengthening of the national movement'.

For those who held firmly to the concept of the authoritarian state it was natural in this situation to seek an arrangement with Hitler and his party. The desire for an authoritarian programme made it logical for them to team up with Hitler, if only because it was clear, after the fiasco of the Papen government and in view of Schleicher's policy of 'reconciliation', that the anti-democratic and 'anti-Marxist' objectives could only be achieved on a plebiscitary basis, and that meant by the NSDAP. This being so, the attempt at a new version of the 'Harzburg front' was bound on this occasion to give Hitler and his party undisputed predominance.

The contacts, soundings and negotiations of the January weeks cannot be described in detail here. Papen, it is known, took the initiative. It has rightly been emphasized that his growing activity from mid-December onwards was largely due to wounded ambition and a desire for revenge: he could not forgive his former friend Schleicher for having brought his chancellorship to an end. But it must not be overlooked that, as we have seen, in addition to personal motives, very specific interests lay behind the manoeuvres with which Papen sought to oust Schleicher and bring the NSDAP into the government.

The decisive round in Hitler's fight for power opened on 4 January 1933, when he met Papen at the latter's suggestion at the house of the Cologne banker, von Schröder. Papen thought at first of a coalition between the DNVP and the NSDAP, led jointly by himself and Hitler, but by degrees he accepted Hitler's claim to the chancellorship, for which the latter held out stubbornly. At this time Papen was feverishly active, functioning as the chief mediator between the Hitler group, the DNVP leaders and the President's palace, where Hindenburg's son Oskar was beginning to play an important part as an intermediary and was working for a Hitler–Papen solution. In the middle of January the President instructed Papen 'personally and in strict confidence' to explore the possibility of forming a new government. This was a turning-point: the palace swung towards Papen and therefore Hitler, while Hindenburg and Schleicher rapidly became estranged.

At the same time the special interests continued to lobby Hindenburg against Schleicher. The executive of the Agrarian League filled Hindenburg's ears with complaints against Schleicher and advocated a new government including the NSDAP. On this occasion it was clear that Hindenburg had much sympathy for the ideas and proposals of the big landowners.

The final decision came when Schleicher applied for, and was refused, a dissolution of the Reichstag; he was thus obliged to tender his resignation on 28 January so as to avoid a defeat in the Reichstag, summoned for the 31st. At the Cabinet meeting on 28 January Schleicher reported on his short interview with the President. To his request for a dissolution Hindenburg had replied 'that the present Cabinet had not succeeded in gaining a parliamentary majority. He hoped he would now get a government that would be able to give effect to his ideas.'

The way was now free for Papen, and on 30 January Hindenburg administered the oath to the Hitler Cabinet, in which three National Socialists were 'fenced in' by nine conservatives, including Papen as Vice-Chancellor and Hugenberg as Minister for the Economy and Agriculture. As rumours had been spread concerning plans for a putsch by the Reichswehr leaders the ceremony took place in a hectic atmosphere, in which the last hesitations about Hitler's appointment were quickly swept away.

While the appointment of the Hitler government was not a *coup d'état*, it did not constitute the assumption of power by a coalition with a parliamentary majority. The Cabinet was a presidential one, like all its predecessors since 1930; yet from the beginning this government was of a radically different kind. The man now in power had behind him a completely subservient, dynamic mass party and a paramilitary organization numbering hundreds of thousands. In all the years of unscrupulous struggle against the Weimar state he had not concealed the fact that his object was to destroy the republic, to abolish democracy, and ruthlessly to suppress and persecute all his political opponents. The very first hours of the new regime showed clearly what was in store; however, they lie outside the subject of this work.

In the view of the evil consequences of National Socialist rule for Germany and the world, an account of the Weimar Republic is bound to consider whether the failure of German democracy – and a failure which resulted in Hitler's party seizing power – was inevitable, or what alternatives existed, perhaps up to the last moment. To what extent were structural factors, self-seeking groups and decisions by individual leaders responsible for the destruction of the Weimar state and the establishment of the Nazi regime? These are not simple questions to answer, and it is not surprising that very different explanations have been, and still are, put forward.

Certainly the first German republic was encumbered by a basic weakness due to the circumstances of its foundation. In the form it took in 1919, parliamentary democracy was truly accepted and zealously defended by only a minority of the population, while a great many others remained indifferent, sceptical or openly hostile. Even during the initial phase, anti-democratic forces on the right and extreme left organized to defeat the republic. In these circumstances it must be regarded as a minor miracle and a considerable achievement by the republican statesmen that they managed to steer the Weimar democracy through the complex domestic and foreign problems of its early years and finally brought about a remarkable degree of political and economic normalization. But even in those years of relative stabilization the development set in which led to a rapid disintegration of the political system after 1929: namely the rejection by large sections of the bourgeoisie, and especially the old élite classes, of the pluralistic system and the initial compromise of 1918–19, whereby the Weimar state was founded on co-operation between the Social Democratic workers and the democratic middle class. A major part of this compromise – the adjustment of interests in a partnership between capital and labour – was gradually abandoned by the employers after the Ruhr ironworks dispute at the end of 1928. In this light, the events and decisions of 1929–30 acquire significance as the real prelude to catastrophe. The shift to a presidential regime and the abandonment of parliamentary government greatly weakened the position of elements loyal to the state and to republican forms. This took place even before the effects of the world depression increased social fears immeasurably and sapped the loyalty of large sections of the population to the existing system. In this way the extreme nationalist and anti-democratic NSDAP received the boost which transformed it into a mass movement. But despite all its success in mobilizing the masses and at the polls, the NSDAP was only victorious in the end because the old élites of the industrial and landowning classes, the military aristocracy and the upper middle class, were determined to replace Weimar by an authoritarian system and believed they could use the Nazi movement for their own purposes. They did not, of course, want a totalitarian dictatorship of the kind introduced on 30 January 1933, but they regarded the NSDAP as an acceptable ally in the fight against democracy, against the parliamentary system and the organized working class.

It can no doubt be said that the Nazi seizure of power was not objectively inevitable even after the summer of 1932. But, given the attitudes, aims and relative strength of the parties and individuals concerned, and the degree to which the constitution had been undermined, the trend towards a Hitler solution was unquestionably very strong from then on. To prevent recourse to this supposed remedy for the crisis to the system would have required a high degree of political imagination and sense of responsibility, especially on the part of those individuals who filled the power vacuum caused by the switch to a presidential regime. But it was precisely this group who were lukewarm about the maintenance of a democratic system in Germany. They were bent on introducing an authoritarian form of state and society, and this reduced the range of possible political combinations so severely that they could hardly avoid coming to terms with Hitler's party. Significantly, this arrangement came about at a time when the NSDAP had suffered considerable setbacks, and while – in the opinion of influential anti-republican circles – under Schleicher's chancellorship an alliance was taking shape which might have made it possible for the workers' movement to return to the political arena. To prevent this the pact with the Nazis was concluded, on the ideological basis of a common front against organized labour and the republican system.

Certainly it must not be recognized that the democratic parties showed little skill in coping with the crisis. The inflexibility and lack of imagination of the SPD and trade-union leaders, and their feeble reaction to Papen's *coup d'état* in Prussia, are of importance here, as is the rightward trend of the Centre Party which made the idea of a coalition with the NSDAP acceptable to it in principle. All groups of the democratic centre and left harboured political illusions and misjudgements as to the Nazi danger, and in the end took refuge in an attitude of fatalistic expectation. But the weakness of those who, by their historical mission and in their own estimation, were called on to defend the rule of law and the parliamentary constitution is not to be judged on the same level as the behaviour of those who set out to destroy the republic and German democracy, and who succeeded in doing so thanks to a combination of the most varied circumstances. We can hardly agree with Karl Dietrich Erdmann that 'the Weimar democracy was not destroyed by its adversaries, but by itself'. The downfall of the republic is not to be imputed first and foremost to the working class and its organizations, the dwindling group of middle-class democrats loyal to the republican regime, or the camp of political Catholicism, but to the nationalist and authoritarian opponents of the Weimar democracy who mounted a major offensive against the state and destroyed it by unscrupulous methods.

PART TWO

Basic Problems and Trends of Research

1

The Weimar Republic as a Subject of Historical Research

Few periods of German history present such difficult problems of interpretation and evaluation as the Weimar years. No attempt to elucidate the history of those fourteen years and 'place' the republic in its context can ignore what came after Weimar. The National Socialist dictatorship erected on the ruins of the first German democracy filled Germany and Europe with destruction and terror on a previously unimaginable scale; it ruined Germany's moral reputation throughout the world and brought about the end of the German national state. The scholar's perspective is necessarily determined by these direct and indirect consequences of the failure of Weimar democracy. As Karl Dietrich Erdmann wrote in 1955: 'All research into the history of the Weimar Republic is necessarily governed, whether expressly or otherwise, by the question as to the causes of its collapse' [93*: 'Die Geschichte der Weimarer Republik als Problem der Wissenschaft', p. 5]. This is still the case, and there seems to be no prospect of it changing.

The central question thus formulated has been answered by scholars in very different ways. But at least one tendency is clear nowadays, namely, to abandon the single-cause explanations which were originally popular – for example, proportional representation, the German national character, the world depression, or the role of the Reichswehr – in favour of theories involving a combination of several causes. In so far as such explanations lay very different weight on the respective elements – for example, structural factors, the strength and aims of anti-democratic forces, the viability of parliamentary democracy and the party system, and the role of personalities in the last phase of the republic – we are presented with a broad spectrum of judgements which will be discussed in the following sections.

We should first take note of the initial conditions and earliest stages of research into the Weimar period. Such research could not be begun until relatively late, that is, only after 1945; but from then onwards conditions were unusually favourable for an intensive study of the first German democracy, based on a wide range of sources.

The reason why research was long in starting is a simple one. Before 1933

* This and similar references relate to the Bibliography, pages 204 ff.

the republican period was not yet a subject of academic history. Many historians, no doubt, took a stand on political questions and general contemporary problems, but they did so not on the basis of a thorough study of the origins and development of the republic, but as 'scholars engaged in politics'. The great majority of them made no secret of their reservations *vis-à-vis* the republic and the parliamentary and party system; among professional historians it was only a few eccentrics who stood up firmly for the Weimar democracy. Thus it came about – and this is certainly one of the gravest faults of Weimar historiography – that the established historians of the time did nothing to refute the 'stab in the back' legend, although there was already plenty of source material for the purpose [438: Faulenbach, *Ideologie des deutschen Weges*, esp. pp. 248 ff., 309 ff.].

In the twelve years of Nazi rule from 1933 onwards a scholarly analysis of the Weimar period was out of the question, and professional historians avoided the theme. The sacrosanct official version of the recent past was basically that expressed in Nazi slogans of the 'time of struggle'. Conforming to the Führer's own directives, official propaganda painted a horrific picture of the Weimar 'system': the republic was the work of the 'November criminals' and a result of the 'stab in the back', a morass of corruption, degeneracy, national humiliation, ruthless persecution of the honest 'national opposition' – fourteen years of rule by Jews, Marxists and 'cultural Bolsheviks', who had at last been swept away by the National Socialist movement under Adolf Hitler and the victory of the 'national revolution' of 1933. Some elements of this stereotype, it should not be forgotten, lived on after 1945; for the National Socialist picture of the Weimar Republic was a product of resentments, traumas and phobias which, in a somewhat less violent form, were common in rightist circles both before and after 1933. Consequently, historians writing about the Weimar Republic had much to do in the way of educating their readers and dispelling rooted prejudices; this was so for a long time after 1945, and is still to some extent the case today.

Historians in exile, who before 1933 had mostly been liberal-democratic defenders of the Weimar Republic, were naturally concerned to inquire into the rise of fascist movements and the National Socialist seizure of power. But this question rather served as a general framework within which they studied the history of ideas. Fact-filled investigations of the Weimar period remained a rarity, as did detailed analyses of politics, economics and society in post-1918 Germany. A. Rosenberg's *Geschichte der Deutschen Republik* [Carlsbad, 1935; English translation, bibliography, no. 112)] was an important advance, but one which could not be acknowledged in Germany at the time of its publication; the same was true of F. Stampfer's comprehensive history of the Weimar Republic [Carlsbad, 1936; no. 119].

The state of knowledge of the Weimar Republic at the end of the Third Reich in Germany was well described in July 1945 by F. Friedensburg in the preface to his work on the republic, which was completed in manuscript in 1934 but could not be published until 1946:

> The face of the Weimar Republic is practically unknown to the younger generation and is distorted for older people by the incessant propaganda of the Hitler period, which had constantly to accuse its predecessors of mistakes and crimes so as to lend colour to its own mendacious boasting ... Even in historical literature there is as yet no objective account of the fateful years between 1918 and 1933. [98: *Die Weimarer Republik*, p. 7]

There was not much change in this respect in the first years after 1945, despite the memoirs of numerous political figures of the Weimar period: Noske [1947; no. 70], Brüning (*Ein Brief*, 1947), Keil [1948; no. 61], Curtius [1948; no. 53], Löbe [1949; no. 65], O. Braun [2nd edn, 1949; no. 49], Severing [1950; no. 82]. Two general accounts in English were hardly noticed [S. W. Halperin, *Germany Tried Democracy* (New York, 1946) and G. Scheele, *The Weimar Republic* (London, 1946)]. The works of émigré German historians and political scientists were received with hesitation. A new edition of Stampfer's *Die ersten 14 Jahre der deutschen Republik* was published in 1947, a German translation of A. Brecht's *Prelude to Silence* (1944) appeared in 1948; Rosenberg's history, on the other hand, was not republished until 1955. No academic works on the Weimar Republic came from historians who had stayed in Germany after 1933 – a clear proof that they had not been keeping any manuscripts hidden in their desks to be published after the collapse of the Third Reich. The only two works of this kind came from authors who were not professional historians. F. Friedensburg, who published *Die Weimarer Republik* [98] in 1946, was a lawyer who had been active in the Weimar period as a senior functionary and liberal politician; L. Preller, who in 1949 published his *Sozialpolitik in der Weimarer Republik* [531], written during the Third Reich, had been a leading exponent of the theory and practice of social policy during the republic.

The 'lessons of Weimar' played a prominent part in the deliberations of the Parliamentary Council which prepared the Basic Law of the Federal Republic of Germany in 1948–9 [see F. K. Fromme, *Von der Weimarer Verfassung zum Bonner Grundgesetz* (Tübingen, 1960)]. However, in the short term at least, these discussions had no stimulating effect on historical scholarship. Surprisingly, the constitutional debates of the Weimar National Assembly were not even subjected to thorough historical analysis, although there was no lack of sources for the purpose.

The Weimar Republic became a subject of intensive historical research in the 1950s. Various circumstances combined to arouse lively interest, not only on the part of specialists, in the development and failure of the first German democracy. At the same time, the availability of relevant sources increased from year to year.

The loss of official archives due to the war, though considerable, was less than was supposed for a year or two after 1945. Most of the material fell into the victors' hands [see J. Henke, 'Das Schicksal deutscher zeitgeschichtlicher Quellen in Kriegs- und Nachkriegszeit', *VfZg*, vol. 30 (1982), pp. 557–620]. From the 1950s onwards the Western Allies returned the captured archives to the Federal Republic so that, for example, the documents of the Reich Chancellery and the Foreign Ministry – to name two basic sources – were made available to researchers. The USSR transferred the documents captured by it to the central archives of the German Democratic Republic, where they could be used by East German historians and some scholars from Western countries. In addition many important unofficial sources, especially the posthumous papers of leading Weimar politicians, which had survived Nazi rule and the hazards of war, now found their way into the archives and were available for research. Thus by degrees, from the end of the 1950s onwards, there developed a body of sources for the academic study of the Weimar Republic. Within a shorter interval than is usually the case, it became possible for students to use all the extant archive material, and not only such parts of it as were selectively made available.

From the beginning, not only West and East German historians made use of the material. The history of the Weimar Republic is a popular theme of international historiography; in particular, American and British scholars have produced important works and taken a valuable part in the debate.

If the research undertaken on a broad front in the 1950s concentrated on the final phase of the Weimar Republic, there was a natural reason for this. Historians could no longer avoid contributing to the process of 'coming to terms with the past', and it was their business to find convincing answers to questions regarding the causes and conditions of the Nazi seizure of power. This involved a thorough analysis of the fateful developments and decisions of, in particular, the years after 1929. It is thus hardly accidental that this was the subject of the first scholarly monograph on the history of the Weimar Republic: in 1955 K. D. Bracher published *Die Auflösung der Weimarer Republik* [86], which is still unsurpassed as a work of research. Bracher first described the numerous structural handicaps of the Weimar Republic, after which he traced with precision the phases of its 'dissolution' from 1930 onwards and the responsibility of certain individuals and social groups. He vigorously opposed the idea that the end of the republic was due to sudden, unpredictable forces and fateful events; instead, he saw the Nazi seizure of power as the last step in a development that was directed by tangible power groups and tendencies, favoured by domestic and external events and finally made possible by momentous errors and failures. From this point of view, central importance attached to the efforts to introduce a presidential regime. It was partly due to these manoeuvres, which dated from before the collapse of the 'great coalition' in March 1930, that no attempt was thereafter made to form a new government on a parliamentary basis. Thus the protagonists and upholders of the system of presidential government were severely criticized in Bracher's work.

Bracher's explanation and description of the break-up of the republic met with much assent but also raised some objections. These related to Bracher's method of structural analysis, which was still somewhat alien to German historiography at the time, and also to his treatment of particular questions of fact. Thus, for example, A. Brecht objected to Bracher's criticism of the passivity of the Prussian government and the Social Democrats at the time of Papen's coup on 20 July 1932 [A. Brecht, 'Die Auflösung der Weimarer Republik und die politische Wissenschaft', *Zeitschrift für Politik*, vol. 2 (1955), pp. 300 ff.; cf. also page 185 below]. The main point of contention, however, was still the transition to a presidential system and the question of Brüning's personality and policy. W. Conze, in particular, took issue with Bracher's view of Brüning's presidential government. Before Bracher's work appeared, Conze had already argued that the party state and parliamentary democracy had come to a dead end by 1929–30, and that Hindenburg's appointment of a presidential Cabinet was the only possible solution that remained [298: Conze, 'Die Krise des Parteienstaates in Deutschland 1929/30']. Conze, expanding this view in reply to Bracher's criticism of Brüning, interpreted the latter's policy as the last attempt to save democracy in Germany. We shall return in another context to the controversy which still continues on this subject and to the further works published in the 1950s on the final stage of the Weimar Republic (see below, pages 179 ff.).

Whereas research in the 1950s was primarily devoted to the last phase of the republic, from the beginning of the 1960s interest shifted to its initial phase. This followed logically enough from considerations thrown up by the intensive discussion of the causes of the republic's downfall. If, after 1929–30, the Weimar democracy was unable to stand up to the political and economic crisis and was rapidly swept away, this could only have been because of the severe structural defects that had encumbered it from its foundation onwards, in the constitutional and in the social spheres. Parties which were repeatedly unable to form parliamentary majorities capable of working and governing; a Reichswehr which gave its loyalty solely to an abstract idea of the state and not to the republic in its actual form of a parliamentary democracy, and which was not without sympathy for nationalist paramilitary organizations; a judiciary wedded to the ideas and values of a pre-democratic conservative political and social order; employers' organizations making ruthless use of their power after the abandonment of the pact of November 1918 with the trade unions; educational institutions largely dominated by anti-democratic ideas and intolerant nationalism – these were only some of the disabling factors, to which Bracher's impressive analysis had once more drawn attention. It was natural to inquire, therefore, whether such handicaps had necessarily to be accepted at the time of the foundation of the republic, or whether it would have been possible in

1918–19 to erect it on a more solid basis. Hence attention came to focus on the initial, revolutionary phase of the republic which had until then scarcely been explored by scholars.

How far this area had previously been neglected can be clearly seen from the general accounts of the Weimar Republic published in the 1950s. All the authors treat the revolutionary months of 1918–19 very briefly and as an uncontroversial subject: this is true of the textbook-type accounts by A. Schwarz [118] and W. Conze [89]. In E. Eyck's two-volume *History of the Weimar Republic* [97], written from a liberal-democratic point of view and still to be read with profit, the events between 9 November 1918 and the meeting of the National Assembly in February 1919 occupy only twenty pages. The revolutionary period was also treated fairly briefly in K. D. Erdmann's contribution of 1959 to Gebhardt's *Handbuch der deutschen Geschichte* (8th edn). Erdmann formulated clearly the interpretation which was not only dominant but almost universal in the 1950s, when he entitled the relevant chapter of his work 'A Republic of Councils or a Parliamentary Democracy?' In 1955, in a very stimulating study, he had argued that the choice in 1918–19 was strictly limited to 'social revolution in alliance with the forces pressing for a proletarian dictatorship, or a parliamentary republic in alliance with conservative elements such as the old officer corps' [93: 'Die Geschichte der Weimarer Republik als Problem der Wissenschaft', p. 7].

Erdmann's version of the alternatives of 1918–19 can be taken as typical of the judgement of the revolution by West German historians in the 1950s. It provided a stimulus for more detailed study of the situation in the revolutionary years, affording as it did a clear contrast to A. Rosenberg's view, which was put forward in 1935 [112] but of which greater notice was now taken. To Rosenberg the situation of 1918–19 seemed much opener than it did to Erdmann: he believed that the broad middle section of the social democratic working class had had a real opportunity to become the social backbone of the republic. Accordingly, his account centred on the question of why it had not been possible to hold the great majority of the workers' movement together for united action; and he found the answer equally in the policy of the Majority Socialist leaders and the revolutionary strategy of the extreme left wing of the workers' movement.

This clear-cut opposition of views between Erdmann and Rosenberg provided a starting-point for the intensive study of the revolutionary period which took place in the 1960s and 1970s, based on a wide range of sources. For a full decade the initial phase of the republic became a central theme of research. Several studies questioned the view, until then accepted, that the only alternatives in 1918–19 were either the Bolshevization of Germany, or an alliance between the Majority Socialists and the traditional élites to maintain order and set up a parliamentary republic. As most of these works emphasized, at least in the first weeks of the revolution there was a much broader range of possibilities open, and a real opportunity, though it was not used, of establishing the Weimar democracy on a sounder footing. In the next section we shall discuss more fully these studies and the 'new picture' of the revolution of 1918–19 that came to prevail in the 1960s and 1970s.

While research in the 1950s centred on the final phase of the republic, and in the 1960s and early 1970s on its initial phase, studies of its middle period cannot be related so closely to any particular date. The period is somewhat lacking in drama compared to the years before and after, and for some time historians paid no great attention to it. However, in the 1960s it finally became the object of specialized study on a wide front, and this has continued up to the present. Apart from party and parliamentary history, much research is naturally devoted to German foreign policy in the 'Stresemann era'. Still more attention, however, has been, and still is, given to the complex problems of economic policy and social development in the 1920s – an impressive review of the work done in this field up to the mid-1970s can be found in the Bochum symposium *Industrielles System und politische Entwicklung in der Weimarer Republik* [523].

Although 'Weimar culture' is unquestionably a credit item in any assessment of the republic, it was for a long time badly neglected by historians. Only since the 1970s has there been a change, and there is good reason to believe that interest in this subject had not yet reached its peak – an interest not confined to major artistic and scientific achievements, but including the problems of 'mass culture' in the democratic age. To this area belong such matters as the use of leisure, changes in relations between the sexes, and the rapid rise of the new mass media, the cinema and radio.

While the initial and final phases of the republic have been, and still are, the subject of intensive controversy, there has hitherto been more unanimity as regards the middle period. Naturally there are appreciable differences of opinion over some important questions and the emphasis to be laid on different connections of events, but these divergences remain within moderate bounds.

The question which, explicitly or not, predominates in many studies and debates concerning the middle period of the republic is: what possibilities existed during the 'peaceful' years, and what use was made of them, to complete the stabilization of the Weimar democracy and render it proof against future crises? To the question of why this did not succeed, careful and convincing answers have been given by studies of such subjects as the parties and the party system, areas of social conflict, and the position of the Reichswehr. The general conclusion is that the temporary stabilization of the republic after 1923 was a highly relative phenomenon. The developments that were to prove uncontrollable after the outbreak of the political and economic crisis can be discerned, in embryo and in their first development, in the so-called 'stable' period. Thus the division between an initial, a middle and a final phase of the republic is not to be taken as corresponding to radically different phases in the development of the state and society in Weimar Germany.

Surveying the history of research into the Weimar period we may conclude that, on the whole, the fourteen years of the first German democracy are among the best-researched periods of German history. The profusion of works is such that even the specialist can scarcely encompass them all, and new studies are constantly being added. These are currently listed in the *Bibliographie zur Zeitgeschichte* [124]; the titles there recorded, up to 1980, now also conveniently appear in the *Bibliographie zur Zeitgeschichte 1953–1980* [125]. P. Stachura's annotated bibliography [135], published in 1977, contains over 3,000 titles; even selected bibliographies like those by W. Benz [123] and Bracher, Jacobsen and Funke [126], comprise many hundreds. Brief summaries of 1,035 articles will be found in the bibliography *The Weimar Republic* published by ABC-Clio Information Services [122].

The work of presenting important collections of sources in painstaking editions is also proceeding rapidly. To begin with, we should mention two sets of volumes which, when complete, will cover the whole Weimar period. The *Akten der Reichskanzlei* [13] contain not only minutes of Cabinet meetings but numerous documents relevant to decision-making at Reich level. Foreign policy in all its breadth and complexity is documented in *Akten zur Deutschen Auswärtigen Politik* [1]: of Series A (November 1918–November 1925) five volumes have so far been published, covering the period as far as February 1922, while Series B (December 1925–January 1933) is already complete in twenty-one volumes. Besides the above, there are further editions of sources which contain in convenient form a wealth of material relating to key problems of the initial and final phases of the republic [see especially 14, 15 and 16].

If the Weimar period as a whole can be described as relatively well researched, it must at once be added that many individual problems and whole areas of interpretation still call for fuller investigation. This applies especially to important aspects of economic development and social issues, but also to the wide field of ideologies and their effects on the 'political culture' of Weimar Germany. But at present it is probably less urgent to increase our knowledge by further highly specialized studies than to meet the need for syntheses – on an intermediate level between monographs and general surveys – giving an accurate and concise picture of the results of specialized research on particular topics. This has recently been done in model fashion by P. Krüger for the foreign policy of the Weimar Republic [251] and by H. A. Winkler for the workers' movement [423, 424]. The production of further such syntheses is probably the most urgent task for historians of the Weimar period.

At the present time, in the midst of worldwide economic difficulties and in a rapidly intensifying atmosphere of crisis, interest in the Weimar Republic is once more concentrating on its final phase. This latest trend confirms a phenomenon that comes to notice repeatedly in our brief review and is in a sense typical of, at any rate, West German historians' concern with the Weimar state. The approach, questions and viewpoints of our historians are considerably, though not exclusively, prompted by a comparison between the first, unsuccessful German democracy and the trends and problems of the Federal Republic. Some may regret this close association between yesterday and today because it prevents a wholly detached view of the Weimar Republic; others may welcome it because it makes Weimar Germany a piece of the living past, not merely of antiquarian interest. In any case, the interrelation of the two subjects is a fact which has to be accepted. The history of the first German republic is 'recent history' to us and will remain so as long as the German present is subject to the direct and indirect effect of the Weimar years.

2

The Revolutionary Origins of
the Republic

As the above outline shows, West German historians, in particular, were fairly slow in turning their attention to the revolutionary initial phase of the republic. However, from the early 1960s onwards the study of this field developed rapidly and for over a decade it was a popular subject of research, with many studies calling in question the view of the revolution that had until then prevailed.

The view almost universally accepted, except by Marxist historians, in the first years after 1945 was that only the co-operation of the Majority Socialists under Ebert with the imperial officer corps and the old bureaucracy made possible the military overthrow of the revolutionary forces, thus paving the way for a parliamentary republic and saving Germany from Bolshevism. This interpretation – probably expressed most clearly by K. D. Erdmann, see page 134 above – was based on the liberal-democratic view of the revolution that developed in Weimar days and was largely adopted by the Social Democrats before 1933: namely, that the events between November 1918 and the spring of 1919 were a defensive action against Bolshevism, fought jointly and successfully by the champions of Weimar democracy. After the end of the Nazi dictatorship such an interpretation of the political and social issues of 1918–19 was attractive for several reasons. In the first place it emphasized the tradition linking the upholders of the Federal Republic with the Weimar democrats. Secondly, it involved a very favourable estimation of the actions of the Social Democrats in 1918–19, especially those of Friedrich Ebert. After the Social Democrats had been slandered mercilessly for years by the National Socialists, such an appreciation of their policy was certainly significant. Moreover, this interpretation of the crisis of 1918–19 was not devoid of topical implications; at the time when the cold war was beginning, it was a welcome opportunity to insist on the connection between defending democracy and combating communism.

The interpretation of the revolution which held almost undisputed sway in the West after 1945 was based on the assumption, which had never been verified from the sources, that the extreme left wing of the workers' movement, given its potential strength and the fluid situation during the revolutionary weeks, had had a serious chance of stopping or even reversing the trend towards a parliamentary republic, preventing the convening of the National Assembly, and bringing about a complete social upheaval on the Bolshevik model. In other words, the potential and opportunities of the 'forces working for a proletarian dictatorship' were rated relatively high. In this respect the 'bourgeois' interpretation of the revolution that prevailed in the 1950s was, paradoxically, to some extent in line with the dogmatic Marxist-Leninist one which was also current at that time and which attributed a role of the first importance to the Spartacus Union.

For Marxist-Leninist historians, especially in East Germany, the revolutionary months of 1918–19 were the subject of a comprehensive analysis related to the present day; basic 'lessons' were to be drawn from it for the fight against 'imperialism', and the treatment of the subject reflected current political strategy. It was probably not by chance that the leaders of the Socialist Unity Party (SED) in the 1950s chose the assessment of the November revolution as a key instance for the purpose of demonstrating to East German historians the leading role of the Party in the interpretation of historical events. In July 1958 the Central Committee of the SED adopted 'Theses' on the November revolution [reprinted in *Zeitschrift für Geschichtswissenschaft*, vol. 6 (1958), special number, pp. 1–27; extracts in 154: Kolb (ed.), *Vom Kaiserreich zur Weimarer Republik*, pp. 369–85]. Whereas originally many communist historians had held that the November revolution was an unsuccessful proletarian revolution, the theses of 1958 laid down that it was 'by its character a bourgeois-democratic revolution, carried out to some extent with proletarian means and methods'. The fact that Germany in 1918–19 had not undergone a 'proletarian revolution', although the objective condition for such a revolution existed, was attributed to the insufficient maturity of the 'subjective element'. The masses were not organized to such an extent that they could take up the fight for power with the prospect of success; in other words, what was still lacking in Germany at that time was a 'militant Marxist-Leninist party'. Thus the presence of such a party, capable of action, was the criterion determining the character of the revolution, and the chief prerequisite for the victory of the proletarian revolution. Consistently with this theory, the foundation of the KPD was declared to have been the turning-point in the history of the German workers' movement.

Thus Marxist-Leninist historians are given clear terms of reference within which to assess the policies and aims of the respective political groups. While the SPD leaders are accused of 'betrayal' and the Independent Socialists of uncertainty and incompetence, only the political struggle of the Spartacus Communists is treated with approval; the strength of the Spartacus Union and its influence on events is much exaggerated, and its tactical mistakes are glossed over. Thus in Marxist-Leninist historiography the Spartacus Communists appear as the only true revolutionaries, the vanguard setting a course for the militant proletariat. At the same time, a line of continuity and essentially 'correct' policy is established for the German Communists from the very beginning.

[On the problem of the November revolution and East German historiography in general see A. Decker, 'Die Novemberrevolution und die Geschichtswissenschaft in der DDR', *IWK*, vol. 10 (June 1974), pp. 269–99, and A. Dorpalen, *German History in Marxist Perspective* (London, 1985), pp. 308ff.].

Although East German historians concerned with the revolution of 1918–19 keep strictly within the dogmatic guidelines of the 1958 Theses, their works are by no means unprofitable, especially as they often use sources to which Western scholars have only limited access. Useful studies, for instance, have been devoted to such general subjects as the people's militias [164] and home guard [567]; of particular interest, especially during the 1960s, was the light thrown on regional and local events [see, e.g., H. Dähn, 'Die lokale und regionale Revolutions- und Rätebewegung 1918–19 in der DDR-Geschichtsschreibung', *AfS*, vol. 15 (1975), pp. 452–70].

When, around 1960, West German researchers began to review current ideas as to the course of the revolution, the potential forces and options for decision during the winter months of 1918–19 in the light of sources that had meanwhile become available, they set out from the central premiss of the interpretation of the revolution that was then dominant. Only a close examination of the power relationships and objectives within the revolutionary movement could show what was the potential strength of the left wing and what scope it had for action, and whether it was true that the Bolshevization of Germany was a real possibility and an imminent threat in those months.

In connection with this question as to the motives, structure, objectives and methods of the revolutionary movement, interest centred on the workers' and soldiers' councils, which were the real representatives of the revolutionary movement from the beginning of November 1918 and also in 1919. The view taken of the councils in retrospect was coloured by the fact that is in general characteristic of the German revolution of 1918–19: its contemporaries had lost no time in dismissing the revolutionary events from memory, or else they distorted them massively in the interests of political opportunism and self-justification. The principal cause of this process, which set in on a broad front as early as 1919, was no doubt the fact that none of the great political camps could identify with the revolution in the way that it took place and came to an end; in one way or another it was an embarrassment to all political groups. This affected the assessment of the workers' and soldiers' councils: in retrospect they came under suspicion of Bolshevism, they were branded as the instruments of a leftist radical minority, and their activity during the revolutionary months was almost invariably condemned. This hostile view proved extremely long-lived, during and since the period of the Third Reich: A. Rosenberg (cf. page 134 above) was for a long time quite alone in his opinion that the councils had afforded an opportunity 'to found a democracy to succeed to the revolution' [112: *History of the German Republic,* p. 89]. Only at the end of the 1950s did Rosenberg's view begin to command sympathy, and stimulated the scholarly discussion which now began.

This discussion took place because the new investigations of the revolution, based on a wide range of sources [especially 141, 144, 147, 151, 153, 154, 155, 159, 161, 165, 170, 171, recently 156, also numerous local and regional studies], led to noteworthy results, which not only altered the traditional picture of the councils but also called in question the prevalent interpretation of the revolution as a whole. Two sets of conclusions are important here.

(1) By ascertaining precise facts as to the composition of both the workers' and the soldiers' councils, it was shown beyond doubt that the great majority of the former were dominated by Majority Socialists and moderate independents, while in the soldiers' councils not only Social Democrats but also bourgeois elements exercised considerable influence. Contrary to what was widely supposed, the extreme left (the Spartacus Union and the Bremen left-wing radicals) had representatives of their own in only a few of the workers' councils, and had no great influence except in two or three large cities. Altogether, the councils in about three-quarters of the big cities were led by Majority Social Democrats, either alone or together with members of the moderate Independent Social Democrats who were prepared to co-operate. This dominance of the SPD and the moderate USPD result from the fact that when the workers' councils were improvised in November the councils in each town or region were as a rule constituted, by election or delegation, in a manner reflecting the political orientation of the local workers. The SPD and USPD had a huge majority in the workers' and soldiers' councils; the extreme left, by contrast, was largely isolated within the revolutionary mass movement of November–December, relatively few in number and weak in organization. The discovery of these facts marked the real turning-point in studies of revolutionary movement and the councils of 1918–19. They were a clear refutation of the view put forward or suggested again and again as late as the 1950s, that the councils in November–December 1918 were the instruments of leftist-radical minorities or harbingers of a Bolshevik revolution. In addition, it was now possible to form a correct understanding of the practical activity of the councils in the local sphere and their objectives concerning a political and social new order after the fall of the empire. An overwhelming majority of the councils saw themselves not as opponents of the Social Democratic coalition government of the Reich and *Länder*, formed by the SPD and the USPD, but as the local and regional agents of those governments. On the main question of the first revolutionary weeks, namely, whether to make 'a National Assembly or a system of councils', they took up an unambiguous position: they were in favour of electing a National Assembly as soon as possible, hence they were in favour of parliamentary democracy. At the same time, they put forward a number of demands from a Social Democratic viewpoint, involving an extensive reform of the political and social order: 'democratization' of the administration, far-reaching changes in the army, socialization of industries 'ripe for the purpose'.

(2) Closer analysis also showed that the revolution and the movement to form councils in 1918–19 had gone through several phases that need to be clearly distinguished. The first phase was from the overthrow of the empire to the break-up of the

government coalition of the SPD and USPD at the end of December or, at the latest, to the January riots and the election to the National Assembly. During that phase the councils represented a broad popular movement which was composed mainly of workers and soldiers. The great majority of politicians who belonged to the councils did not want to erect them into a system of government; they regarded the councils as temporary institutions, and pressed for the early election of a National Assembly. In those weeks the great majority of the councils co-operated loyally with the revolutionary governments in the Reich and *Länder*.

The second phase of the revolution, which began in January 1919 and culminated in the spring, was marked by a rapid radicalization of large numbers of the working class, who – disappointed by the non-appearance of the changes they had demanded and expected in the military system, the bureaucracy and heavy industry – now took a decided stand against government policy. This was a time of increasingly sharp confrontation between the radical mass movement and the Reich government, which asserted its authority by means of military force. In these months the mass movement was developing largely outside the councils, which were no longer so representative as in November and December and were rapidly losing their influence. Only in this second phase did a true 'councils ideology' develop. The 'councils movement' of the spring of 1919, which was largely dominated by the USPD, was partly inside and partly outside the councils as then established; it regarded them as organizations of the class struggle and wished to see them institutionalized as part of the socialization programme. The general conviction of recent research is that the mass movement of the spring of 1919, which was much more radical than that of the previous November, acquired its strength only in the course of the revolution and because of the way in which the revolution developed.

On the basis of these conclusions, which are now scarcely disputed by scholars, research in the 1960s and early 1970s took the further step of re-examining the political alternatives available in 1918–19 and the amount of freedom enjoyed by the revolutionary government. Significant works are those by Carsten [141], Kluge [151], Kolb [153], Lehnert [156], Matthias [159], Miller [161], Oertzen [165] and Rürup [170]. Their argument may be summarized as follows. On the one hand, the social basis for a new order in the first weeks of the republic went further than is suggested by the political consolidation from the beginning of January 1919 onwards. On the other, the 'forces pressing for a proletarian dictatorship' (cf. page 134 above) were, in the decisive weeks of revolutionary transition between November 1918 and January 1919, less strong in reality than they appeared to many contemporaries, some excitable journalists and a considerable number of active politicians, and less strong also than they were sometimes made out to be by interested parties. In view of these facts it is impossible to maintain the earlier opinion that in the winter of 1918–19 there was an imminent danger in Germany of Bolshevik rule or a proletarian dictatorship. This has a bearing on the question of the options open to the political decision-makers. Given the new domestic order after the fall of the empire they certainly had more freedom of action, whatever its exact extent, than is assumed by those who see only one possible choice at that time: either the Bolshevization of Germany, or co-operation between the Majority Socialists and the traditional power élites to maintain order and set up a parliamentary republic. The courses open to the revolutionary government would, for instance, have included taking a firm line with the old army leaders, making preparations to socialize the mines at least, and using the potential strength of the workers' and soldiers' councils to support a Social Democratic programme of reform. But the SPD leaders, in particular, refused to embark on such a course. This was not primarily under pressure of circumstances but because, first, they trusted the old élites to remain loyal to the new holders of power and, secondly, they basically distrusted the spontaneous mass movement. That movement was certainly to some extent amorphous, but in November and December it was largely sustained by members and supporters of the Social Democrats and its political demands were within the Social Democratic range. It was not least because of the line taken by the SPD leaders that what had begun in November 1918 as a democratic people's movement ended in the following spring in radicalization and the acceptance of failure.

In this interpretation of the revolution — which may be called a revisionist one — criticism is directed, above all, at the Majority Socialist leaders headed by Friedrich Ebert. But it must be emphasized that this criticism is quite different from the Communist polemic against the Social Democrats. It does not blame the Majority Socialists for failing to work towards a proletarian dictatorship, which they wished no part of, or for lacking Lenin's revolutionary vision. The criticism is rather that expressed in the question: 'Why did this party, with the means at its disposal, not achieve its ends?' [161: Miller, *Die Bürde der Macht*, p. 101].

The reassessment of the German revolution of 1918–19 that was elaborated in the 1960s and early 1970s [and is best summarized in 170: Rürup, *Probleme der Revolution in Deutschland 1918/19*] found extremely rapid acknowledgment and can now be regarded as the 'prevailing doctrine'. This, however, is the case only as far as academic discussion is concerned. In manuals and many school textbooks the old theory is maintained, either unchanged or with slight modification [cf., e.g., 94: K. D. Erdmann's 'Die Weimarer Republik', or his lecture of 1979, *Rätestaat oder parlamentarische Demokratie* (Copenhagen, 1979)]. It is noteworthy, however, that the critics of the 'revisionist' interpretation seldom attacked it frontally until about the end of the 1970s, but confined themselves to questioning it occasionally without going fully into the arguments. It could, in fact, hardly be disputed that the new interpretation followed convincingly from what had been ascertained as to the character, objects and phases of the revolutionary movement.

At the same time, the discussion of such difficult questions as the freedom of action, potential forces and options available in 1918–19 is bound to be to some extent hypothetical; it cannot be decided by simply looking at the evidence of sources, as can the question of the composition of the workers' and soldiers' councils. It was therefore to be expected that the interpretation that now holds the field would be challenged sooner or later; and it has in fact been strongly criticized in some works since the end of the 1970s. Those who do so do not cite new sources, and they accept at least in part the results of more recent research, but they express decided reservations, in particular as regards the councils' 'democratic potential'. Thus W. J. Mommsen doubts 'whether the workers' and soldiers' councils really aimed throughout at an effective democratization of the administration'; he does not see them as embodying any constructive potential for a new order, and characterizes the movement as an amorphous social protest ['Die deutsche Revolution 1918–1920', *GG*, vol. 4 (1978), pp. 362–91; quotation, p. 372]. E. Jesse and H. Köhler even speak of the 'invention of a "councils movement" ' by recent research. In their view 'the independence and effective role of the democratic councils as the representatives of a new democratic potential is by no means proven'; rather it is the case that 'an amorphous collection of individual councils with very different political views . . . has been elevated to the status of a united movement' ['Die deutsche Revolution 1918–19 im Wandel der historischen Forschung', *Aus Politik und Zeitgeschichte*, B45/78, 11 November 1978, pp. 3–23, esp. p. 18]. However, the objections expressed by Mommsen and by Jesse and Köhler to the description of the councils as a 'democratic potential' are themselves open to criticism. As R. Rürup points out,

> they evidently associate 'democratic potential' with the notion that the councils should immediately have introduced and carried through the necessary processes of democratization, and formulated detailed programmes and strategies for that purpose. But all that recent researchers mean by the term is that, contrary to earlier belief, the councils were definitely on the side of democracy and, given their actual power, could have lent firm support to a policy of democratization by the Reich and *Land* governments. ['Demokratische Revolution und "dritter Weg" ', *GG*, vol. 9 (1983), pp. 278–301; quotation, p. 295]

Further discussion will have to show whether the arguments advanced by Mommsen and by Jesse and Köhler can seriously threaten the 'revisionist' findings based on numerous well-documented monographs. But Jesse and Köhler, who go furthest in that direction, themselves concede that there can be no question of a 'return to the position of the 1950s'. 'The councils were not predominantly Communist, nor can the policy of the Majority Socialists be described as praiseworthy and fortunate in all respects.' As to the freedom of action enjoyed by the Majority Socialist leaders, which is still the subject of disagreement, H. A. Winkler has recently found a way of defining this which may prove to express the consensus of all concerned in the discussion.

First: the governing Social Democrats could not, without provoking chaos, avoid some degree of co-operation with leading elements of the old regime. Secondly: the extent of that co-operation, and hence the political and social continuity between the monarchy and the republic, was considerably greater than the situation required. In other words, if the Social Democrats had shown a stronger degree of political will, they could have altered more and would not have had to preserve so much. [*GG*, vol. 8 (1982), p. 5. For Winkler's intermediary position in general see idem: 176 and 423]

In further discussion, however, historians should avoid giving the impression that the 'revisionist' interpretation of the options of 1918–19 amounts to advocating a policy of the 'third way' – a suggestion at present frequently met with, for example, throughout the work by Jesse and Köhler. The vague, over-simple idea of a 'third way' could not be less appropriate to the revised interpretation of the revolution. In the first place, it implies that the 'dictatorship of the proletariat' was a feasible alternative, or a threatening eventuality, in 1918–19, whereas research has proved the contrary. Secondly, the term 'third way' suggests that the object would have been to create a political system beyond parliamentary democracy, or an economic system that was neither capitalist nor socialist. It was not a question of this, however, but of a broad scale of measures designed to establish the republic on a democratic foundation, and perfectly compatible with the choice of a parliamentary democracy. What recent research shows to have been possible and desirable is not a 'third way', such as, for instance, a permanent institutionalization of the councils, but *another* way, namely that of taking full advantage of the opportunities to ensure that the republic developed on democratic lines. It can scarcely be helpful to use the term 'third way' for the whole spectrum of domestic possibilities between a 'dictatorship of the proletariat', on the one hand, and the SPD leaders' pragmatic co-operation with the élite of the old regime on the other; accordingly, this confusing term should be eliminated from the discussion as soon as possible.

A general view of studies of the 1918–19 revolution in the 1960s and 1970s may give the impression that too much attention was devoted to the workers' and soldiers' councils and too little to other important aspects of the period between the fall of the empire and the convening of the National Assembly. This impression, however, is only partly correct. Two points should not be overlooked.

First, the councils and the revolutionary movement are certainly a major subject of research, and it cannot be denied that there has been a certain danger of turning the councils into the key question of the revolution; this was, at most, only indirectly the case, as S. Miller points out [161: *Die Bürde der Macht*,

p. 120]. But from the point of view of research planning it was right and necessary, in studying the period, to begin by analysing the councils as the most important elements of the revolutionary movement, and to re-examine old stereotypes. Now that the gaps in our information have been filled, it would be wrong to continue to put the councils in the forefront of research or to treat them as an all-decisive factor in the events of the revolutionary months. It should also be noted that interest in the councils and the revolutionary movement of 1918–19 was genuinely historical and not inspired by current politics. All the important evidence had already been studied when, unexpectedly, the question became topical after 1968 and some sections of the student movement began to discuss the theory of councils as a modern-day problem. This 'politicization' of the subject made it harder, rather than easier, to consider the problems of the 1918–19 revolution in a calm and factual manner.

Secondly, while in the 1960s and 1970s much interest was concentrated on the councils and the revolutionary movement, and on the conclusions that might be drawn as a result concerning the revolution as a whole, researchers were at the same time also examining a much broader spectrum of the aspects and problems of the initial phase of the republic. Many works dealt with the question of the armed forces and the policy of the High Command during the revolutionary months [151, 168, 557, 563, 576, 577]; with economic problems and the organizational alternatives after the fall of the empire and in the transition from war to peace [e.g., 143, 146, 172, 177]; and with preparations for the peace negotiations in the winter months of 1918–19 [186, 190, 206, 215]. Another important area is that of parties and the party system in the phase following the collapse of the empire. The re-formation and development of particular parties was studied in depth (see page 152 below), as was the reorientation of the trade unions [e.g., 139, 379, 396, 403, 542] and the behaviour of organized industrial and agrarian interests during the revolutionary period [e.g., 409, 485, 487, 493]. Numerous studies deal with the reaction of the Protestant churches to the revolution and the abrogation of the episcopal status (*summus episcopatus*) of local rulers [e.g., 160, 346, 370, 392, 425]; the attitude of the Catholic church in the revolutionary months has not yet been studied in detail. Other important areas that await further study include the press and journalism during the winter months of 1918–19, and the effects of war and revolution on the social fabric. But, on the whole, it is true to say that the intensive research of the past twenty-five years has thrown a considerable amount of light on the political, economic and social issues and new departures of the revolutionary months. From the various separate pieces of the mosaic it would not be difficult to form a combined, many-faceted picture. A comprehensive account of the German revolution of 1918–19, based on the results of numerous specialized studies, is an urgent desideratum, especially as such accounts have already been produced by Marxist-Leninist historians [142, 150]. For some time past the final period of the Weimar Republic, as opposed to its beginnings, has once more become the centre of academic and public interest, as the question of missed opportunities in the establishment of a democratic state has appeared less urgent than the question of the governability of such a state in times of economic crisis and political uncertainty; but the revolution of 1918–19 remains one of the chief pivots of recent German history and a central theme for historical research and reflection.

3

The Reich Constitution, the Party System, and the Reichswehr

Scholars have so far shown only moderate interest in the genesis of the Reich constitution in 1918–19: a surprising fact when one considers the enormous importance of the constitution in general, and some of its clauses in particular, for the further development of the republic and finally its downfall. We can only speculate as to the reasons for this neglect. However, it may be pointed out that the constitutional debates of the National Assembly did not give rise to any spectacular basic controversy of the kind that fascinates contemporaries and historians alike, such as those of the German National Assembly of 1848–9. This was because, when the National Assembly convened in February 1919, the principal constitutional decisions had already been taken: for a republic and parliamentary democracy, for a federal as against a centralized system, and for a 'strong' presidential power as against purely parliamentary rule.

These fundamental decisions, taken between November 1918 and February 1919, were sanctioned by the National Assembly when, in the first few days of its existence, it approved the law on the Provisional Exercise of State Power which had been negotiated between the Reich government and the Committee of States of the *Land* governments. This formed the basis of the constitutional structure erected by the National Assembly. The principle of a central system of government and the respective powers of the President, Cabinet and Reichstag were scarcely touched on in the parliamentary debates, and the details were also not considered in much depth [308: Haungs, *Reichspräsident und parlamentarische Kabinettsregierung*, p. 22].

The constitution-making process thus includes both the preparatory work and decisions during the transition period from November 1918 to February 1919, and the debates in the National Assembly. Both these stages must be taken into account in studying the origin and final shape of the Weimar constitution. There is as yet no comprehensive monograph on the subject. The earlier account by W. Apelt, who himself took part in drafting the constitution, was based on a relatively narrow range of sources [138]; E. R. Huber [149, pp. 1178–1243] deals with the actual discussions in a fairly summary manner. Attention should be drawn to the close analysis of problems by R. Rürup ['Entstehung und Grundlagen der Weimarer Verfassung', in 154: Kolb (ed.), *Vom Kaiserreich zur Weimarer Republik*, pp. 218–43].

The most important works on the preparation of the constitution deal with particular aspects. Thus R. Schiffers [331] examines the genesis of the 'plebiscitary elements' of the constitution; G. Schulz [333], E. Eimers [300] and W. Benz [293] study in detail the relations between the Reich and the *Länder* during the revolutionary months and the part played by the *Länder* in the constitutional debate; E. Portner [166] and L. Albertin [339] examine the constitutional policy of the liberals, R. Morsey [388] that of the Centre; H. Potthoff [167] sketches the attitude of the leftist parties in the discussions; while W. J. Mommsen [674] analyses the part played by Max Weber in the preparation of the draft. Other important themes still await attention, such as the constitutional debate outside the National Assembly, discussions within the parties and outside Parliament, the genesis of the different articles in the section on fundamental rights, the precise origins of Article 48 and contemporary ideas of its significance and scope.

Thus the present state of research can hardly be considered satisfactory. However, important questions have been cleared up on the basis of existing special studies, for example the debates on the draft constitution between the Reich and *Land* governments at the end of January and beginning of February 1919, or the motives and considerations that led to the concept of a plebiscitary Reich presidency. As we now know, it was the Liberals who developed this concept and secured its adoption, because they were deeply mistrustful of purely parliamentary rule and desired a system based on the separation and balance of powers; instead of constitutional monarchy, there was to be a 'constitutional democracy'. The Majority Socialists did not take a determined stand against the fateful mixture of the presidential and the parliamentary system. Despite much criticism from their own ranks they accepted the idea of a plebiscitary president, which was championed by H. Preuss as well as Max Weber; thus they set up a dualistic system which was 'fundamentally ambiguous' (D. Sternberger) and, among other things, was calculated to weaken the compulsion to form parliamentary majorities.

Another element of the constitution that was virtually decided on before the National Assembly met was proportional representation. This was decreed by the revolutionary government in November 1918, and was applied in the election to the National Assembly. The Assembly, without any fundamental debate on electoral methods, incorporated proportional representation in the constitution. This was generally expected and was in no way considered to be 'revolutionary'. The SPD had fought for its adoption for decades and now made it a *sine qua non*. But the bourgeois parties and groups were also in favour, as under current condition it seemed that an overwhelming predominance of the SPD would be less likely under proportional representation than under the previous majority system. It was not only in Germany that proportional representation was thought of in those days as the most 'up-to-date' electoral system; most other European countries also adopted it in the 1920s.

In the last years of the Weimar Republic the debate on electoral methods was intensified, with a view to improving the existing system; but the latter was only subjected to strong criticism after 1945, when statesmen, political scientists and historians agreed in blaming proportional representation for the deficiencies of the Weimar parliamentary system and the collapse of democracy. Proportional representation, it was argued, had encouraged the formation of new parties and splinter parties; the multiplicity of groups had made it harder to form governments and had finally led to a breakdown of the system. F. A. Hermens, the most determined and persistent critic of proportional representation, argued in numerous publications that it was the real cause of the collapse of the Weimar Republic [e.g., *Demokratie oder Anarchie?* (Frankfurt on Main, 1951) with approving prefaces by A. Weber and C. J. Freidrich]. According to Hermens, if the majority system had been in force 'the NSDAP would certainly not have been a factor of national importance in 1932 and would probably have long since died of political anaemia' [ibid., p. 229]. The arguments of Hermens and his followers were scarcely disputed in the 1950s and were accepted by historians, sometimes in a less emphatic form (e.g., E. Eyck, and A. Schwarz). In 1964 K. D. Bracher spoke of the 'widespread view' that a voting system based on relative majorities might have saved the Weimar Republic and prevented the victory of National Socialism ['Probleme der Wahlentwicklung in der Weimarer Republik', in 297: Büsch, Wölk, and Wölk (eds), *Wählerbewegungen in der deutschen Geschichte*, p. 629].

The argument has since quietened down. It lost its politically sensitive character inasmuch as the development of the Federal Republic showed that proportional representation is by no means incompatible with a stable parliamentary system. Looking back on the controversy as to the connection between the electoral system and the failure of the Weimar democracy, certain points may be noted:

(1) It is not only difficult, but highly questionable from the point of view of method, simply to recalculate the electoral results of the Weimar period in terms of majority voting, as parties' voting tactics are certainly different under the two systems. As H. Fenske rightly observes in his criticism of Hermens, one would need the courage to rewrite the history of Weimar from the first day onwards in terms of a different electoral system; in short, 'one would be relying solely on fictions' [305: *Wahlrecht und Parteiensystem*, p. 34].

(2) A relative majority system could not have saved the republic from dangers arising from radical changes of view by the electorate. We may agree with E. R. Huber that 'proportional representation in the Weimar Republic was certainly not the cause of the rapid rise of the radical parties' [104: *Deutsche Verfassungsgeschichte*, Vol. 6, p. 133]. Thus considerable doubt attaches to the view recently put forward by E. Schanbacher in support of Hermens, that proportional representation was 'a main cause of the triumphant advance of the National Socialists in the parliamentary elections from 1929 onwards and,

consequently, of Hitler's appointment as Chancellor on 30 January 1933' [330: *Parlamentarische Wahlen und Wahlsystem*, p. 231].

(3) The role of splinter parties in the Weimar period is often much exaggerated. The functioning of the parliamentary system was less impaired by the existence of a few small parties than by the difficulty of forming coalitions among the larger ones. This difficulty, as Fenske points out, was largely due to the way in which 'anti-Marxism' gained ground among the bourgeois parties.

> These pronounced anti-Marxist positions were the real germ of disease in the German party system of the Weimar period, and it was particularly serious that they were not confined to the conservatives but also affected the National Liberals. They are far more important than the fragmentation due to the electoral system or the formal legacy of constitutionalism in the construction of the constitution. [305: p. 345; cf. also pp. 281, 349]

Parties and the party system in the Weimar period are a wide field to which research has devoted special attention for over two decades. Interest in the development of the German party system after 1918 had already been displayed in the years before 1933. Thus L. Bergsträsser in the fifth and sixth editions (1928, 1932) of his *Geschichte der politischen Parteien in Deutschland* [343] dealt with the development of parties since the foundation of the republic, and in 1932 S. Neumann published a pioneering study of the history and structure of the Weimar parties [390] which is still among the best descriptions of the parties of those years, their structure, programmes, politico-social background and general place in political life. K. D. Bracher, who edited Neumann's study in 1965, rightly placed it on a par with A. Rosenberg's *History of the German Republic* [112]. Neumann, as a social scientist of historical inclination, developed Max Weber's theory of types into a typology of parties which made possible a precise structural analysis and comparative description of the German parties, in the Weimar period at least, and which has since become widely accepted. He distinguishes the liberal 'party of representation', rooted in nineteenth-century tradition, whose members and supporters scarcely come into action except at election time, from the modern 'party of integration', characterized by the constant activity of its members, a high degree of bureaucratization, complete involvement of the individual in the organization, and the permeation by it of all spheres of life. Neumann further distinguishes two variants of the party of integration: the 'democratic' (SPD, Centre) and the 'absolutist' (NSDAP, KPD).

Neumann's important contribution to the study of German political parties could not exercise much influence at first, as under the Third Reich the Weimar parties were taboo as a theme of academic research. After 1945 the study of the Weimar party system did not get under way at once; in 1956 Neumann observed that the Weimar party landscape was a *terra incognita* [*Modern Political Parties*

(Chicago, 1956), p. 354]. However, things changed very quickly in the following years: in the 1960s and 1970s a large number of studies of Weimar party history were published, so that one can certainly no longer speak of a *terra incognita*.

As early as 1960 E. Matthias and R. Morsey edited a comprehensive work, *Das Ende der Parteien 1933* [385], which set standards for future studies of party history. The careful studies, based on the sources then available, of the structure and policies of the chief parties during the 'crisis of the party state' combine to form a differentiated picture of the party landscape at the end of the republic and in the first weeks of the Third Reich. The work emphasized not only the insoluble difficulties that confronted the main parties of the state, but also the confusion and lack of purpose with which the republican parties reacted to the institution of the presidential regime and the challenge of the National Socialist movement. This major work was compiled in connection with extensive research by the Commission for the History of Parliamentarianism and the Political Parties: this body, founded in 1951, became a centre of research in the Federal Republic, publishing from the late 1950s onwards a series of basic editions of sources and numerous monographs on the history of parliament, parties and associations.

By far the greater number of studies of party history in the Weimar period are devoted to single parties, their organization and policies; to some extent also to the formation of policies and the effects of social processes on the composition of party membership and its electoral following. As against this, relatively few works deal explicitly with the general development of the party system between 1918 and 1933. Two subjects of the greatest importance call for thorough study and analysis: the continuity, to a large extent, of the German party system before and after the upheaval of 1918–19, and its rapid break-up from 1928 onwards.

The party system of imperial times remained essentially unaltered during the revolutionary months of 1918–19. Some parties changed their names, and the political left split into two rival parties; but the four main political currents – the conservatives, the Centre, the liberals and the Social Democrats – were represented in 1919 in about the same relative strength as in the Reichstag election of 1912. It is generally accepted today that the structure of the party system hardly suffered any change in the transition from the monarchy to the republic, so that we can speak of a continuity of the party system. G. A. Ritter, differentiating somewhat, refers to the 'continuity and re-forming of the German party system in 1918–20' [400]. He points to some changes in the inner structure and behaviour of the parties, resulting mainly from the change in the electoral system. This called for the mobilization of scattered votes and therefore required a party organization extending over a wide area, which led to shifts in the reservoir of voters. But Ritter also regards continuity as the dominant feature of the party system in the transitional period.

Credit is due to R. M. Lepsius, whose study 'Parteiensystem und Sozialstruktur' [380] was first published in 1966, for not only emphasizing the stability of the party system between 1871 and 1928 but also giving a convincing explanation of the phenomenon. He attributed it to the direct link between party formations and the more or less distinct social milieux with which each of them was associated. The political integration and organization of society depended not only on class interests but also on a complex configuration of religious, regional, social and economic factors [ibid., p. 67]. None of the great party groupings was strictly homogeneous from the class point of view, but each had a 'socio-moral milieu' on which it depended. Hence the party system disintegrated when these milieux gradually dissolved as a result of industrialization, growing mobility and social differentiation. The loosening of ties to the respective milieux in the 1920s was felt by the Centre and SPD as well as the other parties, but the real breakdown affected the middle ground of politics.

This did not happen overnight, however. In 1920 the lower middle class showed a rightward tendency, which increased in 1924; in 1928, on the other hand, middle-class and peasant 'interest parties' scored considerable electoral successes. It can be said that large sections of the middle class had ceased to be 'liberal' and were looking for a new political home. Thus the party system began to break up before the world depression set in, before the German political crisis and the significant rise of the NSDAP; afterwards, however, the latter's rapid development into a mass party greatly accelerated the process of dissolution. In 1928–9 it was indeed not yet clear – as H. A. Winkler has shown in his basic study *Mittelstand, Demokratie und Nationalsozialismus* [546] – that the bulk of the lower middle class would turn to National Socialism as the alternative to parliamentary democracy [ibid., p. 159]: that class, after all, was not the only one to which Nazi propaganda was addressed. But the situation was altered by the depression, so that the middle-ground parties, apart from the Centre, lost the great bulk of their voting support in 1930–2 and disappeared almost completely from the political scene.

Seeing that the German party system had been relatively stable for over sixty years, its break-up within a few years is a highly dramatic phenomenon. Some aspects of it have been elucidated, but a comprehensive analysis is still lacking. More light might be thrown by research into the connection between the party system and changes in political mentality due to social shifts during the middle period of the republic – another reason why further study of that period is required.

The history, structure and policies of individual parties during the Weimar period is the subject of a large number of works – it would be beyond our scope to discuss them or even enumerate their titles and principal themes. We can merely make the general observation that only in the case of the smaller parties do we at present have accounts of the whole period of their existence (which is often relatively short); whereas the numerous accounts of the major parties are confined to particular stages of their development between 1918 and 1933, or some aspects of their political activity. For practically all the important parties, their internal development and political activity in the initial and final phases of the republic have been much more thoroughly studied than the middle phase. This applies to the Centre [291, 292, 350, 373, 388, 389], the Liberal parties [e.g., 166, 339, 362] and the DNVP [363, 367, 382, 412, 414, 657]; largely also to the SPD [161, 375, 384, 386, 423; for the middle period see now 424: Winkler, *Der Schein der Normalität*]. For an assessment of the political strategy and tactics of these parties in the middle years of the republic, reference should therefore be made to the important studies by M. Stürmer [336] and P. Haungs [308] on the coalitions of 1923–9. This history of the KPD is fairly well researched for the whole period of the republic [340, 342, 352, 353, 416, 417, 418, 419].

Despite the large number of valuable works on the organization, development and policies of the individual parties, there are still many gaps to be filled. As we have already pointed out, overall accounts of the major parties are lacking. Also, for instance, we know far too little about the parties' regional organization, the social composition of their membership and constituents (and the changes in this respect between 1918 and 1932), and their leading personnel, apart from H. Weber's exact prosopography of the administration of the KPD from 1918 onwards [417]. We also lack studies of the leading parliamentarians of the Weimar period; surprisingly, there is no adequate political biography of any of the Reich chancellors. Altogether it seems as if the classical investigation of the parties, as it was pursued in the 1960s and 1970s with great intensity and with considerable success in terms of quality and quantity, has since been replaced by an approach more oriented towards social history, more particularly questions of the structure and behaviour of the electorate.

There has also been a change for some years past in the perspective from which problems of the armed forces and military policy are treated. For a long time research concentrated on questions, which were also central to any politico-historical discussion, of the relationship between the Reichswehr and the republic, the extra-constitutional influence of the military in politics, and the degree of responsibility falling on the Reichswehr and its leaders for the downfall of the Weimar democracy. Since the mid-1960s, however, these themes have receded into the background. Instead, interest has centred – within the framework of general theorizing as to the relationship of the military, society and politics in the modern industrial state – on the problem of rearmament and the attempts to create a 'military-industrial complex' in the Weimar Republic. [On the development of research and the new lines of inquiry, see the instructive remarks by K.-J. Müller in *The Army, Politics and Society in Germany, 1933–1945* (Paderborn, 1979; 3rd edn 1981; Eng. trans., Manchester, 1987, pp. 16 ff.]

Studies of the Reichswehr have at all times had a marked relevance to present-day questions. In the 1950s decisive stimuli were received from the debate on

German rearmament and membership of the Western military alliance. The place of the armed forces in a parliamentary democracy was a topical issue, and naturally aroused interest in the controversial relationship between the Reichswehr and the republic in Weimar times. In this first phase of Reichswehr historiography two fundamental positions took shape, which in developed form still confront each other.

The anti-Reichswehr interpretation of the 1950s and 1960s was expressed more particularly in the works by W. Sauer ['Die Reichswehr', in 86: Bracher, *Die Auflösung der Weimarer Republik*] and F. L. Carsten [557]. It emphasized, as the main component of Reichswehr policy, the determination of the military leaders to obtain and preserve an autonomous position of power for the Reichswehr in the republican state. The officer corps formed by the imperial army could not bring itself to accept parliamentary democracy, and organized the Reichswehr as a 'state within the state', independent of the society and politics of the republic. This autonomous position of the Reichswehr weakened the democratic order and contributed to the downfall of the republic. As against this, a more favourable view of the role of the armed forces was taken by H. J. Gordon [563] and H. Meier-Welcker [667]. These writers held that Seeckt could not be accused of exercising undue political influence; on the contrary, he was loyal to the state and did much to consolidate the republican order. The Reichswehr, under Seeckt at least, had come to terms with the republic, becoming, as it were, republican by conviction if not by sentiment, and would have remained so if the political leaders had shown more sympathy towards the armed forces and more understanding of Germany's security needs. R. Wohlfeil attempted to reconcile these conflicting views, which can be called liberal and conservative, in his contribution to the *Handbuch zur deutschen Militärgeschichte* [580]. This takes a line of cautious revisionism, showing understanding for an interpretation such as Meier-Welcker's and toning down Carsten's criticism. It offers a synthesis of research as it stood at the end of the 1960s. [Cf. also the comprehensive survey of M. Geyer, 'Die Wehrmacht der Deutschen Republik ist die Reichswehr', *MGM* 1973/2, pp. 152–99].

The argument was given a different direction by A. Hillgruber in his study of 1974, 'Militarismus am Ende der Weimarer Republik und im "Dritten Reich" ' [in 242: idem, *Grossmachtpolitik und Militarismus im 20. Jahrhundert*, pp. 37–51]. Referring to M. Geyer's research, which had not then been published, Hillgruber pointed out that from the end of the 1920s onwards the army leaders developed and propagated new social conceptions of a militarist kind, tending towards a fusion of the military and the civilian sector and ultimately a totalitarian military state (*Wehrstaat*). This new perspective was developed in the following years, especially by M. Geyer [562] and E. W. Hansen [565], and at an international symposium in 1977 [570]. Thus interest shifted from the 'Seeckt era', on which it had previously concentrated, to the period from 1926 onwards when, in connection with the new concept of 'home defence' and the ambitious rearmament programme, the Reichswehr introduced the idea of 'militarization of the home front' – an 'extension of the military sphere', blurring the organizational boundaries between the military and civil society, with a view to total preparation for total war. As M. Geyer, in particular, pointed out, this new armament policy presupposed the social and political stabilization of the Weimar Republic and required a compromise between the Reichswehr and the civil power. Hence the Reichswehr leaders abandoned Seeckt's attitude of aloofness towards the republic and its institutions; their military and armaments policy was increasingly pursued in alliance with the government rather than independently of it. Thus the traditional idea of the Reichswehr as a 'state within the state' is expressly called in question.

This significant reinterpretation of the Reichswehr and its policy has in many ways supplemented and modified the general picture of military, social and political conditions in the Weimar state. However, the new concept of an 'extension of the military sphere' should not be taken to mean that the military and armaments policy was a social process initiated and impelled primarily by functional necessity, rather than one fully controlled by the military and political decision-makers. Important results of earlier research are still relevant, for example, evidence of the marked hostility of army leaders to the constitutional form of parliamentary democracy. The political aims and ambitions of the Reichswehr chiefs, and their consequent manoeuvres in 1929–32, which were in no way forced by events, were factors of the first rank in the disruption of the Weimar Republic and must not be lost to view.

4
Problems of Economic and Social Development

Historians after 1945 turned only with hesitation to problems of economic and especially social development in Weimar Germany. Until the 1960s the main interest was in political history, parties, state institutions and political crises. Themes of social history were seldom treated, a work such as L. Preller's of 1949 [531] remaining an exception. If the social history of the Weimar Republic was for a long time overshadowed by party-political history or the analysis of crises, this was no doubt partly because, with the end of Weimar and the Nazi seizure of power, a particular line of research was abruptly broken off: namely, a historically oriented social science, which had begun to develop a set of tools for the investigation of questions of social history, making use of the 'young' disciplines of sociology and political science, in the tradition of Lujo Brentano and Max Weber. Hence in Germany after 1945 there was far less continuity in the field of social history than of political history; institutional conditions were less favourable, and methodical training was much less in evidence. Thus it was certainly no accident that the decisive stimulus towards the treatment of Weimar social history came first of all from other Western countries, especially the USA. Later, during the 1960s, German historians began to devote their attention to economic and social problems of the Weimar Republic.

An attempt to draw up a 'progress report' in this respect was made by the symposium on 'the industrial system and political development in the Weimar Republic', held at Bochum in June 1973 and attended by historians, economists and political scientists. Political developments were by then relatively well documented, and the debate was intended to centre on their socio-economic background. The symposium led to a new emphasis and a change of viewpoint in academic discussion of the Weimar Republic. The record of the proceedings [523], which runs to 1,000 pages, presents numerous contributions and reports of discussions in sessions devoted to individual themes: economic growth, changes in economic structure and in the industrial system; social policy and social conflict in the Weimar Republic; financial policy and its effects on social issues; the international framework and the role of reparations policy; economic pressure groups representing industry, the agrarian interest or the middle class; state interventionism and 'special interest' policy in the period of crisis. This list of subjects shows that central elements of economic and social development were singled out, and despite disagreements in detail there was one noteworthy consensus: a principal weakness of the political system of the Weimar Republic lay in the contrast between 'far-reaching social intervention by the state and the almost unlimited autonomy of big business in matters of price-fixing and market policy' [H. Mommsen, in 523: p. 614]. Economic and social policies were more or less independent of each other. In the demobilization phase of 1918–19 the great industrial interests, especially those of heavy industry, secured a dominating influence over economic policy. In return they made concessions to the trade unions and parties, especially the Social Democrats, in the field of social policy which, however, they did not regard as irrevocable. To this extent the arrangement between the political and the industrial system rested on a very unequal basis [L. Albertin, in 523: p. 673]. When, as a result of economic crises and mass unemployment, economic rivalries became more intense and the position of the trade unions was permanently weakened, important business interests went back on the 'arrangement', pursued a policy of 'class struggle from above' and worked for an authoritarian constitution outside the parliamentary system. The Bochum symposium showed clearly how explosive the field of social policy had been in Weimar days, even well before 1929–30.

In the following years useful monographs were written on several themes that had been discussed briefly at Bochum or noted as deserving research. Thus we are now well informed on the agrarian associations and their influence on the parties, bureaucracy and economic policy; the chief works are those by M. Schumacher [409], J. Flemming [493] and D. Gessner [355]. As Schumacher shows, the agrarian bloc after 1918, in spite of a perceptible loosening of the agrarian-industrial 'common front', contributed much more than is often supposed to the stabilization and consolidation of pre-revolutionary structures in Germany. The unity and effectiveness of the agrarian camp was not seriously endangered by the revolution and the republican order [409: *Land und Politik*, p. 503]. Apart from the less important bodies representing small farmers, the traditional agrarian associations were among the mainstays of right-wing conservative anti-parliamentarianism under the Weimar Republic. Gessner, whose account concentrated on the final phase of the republic, detects in the case of some agrarian-conservative groups a pragmatic readiness to co-operate with the Weimar state, and would thus extend the spectrum of conservative policy 'in the direction of conservative governmentalism' [355: *Agrarverbände in der Weimarer Republik*, p. 265]. It must, however, be noted that even the 'governmentalists' in the agrarian associations were far from sincerely accepting the parliamentary republic. If, especially after the outbreak of the agrarian crisis in 1927–8, they showed more anxiety to come to an arrangement with the government and the civil service, it was because they needed state subsidies and protectionist measures. In Brüning's time they pursued this line intensively and not without success, with the clear objective of using the authoritarian state to further their own protectionist interests.

Since the Bochum symposium considerable progress has also been made in investigating the history of the trade unions, industrial associations and interest groups. The studies published in the last ten years on the development and policy of the Free Trade Unions and the Christian Trade Unions have concentrated on the transition from empire to republic and the problems of adaptation to the altered conditions of trade union activity in the first years of the republic [139, 327, 379, 396, 403, 542], while studies of industrial interests and employers' policy under Weimar have concentrated on heavy industry. In particular, B. Weisbrod, following C. Maier, has shown clearly that the influence of heavy industry in the Weimar years was based on its 'power of veto'. Despite some severe setbacks and its insufficient ability to achieve particular objectives, this enabled heavy industry to impose 'restrictive conditions' on the political system, 'which seriously threatened its power of integration and direction and did much to undermine its social content and democratic structure' [544: Weisbrod, *Schwerindustrie in der Weimarer Republik*, pp. 17 f.]. The 'special interest policy' of heavy industry throughout the Weimar period has been to a great extent illuminated by several solid works [485, 487, 500, 525, 537, 541, 634, 670], but we still lack comprehensive accounts (such as exist for the imperial period) of the great associations representing big business – the Reichsverband der Deutschen Industrie, the Vereinigung der Deutschen Arbeitgeberverbände, the Deutscher Industrie- und Handelstag, and the Langnam-Verein, to name only the most important. In addition, more research is needed into the activities, methods and organization of branches of the economy outside the sector of heavy industry.

On the whole, however, the present state of research enables us to make considerably more precise statements than were possible ten years ago about the course of socio-political conflict in the Weimar period, its main issues, strategies and dimensions. In the light of recent research, the two decisive issues in the development of relations between employers and workers were the creation of the Central Working Association in 1918–19 and the Ruhr ironworks dispute of 1928. Hence these two areas of problems are examined thoroughly in the relevant studies.

The picture arrived at is that the decision in the autumn of 1918 to co-operate on a basis of social partnership was taken by the employers and unions for different reasons and with different aims. The creation of the Central Working Association in November 1918 was made possible by the willingness of the unions to embark on a policy of 'small steps' rather than go for drastic alterations in the social balance of power; the employers, on the other hand, were prepared to make concessions so as to fob off the demand for socialization and stabilize their own position. The community of intent between the two sides soon lost its integrative force, and finally broke down at the beginning of 1924. The social conflict escalated during the phase of economic recovery when heavy industry, in particular, turned away from the November concessions; its leaders systematically opposed union claims for parity in management and social reforms, especially the eight-hour day, and supported all political groups which promised to steer the republic into authoritarian channels.

In the unanimous view of recent research, the Ruhr dispute of 1928 was the real turning-point in the social conflict of the Weimar period. With the lock-out of 250,000 workers the bosses took the offensive against the social elements of the Weimar constitution, aiming to break the power of the unions, defeat the compulsory arbitration system, and put an end to state intervention in social policy. In so doing they did not hesitate to create a *fait accompli* in opposition to the Reichsverband der Deutschen Industrie and the Vereinigung der Deutschen Arbeitgeberverbände, which had been prepared to compromise with the unions. The Ruhr dispute – which the earlier literature at best mentions only incidentally, apart from Preller's *Sozialpolitik in der Weimarer Republik* [531] – has gradually been recognized as a conflict of the greatest significance; this was first pointed out in E. Fraenkel's stimulating analysis of 1967 [494]. The 'discovery' is of special importance because, along with other findings, it tends considerably to modify the current picture of the so-called 'stabilization phase', as showing how explosive the social situation was before the world depression, and to what extent the consensus was already broken.

For many years economic and social historians have devoted great and increasing attention to the German inflation. At a congress in 1976 G. D. Feldman described research on the inflation that began in 1914 and lasted almost a decade as like 'crossing a historiographic desert with a few oases' [483: Büsch and Feldman (eds), [Historische Prozesse der deutschen Inflation 1914–1924, p. 3]. Since then the number of oases has increased a good deal, but on the whole it is still true that the field of research is 'wide open' [ibid., p. 211]. Four main aspects may be pointed out here.

(1) It is agreed today that the inflation must be considered as a process that began in 1914, immediately after the outbreak of war; it went through many phases – during some of which the currency was relatively stable, while during others it fell rapidly – and culminated in the 'hyperinflation' beginning at the end of 1922. The term 'hyperinflation' for the final phase has become generally accepted by historians. It is further agreed that inflation took a decisive turn in 1916, when government expenditure exceeded the revenue from domestic loans; and that hyperinflation dates from the last months of 1922, *before* the occupation of the Ruhr and the beginning of passive resistance. In the minds of contemporaries, on the other hand, the early phases were wholly eclipsed by the searing experience of hyperinflation, and the chaotic phase of total devaluation of the currency was equated with the whole development of events since the First World War. Whereas historians formerly concentrated entirely on the months of hyperinflation, and its politically and socially destabilizing effects, this no longer appears to modern research as the most interesting period of inflation; it is emphasized that hyperinflation is not the single standard by which the process should be evaluated.

(2) The inflation was long depicted as a politico-economic mistake of the first order. Recently, economic historians in particular have tended to take a much more positive view, at least of the period prior to hyperinflation. When the possible consequences of a different strategy, such as an earlier stabilization, are considered, inflation accompanied by full employment and economic growth up to the end of 1922 appears as a 'lesser evil', since it saved Germany from being involved in the 'world economic crisis' of 1920–1. Whereas in Britain in 1921 over 20 per cent of workers were unemployed, in Germany at that time there was practically full employment with rising wages, adjusted ever more frequently to rising price levels. (On the other hand, economic historians take very different views as to whether the boom associated with inflation was favourable to German economic growth in the long run.) According to C.-L. Holtfrerich, the Germany economy at that time made an important contribution to the relatively rapid overcoming of the economic crisis in the USA, Britain and other countries [508: *The German Inflation, 1914–1923*, pp. 210 ff., 220, 332]. Holtfrerich gives a further reason for regarding the inflationary policy down to 1922 as a 'rational strategy . . . in the national interest': by the summer of 1922 large amounts of short-term foreign money, especially from the USA, were invested in Germany; thus the creditors' losses from devaluation were borne in part by foreigners [ibid., pp. 298, 333 f.]. Finally, the inflation afforded the possibility – admittedly a very dubious one politically – of, so to speak, exporting economic grievances, because many in Germany blamed the situation primarily on the Allies' reparation demands.

Although the effective German obligations were not in fact so drastic as to be the main cause of the inflation process, this makes no difference to the fateful pattern of postwar decisions . . . In view of the virtually unlimited Allied claims, every German government had to fear that if it took the political risk of reducing real incomes at home, this would only enable the Allies to ask for more. [K. Borchardt, in 85: Aubin and Zorn (eds), *Handbuch der deutschen Wirtschafts- und Sozialgeschichte*, Vol. 2, p. 700]

For such reasons as these, Holtfrerich and other economic historians argue that the inflation was unavoidable for compelling reasons of home and foreign policy; a policy of stabilization in Germany after 1918, with its inevitable economic and social consequences, would have destroyed the parliamentary democratic system of government before 1923. This amounts to a basic questioning of current ideas concerning German financial and reparations policy in 1919–23. But it may be wondered whether it is legitimate to draw so sharp a distinction between the period of ordinary inflation, regarded as beneficial on the whole, up to the end of 1922, and the ensuing hyperinflation with its acute economic, social and political implications; and it remains to be seen whether historical scholarship will adopt this reinterpretation of the German inflation, based primarily on economic and financial arguments.

(3) The belief that the inflation process was deliberately manipulated by individual industrialists (such as Stinnes) or particular groups in society plays a large part in earlier literature. Recent research does not support the wholesale thesis of conscious manipulation, but takes the view that inflation profiteers such as big business men came only gradually to turn the situation to their own ends. 'They exhibited very different, and by no means always consistent, styles of behaviour, their decisions clearly reflecting each particular phase of the inflation' [490: Feldman, Holtfrerich, Ritter and Witt (eds), *Die deutsche Inflation*, p. 8]. Hence the different processes of learning and adaptation should, it is suggested, be more closely studied.

> Not until late in 1922 did practically all groups of German society begin to reckon in gold marks or foreign currency, so that in practice, if not in theory, the principle that 'a mark is a mark' was abandoned. In this way domestic prices were raised to the world market level and the occasion for a fresh round of inflation was removed. Thus the extent to which different groups exploited the situation to their own advantage was a question of their learning to do so, and time played an important part in this. In other words, it must be clearly indicated who learnt about the effects and opportunities of inflation from whom, and when. [ibid.]

(4) This leads to a further central problem: the question as to who gained and who lost by the inflation has been intensively discussed in the latest research. It is of great importance since, in the opinion of many historians, a direct or indirect connection exists between the traumatic experience and social consequences of hyperinflation on the one hand and, on the other, the rise of National Socialism and Hitler's victory. A direct connection, since the inflation turned part of the middle class into a proletariat, politically disoriented and susceptible to Nazism; and an indirect one, since during the world depression the German government dared not take the necessary measures to alleviate unemployment for fear of causing another inflation [479: Borchardt, *Wachstum, Krisen, Handlungsspielräume der Wirtschaftspolitik*, pp. 151 f.]. It is hard to give precise indications of the effects of the inflation on the incomes and fortunes of different social groups, because statistical data are incomplete; the official figures are inadequate from the point of view of method, or sometimes actually falsified. But, as recent studies have shown, if the existing data are carefully used and evaluated – for example, wage-scales differentiated by occupational groups which are available for some regions, such as Hamburg and Thuringia – it is possible to arrive at conclusions which substantially modify the usual picture of the social consequences of the inflation, based chiefly on contemporary opinions.

Economic and social historians are agreed in their view that the widespread belief as to the 'destruction of the middle class' by the inflation is untrue. The 'middle class' consisted of very different groups which were affected in very different ways by the almost complete devaluation of the currency and consequent wiping out of all debts, including those incurred by public bodies. While savers, mortgagees and bondholders lost their wealth and the *rentier* class disappeared entirely, small tradesmen, shopkeepers and craftsmen did good business and suffered scarcely at all from the inflation, and farmers were on the whole unaffected [483: Büsch and Feldmann (eds), *Historische Prozesse der deutschen Inflation 1914–1924*, pp. 54 f., 61, 79, 217].

It cannot be denied, however, that the redistribution of wealth within the middle class hastened the dissolution of the German bourgeoisie as a social and political factor; it accentuated the conflicts of wealth within the bourgeois parties and had a lasting effect on the configuration of the party system [ibid., pp. 264 f., 288 ff.].

There is disagreement as to the effect of the inflation on real wages and salaries. Until recently, both Marxist and non-Marxist historians have generally believed that the impoverishment of the working class which began during the war continued in 1919–23. This, however, is now being called in question: it is suggested that the level of real wages did not fall steadily during the inflation, but that after 1918–19 the workers' standard of living improved measurably in certain important areas [W. Abelshauser, 'Verelendung der Handarbeiter?', in H. Mommsen and W. Schulze (eds), *Vom Elend der Handarbeit* (Stuttgart, 1981), pp. 445–76]. Officials' salaries, according to the latest research, apparently did not decrease as the inflation progressed; after reaching a low in March 1920, in the next year or two they improved for a while in real terms. Before 1914 there had already been a tendency for the salaries of different groups to approximate to one another; this was much increased by the war and inflation, giving rise to jealousy and resentment on the part of higher officials, who felt their social status to be impaired [A. Kunz, 'Verteilungskampf oder Interessenkonsensus? Einkommensentwicklung und Sozialverhalten von Arbeitnehmergruppen in der Inflationszeit 1914 bis 1924', in 490: Feldmann, Holtfrerich, Ritter and Witt (eds), *Die deutsche Inflation*, pp. 347–84; and idem, 517: *Civil Servants*]. The levelling tendency was not confined to official salaries: differentials between adolescents and adults, male and female, skilled and unskilled workers were greatly reduced during the inflation years.

These references to some recent studies of the inflation and its effects show that research into economic and social developments after 1918 is to a large extent in a state of flux, and that many older judgements are in need of revision. While only provisional conclusions can be drawn at present, a major project on the inflation period is under way (8 vols to date, published in the series Beiträge zu Inflation und Wiederaufbau in Deutschland und Europa 1914–24, Munich) and it can be expected that further important data and broader-based findings will soon be available.

Such results may also provide the stimulus for a more intensive study of some problems that are still quite inadequately researched, concerning social history and population movements after 1918. To mention only some desiderata: we know far too little about social divisions among the population, changes in the occupational structure, the extent and nature of women's work, the effects of rationalization on the labour market, urbanization and the flight from the land, the falling birth-rate, age structure and urban population [on population movements, see the references in K. J. Bade, 'Arbeitsmarkt, Bevölkerung und Wanderung in der Weimarer Republik', in 120: Stürmer (ed.), *Die Weimarer Republik*, pp. 160–87].

There has recently been controversy as to the trend of the German economy during the years of relative stabilization. It was long supposed that the economy in these years took a decided upward turn, which was suddenly reversed after the onset of the world depression and in consequence of it. This view has been challenged with good reasons, notably by K. Borchardt in 'Zwangslagen und Handlungsspielräume in der grossen Weltwirtschaftskrise der frühen dreissiger Jahre', [in 479: idem, *Wachstum, Krisen, Handlungsspielräume*, pp. 165–82]. This study, which aroused much attention, was primarily intended as a defence of Brüning's deflationary policy (to which we shall revert), but forms part of a comprehensive reassessment of economic developments in Germany from 1926 to 1929.

Borchardt's argument may be briefly summarized as follows. After the First World War the German state was living beyond its means. 'Far more than any previous German state' it practised a system of subsidies and the redistribution of wealth. In particular, wage rates in 1925–9 took no account of productivity and thus acted directly as an instrument of redistribution. After the inflation of 1923 wage rises were forced through by the increased strength of the trade unions and the system of compulsory arbitration. Since these could no longer be fully reflected in prices, the result was a 'squeeze on those types of income from which investments are as a rule basically financed' [ibid., p. 178]. Hence the investment rate remained low, and economic growth until 1929 was slow in comparison with what might theoretically have been expected after the considerable losses of growth during and after the war ('relative stagnation'). In consequence, from 1925 onwards and not only after 1929, the unemployment rate was higher than it had ever been in Germany. The recession began at different times in different sectors of the economy, but overall it set in well before the New York stock exchange crash at the end of October 1929. Altogether, Borchardt concludes, the German economy in 1925–9 must be described as an 'abnormal, in fact a sick economy, which could not possibly have gone on in the same way even if the world depression had not occurred' [ibid., p. 179].

This interpretation rapidly gained much assent among economic historians and others, and has already been described as the 'dominant view' [H. A. Winkler in *GG*, vol. 8 (1982), p. 6]. However, some social historians have expressed doubts. Was it actually or mainly because of 'excessively high' wages that labour productivity remained low during the Weimar period, or did other factors play an important part, such as economically unjustified subsidies and the cartellization of German industry, which had 'long put a damper on the entrepreneurial spirit' [ibid., p. 8]? Is it permissible to measure wages (under the heading 'wage movements as a neutral factor in the distribution of wealth') only in relation to current productivity rates, when this means that 'the complex social and political conflicts of interest in Germany between the wars are viewed mainly from the point of view of economic growth and thus of the economy as a whole, so that social and political developments are increasingly thrust into the background'? [A. Kunz, in 490: Feldman, Holtfrerich, Ritter and Witt (eds), *Die Deutsche Inflation*, p. 365. Borchardt's theory of 'excessively high wages' is also attacked by C.-L. Holtfrerich in 'Zu hohe Löhne in der Weimarer Republik?', *GG*, vol. 10 (1984), pp. 122–41].

There is at present a lively debate over Borchardt's argument that economic sense lay all on the employers' side in the years after 1924 and that wage pressure acted as a destabilizing economic and social factor. However, it is generally accepted that the economic situation in Germany was highly precarious even before the world depression. The latter's epochal importance for Germany is indeed accepted, but the German recession began well before the end of 1929; it was aggravated, but not caused, by the New York stock exchange failure; in this sense we may speak of a 'crisis before the crisis'. If these conclusions about the development of the economy in 1924–9 are correlated with what is known about the break-up of the party system or the increased antagonism between capital and labour, we may sum up as follows: recent research is gradually bringing to light the fact that even in the few 'good' years of the Weimar Republic, those of relative stabilization, there was no true stabilization of the political system, economic relations, or the social structure.

5

From the Peace Treaty to the Young Plan: International Relations and Foreign Policy, 1919–30

The interwar power system was given its character by the course, conclusions and effects of the Paris Peace Conference. International relations after 1919 were governed by the conflict over the consolidation, modification or destruction of the status quo established in Paris.

There is scarcely any other peace congress or peace settlement in respect of which opinions have changed so much in the course of a few decades as they have – not least in Germany herself – in regard to the Paris conference and the Treaty of Versailles. In Germany between the wars the peace treaty, the Versailles 'dictat', was *the* great national trauma. Both the genesis and the provisions of the treaty were the object of passionate criticism, often expressed with the greatest vehemence. On no political question were the parties and groups so unanimous as in condemning the peace treaty, particularly the so-called 'war guilt' article, which Germans rejected almost with one voice. Politicians of the left and centre saw the treaty and its effects as one of the main reasons for the desperate state of the German republic. Those of the right, for their part, strove to undermine the democratic republic with their unbridled agitation against the 'dictat' and the 'policy of fulfilment'. In National Socialist propaganda against the republic, the 'shameful peace' played a major role along with the 'stab in the back' and the 'November criminals'.

Only after the convulsions of the Second World War and the catastrophe of 1945 were Germans able to form a less emotional view of the peace settlement of 1919. Against the background of 1945 the Treaty of Versailles appeared relatively 'moderate', since it had allowed Germany to continue to exist as a united national state, and in the long run as a European great power. However, the abandonment of the intellectual attitudes of the 1920s and the earlier drastic condemnation of the treaty was a more or less tacit process, expressed in incidental judgements (see for example, Gerhard Ritter's observation of 1951, pages 33 f. above), without spectacular controversy or elaborate pieces of research. Apparently the German public had lost interest in the Treaty of Versailles. While international research after 1945 devoted much attention to the

Paris conference, German scholars at first made little contribution [213: Viefhaus, *Die Minderheitenfrage und die Entstehung der Minderheitenschutzverträge auf der Pariser Friedenskonferenz 1919*; 181: Dickmann, *Die Kriegsschuldfrage auf der Friedenskonferenz von Paris 1919*]. In the 1970s some West German historians produced monographs based on a wide range of sources, in which German and American aims were analysed in detail and with important new conclusions [206: Schwabe, *Woodrow Wilson, Revolutionary Germany, and Peacemaking 1918–1919* (orig. German edn, 1971); 190: Krüger, *Deutschland und die Reparationen 1918/19*; 186: Haupts, *Deutsche Friedenspolitik 1918–19*]. Despite differences on some points of fact and in their general conclusions, these authors agree that the principal aim of the German government was to preserve the country's economic potential as far as possible intact, so as to use it as an asset in restoring Germany's 'great power' status (cf. page 30 above).

It was, however, not only the defeated nations that criticized the Paris settlement between the wars; in the victorious countries the 'peacemakers' were also much attacked, though for varying reasons and with varying emphasis. In France the treaty was widely regarded as too lenient, because it took too little account of France's need for security against her eastern neighbour. In Britain, on the other hand, at the turn of the year 1919–20 the economist J. M. Keynes, who had been a member of the British delegation to the conference, provided all critics of the treaty with a range of effective arguments in his book *The Economic Consequences of the Peace* [London, 1919; German translation, 1920]. Lloyd George in his own account [*The Truth about the Peace Treaties* (London, 1938, 2 vols)] replied to these critics that they had failed to appreciate the unique circumstances and difficulties of peacemaking after a world war; but by this time his views carried little weight. The 'bad conscience' of the victorious countries went far to create the psychological conditions for the appeasement policy which played into Hitler's hands after the establishment of the Nazi dictatorship.

Since 1945, not only in Germany but also in other countries, the debate has been no longer a matter of attack and defence, but rather of moderate criticism and increased understanding for the formidable task which confronted the statesmen assembled in Paris. This is not only because of greater detachment and the cooling of passions, but is also due to the opening up of a large amount of source material [see, e.g., 6: *Papers relating to Paris Peace Conference*; 29: Mantoux, *Les Délibérations du Conseil des Quatre*]. On this broader basis many important conclusions have been arrived at. These throw light on many connections and make clear how limited the peacemakers' freedom of action was and how many difficult problems faced them in attempting to transform a world war into a system of universal peace [see, e.g., 178: Baumgart, *Vom europäischen Konzert zum Völkerbund*, pp. 56 ff.; K. Schwabe, 'Versailles – nach sechzig Jahren', *NPL*, vol. 24 (1979), pp. 446–75; also the bibliography (down to 1969) in 128: Gunzenhäuser, *Die Pariser Friedenskonferenz 1919 und die*

Friedensverträge 1919–1920]. Four conclusions should be emphasized in particular.

(1) The final terms of peace corresponded not so much to the intentions and desires of the statesmen concerned as to the 'irreparable situation created by the war' [205: Schulz, *Revolutions and Peace Treaties, 1917–1920*, p. 137]. Given the conflict between Wilson's ideological principles and the emphatic demands of old-style power politics, it was at best possible to aim at compromises, and in the view of more recent research this aim was successful. Numerous studies add up to a far-reaching rehabilitation by historians of the peacemakers of 1919. This is true, in particular, of Wilson himself, whose image was overshadowed by the evident contrast between his idealistic programme and certain features of the peace. As P. Birdsall emphasized in 1941 [179: *Versailles Twenty Years After*], Wilson fought hard for the main points of his peace programme and, despite great difficulties, was far from unsuccessful in converting the abstract principles into specific terms. This view of Wilson's attitude and achievement at the conference has since gained large acceptance. Thus, for instance, K. Schwabe, in his detailed study of the American peace strategy, concludes that Wilson, as the conference proceeded, 'came to adopt a policy of practical responsibility', appearing less and less as the "radical ideologue" of his own war speeches but rather as the exponent of a "higher realism" ' [206: *Woodrow Wilson, Revolutionary Germany, and Peacemaking 1918–1919*, pp. 396, 401]. Certainly Wilson had to give up or modify parts of his programme, but we should not for this reason underestimate the influence of his ideas on the peace treaties [205: Schulz, *Revolutions and Peace Treaties, 1917–1920*, p. 147]; they were, in any case, an important counterweight to the demands of some of the victorious countries, and thus enforced compromises that would otherwise hardly have been possible.

(2) It is nowadays more fully realized that the task in Paris really was to deal with the consequences of a *world* war. Germany was indeed the central object of the negotiations, but by no means the only one: the problems ranged from South-Eastern Europe and the Mediterranean, all the way to the Far East. The handling of the German question was overshadowed by the most various international constellations of interests and fronts, and was affected by horizontal lines of division within particular countries. This aspect is brought out in A. J. Mayer's monumental work [195: *Politics and Diplomacy of Peacemaking*], which emphasizes connections that have been overlooked or neglected and provides many new insights. According to Mayer, the polarization of leftist and rightist forces in each nation was the decisive feature of the postwar situation, so that analysis should concentrate on the interrelation between the domestic scene and attitudes to peacemaking. The behaviour of the European and American statesmen can, in his view, only be properly understood as an answer and reaction to events in Russia, given that the containing of Bolshevik Russia was the Allied statesmen's first priority. For this reason Mayer inclines to regard the Allies' German policy as no more than a function of their policy towards

Russia. While the German question was formerly all too often regarded as the chief or even the only focus of the peace negotiations, Mayer goes to the opposite extreme. He certainly exaggerates in playing down the intrinsic importance of Germany at the peace conference and making Russia the primary factor; but he is right in contending that the strategy of 'containing' Bolshevik Russia was an important aspect of international politics in those months. [For arguments against overrating the importance of Russia in this connection see, e.g., 210; Thompson, *Russia, Bolshevism and the Versailles Peace*; 193: Lundgreen-Nielsen, *The Polish Problem at the Paris Peace Conference*; 178: Baumgart, *Vom europäischen Konzert zum Völkerbund*, pp. 106 ff.]

(3) It is realized and admitted today, more clearly than in Weimar Germany, that the German treaty was a compromise – it was not a 'Wilsonian peace', but neither was it a 'Carthaginian peace' (cf. page 33 above). Despite the heavy burdens it imposed, Germany came off more lightly than seemed probable at certain stages of the negotiations. France's extreme demands, prompted by her dire need for security, were firmly opposed by Wilson and Lloyd George and were only partially reflected in the treaty. It is nowadays generally accepted that Versailles left Germany in a position, in the long run, to become an influential power once more; indeed her opportunities in foreign affairs were greater after 1919 than in the Kaiser's or Bismarck's Germany [242: Hillgruber, *Grossmacht politik und Militarismus*, p. 24].

(4) As regards the question of how far the Treaty of Versailles constituted a burden on the Weimar Republic, and to what extent the 'Versailles complex' contributed to the rise of Nazism and the destruction of the republic, recent researchers take a different view from that of most contemporary observers. Typical of the latter is a remark by Otto Braun, for many years minister-president of Prussia. In his memoirs, commenting on the question of how the Hitler dictatorship could have come to power, he used the pithy phrase 'Versailles and Moscow' [49: Braun, *Von Weimar zu Hitler*, p. 5]. In other words, the blame for the destruction of German democracy was due to foreign factors, and to Versailles first and foremost. A similar view was expressed by L. Zimmermann, who concluded his account of German foreign policy in the Weimar era [288, p. 474] with the words: 'Timely revision of the peace treaties would probably have saved the Weimar Republic and saved the peace.' When this was published in 1958 it was already a somewhat anachronistic judgement (but characteristic in so far as the whole book is written from an interwar viewpoint). For investigation of the final phase of Weimar has brought to light such a complication of causes that it is no longer possible to attribute the downfall of the republic simply to Versailles, either as a real handicap or as a psychological factor and propaganda theme [86: Bracher, *Die Auflösung der Weimarer Republik*, p. 17]. No doubt it will never be possible to assess the exact part played by Versailles and its effects in bringing about the rise of Hitler, but it is today no longer regarded as decisive [178: Baumgart, *Vom europäischen*

Konzert zum Völkerbund, p. 134]. The latest contribution to this theme reaches the convincing conclusion that while the general tendency of Versailles was to destabilize the Weimar system,

> in the early stages, when such tendencies were strongest (1919–20 and 1921–3), Versailles did not bring about the downfall of the republic. Its importance, either as a real burden or as a psychological factor, was relatively small by the end of the Stresemann era . . . The main decisions in the transition from the Weimar Republic proper to the presidential regime, and from that to the Third Reich, were not taken for reasons connected with foreign policy or motives related to Versailles. [A. Hillgruber, 'Unter dem Schatten von Versailles', in 95: Erdmann and Schulze (eds), *Weimar*, p. 66]

Just because Versailles was not a 'Carthaginian peace' – because, while Germany ceased for the time being to be a great power, she was in a position once more to become one – the treaty 'exerted no compulsion on the Germans and their social and political leaders to come to terms once and for all with the new situation' [ibid., p. 57]. In this respect Germany's position after 1918 was basically different from that after 1945. In Weimar Germany, revision of the Treaty of Versailles was the chief aim of foreign policy; all relevant political and social forces concurred in this, and the whole population supported them. However, there were important differences of opinion which developed into bitter conflict, as to the timing, priorities and methods of revisionist policy. While the losses of territory in the east were felt as especially painful and were not accepted as a final settlement, in the existing circumstances their recovery could not be in the forefront of German aims. In the first years after the war, the focus of international dispute arising out of Versailles was not territory but the reparations question. The economic and political reorganization of Europe after 1919 was closely bound up with this question, and – if only because of the unavoidable participation of the USA, as the world's strongest economic power – the reparations settlement was crucial to the development of the postwar international system. Accordingly, for many years research has concentrated on this area of problems.

Publications on the subject of reparations are almost too numerous to survey, and represent probably every conceivable viewpoint. Given the far-reaching differences between the various political and economic historians and financial experts who have approached the problem, it is particularly difficult for anyone not fully versed in financial and monetary questions to find his or her way through the jungle of arguments and reach a valid conclusion. As the experts do not even agree as to how much Germany actually paid, it is not surprising that widely contrary views are put forward as to how much she could have paid, given the utmost good will. The debate as to what Germany could have paid under what economic conditions, with what specific modalities as to the raising and transfer of funds, must operate with theoretical models and numerous hypotheses, leading, understandably, to very different results and assessments.

In this situation it is to be welcomed that an expert on German reparations policy has recently produced a study which includes a comparative analysis of figures, the theory of transfers, and the effects of reparations on Germany's external economy and political system [P. Krüger, 'Das Reparationsproblem der Weimarer Republik in fragwürdiger Sicht', *VfZg*, vol. 29 (1981), pp. 21–47]. In this study Krüger also surveys the conclusions of some recent research into French and German reparations policy in 1919–24.

The research in question – chiefly by J. Bariéty [219], W. McDougall [258], S. Schuker [278] and M. Trachtenberg [281] – is based on a thorough use of the French archives released since 1972. This has enabled the authors to add innumerable details and to modify in several important respects the accepted picture of the 'reparations battle' between 1919 and 1924. The conclusion on which they agree is to revise comprehensively the negative view of France's policy towards Germany and the reparations issue, and the general assessment of the power relationship between France and Germany after the First World War. The general view has hitherto been that, in contrast to the comparatively moderate attitude of Britain and the USA, France adopted an extremely harsh attitude towards defeated Germany. These authors, on the contrary, maintain that the French government after 1919 behaved with essential moderation and that much of the responsibility for what went wrong at the peace conference and afterwards is to be laid at the door of the Americans and especially the British (Trachtenberg). A key point in the argument is the estimate of the relative strength of France and Germany after the war. France's aim, they argue, was not to perpetuate French hegemony on the Continent but to maintain a Franco-German equilibrium which had been temporarily secured by the German defeat but remained precarious because, in spite of Versailles, Germany's demographic and economic potential made her superior to France. Bariéty, in particular, interprets French policy in 1919–23 as a series of attempts – by a combination of Rhineland policy, reparations and the general economic provisions of the Treaty of Versailles – to establish an equilibrium of the *structures économiques profondes* and thus achieve an object that was not secured by the treaty itself. Poincaré, in particular, was imbued with the fear of long-term German predominance and did all he could to correct the balance in favour of France. By the occupation of the Ruhr, which he undertook after long hesitation and when all attempts at a negotiated solution had failed, he hoped to safeguard the payment of reparations and exert pressure on the British and Americans to co-operate with France in solving the German problem, including if possible the separation of the Rhineland from Germany (Bariéty, McDougall). This proved a failure. The attempt to bring Germany to her knees resulted in a 'technical victory' over the Ruhr question, but ultimately in defeat for France's revisionist policy. After the cessation of passive resistance in the Ruhr, and with the French financial crisis after the beginning of 1924 (see especially Schuker on this point), France became increasingly dependent on the British and Americans, and Germany's negotiating position improved. The London conference of July–August 1924 drew a line under French efforts to achieve, by any possible means, a revision of the treaty situation in France's favour.

A critique of this new assessment of French postwar policy must begin with the theory concerning the Continental balance of power which offsets France's hegemony after 1918 against the potential strength of Germany. It is hard to relate this to the actual situation after the war. The debate over the new assessment of the power situation in postwar Europe has only just begun [cf. articles in *Journal of Modern History*, vol. 51 (1979), pp. 56–85]. But the recent research can already be credited for throwing light on the detailed course of the reparations battle, especially between the autumn of 1923 and the London conference (Bariéty, Schuker), and for putting beyond doubt the seriousness of France's ambitions on the Rhine in 1919–23 (Bariéty, McDougall). It can be stated even more firmly than before that the London conference and the events leading up to it were the real turning-point in postwar European politics. It may be doubted, on the other hand, whether the extremely favourable picture of French policy as one of relative moderation towards the defeated enemy can be sustained.

Among the controversial aspects of German foreign policy under Weimar has long been the Rapallo treaty of 1922: its origins, the time and manner of its conclusion, its significance and effect on European politics. The 'Rapollo complex' is still with us. In Western minds at that time it conjured up the bogy of a German–Russian conspiracy against the West, and to the present day this fear is revived on occasion [222: Bournazel, *Rapallo*]. The Eastern bloc regards the treaty as a model foundation for relations with capitalist states [e.g., A. Anderle (ed.), *Rapallo und die friedliche Koexistenz* (Berlin, 1963)]. Scarcely any treaty in the present century has been so thoroughly investigated by historians. But, while its genesis, on the German side at least, has been illuminated to a great extent [most recently in 267: Pogge, 'Rapallo – Strategy in Preventive Diplomacy'], the controversy as to its significance continues, since the sources permit various interpretations of the motives of those concerned on the German side.

If historians since the Second World War have devoted special attention to the Rapallo theme, which arouses the interest of a wider public outside academic circles, the reason is no doubt that, much as the international situation has changed since 1945, relations with the Soviet Union are a topical issue of the first order in German politics. West German research in the 1950s and 1960s concentrated on refuting the 'Rapallo legend' of a German–Soviet conspiracy against the rest of Europe. Using fresh source material, Schieder [276], Helbig [240], Erdmann [230], Laubach [318] and Linke [256] reached essentially the same conclusion, namely, that there was no question of a revisionist German–Soviet conspiracy against the West. After 1919 Germany had need of an active Eastern policy if only because of her economic interests; the Rapallo policy was one of political equilibrium, suited to the time and place; the treaty did not imply a German–Soviet alliance 'to burst the fetters of Versailles' [240: Helbig, *Die Träger der Rapallo-Politik*, pp. 5 ff.]; it was not a 'blow against the West' [230: Erdmann, 'Deutschland, Rapallo und der Westen', p. 164], but rather a 'defensive measure by German politicians against what they saw as a danger from the Western powers' [318: Laubach, *Die Politik der Kabinette Wirth 1921/22*, p. 209]. T. Schieder summed up this interpretation by saying that Rapallo was a 'treaty of normalization and liquidation, born of immediate economic and political needs' [276: Schieder, 'Die Entstehungsgeschichte des Rapallo-Vertrags', p. 551].

H. Graml has joined issue with this interpretation [100: Graml, *Europa zwischen den Kriegen*, pp. 137 ff.; 235; Graml, 'Die Rapallo-Politik im Urteil der westdeutschen Forschung'], expressing in strong terms his view that it tends to whitewash the intentions and methods of German foreign policy in general, and particularly as regards the Rapallo treaty. He regards Ago von Maltzan of the German Foreign Ministry as the leading spirit of the Rapallo policy, which in his view was a coolly calculated strategy intended to wreck the 'policy of fulfilment' and its first positive effect on German–Western relations, and to free Germany's hands for a revisionist policy directed especially against Poland. He regards Rapallo as 'a decisive victory for the policy of revision and restoration, and one from which neither Germany nor Europe was to recover' [100: Graml, *Europa zwischen den Kriegen*, p. 151].

Graml's reinterpretation, amounting to a revival of the theory of a German–Soviet 'revisionist' conspiracy, aroused lively controversy. The objection was rightly made that the effect of isolating and overemphasizing a single motive of the German Rapallo policy, namely, the revisionist anti-Polish one, was to 'encourage the monocausal explanation of an extremely complex process in foreign affairs', and to obscure other motives, such as the widespread interest of German business circles in trade with Russia, or the problems connected with Article 116 of the Treaty of Versailles [P. Alter, 'Rapallo – Gleichgewichtspolitik und Revisionismus', *NPL*, vol. 19 (1974), pp. 509 ff.]. It should also be pointed out that it is wrong to draw a sharp distinction between the 'policy of fulfilment' and Maltzan's revisionism, as the former policy also aimed at the revision of Versailles [266: Pogge, 'Grossindustrie und Rapallopolitik', p. 297]. As to the charge, repeated by Graml and many others, that Maltzan deliberately misinformed and finally duped the Foreign Minister, this was refuted by the observation that Rathenau (whose own firm, AEG, was keenly interested in business with Russia) was himself very ready to sign the Rapallo treaty, having worked for an agreement with Russia since 1919. Maltzan, it was suggested, may have taken advantage of Rathenau's death to enhance his own reputation as the 'father of Rapallo' [267: Pogge, 'Rapallo – Strategy in Preventive Diplomacy', p. 143; see also R. Himmer, 'Rathenau, Russia and Rapallo', *Central European History*, vol. 9 (1976), pp. 146–83].

In the light of all these arguments, K. Hildebrand concludes that the immediate reason and one of the strongest motives leading the German delegation to sign the treaty was 'fear of isolation in the realm of power politics'. The treaty made it possible for Germany and the Soviet Union to pursue a joint policy of counterbalancing the Entente: 'the freedom of movement which the treaty conferred on both parties, and the counterweight now created within the framework of the Paris settlement, as matters stood in the first half of the 1920s, enabled Germany and the Soviet Union to create an urgently needed balance *vis-à-vis* the French claim to hegemony' [241: Hildebrand, *Des Deutsche Reich und die Sowjetunion*, pp. 25 ff.].

Surveying the course of German foreign policy after 1922 we may conclude that Graml not only attributes far too great an importance to the Rapallo treaty as a basis factor in post-war German and European politics, but that he also takes a very one-sided view of the intentions and style of German policy. He effectively denies the legitimacy of any kind of revisionist policy on Germany's part, by stating that revisionism was permissible to all the defeated countries and even to dissatisfied victors, with the single exception of Germany, because a German revisionist policy implied a claim to hegemony and was therefore tantamount to endangering the peace of Europe. 'In other words, a revisionist policy on Germany's part meant a return to the law of the jungle, and if this policy succeeded it would destroy the European balance' [100: Graml, *Europa zwischen den Kriegen*, p. 57]. The guiding principle of German foreign policy after 1919 ought therefore, according to Graml, to have been to give up any idea of correcting the results of the war and to work within the system of collective security, as only thus could the peace of Europe be preserved. From today's standpoint this is certainly an important view and one worth discussing, but there was no practical basis for it in the Weimar Republic. Not to mention the right wing, neither the centre nor the political left were prepared to give up all hope of treaty revision; the only question was how soon that attempt should be made, by what methods and with what priorities. This complex of questions lies at the centre of all research into German foreign policy in the Stresemann era.

The personality and policy of Gustav Stresemann have from the beginning been a favourite subject of research into the Weimar period. Initially – before 1933, and also after 1945 – the great majority of published works were by Stresemann's supporters and admirers. The release of his posthumous papers in 1953 led to the first phase of academic interest in his foreign policy; soon afterwards the source basis was enlarged by the opening of the Foreign Ministry archives. [For a list of works of the 1950s and early 1960s see H. W. Gatzke, 'Gustav Stresemann: A Bibliographical Article', *Journal of Modern History*, vol. 36 (1964), pp. 1–13.] A second phase of intensive interest in German foreign policy in the Stresemann era began around 1970. In addition to W. Link's basic work on the American policy of stabilization in Germany, 1921–32 [254], we should mention the studies by M. Walsdorff [283], W. Weidenfeld [285], M.-O. Maxelon [260], J. Jacobson [246], K. Megerle [261], P. Krüger [250, 251] and K.-H. Pohl [268]. These works, written from various points of view and concentrating on various aspects, have systematically illuminated the whole field. Considering how long Stresemann and his policy were a subject of acute controversy, it is remarkable that these recent works establish a far-reaching consensus, in particular on two questions that were formerly much contested: namely, Stresemann's transformation from a nationalist into a 'European', and the general conception of his foreign policy.

(1) Among the standard themes of the literature on Stresemann is that of his development as a politician and statesman: was he a nationalist or a European, an opportunist or an idealist, a sincere advocate of a policy of understanding or a deceitful power-politician? While critics concentrated on his letter of 7 September 1927 to the former crown prince, which was published in 1932 [cf. R. Grathwol, 'Gustav Stresemann: Betrachtungen über seine Aussenpolitik', in 262: Michalka and Lee (eds), *Gustav Stresemann*, pp. 224–9], pro-Stresemann writers formerly distinguished sharply between the nationalist of the First World War and the European statesman of the 1920s; almost without exception, they posited a dramatic conversion at the beginning of the 1920s. On the basis of this interpretation, after 1945 Stresemann was elevated to the status of a 'great European', not on any new evidence but as part of the attempt to establish a respectable tradition of German foreign policy. In the 1950s scholars concentrated on refuting this 'legend' [H. W. Gatzke, *Stresemann and the Rearmament of Germany* (New York, 1954); 672: Thimme, *Gustav Stresemann*], which is now exploded. Almost all recent researchers agree that Stresemann was a coolly calculating realist, nationalist and power-politician, but – this should be emphasized, to counter some exaggerations of the de-mythologizing process – he was no different in that respect from other European statesmen of his time: they, too, were exponents of national power politics and not European integration.

(2) The central objective of Stresemann's foreign policy was the restoration of Germany as a sovereign 'great power' with equal rights. 'Stresemann's basic concept, in respect of its content, was derived from the German aspiration to power before 1914; his strategic methods were adapted to the power situation after 1918' [260: Maxelon, *Stresemann und Frankreich*, p. 297]. The studies of German foreign policy in 1923–9 which appeared in the 1970s proved this convincingly and showed in detail how, in Stresemann's view, the recovery of Germany was possible and should be achieved. If only because of the lack of military power, he firmly rejected war as a means to his political ends, and regarded the path of negotiation and understanding as the only possible one. The main role in his plans was played by Germany's economic potential, not

the least important feature being close economic co-operation with the USA; he realized at an early stage that an American stake in Germany would confirm the interest of the world's leading power in the peaceful evolution of conditions in Europe.

The second basic component of Stresemann's foreign policy was his realization that only by satisfying France's demand for security could the way be opened for the co-operative solution of European problems. Therefore he endeavoured, on the one hand, to achieve a Franco-German compromise based on frontier guarantees and trade agreements and, on the other, he sought by co-operation with Britain and the USA to normalize relations with the Western powers and create an international climate that would make possible a peaceful settlement of outstanding problems. At the same time, he was concerned to avoid taking an unambiguous stand in favour of the West and against the East. Summarizing the results of recent research, W. Michalka describes Stresemann's priorities as follows:

> On the basis of a solution to the question of reparations he aimed to put an end to the occupation of the Ruhr and then of the territory occupied in accordance with the Treaty of Versailles. Closely connected with these aims were the recovery of the Saarland and the abolition of military control in Germany. His next aim was to be the revision of Germany's eastern frontiers. [The Locarno treaty and Germany's entry into the League of Nations] were means to these ends. [262: Michalka and Lee (eds), *Gustav Stresemann*, p. xiv]

This last statement could be elaborated: basically Stresemann regarded all the 'stages' in his foreign policy of 1923–9 (Dawes Plan, Locarno treaties, Treaty of Berlin, membership of the League of Nations, Young Plan) as steps towards the restoration of German power. But he proceeded cautiously, avoiding conflicts, and regarded treaty revision and European peace as interdependent aims to be reconciled by international co-operation – such is the broad consensus of more recent research.

Against this background, views still differ on two points. Was Stresemann's foreign policy in 1923–9 successful in terms of his own ideas and purposes? Secondly, could a revisionist policy, such as his, have achieved its object in the long term without the use of force?

Some scholars (Walsdorff, Megerle, to some extent Weidenfeld and Jacobson) incline to a sceptical view of the effects of Locarno. They consider that Stresemann overestimated the revisionist potential of the treaties; in 1928–9 he had to recognize that his policy had not been a success. Two replies may be made to this. Certainly, the years after 1925 did not bring such rapid and spectacular results in the way of revision as many, including probably Stresemann himself, had hoped for in the initial euphoria. But the view that the Locarno policy was a failure does not do justice to the motives or the actual results of Stresemann's foreign policy. Taking into account the situation of 1923, the relatively short span of six years and an international situation that was far from favourable to Germany, it can be said that Stresemann as Foreign Minister achieved no small results for his country. It must be remembered that the Locarno policy also had a defensive purpose, namely, to prevent a Franco-British entente and the isolation of Germany, and in this respect it was without question highly successful.

Could Germany's further revisionist aims, which Stresemann approved of in principle – and especially the revision of the eastern frontier – have been achieved eventually by other than warlike means, and did Stresemann accept the use of such means if necessary? To this hypothetical question we can only give speculative answers. According to Marxist-Leninist historians: 'Stresemann's long-term policy was one of preparing for warlike expansion . . . He worked towards a war, but always kept in view that armed force as a political instrument was, under certain conditions, not calculated to serve the interests of the classes he represented' [W. Ruge, *Stresemann* (East Berlin, 1965), pp. 226, 223]. On the other hand, recent non-communist authors are predominantly in agreement, for convincing reasons, that Stresemann realized 'that even a militarily strong Germany could not face a confrontation with the Western powers. Hence he had no realistic alternative to the policy of mutual understanding' [260: Maxelon, *Stresemann und Frankreich*, p. 184]. It was also to Stresemann as a realist that 'the political and economic gains that Germany could expect to achieve by peaceful means – including perhaps union with Austria – would, in any case, put her in the front rank of European powers. Why risk such promising prospects for the sake of a military adventure?' [K. Epstein, *Vom Kaiserreich zum Dritten Reich* (Frankfurt, Berlin and Vienna, 1973), p. 198]. In an interesting 'counter-factual analysis', H. A. Turner concludes that even at the crucial stage of a policy of revision *vis-à-vis* Poland, Stresemann would have aimed at a compromise. 'He would in all probability have had to do so if he wanted to retain the support or at least acquiescence of the Western powers, which was a cornerstone of his foreign policy from the beginning' ['Stresemann und die Kontinuität in der deutschen Aussenpolitik', in G. Ziebura (ed.), *Grundfragen der deutschen Aussenpolitik seit 1871* (Darmstadt, 1975), pp. 284–304; quotation p. 302]. Even though a continuity of German power policy and ambition can be traced before and after the breach of 1918, there is a qualitative and fundamental difference between Stresemann's cautious policy of revisionism within the international system, and Hitler's expansionist policy of *Lebensraum* and racial ideology.

It must, however, be noted that in the three years that elapsed between Stresemann's death and Hitler's assumption of power, Stresemann's successors forced the pace of revisionism and departed from his policy of 'channelling revisionist demands into a general understanding with the other great powers and a recognized procedure in accordance with international law' [250: Krüger, 'Friedenssicherung und deutsche Revisionspolitik', p. 257]. In June 1930 von Schubert, who was for many years permanent secretary in the Foreign Ministry and had played an important part in formulating Stresemann's policy, was removed from office and replaced by von Bülow. The latter, previously head of the League of Nations department, was the exponent of an outspokenly nationalist policy, albeit one combined with peaceful intentions; his views on foreign affairs were close to those of Brüning. The methods, aims and priorities of Brüning's foreign policy were distinctly different from Stresemann's, involving an aggressive bid for the early solution of the reparation and armament questions. It would probably be too much to interpret this as a clear and irrevocable departure from Stresemann's policy, but certainly 1930 marked 'the switch to a policy of national self-centredness (*Abgrenzung*) and intensified revisionist claims' [ibid., p. 256]. It was also largely owing to the 'radicalization of international affairs' from 1930/1 onwards that German complaints about the Treaty of Versailles and demands for its revision became louder and shriller with the transition from Stresemann to Brüning and from the latter to the Papen and Schleicher governments [Hildebrand in 220: Becker and Hildebrand (eds), *Internationale Beziehungen in der Weltwirtschaftskrise 1929–1933*, pp. 434, 436].

6

The Last Phase of the Republic

As already mentioned (page 132 above), postwar research concerning the Weimar Republic began by concentrating on its last phase, and with good reason: the object was to investigate the causes and stages of the failure of Weimar democracy and to explain the fateful events that led in January 1933 to the takeover of state power by Hitler and his party. The main interest centred then, as it does now, on the breakdown of the 'great coalition' and the change to presidential government in March 1930, and the development of National Socialism into a mass movement.

Opinions vary as to the causes, scope and effects of the decisions taken for the solution of the government crisis in the spring of 1930 but no one disputes that the appointment of a 'Hindenburg Cabinet' under Brüning was a far-reaching and dangerous transformation of the system of government. Opposing views of Brüning's presidential Cabinet were formulated with great clarity at an early stage. A. Rosenberg, writing in 1935, dated the end of the republic from 1930; after the September election of that year, the Reichstag majority 'abandoned the struggle with the unconstitutional dictatorship . . . The same hour saw the death of the Weimar Republic. Since then one dictatorship has succeeded to another in Germany' [112: *History of the German Republic*, p. 306]. On the other hand, F. Meinecke in 1946 expressed the view that the 'path to the abyss' began only with the dismissal of Brüning, since under his leadership the German people 'could very well have been able to survive the difficult economic and spiritual crisis and to avert the ruinous experiment of the Third Reich' [The German Catastrophe (Cambridge, Mass., 1950), p. 70]. These rival assessments of the Brüning period are not based on a profound study of sources but on the experience of the time, which some evaluated differently from others. The respective views were not researched and argued systematically until the 1950s.

On the one hand, W. Conze then developed the thesis of the inevitability of the change to a presidential system on account of an acute 'crisis of the party-political state' which was essentially the fault of its own exponents. On the other hand, K. D. Bracher maintained that the authoritarian system created by Hindenburg and Brüning could not be justified as the consequence of an irremediable structural crisis of party democracy. If no attempt was made to find a parliamentary solution to the government crisis of 1930, it was only because the President's entourage and the chief army officers, long before the crisis, had decided to introduce a presidential regime and had made firm preparations to do so. Hence Bracher regards Brüning's period of office as the first stage in the dissolution of the Weimar Republic, whereas Conze takes a favourable view of the Brüning experiment for a 'state above party' and considers that the real crash came with Brüning's dismissal 'within a hundred yards of the goal' (cf. page 132 above).

The controversy between Bracher and Conze set off a debate about Brüning that has gone through many phases; it has at times slackened but never subsided, and is still unresolved. Three stages of particular intensity may be distinguished. In the first phase after 1955, prompted by Bracher's criticism of Brüning, the main question was whether the change to a presidential system could or could not have been avoided. What were the motives and aims of the protagonists of the authoritarian course, and what exactly was the importance of the Brüning period in the break-up of the republic? The dispute revived with different emphasis after the publication of Brüning's memoirs [51] in 1970. A third round of the debate was set off at the end of the 1970s by K. Borchardt ['Zwangslagen und Handlungsspielräume in der grossen Weltwirtschaftskrise der frühen dreissiger Jahre' (1979), in 479: idem, *Wachstum, Krisen, Handlungsspielräume*, pp. 165-82]. Borchardt subjected to a critical review the unfavourable assessment of Brüning's deflationary policy which had until then been generally accepted and was even encountered among Brüning's defenders. The main argument thus shifted to the content of Brüning's policies, the question of freedom of action and feasible alternatives for German economic and financial policy during the world depression. This discussion is still in its initial phase.

The debate in the late 1950s and early 1960s produced no agreement between the views of Bracher and Conze. Conze held to his thesis of an incurable 'crisis of the party-political state' in 1929-30 and described the Brüning policy as a last attempt to 'save democracy' ['Brünings Politik unter dem Druck der grossen Krise', *HZ*, vol. 199 (1964), pp. 529-50; 'Die Regierung Brüning', in 102: Hermens and Schieder (eds), *Staat, Wirtschaft und Politik in der Weimarer Republik*, pp. 223-48; 'Die politischen Entscheidungen in Deutschland 1929-1933', in 90: Conze and Raupach (eds), *Die Staats- und Wirtschaftskrise des Deutschen Reichs 1929/33*, pp. 176-252].

In substantial agreement with Conze, W. Besson saw it as the essence of Brüning's policy to 'strengthen the power of the state to do what had to be done' (*Exekution der Sachlichkeit*), but conceded that there was much to be said for the view that 'it was the authoritarian state in the form of the bureaucratic regime governing by emergency decrees which sacrificed the masses to Adolf Hitler by leaving them to themselves' [294: *Württemberg und die deutsche Staatskrise 1928-1933*, pp. 358, 362]. Bracher, on the other hand, vigorously opposed the 'increasing tendency to rehabilitate the presidential solution', and declared that 'the history of the Brüning-Papen-Schleicher system of governing by emergency decrees from 1930 onwards is in a very precise sense the prehistory of the Third Reich, the starting-point of Hitler's dictatorship and the situation that made it possible' ['Parteienstaat, Präsidialsystem, Notstand', in 106: Jasper (ed.), *Von Weimar zu Hitler 1930–1933*, pp. 69 f.]

Despite a tendency which certainly exists, and is deplored by Bracher, to take 'a conservative and all too benevolent view of the presidential regime' [86, preface to 5th edn, 1971], it can be said that the broadening of the source base in the 1960s furnished important arguments for a critical view of the genesis of the first presidential Cabinet. It now became clear that

> the aversion to compromise, shown by the parties at either extreme of the 'great coalition' and the interest groups behind them, was increased by the fact that from the beginning of 1930 there was loud and clear talk behind the scenes of a coming 'Hindenburg government', and to many it seemed only a question of time before the SPD was forced out of the Cabinet . . . Not the least important cause of the failure of the coalition was the fact that a real alternative existed in the shape of a presidential government under Article 48. Thus the switch to a presidential regime in March 1930 was not merely a consequence of the collapse of the 'great coalition', but also one of its causes. [U. Wengst, 'Heinrich Brüning und die "Konservative Alternative" ', *Aus Politik und Zeitgeschichte*, B50/80, 13 December 1980, p. 20]

In the midst of conflicting judgements as to the inauguration of the presidential system and the significance of Brüning's Cabinet for the break-up of the Weimar Republic, a sensation was caused by the publication of Brüning's memoirs [51] at the end of 1970. In them he spoke with great openness of his basic political views and intentions, so that his personality and policy appeared in a new light. The picture he presented of his own opinions and objectives at the time is well summarized by E. Hamburger:

> In foreign policy he was a 'revisionist', determined to break the peace settlement of 1919. In constitutional matters he was a monarchist and an opponent of the democratic republic. Politically he was a conservative in the Centre Party. His deflationary measures were made to serve his foreign policy; so was the fight for arms equality. His efforts were bent on destroying the Versailles system, with the abolition of reparation payments as the first step. In the legislative sphere, from 1930 onwards he took advantage of the increasing impotence of Parliament in order to restore a constitutional order of the Bismarckian type by misusing the system of emergency decrees. In the executive sphere, Hindenburg's re-election was intended to

pave the way for a regency followed by a restoration of the monarchy. In party matters Brüning sought to link his party on a permanent basis with the anti-republican forces in the Reich and in Prussia. ['Betrachtungen über Heinrich Brünings Memoiren', *IWK*, vol. 15 (April 1972), pp. 18–39; quotation, p. 31]

R. Morsey is certainly right in saying that if Brüning's friends and interpreters had been acquainted with his memoirs they would have found it harder to explain his policy during the world depression [*Zur Entstehung, Authentizität und Kritik von Brünings 'Memoiren 1918–1934'* (Opladen, 1975), p. 50]. In his subtle analysis Morsey expressed strong reservations as to the 'reliability' of the memoirs, which is often unthinkingly taken for granted, and as to Brüning's depiction of his own policy as having been consistently planned in terms of long-range objectives. Even since the appearance of the memoirs, W. Conze adheres with few modifications to his basically favourable assessment of Brüning and his policy ['Brüning als Reichskanzler', *HZ*, vol. 214 (1972), pp. 310–34; 'Die Reichsverfassungsreform als Ziel der Politik Brünings', *Der Staat*, vol. 11 (1972), pp. 209–17; see also J. Becker, 'Heinrich Brüning und das Scheitern der konservativen Alternative in der Weimarer Republik', *Aus Politik und Zeitgeschichte*, B22/80, 31 May 1980, pp. 3–17]. But the memoirs have certainly strengthened the position of those who regard March 1930 as the crucial turning-point. Bracher could thus feel confirmed in his view that the introduction of presidential government was 'not a move to save democracy, but part of a conscious plan to bring about a right-wing regime independent of party and parliament and to keep the Social Democrats out of power'. Brüning's policy 'oscillated between the defence of a bureaucratic version of a state based on the rule of law, and paving the way for dictatorship . . . He was not . . . the last chancellor *before* the break-up of the Weimar Republic, but the first chancellor *in* the process of destroying German democracy' ['Brünings unpolitische Politik und die Auflösung der Weimarer Republik', *VfZg*, vol. 19 (1972), pp. 113–23; quotations pp. 119, 122 f.].

In the light of present research it can no longer be doubted that Brüning was well aware of the plans for an authoritarian transformation of the system that were being brewed in Hindenburg's circle and by the army leaders. Admittedly, at the beginning of 1930 Brüning still thought it desirable for the 'great coalition' to remain in being until the autumn of that year, and in March 1930 he endeavoured to bring about a *modus vivendi* between its right and left wing [at least until 18 March: see T. P. Koops, 'Heinrich Brünings "Politische Erfahrungen" ', *GWU*, vol. 24 (1973), pp. 197–221]. But as soon as the coalition broke up he placed himself without reservation at Hindenburg's disposal and willingly – all too willingly, as Conze admits – accepted the President's conditions for the formation of the new government and the policy it was to pursue. The historical importance of the political decisions of those March days of 1930 can hardly be overestimated.

While it was long disputed as to whether the Brüning period was a first stage in the dissolution of the republic or the last attempt to save democracy, from the 1950s onwards there was a high degree of unanimity as to Brüning's economic and financial measures. The deflationary policy which he pursued with ruthless consistency until his dismissal, and which aggravated the crisis, was regarded by almost all economists and historians as having been fatally mistaken. However, the rightness of his judgement and its applicability to Brüning's policy were challenged by K. Borchardt in 1979 in his study entitled 'Zwangslagen und Handlungsspielräume' [479: *Wachstum, Krisen, Handlungsspielräume*, pp. 165–82], thus imparting a new direction to the discussion about Brüning.

Borchardt begins by posing the question whether Brüning's failure to embark on an expansionist, anti-cyclical policy was due to 'incompetence and lack of discernment on the government's part', or whether the political and economic options in 1930–2 left no feasible alternative. In order to answer this question, Borchardt seeks to clarify: (1) when such measures to offset the crisis could and should have been taken, and (2) whether appropriate means were available for the purpose. In Borchardt's view, measures to stimulate the economy could not have been taken before the summer of 1931, so that a timely move against the recession was impossible; at best the bottoming-out of the crisis, which occurred in the summer of 1932, might have been advanced by some months. As to the possible means (deficit financing to create jobs), Borchardt considers that the government ruled out foreign credits because of the likely political conditions; while the creation of money by the Reichsbank was open to many technical and political obstacles, such as the terms of the bank's charter, the impossibility of devaluing the mark on account of the Young Plan, and fear of inflation. 'Because of foreign and domestic constraints, the possibilities of action to stimulate economic activity were, at least during Brüning's period of government, . . . much more restricted than subsequent critics have suggested on the basis of pure economic theory' [ibid., p. 173]. Borchardt's opinion that the German economy was in an abnormal and unhealthy state even before the world depression (cf. page 164 above) supplies him with a further explanation of the reaction to the crisis by Brüning's government and the social groups supporting it. Since premature stabilization measures would have tended to preserve the 'sick' economy, they did not appeal to those who sought to use the crisis as a 'chance to clean up the system' [479: p. 182]. In Borchardt's view, Brüning was faced with constraints 'so tremendous that even today we can offer no real solution to them'; so it is understandable that 'those in charge at that time did not take the measures that it was later thought they should have done' [ibid., pp. 181 f.].

Borchardt's study caused a considerable stir and some disarray, as it called in question much that had long been regarded as economically unchallengeable. Among comments on his account of German economic and financial policy in the years of the slump, particular attention should be given to that by Holtfrerich [509: 'Alternativen zu Brünings Wirtschaftspolitik in der Weltwirt-schaftskrise?']. Holtfrerich shows that pressure in Brüning's own ranks for a revision of the deflationary policy increased after the bank crisis of July 1931, and he asks why Brüning held unswervingly to that policy throughout his term of office despite growing resistance on the home front. The answer, according to Holtfrerich, lay in Brüning's political aims, which were also to a large extent those of the classes supporting him: the consolidation of the public finances, above all the curtailment of social expenditure, and the wiping-out of reparations. To achieve these aims, Brüning needed the depression.

If Brüning found his options limited, it was because of his own scale of priorities: (1) the revision of Versailles, above all the abolition of reparation payments with Allied consent; (2) so as not to bar the way to this, strict observance of international obligations (including the stipulations of the Young Plan as to the gold and foreign currency backing of the mark and the ban on its devaluation); (3) avoidance of inflation; and (4) far behind these, the aim of full employment or even economic growth. [ibid., p. 629].

According to Holtfrerich, if Brüning had chosen to alter his priorities he could have taken active measures to revive the economy in the summer of 1931, before the final cancelling of reparations; and a policy of work creation beginning a year earlier might have changed Germany's political destiny and enabled democracy to survive. Thus Holtfrerich is of the opinion that there was probably no situation of constraint which excluded alternatives [ibid., p. 631].

There is no longer any doubt that Brüning's first priority was the cancelling of reparations. The view already put forward by W. J. Helbich [504] that this was Brüning's aim from the beginning of his government is amply confirmed by the latest research based on all relevant sources [497: Glashagen, Die Reparationspolitik Heinrich Brünings 1930–1931]. The Brüning government cannot be accused of having deliberately aggravated the economic crisis so as to force a solution of the reparations question; but the desperate financial and economic situation in Germany, if not engineered by Brüning, was recognized and used by him as a means of scaling down reparations [ibid., p. 32]. In his policy of putting this ahead of all the country's other vital needs, Brüning was influenced not least by the expectation that if he got rid of reparations it would open the way for early co-operation between himself and the political right, and thus meet the wishes of Hindenburg and the army leaders. Thus there was a connection between reparations, Brüning's stubborn adherence to a policy of deflation, and the objective of a presidential regime. In this way, it is clear that March 1930 not only introduced a momentous transformation of the system of government, but also laid the basis for German economic and financial policy during the great depression.

The political decisions and events from September 1930 to January 1933 were of the first importance in 'making Hitler possible'; accordingly they have been studied exhaustively from this point of view, among others. Some problems that were long controversial have been cleared up in recent years and are now the subject of broad agreement, for example, the motives, stages and responsibilities for Brüning's dismissal (cf. page 118 above). [For the importance of the decree on settlement in eastern Germany see the latest summary by U. Wengst: 'Schlange-Schöningen, Ostsiedlung und die Demission der Regierung Brüning', *GWU*, vol. 30 (1979), pp. 538–51.] On some other matters, however, disagreement still prevails: for example, the SPD's policy of 'toleration' in the Brüning period, or the estimate of Schleicher's government as the last, and presumably the only, alternative to Hitler's takeover [on Schleicher's idea of the 'diagonal front', see most recently 575: Schildt, *Militärdiktatur mit Massenbasis?*].

Still much debated is the reaction of the Prussian government, the SPD and the trade unions to Papen's *coup d'état* against Prussia on 20 July 1932 [as to the propriety of the term, see G. Schulz, ' "Preussenschlag" oder Staatsstreich?', *Der Staat*, vol. 17 (1978), pp. 553–81, esp. pp. 569 ff.]. The controversy on possible forms of resistance to the deposition of the Prussian government has exercised historians of Weimar from the beginning, as Papen's measure of *Gleichschaltung* seemed in retrospect to be a prelude to the Nazi seizure of power. While those directly involved, such as O. Braun and C. Severing, maintained in their memoirs that resistance appeared hopeless and an appeal to mass action would have been irresponsible, in the mid-1950s K. D. Bracher and E. Eyck contended that non-resistance had been a grave mistake. Bracher admitted that resistance by force would probably have been crushed, but

> there remained the possibility of a lasting demonstration, a manifestation of the unbroken will of democracy to assert itself against a temporarily superior force. This might, beyond all justified practical calculations, have made it possible to save a democratic consciousness from the psychological and moral collapse of the republican forces; it might have made the way harder for the new rulers, delayed future developments and lessened their effect. [86: *Die Auflösung der Weimarer Republik*, p. 599]

This view was generally accepted, despite the immediate objection by A. Brecht that judgements as to responsibility must be based on the situation as it had been when actions were performed or left undone, and 'not as it later developed in unforeseeable circumstances' (cf. page 133 above). E. Matthias considered that the decision by the Prussian government and SPD leaders to offer no resistance was a fatal one even though the republican 'stronghold' of Prussia could not have held out in the end. 'On 20 July the last chance of widening the base of republican resistance in a rightward and leftward direction was thrown away; and the effect of total defeat could not have been more devastating than the political and psychological consequences of failing to act' [385: *Das Ende der Parteien*, pp. 127, 144]. H.-P. Ehni actually described the balance of forces as 'not by any means so hopeless', and accused the SPD leaders of 'a fatal trust in legality' and 'legalistic immobility' [299: *Bollwerk Preussen?*, pp. 270 f.]. The only exception to this consensus in the 1960s was K. Rohe in his book on the Reichsbanner, in which he stated that the reasons for not resisting were politically compelling and convincing: 'The actual power situation at the time of Papen's action – which moreover was legitimate in a formal sense – was so completely in the Reich government's favour that resistance by force could only have appeared to the left as an act of political suicide. Any sacrifice must have seemed useless from the start.' No alternative course was open on 20 July, 'in so far as it can be taken as a principle of sensible political action that every risk must be proportionate to the likely results of action' [573: *Das Reichsbanner Schwarz Rot Gold*, p. 437]. Similar arguments, and some additional ones, are used by H. Schulze in his biography of Otto Braun, published in 1977 [644: *Otto Braun*, pp. 745 ff.].

Historians generally are still critical of the Prussian government and the SPD leaders, and the latter's passivity is, on the whole, strongly criticized by surviving witnesses of the event. But recently a change of perspective seems to be adumbrated. It is hardly in dispute that the foundations of the 'Prussian bulwark' were already much undermined by the summer of 1932, and an attempt at armed resistance would not only have been condemned to rapid failure but would almost certainly have led to an authoritarian military dictatorship, at least for a time. In addition, greater weight is laid on the reasons for holding that the SPD's decision not to call on the masses to fight was politically the right one: for example, the destabilization of the workers' movement by reason of high unemployment, the party's attrition in the 'war on two fronts' against right-wing radicalism and the KPD, and the lack of a rousing battle-cry. It is also highly questionable whether the moment for a 'last stand' had already come in July 1932. [For the present state of the debate on this, see H. Grebing, 'Flucht vor Hitler?' *Aus Politik und Zeitgeschichte*, B 4–5/83, 29 January 1983, pp. 26–42.]

On the other hand, the most recent research shows clearly that Papen's action against Prussia was, to a much greater extent than had been supposed, 'the beginning of a switch from the liberal and democratic state of the Weimar Republic to the totalitarian dictatorship of the Third Reich'. The coup of 20 July 1932 was followed by a 'complete reorganization of the political police, who, instead of protecting the republican constitution and the rule of law, became the instrument of a reactionary and authoritarian regime on a pre-revolutionary and anti-democratic basis'. More particularly in respect of the political police, a high degree of continuity – organizational, practical and personal – can be traced from Papen's commissar regime to that of Hitler and

Göring [306: Graf, *Politische Polizei swischen Demokratie und Diktatur*, pp. 89 f].

The final phase of the Weimar Republic was overshadowed by the triumphant rise of the National Socialist movement from 1929–30 onwards. It is certainly a major responsibility of historians to explain convincingly the causes and stages whereby the party became a mass movement and an important factor in the domestic arena. During the first two decades after 1945, however, research concentrated on the party's early history in Bavaria in 1919–23 and on Hitler's personality. [On the problems of Hitler biography and the study of his character and opinions see, most recently, A. Hillgruber, *Endlich genug über Nationalsozialismus und Zweiten Weltkrieg?* (Düsseldorf, 1982), pp. 11 ff., and G. Schreiber, 627: *Hitler*]. Only in the late 1960s did interest shift to some extent to the years after the party's re-foundation in 1925. The monographs by J. Nyomarkay [622], D. Orlow [623], W. Horn [606] and A. Tyrell [637, cf. 39], which appeared within a short time of each other, deal thoroughly with the internal development and structure of the NSDAP and the formation of a new type of party based on the Führer ideology and the Führer principle (cf. page 98 above), while the work by P. Hüttenberger [607] describes the *Gauleiter* system, the most important party cadre during the 'time of struggle'.

Other studies seek to discover on what the attraction of the NSDAP was based and what were the real causes of its mass following. In this connection M. Broszat draws attention to the psychological attitudes related to age, experience, or social origin to which for a long time too little heed was paid in comparison with 'objective' socio-economic data, such as origin, occupation, and so on, which are easier to ascertain but often less informative (cf. page 105 above). To Broszat the mass appeal of the NSDAP seems 'undramatic' and 'sudden in appearance only', because the new, anti-Marxist and anti-liberal, catch-all party to a great extent simply took over and united 'what had already existed far and wide, though in a scattered form, in the way of ideology and sectional interest with a political potential'. The watchword of a 'national community' (*Volksgemeinschaft*) proved the most effective element of National Socialist propaganda, and the party became highly popular with the younger generation, in particular, thanks to widespread social discontent [586: 'Zur Struktur der NS-Massenbewegung', pp. 59 ff.; cf. idem 585: 'Soziale Motivation und Führerbindung des Nationalsozialismus'].

In J. Kocka's view the attraction that National Socialism exerted on very different social groups was due primarily to the movement's 'Janus-like character'. 'National Socialism made it possible to be simultaneously, on the one hand, radical and anti-élitist, opposed to capitalists and "big shots", and, on the other, fiercely anti-socialist, nationalistic and conscious of one's social standing.' The fact that large sections of German society were attracted by this dualism – National Socialism was both dynamic and anti-modern, reactionary and revolutionary, opposed to capitalism and also to socialism – is attributed by Kocka to the persistence of strong pre-industrial, pre-capitalist and pre-bourgeois traditions [614: 'Ursachen des Nationalsozialismus', pp. 10 f.]. A further theory of the nature of the National Socialist movement, its conception of itself and its cohesive force, has recently been put forward by the American historian J. M. Rhodes, who interprets it as a secular, chiliastic phenomenon [624: *The Hitler Movement*].

Works describing the NSDAP as a whole, and the origins of its mass membership are supplemented by more specialized studies dealing, on the one hand, with particular cities and regions [e.g., 581, 583, 602, 604, 621, 625] and, on the other, with the organizational 'infrastructure', for example, the SA [582, 591, 609, 638], the SS [615], the agrarian advisers [595], the youth organizations and the Students' Association [628, 590, 596]. This organization network is, in particular, in need of further investigation, as it enabled the Nazis to penetrate the most varied sections of society and, in some cases, to infiltrate bourgeois associations and institutions (cf. pages 101–3 above); it thus played an important part in making possible the spectacular Nazi advance from 1930 onwards. For some years past, research into the Nazi rise to power has concentrated on two themes: electoral developments, and relations between the NSDAP and the industrial world, especially heavy industry.

Certainly, it was not by election that Hitler came to power. But it is equally true that he would not have done so but for the elections, in particular the National Socialist successes of 1932. In view of this fact it is surprising that the shift of voters to the NSDAP was for some time not analysed on a scientific basis; such analysis was replaced by 'electoral folklore' (J. W. Falter), a mixture of true, half-true and completely false assertions. The view – based partly on contemporary studies – which prevailed for a long time, and still does, is that National Socialism was a middle-class phenomenon: the party consisted mainly of members of the old and new middle class, that is, craftsmen, small tradesmen, medium-sized farmers, employees and officials, in so far as voters in these categories were not Catholic supporters of the Centre or the BVP. As against this, it was thought, the upper and upper-middle classes were largely immune to National Socialism; so was the working class, except that the Nazis had some success with the unemployed. This interpretation was condensed by the American sociologist S. M. Lipset into a theory of Fascism as 'extremism of the centre' [' "Fascism" – Left, Right and Center', in *Political Man – the Social Bases of Politics* (Garden City, NY, 1960), pp. 127–79; cf. an early criticism of this theory by H. A. Winkler, 'Extremismus der Mitte?', *VfZg*, vol. 20 (1972), pp. 175–91].

The analysis of the political origin and social background of NSDAP voters with the help of modern methods of studying electoral history did not get under way until the 1970s. Important results were contained in several (unpublished) American theses [titles and conclusions in 589: Falter, 'Wer verhalf der NSDAP zum Sieg?', pp. 8 ff], and a large-scale research project under

J. W. Falter promises further important results that are already known in outline [ibid.]. So far the following may be stated.

(1) The shift of voters to the NSDAP, especially in the election of September 1930, cannot be sufficiently explained and interpreted either by means of the class theory of Lipset and others, or by the theory of the masses put forward by Bendix and others (cf. page 108 above). [For a presentation and critique of these two positions, see Falter, ibid., pp. 4 ff., and idem, 'Radikalisierung des Mittelstandes oder Mobilisierung der Unpolitischen?', in P. Steinbach (ed.), *Probleme politischer Partizipation im Modernisierungsprozess* (Stuttgart, 1982), pp. 438–69.] The shifts of voters to the NSDAP appear today considerably more complex than either theory assumes; the social basis of the party's electoral support was neither so static nor so narrow as was long supposed [588: Childers, *The Nazi Voter*].

Recent research indicates that in each of the Reichstag elections of 1930, July 1932 and 1933 the NSDAP had more success than any other party in gaining voters who had not cast a vote at the previous poll. By far the most of these, however, had in the past voted for the DNVP, the bourgeois middle-ground parties or the special-interest and regional parties; some had even voted for the SPD. Like the Centre and the BVP, the KPD was virtually immune to Nazi attraction. It is thought that of all those who voted for the NSDAP in September 1930, about 14 per cent had done so in 1928, while 23 per cent had not voted at the 1928 election; 31 per cent had voted for parties of the bourgeois middle ground, 21 per cent for the DNVP, 9 per cent for the SPD and 2 per cent for smaller parties [T. Schnabel, 'Wer wählte Hitler?', *GG*, vol. 8 (1982), pp. 116–33, here p. 121].

(2) As to the social origins of those who voted for the NSDAP, the customary view that Hitler came to power on the votes of the petty bourgeoisie cannot be sustained in this form. R. F. Hamilton has shown by a careful analysis of results in the individual wards of fourteen cities that the NSDAP was more than averagely successful in districts inhabited by the upper and upper-middle classes, which, in some cases – for example, Berlin, Hamburg, Essen and Dortmund – actually gave it its highest percentage for the city in question ['Die soziale Basis des Nationalsozialismus', in J. Kocka (ed.), *Angestellte im europäischen Vergleich* (Göttingen, 1981), pp. 354–75; also 603: Hamilton, *Who Voted for Hitler?*]. It is also of interest that the NSDAP obtained results well above its average among voters registered as being on their summer holidays, who were probably among the better-off members of society [603: pp. 220 ff.].

Among the working class, too, the NSDAP gained considerably more votes than was once supposed. Two points are to be noted here. First, even before 1930 a sizeable number of workers had not voted for either of the 'working-class parties', the SPD or the KPD. Thus it is estimated that in December 1924 the DNVP received about 2·2 million workers' votes [413: Stupperich, *Volksgemeinschaft oder Arbeitersolidarität*, p. 35]. It is to be supposed that the NSDAP was especially able to attract such ex-supporters of the conservative or bourgeois parties. Secondly, the NSDAP could make inroads particularly among classes with whom the independent trade unions and workers' parties had had little success: with farm labourers, homeworkers, employed craftsmen and workers in small concerns and some branches of the public service (post, railway, municipal enterprises). On the other hand, industrial workers, especially those in heavy industry, remained largely impervious to Nazi attraction.

(3) A further important result of the latest studies is that, contrary to the usual belief, the NSDAP did not make wholesale gains among the unemployed. The latter, who in 1932–3 comprised about a third of all workers, voted for the KPD and (to a less extent) the SPD rather than the NSDAP, which registered appreciable gains only among out-of-work white-collar employees. Thus the common view that the unemployed contributed significantly to the electoral success of the NSDAP is not confirmed but refuted by research. [See, e.g., H. Prohasky, 'Haben die Arbeitslosen Hitler an die Macht gebracht?', *GWU*, vol. 33 (1982), pp. 609–37; J. W. Falter, 'Politische Konsequenzen von Massenarbeitslosigkeit', *PVS*, vol. 25 (1984), pp. 275–95.]

J. W. Falter sums up these conclusions as follows:

> Undoubtedly the middle-class element predominated among those who voted for the NSDAP from 1930 onwards. But, with its extreme nationalism and its ideology of the 'racial community', the NSDAP was able to draw its forces from all sections of the population – clerks and workers, peasants and officials, professionals and housewives, young and old, Protestants and the unemployed, and so on – in such numbers that it deserved the name of a 'people's party' more than any other political groups during these years. [589: 'Wer verhalf der NSDAP zum Sieg?', p. 19]

The question of relations between big business and the Nazis before 1933 was for a long time much neglected by scholars in West Germany and in the West as a whole. This was a considerable disadvantage when, in the late 1960s, the interpretation of National Socialism in terms of fascism became popular, as this necessarily focused attention on the relationship between capitalism and fascism. In the absence of source-based, non-Marxist studies of the relations between heavy industry and the NSDAP in the last phase of the republic, East German scholars were at first able to dominate the discussion in West Germany with a series of publications. Their intellectual offensive was based on the Soviet-Marxist 'agency theory', to the effect that the Nazi seizure of power was engineered by German heavy industry. Hitler, on this view, became 'the political candidate, carefully built up at great expense', of a 'Nazi group' of industrialists, bankers and big landowners, who wanted him to be chancellor and brought about his appointment [E. Czichon, *Wer verhalf Hitler zur Macht?*

(Cologne, 1967), p. 32]. East German historians indeed admit that German heavy industry before 1933 did not act as a single monopoly-capitalist bloc (as the Comintern used to assert in its time), but was divided into rival wings and groups (which are defined and characterized in varying ways); but ultimately it was a majority group of 'representatives' of industry who placed Hitler in power. From this point of view fascism appears as a 'completely monocausal act of purchase' [E. Hennig, 'Industrie und Faschismus', *NPL*, vol. 15 (1970), pp. 433–49; quotation p. 439].

By way of reaction to these views, from the end of the 1960s onwards non-communist research, in its turn, took up the theme of 'industry and National Socialism'. Credit belongs to the American historian H. A. Turner for a number of critical and empirical studies which have thrown light on the extent of financial support given by industry to the NSDAP. [For a summary of these studies see 634: *Faschismus und Kapitalismus in Deutschland.*] Turner was able to expose as legends various assertions that had been repeated so often as to be counted as facts, and to cast doubt upon the cogency of some pieces of evidence that had been regarded as 'key documents'. According to Turner, even in 1932 – not to speak of previous years – the NSDAP received only a very modest share of the 'political funds' distributed by heavy industry; these donations amounted to very little in comparison with those from other sources, for example, small and medium-sized firms as well as foreign donors, or with the sums the party derived from its own resources [cf. 619: Matzerath and Turner, 'Die Selbstfinanzierung der NSDAP 1930–1932'; and now Turner's comprehensive study, 636: *German Big Business and the Rise of Hitler*].

Turner's conclusions aroused fierce controversy, which developed into a regular 'documentary battle' (G. D. Feldman). D. Stegmann charged Turner with neglecting structural aspects that were relevant from the point of view of social history; according to Stegmann, the pro-Hitler wing of heavy industry worked hard and successfully to pave the way for his chancellorship [see, e.g., 632: 'Zum Verhältnis von Grossindustrie und Nationalsozialismus 1930–1933']. Turner, in reply, accused Stegmann of sometimes using sources arbitrarily, misinterpreting archive material and arriving at conclusions that did not hold water [635: 'Grossunternehmertum und Nationalsozialismus 1930–1933']. The vehemence of this dispute and the disparity of conclusions were not only due to differences of method and standards of judgement, but also to the fact that the questions and object of research were not clearly enough formulated, so that the respective arguments to some extent missed their aim. Two aspects of the whole complex should in fact be carefully distinguished: (1) the financing of the NSDAP – the question as to what absolute and relative share was provided by industry, especially heavy industry; (2) the part played by heavy industry and the key industrial associations in the final phase of the Weimar Republic. The latter question involves, over and above elucidation of the position regarding subsidies, a full analysis of the self-regarding policy of heavy industry and its share in the destruction of parliamentary democracy, the collapse of the republic and the facilitation of the Nazi 'seizure of power'. While Turner concentrates on the first question, Stegmann is chiefly concerned with the second; this divergence, however, was not brought out with sufficient clarity by either adversary.

As to the first question, as matters stand at present the argument may be regarded as closed. Unless any new sources come to light and call for fresh conclusions, it can be taken as proven that big business did not make any decisive material contribution to the rise of National Socialism and the Nazi electoral successes. 'There is so far no evidence that the NSDAP, in the last phase of the Weimar Republic, received continuous and massive, let alone decisive financial help from German heavy industry' [T.Trumpp, 'Zur Finanzierung der NSDAP durch die deutsche Grossindustrie', *GWU*, vol. 32 (1981), pp. 223–41; quotation, p. 233]. On the other hand, Turner's statement that financial grants from the business world were 'predominantly aimed *against* the National Socialists' [634: *Faschismus und Kapitalismus in Deutschland*, p. 25] needs to be corrected in the sense that the subsidies of heavy industry to the DNVP, the DVP and other small parties of the right were not directed so much 'against the National Socialists' as against the left and, in a wider sense, against parliamentary democracy. Financial contributions from heavy industry did not enable the right-wing parties to succeed in the elections of 1932. Accordingly, G. D. Feldman rightly concludes that money did not transform itself into political power: 'The industrialists did not manage to create a political party with a broad bourgeois base, which . . . would have given industry more solid support, . . . nor did they win favour with a majority of the population through their efforts to buy the press' ['Aspekte deutscher Industriepolitik am Ende der Weimarer Republik 1930–1932', in 507: Holl (ed.), *Wirtschaftskrise und liberale Demokratie*, pp. 103–25; quotation p. 118].

Thus there can hardly be any doubt today that heavy industry's direct financial contribution to the NSDAP was a relatively small one. Much more complex, and harder to answer, is the question as to how far industry, especially heavy industry, helped to prepare the way for Hitler's chancellorship through its political activities and by directly or indirectly influencing those in control during the period of presidential Cabinets. In particular, it is still disputed as to how far heavy industry was truly represented by its pro-Hitler wing in 1932, and how effective the latter's activities were in the last months and weeks before 30 January 1933. (Turner and Stegmann take completely opposite views of, in particular, the importance of the Keppler circle and of Schacht's office, also the genesis and significance of the industrialists' petition to Hindenburg in November 1932.) Although the argument is still in full swing, some points may be taken as established.

(1) In the last months before the Nazi seizure of power, it was evidently less than ever the case that a single individual could speak or act as a representative

of big business as a whole [310: Hentschel, *Weimars letzte Monate*, p. 133]. It can scarcely be disputed any longer that 'heavy industry' was *not* essentially involved in arranging Papen's interview with Hitler on 4 January 1933 [ibid., p. 136, agreeing with Turner and others against Stegmann].

(2) Note should be taken of G. D. Feldman's point that the long predominance of heavy industry, which was still unbroken in the 1920s, had the effect of driving important parts of the business world, especially medium and smaller enterprises, towards right-wing radicalism, thus destroying potential reserves of support for a liberal democratic policy. 'In this sense heavy industry bears more responsibility for the support given to Hitler by German industry as a whole than can be inferred simply from its direct influence' ['Aspekte deutscher Industriepolitik am Ende der Weimarer Republik 1930–1932', in 507: Holl (ed.), *Wirtschaftskrise und liberale Demokratie*, p. 115].

(3) After Schleicher's government declaration and the rescinding of the emergency decrees of 4 and 5 September 1932 (which had gravely modified the labour laws to the workers' disadvantage), the group of heavy industrialists led by Reusch insisted on the abandonment of Schleicher's plans and worked for a return to Papen's authoritarian regime. That is to say, while not fully cognizant of Papen's manoeuvres since the end of December, they endeavoured to put an early end to Schleicher's chancellorship. Until recently the dominant view has been that the industrialists were more or less agreed in opposing Schleicher, but K. Neebe has now shown that the Reichsverband der Deutschen Industrie and the Deutscher Industrie- und Handelstag were still behind Schleicher in January 1933; thus Hitler became Chancellor at a time when 'the industrial front was split' [525: *Grossindustrie, Staat und NSDAP 1930–1933*, p. 201]. To this extent it appears that heavy industry was less responsible for bringing Hitler to power than is often supposed; but its chief representatives no doubt hardly saw any reason to oppose a take-over of the government by Hitler [310: Hentschel, *Weimars letzte Monate*, p. 138]. The business world did not create Hitler's government and the great majority of big business men were not trying, in or before January 1933, to bring a Nazi government to power. But, by their opposition to parliamentary democracy and preference for an authoritarian system, the bosses had accelerated the break-up of the Weimar Republic and played into the hands of a dictatorship. Hence the business world in general, and big business in particular, bears a large share of responsibility for Hitler's accession to power and for Nazi rule.

What made Hitler possible? Was the Nazi 'seizure of power' inevitable in the circumstances that prevailed? Every discussion of the collapse of Weimar circles round these questions, which have received very different answers from researchers up to the present. Certainly, the monocausal explanations which at first prevailed, attributing the rise of Nazism and Hitler's assumption of power to a single cause or a single main cause, are by now discarded, as all such simplistic accounts have proved inadequate. Historians today at least agree that

	National Assembly 19. 1. 1919	1st Reichstag 6. 6. 1920	2nd Reichstag 4. 5. 1924	3rd Reichstag 7. 12. 1924
Number entitled to vote (in millions)	36·766	35·949	38·375	38·987
Votes cast (in millions)	30·524	28·463	29·709	30·704
Size of poll (%)	83·0	79·2	77·4	78·8
Total no. of seats[a]	421 (423)[b]	459	472	493
DNVP	3·121 10·3% **44**	4·249 15·1% **71**	5·696 19·5% **95**	6·206 20·5% **103**
NSDAP (in 1924: NS-Freiheitsbewegung)	—	—	1·918 6·5% **32**	0·907 3·0% **14**
Wirtschaftspartei/ Bayer. Bauernbund	0·275 0·9% **4**	0·218 0·8% **4**	0·694 2·4% **10**	1·005 3·3% **17**
Deutsch- Hannoversche Partei	0·077 0·2% **1**	0·319 1·1% **5**	0·320 1·1% **5**	0·263 0·9% **4**
Landbund	—	—	0·574 2·0% **10**	0·499 1·6% **8**
Deutsches Landvolk	—	—	—	—
Deutsche Bauernpartei	—	—	—	—
Christlich-sozialer Volksdienst	—	—	—	—
DVP	1·345 4·4% **19**	3·919 13·9% **65**	2·694 9·2% **45**	3·049 10·1% **51**
Zentrum (Centre) (in 1919: Christliche Volkspartei)	5·980 19·7% **91**	3·845 13·6% **64**	3·914 13·4% **65**	4·119 13·6% **69**
BVP	—	1·238 4·4% **21**	0·946 3·2% **16**	1·134 3·7% **19**
DDP (from 1930: Deutsche Staatspartei)	5·641 18·5% **75**	2·333 8·3% **39**	1·655 5·7% **28**	1·920 6·3% **32**
SPD	11·509 37·9% **163 (165)[b]**	6·104 21·7% **102**	6·009 20·5% **100**	7·881 26·0% **131**
USPD	2·317 7·6% **22**	5·046 17·9% **84**	0·235 0·8% —	0·099 0·3% —
KPD	—	0·589 2·1% **4**	3·693 12·6% **62**	2·709 9·0% **45**
Others	0·131 0·5% **2**	0·332 1·1% —	0·930 3·1% **4**[d]	0·598 2·0% —

Source: *Statistisches Jahrbuch für das Deutsche Reich*, vol. 52 (Berlin, 1933), p. 539.
Note: The figures against each party indicate, first, the number of votes obtained (in millions), then its percentage of the poll, then (in bold type) the number of seats it held at the beginning of the session.

[a] The total number of seats varied from one Parliament to another, as it depended on the number of votes cast: see Bibliography, no. 337, pp. 145 ff., 361 ff.

[b] Two additional SPD members were elected by the Eastern Army on 2 February 1919, bringing the total to 423 and the strength of the SPD to 165.

Results 1919–33

	4th Reichstag 20. 5. 1928			5th Reichstag 14. 9. 1930			6th Reichstag 31. 7. 1932			7th Reichstag 6. 11. 1932			8th Reichstag 5. 3. 1933		
	41·224			42·957			44·226			44·374			44·685		
	31·165			35·225			37·162			35·758			39·654		
	75·6			82·0			84·1			80·6			88·8		
	491			577			608			584			647		
	4·381	14·2%	73	2·458	7·0%	41	2·177	5·9%	37	2·959	8·3%	52	3·136	8·0%	52
	0·810	2·6%	12	6·409	18·3%	107	13·745	37·3%	230	11·737	33·1%	196	17·277	43·9%	288
	1·397	4·5%	23	1·362	3·9%	23	0·146	0·4%	2	0·110	0·3%	1	—		
	0·195	0·6%	3	0·144	0·4%	3	0·047	0·1%	—	0·064	0·2%	1	0·048	0·1%	—
	0·199	0·6%	3	0·194	0·6%	3	0·097	0·3%	2	0·105	0·3%	2	0·084	0·2%	1
	0·581	1·9%	10	1·108	3·2%	19	0·091	0·2%	1	0·046	0·1%	—	—		
	0·481	1·6%	8	0·339	1·0%	6	0·137	0·4%	2	0·149	0·4%	3	0·114	0·3%	2
	—			0·870	2·5%	14	0·364	1·0%	3	0·403	1·2%	5	0·383	1·0%	4
	2·679	8·7%	45	1·578	4·5%	30	0·436	1·2%	7	0·661	1·9%	11	0·432	1·1%	2
	3·712	12·1%	62	4·127	11·8%	68	4·589	12·5%	75	4·230	11·9%	70	4·425	11·2%	74
	0·945	3·1%	16	1·005	3·0%	19	1·192	3·2%	22	1·095	3·1%	20	1·074	2·7%	18
	1·505	4·9%	25	1·322	3·8%	20	0·371	1·0%	4	0·336	1·0%	2	0·334	0·9%	5
	9·153	29·8%	153	8·577	24·5%	143	7·959	21·6%	133	7·248	20·4%	121	7·181	18·3%	120
	0·021	0·1%	—	—			—			—			—		
	3·264	10·6%	54	4·592	13·1%	77	5·283	14·3%	89	5·980	16·9%	100	4·848	12·3%	81
	1·445	5·5%	4[e]	0·804	2·3%	4[f]	0·244	0·7%	1[g]	0·299	0·8%	—	0·005	—	—

[c] Results of the election on 6 June 1920, together with those of 20 February 1921 in constituency no. 1 (East Prussia) and no. 14 (Schleswig-Holstein) and 19 November 1922 in constituency no. 10 (Oppeln).

[d] Deutschsoziale Partei.

[e] Sächsisches Landvolk 2, Volksrechtspartei 2.

[f] Konservative Volkspartei.

[g] Volksrechtspartei.

the collapse of the republic and the Nazi 'seizure of power' can only be plausibly explained in terms of a very complex range of causes. Among these, the following must be taken into account: (1) the institutional framework, for example, the President's constitutional rights and options, especially in the absence of clear parliamentary majorities; (2) economic developments, with their effect on the political and social balance of power; (3) the pecularities of German political culture (partly responsible, for example, for the disaffection of the élite classes who, for the most part, were hostile to the pluralistic party, democracy of the republic); (4) changes in the social fabric, especially in the 'middle class', with consequences, *inter alia*, for its political orientation and electoral behaviour; (5) ideological factors (the German authoritarian tradition; extreme nationalism, exacerbated by defeat in war, by the 'stab in the back' legend and by propaganda against the 'war guilt' charge; the yearning for a 'strong man', which prepared the way for a charismatic 'leader' cult such as Hitler's); (6) factors of mass psychology, for example, the effect of propaganda enhanced by the rootlessness and political instability of large sections of the population; and (7) the role of certain key personalities, in particular Hindenburg, Schleicher and Papen.

Our answer to the question as to what brought down the Weimar Republic and made Hitler possible will largely be qualified by the weight attached to the different components, and how they are woven into a consistent whole; for this weighting and combining is not dictated by the sources, but is the task of the interpreting historian. How it is performed will depend on shifts of interest and the viewpoint of the individual inquirer or of a whole generation of researchers, determined by their horizon of experience, scale of values and standards of judgement. Because this is so, particular events, situations and connections are judged differently, and for the past thirty-five years interest in the Weimar Republic has concentrated first on one major aspect and then on another, as we have seen several times in the present survey.

These remarks are not intended as a plea for any far-reaching modification of the historical verdict on Weimar and its end, but only to point out why it can, and must be, the case that differently stressed answers are legitimately given by historians to a questions such as that regarding the causes and conditions of the Nazi 'seizure of power' and the circumstances that made it possible. The phrase 'differently stressed' is used advisedly, since there can be nothing casual or arbitrary about the historian's judgement. As our survey has also shown with many examples, in the past decades research into the Weimar Republic has achieved important results, has cleared up many facts and has refuted a whole range of assertions and suppositions that were long taken for granted. The limits within which interpretation is still possible are set by the body of research thus created.

Chronology

1918

29 Sept.	Army High Command calls for immediate armistice and establishment of a parliamentary regime.
3–4 Oct.	Germany proposes armistice to President Wilson.
28 Oct.	Adoption of parliamentary constitution; mutiny of the High Seas Fleet at Wilhelmshaven. Czechoslovak republic proclaimed in Prague.
3 Nov.	Armistice between Austria-Hungary and the Allies; sailors' rebellion at Kiel.
3–9 Nov.	Rebellion spreads in Germany, soldiers' and workers' councils formed in many cities.
9 Nov.	Abdication of William II; proclamation of the German republic.
10 Nov.	Formation of Council of People's Representatives (SPD–USPD); Ebert–Groener agreement.
11 Nov.	Armistice signed at Compiègne. Poland an independent republic.
12 Nov.	German Austria proclaims itself part of the Reich.
15 Nov.	Central Working Association agreement between heavy industry and trade unions.
14 Dec.	'Khaki election' in Britain.
16–20 Dec.	Congress of councils in Berlin; decision to hold election to National Assembly on 19 Jan. 1919.
28–9 Dec.	USPD members withdraw from Council of People's Representatives.

1919

1 Jan.	Foundation of KPD (German Communist Party).
5–11 Jan.	Street fighting in Berlin (Spartacist rising).
15 Jan.	Murder of Karl Liebkneckt and Rosa Luxemburg.
18 Jan.	Peace conference opens in Paris (without the defeated Central Powers).
19 Jan.	Election of National Assembly.
6 Feb.	Opening of National Assembly in Weimar.
11 Feb.	Friedrich Ebert elected Reich President.
13 Feb.	Scheidemann Cabinet ('Weimar coalition') of SPD (Social Democrats), DDP (left-wing Liberals) and Catholic Centre.
21 Feb.	Murder of Bavarian minister-president, Kurt Eisner.
Feb.–May	Disturbances, strikes and riots in many parts of Germany.
2–6 Mar.	Founding congress of the Third International (Comintern) in Moscow.
21 Mar.–1 Aug.	Soviet republic in Hungary (Béla Kun).
7 Apr.–2 May	Soviet republic in Munich.
7 May	Peace terms communicated to German delegation at Versailles.
16 June	Allied ultimatum concerning acceptance of peace treaty.
20 June	Scheidemann Cabinet resigns; government formed by Bauer (SPD and Centre).
28 June	Peace treaty signed at Versailles.

11 Aug.	Weimar constitution comes into force.
Sept.	Allies withdraw intervention forces from Russia.
10 Sept.	Peace treaty between Austria and the Allies (St Germain).
Nov.	Beginning of civil warfare in China (to 1926).
16 Nov.	Electoral victory of Bloc National in France.
18 Nov.	Hindenburg's evidence to National Assembly committee of inquiry ('stab in the back' legend).
27 Nov.	Peace treaty between Bulgaria and the Allies (Neuilly).

1920

10 Jan.	Treaty of Versailles comes into force.
1 Mar.	Admiral Horthy elected regent of Hungary.
13–16 Mar.	Kapp–Lüttwitz putsch; government flees to Dresden and Stuttgart; general strike proclaimed by unions; putsch collapses.
Mar.–Apr.	Fighting in the Ruhr district and central Germany.
19 Mar.	US Senate refuses to ratify Treaty of Versailles or approve US membership of League of Nations.
Mar.–Oct.	Russo-Polish war.
4 June	Peace treaty between Hungary and the Allies (Trianon).
6 June	Reichstag election ('Weimar coalition' suffers considerable losses); bourgeois minority government formed by Fehrenbach (Centre, DDP and DVP [National Liberals]).
10 Aug.	Peace treaty between Turkey and the Allies (Sèvres).
14 Aug.	Formation of the 'little Entente' (Yugoslavia and Czechoslovakia), joined by Romania in June 1921.
16 Oct.	Split of the USPD.
4–7 Dec.	Left wing of the USPD joins the KPD.
Dec.	Greco-Turkish war (to 1922).

1921

24–9 Jan.	Paris conference: German reparations payment set at 269,000 million gold marks.
19 Feb.	Franco-Polish treaty of mutual assistance.
21 Feb.–14 мar.	London conference on reparations; threat of sanctions against Germany.
8 Mar.	Allied troops occupy Duisburg, Ruhrort and Düsseldorf.
8–16 Mar.	Russian Communist Party congress adopts New Economic Policy.
18 Mar.	Polish–Soviet frontier fixed by peace treaty of Riga.
20 Mar.	Plebiscite in Upper Silesia; KPD's 'March operation' (*Märzaktion*) in central Germany.
27 Apr.	German reparations fixed at 132,000 million gold marks.
2 May	Fighting breaks out in Upper Silesia.
5 May	Allied ultimatum demands acceptance by Germany of 'London payments plan'.
10 May	Wirth government; Reichstag accepts London ultimatum. Beginning of 'policy of fulfilment'.
24–5 Aug.	USA signs peace treaties with Germany and Austria.
26 Aug.	Erzberger murdered.
12 Oct.	League of Nations Council partitions Upper Silesia between Germany and Poland.
5 Nov.	'Great coalition' government (SPD, Centre, DDP, DVP) formed in Prussia under Otto Braun (SPD).

12 Nov. 1921– Washington conference (naval limitation agreement; independence of
6 Feb. 1922 China guaranteed).

1922

6–13 Jan.	Cannes conference (decision to hold a world economic conference at Genoa).
18 Jan.	Poincaré government in France.
10 Apr.–19 May	Genoa conference.
16 Apr.	Treaty of Rapallo between Germany and the Soviet Union.
24 June	German Foreign Minister Rathenau murdered by right-wing extremists.
18 July	Reichstag approves Law for the Protection of the Republic.
7–14 Aug.	London conference; Poincaré demands 'productive pledges' from Germany in return for a moratorium.
Aug.	Acclerated inflation in Germany.
24 Sept.	Remnant of USPD merges with SPD.
10 Oct.	Greco-Turkish armistice after Greek defeats; failure of Lloyd George's Near East policy.
23 Oct.	Bonar Law (Conservative) succeeds Lloyd George as Prime Minister.
24 Oct.	Ebert's term of office prolonged by constitutional amendment until 1 July 1925.
28 Oct.	March on Rome: beginning of fascist seizure of power in Italy: Mussolini premier.
14 Nov.	Wirth government resigns; bourgeois minority government formed by W. Cuno, head of Hamburg–America shipping line.

1923

10 Jan.	Lithuanians invade Memel territory.
11 Jan.	Occupation of Ruhr by French and Belgian troops.
13 Jan.	'Passive resistance' proclaimed; beginning of struggle over the Ruhr.
22 May	Stanley Baldwin becomes British Prime Minister.
24 July	Greco-Turkish peace treaty of Lausanne; Greece abandons claims on Turkish mainland.
12 Aug.	Fall of Cuno government; 'great coalition' (SPD, Centre, DDP, DVP) under Gustav Stresemann (DVP).
13 Sept.	Military dictatorship of Primo de Rivera in Spain.
26 Sept.	Passive resistance in the Ruhr broken off; state of emergency proclaimed in Germany; peak of inflation.
Oct.	Separatist movements in Rhineland and Palatinate.
16 Oct.	Deutsche Rentenbank established to stabilize the currency.
end of Oct.	Deposition of SPD–KPD government in Saxony; conflict between Bavaria and the Reich government; failure of communist attempt at a rising ('German October').
3 Nov.	SPD ministers withdraw from Reich government owing to events in Saxony and Bavaria.
8–9 Nov.	Hitler–Ludendorff putsch in Munich; Ebert confers Reich executive authority on General von Seeckt.
15 Nov.	Rentenmark introduced at a value of 1 billion (a million million) paper marks.
23 Nov.	Fall of Stresemann government. He remains Foreign Minister in bourgeois minority government of Wilhelm Marx (Centre, DVP, DDP, BVP [Bavarians]).
30 Nov.	Reparation Commission decides to appoint an international committee of

experts to report on Germany's ability to pay (chairman: the American financial expert Charles G. Dawes).

1924

21 Jan.	Lenin dies.
22 Jan.	First British Labour government (minority) under Ramsay MacDonald.
25 Jan.	Franco-Czechoslovak treaty of alliance.
27 Jan.	'Adriatic treaty' between Italy and Yugoslavia.
1 Feb.	Britain recognizes Soviet Union.
13 Feb.	End of state of emergency in Germany.
1 Apr.	Hitler sentenced to five years' fortress detention.
9 Apr.	Publication of Dawes Plan for provisional settlement of German reparation payments.
16 Apr.	German government accepts Dawes Plan.
4 May	Reichstag election (losses by government parties and SPD, gains by DNVP [Nationalists], Völkische Partei and KPD).
11 May	Electoral victory of Cartel des gauches in France; Herriot becomes Premier, Briand Foreign Minister.
17 May	Memel statute adopted.
16 July–16 Aug.	London conference adopts Dawes Plan.
29 Aug.	Dawes Plan approved by Reichstag.
2 Oct.	Geneva Protocol 'for peaceful settlement of international disputes'; ineffective, as rejected by British government.
24 Oct.	France recognizes Soviet Union.
29 Oct.	Massive electoral victory of Conservatives under Baldwin, who forms government in Nov.
7 Dec.	Reichstag election following dissolution (losses by radical parties).
17 Dec.	Hitler prematurely released.
Dec.	Military dictatorship in Lithuania.

1925

5 Jan.	Allies postpone evacuation of first Rhineland zone (Cologne), due on 10 Jan., on account of German violation of disarmament terms.
15 Jan.	Hans Luther forms first 'bourgeois bloc' government, including DNVP.
20 Jan., 9 Feb.	Stresemann addresses memorandum on security to British and French governments.
21 Jan.	Japan recognizes Soviet Union; neutrality pact.
27 Feb.	Re-foundation of NSDAP (Nazi Party).
28 Feb.	Ebert dies.
26 Apr.	Hindenburg elected President.
4 June	Conference of Ambassadors note to Germany concerning disarmament.
14 July	Evacuation of Ruhr district begins (completed 1 Aug.).
25 Aug.	Evacuation of Düsseldorf, Duisburg, Ruhrort.
5–16 Oct.	Locarno conference; treaties initialled.
25 Oct.	DNVP ministers withdraw from government.
27 Nov.	Reichstag approves Locarno treaties.
30 Nov.	Evacuation of Cologne zone begins (completed 31 Jan. 1926).
1 Dec.	Lacarno treaties signed in London.

1926

19 Jan.	Second Luther Cabinet (bourgeois minority government, without DNVP).

24 Apr.	German–Soviet treaty of friendship and neutrality ('Berlin treaty').
3–12 May	General strike in Britain ends in workers' defeat.
5 May	Hindenburg's 'flag decree'.
12 May	Luther government resigns over flag dispute; Marx forms bourgeois minority government.
12–15 May	Marshal Pilsudski's *coup d'état* in Poland.
20 June	Plebiscite on expropriation of former princes.
8 Sept.	Germany becomes member of League of Nations.
17 Sept.	Stresemann–Briand conversation at Thoiry.
6 Oct.	Seeckt dismissed from post as chief of army command.
19 Oct.–18 Nov.	Imperial conference in London: Dominions defined as 'autonomous communities . . . freely associated as members of the British Commonwealth of Nations'.
10 Dec.	Stresemann awarded Nobel Peace Prize.
17 Dec.	Marx Cabinet falls.

1927

29 Jan.	Fourth Marx Cabinet, this time including DNVP: second 'bourgeois bloc' government.
31 Jan.	Inter-Allied Military Commission withdrawn from Germany.
4–23 May	World economic conference at Geneva.
27 May	Anglo-Soviet relations broken off (British charges of espionage and propaganda); resumed Oct. 1929.
16 July	German law on employment exchanges and unemployment insurance.
17 Aug.	Franco-German commercial treaty.

1928

16–18 Jan.	Conference on proposed re-delimitation of *Länder* boundaries.
15 Feb.	Government coalition splits over Education Bill.
20 May	Reichstag election (gains by the left, losses by DNVP and bourgeois middle-ground parties).
29 June	'Great coalition' government formed by Hermann Müller (SPD).
27 Aug.	Briand-Kellogg pact outlawing war; 54 states accede by the end of 1929.
Sept.	League of Nations sessions dealing *inter alia* with evacuation of the Rhineland and question of a final reparations settlement.
Oct.–Dec.	Ruhr ironworks dispute.
Oct.	First Soviet Five-Year Plan.
20 Oct.	Alfred Hugenberg elected leader of DNVP.
9 Dec.	Monsignor Kaas leader of Centre Party.

1929

9 Feb.	Litvinov Protocol (non-aggression pacts linking the Soviet Union, Romania, Poland, Latvia and Estonia).
11 Feb.	Lateran treaties between Italy and the Holy See.
11 Feb.–7 June	Paris conference for revision of Dawes Plan, chaired by the US economist Owen D. Young.
24 Mar.	Parliamentary election in Italy under law of 12 May 1928 (single list): plebiscitary acceptance of fascist regime.
7 June	Young Plan signed by experts.
9 July	'Reich Committee' formed under Hugenberg and representing DNVP, Stahlhelm and NSDAP; beginning of campaign by nationalist right against the Young Plan.

16 July	Poincaré resigns.
6–31 Aug.	First conference at The Hague on the Young Plan.
4–5 Sept.	Briand proposes to the League of Nations Assembly his plan for a 'united States of Europe' (customs and economic union).
3 Oct.	Death of Stresemann.
end of Oct.	Crash on New York stock exchange; beginning of world economic depression.
6 Dec.	Memorandum against Young Plan by Schacht, president of the Reichsbank.
21 Dec.	Stalin's fiftieth birthday celebrations; beginning of the 'personality cult'.
22 Dec.	Failure of nationalist petition against the Young Plan.

1930

3–20 Jan.	Second conference at The Hague on the Young Plan.
21 Jan.–22 Apr.	London naval conference.
23 Jan.	Wilhelm Frick first Nazi member of a government (Thuringia).
7 Mar.	Schacht resigns as Reichsbank president; succeeded by Hans Luther.
12 Mar.	Reichstag adopts Young Plan legislation.
27 Mar.	Müller Cabinet resigns.
29 Mar.	Heinrich Brüning appointed Chancellor; first presidential government.
17 May	Briand's memorandum on Europe.
30 June	Evacuation of Rhineland by Allied troops completed ahead of scheduled date.
16 July	Reichstag annuls government decree on 'safeguarding the national economy and finances', and is dissolved.
14 Sept.	Reichstag election; large gains especially by NSDAP.
25 Sept.	'Legality oath' by Hitler at Leipzig trial of Reichswehr officers from Ulm, accused of high treason.
1 Dec.	Several (deflationary) emergency decrees.

1931

Feb.	Nearly 5 million unemployed.
20 Mar.	German government announces plan for a customs union with Austria, which is prevented mainly by French veto.
13 Apr.	Fall of Spanish monarchy.
11 May	Failure of Austrian Credit-Anstalt threatens economic and political stability throughout Europe.
20 June	President Herbert Hoover proposes a year's moratorium on all international debts.
6 July	Hoover moratorium declared.
13 July	Failure of Darmstädter und Nationalbank (Danat-Bank); banking crisis in Germany.
18 Sept.	The Japanese capture Mukden and occupy Manchuria.
6 Oct.	Further emergency decree on 'safeguarding the national economy and finances'.
9 Oct.	Second Brüning Cabinet.
11 Oct.	Rally of the 'national opposition' at Bad Harzburg (the 'Harzburg front').
8 Dec.	Fourth emergency decree on 'safeguarding the national economy and finances'.
11 Dec.	The Statute of Westminster grants full self-government to the British Dominions.

| 16 Dec. | Formation of the 'iron front' (SPD, ADGB [trade unions], workers' sporting associations, and the Reichsbanner Schwarz-Rot-Gold). |

1932

Feb.	German unemployment reaches its peak (6,128,000).
2 Feb.	Disarmament conference opens at Geneva.
18 Feb.	Japan creates the puppet state of Manchukuo out of occupied Manchuria.
10 Apr.	Hindenburg re-elected President.
13 Apr.	SA and SS banned.
24 Apr.	Landtag elections in Prussia, Bavaria, Württemberg, Anhalt and Hamburg. Large NSDAP gains everywhere; the 'Weimar coalition' under Otto Braun (SPD), governing in Prussia since 1925, loses its majority.
12 May	Groener forced to resign from the post of Defence minister.
20 May	Dollfuss government in Austria.
30 May	Brüning Cabinet resigns. Government of 'national concentration' formed by Franz von Papen, with Schleicher as Defence Minister.
4 June	Reichstag dissolved.
16 June	Ban on SA lifted.
16 June–9 July	Lausanne conference; end of reparations.
5 July	Antonio Salazar becomes Prime Minister of Portugal.
20 July	'Prussia coup' by von Papen and Schleicher. Interim Prussian government dismissed and Papen appointed Reich Commissioner. The deposed government appeals to the High Court.
22 July	Germany withdraws from the Geneva conference on disarmament.
25 July	Soviet-Polish non-aggression pact.
31 July	Reichstag election; NSDAP the largest party.
13 Aug.	Hindenburg refuses Hitler's demand to be appointed Chancellor.
4 Sept.	Emergency decree 'to reanimate the economy'.
12 Sept.	Reichstag passes a vote of no confidence in the Papen government, and is dissolved.
25 Oct.	Court verdict on the Prussian coup: Reich Commissioner to continue exercising authority in Prussia; Otto Braun government to represent Prussia in the Reichsrat.
6 Nov.	Reichstag election; NSDAP loses votes but remains largest party.
17 Nov.	Papen Cabinet resigns.
29 Nov.	Franco-Soviet non-aggression pact.
2 Dec.	Kurt von Schleicher forms presidential government.
11 Dec.	Five-power declaration acknowledging Germany's equality of rights in respect of disarmament.

1933

4 Jan.	Hitler and Papen meet in Cologne: soundings for the formation of a joint Cabinet.
28 Jan.	Schleicher resigns, having lost Hindenburg's confidence.
30 Jan.	Hitler appointed Chancellor at the head of a presidential government.

Bibliography

Note

(1) Works published before 1970 are cited sparingly, as the earlier literature can easily be traced through the bibliographies of later works.
(2) Subtitles are only given when they elucidate the main title.
(3) As a rule the latest edition is cited; occasionally also the date of the first edition, when it is of importance for the history of research.
(4) In cases where English translations of German works exist, these are cited in preference to the originals, but are preceded by an asterisk.

A   Sources

I   Documents on Foreign Policy and Treaty Texts

1 *Akten zur Deutschen Auswärtigen Politik* (ADAP) *1918–1945: Serie A, 1918–1925* (1982 ff.) 9 vols to date (to 6 April 1924); *Serie B, 1925–1933* (1966 ff.), 21 vols.
2 *Documents on British Foreign Policy, 1919–1938: Series I, 1919–1925* (1947 ff.), 27 vols to date; *Series IA, 1925–1929* (1966 ff.), 7 vols to date; *Series II, 1929–1938* (1946 ff.), so far 21 vols.
3 *Documents diplomatiques français 1932–1939, Série 1, 1932–1935* (1964 ff.) vols 1 ff.
4 *Dokumenty vneshney politiki SSSR* (1957 ff.), 21 vols to date (1917–38).
5 *Foreign Relations of the United States* (1935 ff.), 37 vols (1920–33).
6 *Papers relating to the Foreign Relations of the United States, Supplement, Paris Peace Conference 1919*, 13 vols (1942 ff.). 261.
7 *I Documenti diplomatici Italiani, Serie 6, 1918–1922* (1956 ff.), 2 vols to date; *Serie 7, 1922–1935* (1953 ff.), so far 11 vols.
8 *Documents diplomatiques belges 1920–1940* (1964 ff.), vols 1–3 (1920–36).
9 *Deutsch-sowjetische Beziehungen von den Verhandlungen in Brest-Litovsk bis zum Abschluss des Rapallo-Vertrages*, 2 vols (East Berlin, 1967–71).
10 *Locarno-Konferenz 1925. Eine Dokumentensammlung* (East Berlin, 1962).
11 *Der Friedensvertrag zwischen Deutschland u. den Alliierten und Assoziierten Mächten nebst dem Schlussprotokoll und der Vereinbarung betr. die militärische Besetzung der Rheinlande. Amtlicher Text der Entente u. amtliche deutsche Übertragung. Im Auftrage des Auswärtigen Amtes* (Charlottenburg, 1919). (English, French and German texts of the Treaty of Versailles.)
12 *Konferenzen und Verträge. Vertrags-Ploetz* (. . .), *Teil II*, 4. Bd.: Neueste Zeit 1914–1959, 2nd edn (Würzburg, 1959).

II   Collections of Documents; Year-Books

13 *Akten der Reichskanzlei, Weimarer Republik* (Boppard, 1968 ff.):

Das Kabinett Scheidemann, ed. by H. Schulze (1971).

Das Kabinett Bauer, ed. by A. Golecki (1980).

Das Kabinett Müller I, ed, by M. Vogt (1971).

Das Kabinett Fehrenbach, ed. by P. Wulf (1972).

Die Kabinette Wirth I u. II, ed. by I. Schulze-Bidlingmaier, 2 vols (1973).

Das Kabinett Cuno, ed. by K.-H. Harbeck (1968).

Die Kabinette Stresemann I u. II, ed. by K. D. Erdmann and M. Vogt, 2 vols (1978).

Die Kabinette Marx I u. II, ed. by G. Abramowski, 2 vols (1973).

Die Kabinette Luther I u. II, ed. by K.-H. Minuth, 2 vols (1977).

Die Kabinette Marx III u. IV, ed. by G. Abramowski, 2 vols (1988).

Das Kabinett Müller II, ed. by M. Vogt, 2 vols (1970).

Die Kabinette Brüning I u. II, ed. by T. Koops, 3 vols (1982/90).

Das Kabinett von Papen, ed. by K.-H. Minuth, 2 vols (1989).

Das Kabinett von Schleicher, ed. by A. Golecki (1986).

14 *Quellen zur Geschichte des Parlamentarismus und der politischen Parteien* (Düsseldorf, 1959 ff.):

First series: *Von der konstitutionellen Monarchie zur parlamentarischen Republik.*

Vol. 2, *Die Regierung des Prinzen Max von Baden*, ed. by E. Matthias and R. Morsey (1962).

Vol. 6, *Die Regierung der Volksbeauftragten 1918/19*, introd. by E. Matthias, ed. by S. Miller with the assistance of H. Potthoff (1969).

Vol. 10 *Die Regierung Eisner 1918/19. Ministerprotokolle und Dokumente*, ed. by F. J. Bauer (1987).

Second Series: *Militär und Politik.*

Vol. 2, *Zwischen Revolution und Kapp-Putsch. Militär und Innenpolitik 1918–1920*, ed. by H. Hürten (1977).

Vol. 3, *Die Anfänge der Ära Seeckt, Militär und Innenpolitik 1920–1922*, ed. by H. Hürten (1979).

Vol. 4, *Das Krisenjahr 1923. Militär und Innenpolitik 1922–1924*, ed. by H. Hürten (1980).

Third Series: *Die Weimarer Republik*

Vol. 1, *Erinnerungen und Dokumente von Joh. Victor Bredt 1914 bis 1933*, ed. by M. Schumacher (1970).

Vol. 2, *Parlamentspraxis in der Weimarer Republik. Die Tagungsberichte der Vereinigung der deutschen Parlamentsdirektoren 1925 bis 1933*, ed. by M. Schumacher (1974).

Vol. 3, *Staat und NSDAP 1930–1932. Quellen zur Ära Brüning*, introd. by G. Schulz, ed. by I. Maurer and U. Wengst, 2 vols (1977).

Vol. 4, *Politik und Wirtschaft in der Krise. 1930–1932. Quellen zur Ära Brüning*, introd. by G. Schulz, ed. by I. Maurer and U. Wengst, 2 vols (1980).

Vol. 5, *Linksliberalismus in der Weimarer Republik. Die Führungsgremien der Deutschen Demokratischen Partei und der Deutschen Staatspartei 1918–1933*, intro. by L. Albertin, ed. by K. Wegner (1980).

Vol. 6, *Die Generallinie. Rundschreiben des Zentralkomitees der KPD an die Bezirke 1929–1933*, ed. by H. Weber (1981).

Vol. 7, *Die SPD-Fraktion in der Nationalversammlung 1919–1920*, introd. by H. Potthoff, ed. by H. Potthoff and H. Weber (1986).

15 *Quellen zur Geschichte der deutschen Gewerkschaftsbewegung im 20. Jahrhundert* (Cologne, 1985 ff.):

Vol. 1, *Die Gewerkschaften in Weltkrieg und Revolution 1914–1919*, ed. K. Schönhoven (1985).

Vol. 2, *Die Gewerkschaften in den Anfangsjahren der Republik 1919–1923*, ed. by M. Ruck (1985).

Vol. 3, *Die Gewerkschaften von der Stabilisierung bis zur Weltwirtschaftskrise 1924–1930*, ed. by H. A. Kukuck and D. Schiffmann (1986).

Vol. 4, *Die Gewerkschaften in der Endphase der Republik 1930–1933*, ed. by P. Jahn (1988).

16 *Quellen zur Geschichte der Rätebewegung in Deutschland 1918/19* (1968 ff.):

Vol. 1, *Der Zentralrat der deutschen sozialistischen Republik. Vom ersten zum zweiten Rätekongress*, ed. by E. Kolb with the assistance of R. Rürup (Leiden, 1968).

Vol. 2, *Regionale und lokale Räteorganisationen in Württemberg 1918/19*, ed. by E. Kolb and K. Schönhoven (Düsseldorf, 1976).

Vol. 3, *Arbeiter-, Soldaten- und Volksräte in Baden 1918/19*, ed. P. Brandt and R. Rürup (Düsseldorf, 1980).

17 *Ursachen und Folgen. Vom deutschen Zusammenbruch 1918 und 1945 bis zur staatlichen Neuordnung Deutschlands in der Gegenwart*, ed. by H. Michaelis and E. Schraepler with the assistance of G. Scheel, Vols 1–9 (Berlin, 1958 ff.) (to 1933).

18 *Dokumente und Materialien zur Geschichte der deutschen Arbeiterbewegung*, ed. by Institut für Marxismus-Leninismus beim Zentralkomitee der SED, Series 2, 1914–1945 (1957 ff.).

19 Benz, W. (ed.), *Politik in Bayern 1919–1933. Berichte des württembergischen Gesandten Carl Moser von Filseck* (Stuttgart, 1971).

20 Berthold, L., and Neef, H., *Militarismus und Opportunismus gegen die Novemberrevolution. Das Bündnis der rechten SPD-Führung mit der Obersten Heeresleitung November u. Dezember 1918. Eine Dokumentation* (East Berlin, 1958; rev. and enlarged 2nd edn 1978).

20a Deuerlein, E. (ed.), *Der Hitler-Putsch*. Bayerische Dokumente zum 8/9 November 1923 (Stuttgart, 1962).

21 Flemming, J., Krohn, C.-D., Stegmann, D., and Witt, P.-C. (eds), *Die Republik von Weimar*, 2 vols (Königstein and Düsseldorf, 1979).

21a Flemming, J., Saul, K. and Witt, P.-C. (eds), *Familienleben im Schatten der Krise. Dokumente und Analysen zur Sozialgeschichte der Weimarer Republik* (Düsseldorf, 1988).

22 Holl, K., and Wild, A. (eds), *Ein Demokrat kommentiert Weimar. Die Berichte Hellmut von Gerlachs an die Carnegie-Friedensstiftung in New York 1922–1930* (Bremen, 1973).

23 Hubatsch, W., *Hindenburg und der Staat. Aus den Papieren des Generalfeldmarschalls und Reichspräsidenten von 1878 bis 1934* (Göttingen, 1966).

24 Huber, E. R. (ed.), *Dokumente zur deutschen Verfassungsgeschichte*, Vol. 3: *Dokumente der Novemberrevolution und der Weimarer Republik 1918–1933* (Stuttgart, 1966).

24a Huber, E.R., and Huber, W. (eds), *Staat und Kirche in der Zeit der Weimarer Republik* (West Berlin, 1988).

25 Jäckel, E., and Kuhn, A. (eds), *Hitler. Sämtliche Aufzeichnungen 1905–1924* (Stuttgart, 1980).

26 Kaes, A. (ed.), *Weimarer Republik. Manifeste und Dokumente zur deutschen Literatur 1918–1933* (Stuttgart, 1983).

27 Kahlenberg, F. P. (ed.), *Die Berichte Eduard Davids als Reichsvertreter in Hessen 1921–1927* (Wiesbaden, 1970).

28 Könnemann, E. (ed.), *Arbeiterklasse siegt über Kapp und Lüttwitz. Quellen* (. . .) (East Berlin, 1971).

28a Longerich, P. (ed.), *Die Erste Republik. Dokumente zur Geschichte des Weimarer Staates* (Munich, 1992).

29 Mantoux, P. (ed.), *Les Délibérations du Conseil des Quatre (24 mars–28 juin 1919)*, 2 vols (Paris, 1955).

30 Michalka, W., and Niedhart, G. (eds), *Die ungeliebte Republik. Dokumentation zur Innen- und Aussenpolitik Weimars 1918–1933* (Munich, 1980).

31 Morsey, R., and Ruppert, K. (eds),*Die Protokolle der Reichstagsfraktion der Deutschen Zentrumspartei 1920–1925* (Mainz, 1981).

32 Morsey, R. (ed.), *Die Protokolle der Reichstagsfraktion und des Fraktionsvorstandes der Deutschen Zentrumspartei 1926–1933* (Mainz, 1969).

33 Richarz, M. (ed.), *Jüdisches Leben in Deutschland. Selbstzeugnisse zur Sozialgeschichte 1918–1945* (Stuttgart, 1982).

34 Ritter, G. A., and Miller, S.(eds), *Die deutsche Revolution 1918–1919. Dokumente*, 2nd rev. and enlarged edn (Hamburg, 1975).

35 Schüddekopf, O.-E., *Das Heer und die Republik. Quellen zur Politik der Reichswehrführung 1918–1933* (Frankfurt, 1955).

36 Schulze, H. (ed.), *Anpassung oder Widerstand? Aus den Akten des Parteivorstands der deutschen Sozialdemokratie 1932/1933* (Bonn–Bad Godesberg, 1975).

37 Stehkämper, H. (ed.), *Der Nachlass des Reichskanzlers Wilhelm Marx*, 4 vols (Cologne, 1968).

38 Treuu, W., *Deutsche Parteiprogramme seit 1861*, 4th edn (Göttingen, 1968).

39 Tyrell, A., *Führer befiehl . . . Selbstzeugnisse aus der 'Kampfzeit' der NSDAP* (Düsseldorf, 1969).

40 Vogt, M. (ed.), *Die Entstehung des Youngplans. Dargest. vom Reichsarchiv 1931–1933* (Boppard, 1970).

41 Weber, H. (ed.), *Der Gründungsparteitag der KPD. Protokoll und Materialen* (Frankfurt, 1969).

41a Weber, M., *Zur Neuordnung Deutschlands. Schriften und Reden 1918–1920*, ed. by W.J. Mommsen assisted by W. Schwentker (Tübingen, 1988) (Vol. I/16: Max Weber-Gesamtausgabe).

42 *Schulthess' Europäischer Geschichtskalender*, new series, Vols 34–49 covering 1918–33 (Munich, 1922–34).

43 *Deutscher Geschichtskalender*, founded by K. Wippermann, Vols 35–49 covering 1919–33 (Leipzig, n.d.). Supplementary vols: *Die deutsche Revolution*, 2 vols (1919); *Vom Waffenstillstand zum Frieden von Versailles* (1919); *Die deutsche Reichsverfassung vom 11. Aug. 1919* (1919).

III Stenographic Reports and Statistics

44 *Allgemeiner Kongress der Arbeiter- und Soldatenräte Deutschlands vom 16. bis 21. Dezember 1918 im Abgeordnetenhaus in Berlin. Stenographische Berichte* (Berlin, 1919; repr. Glashütten, 1972).

45 *II. Kongress der Arbeiter-, Baueren- und Soldatenräte Deutschlands am 8. bis 14. April 1919 im Herrenhaus zu Berlin. Stenographisches Protokoll* (Berlin, 1919; repr. Glashütten, 1975).

46 *Verhandlungen der verfassungsgebenden Deutschen Nationalversammlung. Stenographische Berichte*, vols 326–43 (Berlin, 1919–20).

47 *Verhandlungen des Deutschen Reichstages, 1920–1933*, vols 344–457 (Berlin, 1920 ff.).

48 *Statistisches Jahrbuch für das Deutsche Reich*, ed. by Statistischem Reichsamt, vols 34 (Berlin, 1919) to 53 (Berlin, 1934). Cf. no. 304.

IV Selected Memoirs, Diaries and Letters

49 Braun. O., *Von Weimar zu Hitler* (New York, 1940; 2nd edn, Hamburg, 1949).

*50 Brecht, A., *The Political Education of Arnold Brecht. An Autobiography, 1884–1970* (Princeton, NJ, 1970).

[Bredt: see no. 14, third series, vol. 1]

51 Brüning, H., *Memoiren 1918–1934* (Stuttgart, 1970).
52 Brüning, H., *Reden und Aufsätze eines deutschen Staatsmanns*, ed. by W. Vernekohl with the assistance of R. Morsey (Münster, 1968).
53 Curtius, J., *Sechs Jahre Minister der Deutschen Republik* (Heidelberg, 1948).
54 D'Abernon (Edgar Vincent, Lord), *An Ambassador of Peace. Pages from the Diary of Viscount D'Abernon, Berlin, 1920–1926* (London, 1929–30).
55 Ebert, F., *Schriften, Aufzeichnungen, Reden*, ed. by F. Ebert jun., 2 vols (Dresden, 1926).
56 Feder, E., *Heute sprach ich mit . . . Tagebücher eines Berliner Publizisten 1926–1932*, ed. by C. Lowenthal-Hensel and A. Paucher (Stuttgart, 1971).
57 Gessler, O., *Reichswehrpolitik in der Weimarer Zeit*, ed. by K. Sendtner (Stuttgart, 1958).
*58 Goebbels, J., *The Early Goebbels Diaries. The Journal of Joseph Goebbels from 1925–1926*, ed. by H. Heiber (London and New York, 1963).
59 Groener, W., *Lebenserinnerungen. Jugend, Generalstab, Weltkrieg*, ed. by F. Frhr. Hiller von Gaertringen (Göttingen, 1957).
60 Heuss, T., *Erinnerungen 1905–1933* (Tübingen, 1963).

Hindenburg: see no. 23

Hitler: see no. 25

61 Keil, W., *Erlebnisse eines Sozialdemokraten*, 2 vols (Stuttgart, 1947–8).
*62 Kessler, H. K. Graf von, *The Diaries of a Cosmopolitan. Count Harry Kessler, 1918–1937*, ed. by C. Kessler (London, 1971).
63 Köhler, H., *Lebenserinnerungen des Politikers und Staatsmannes 1878–1949*, ed. by J. Becker with the assistance of F. Zilken (Stuttgart, 1964).
*64 Krebs, A., *The Infancy of Nazism. The Memoirs of ex-Gauleiter Albert Krebs, 1923–1933*, ed. by W. S. Allen (New York, 1976).
65 Löbe, P., *Erinnerungen eines Reichstagspräsidenten* (West Berlin, 1949).
66 Luppe, H., *Mein Leben*, edited from his papers by the Stadtarchiv Nürnberg in collaboration with M. Heinsen-Luppe (Nuremberg, 1977).
67 Luther. H., *Politiker ohne Partei. Erinnerungen* (Stuttgart, 1960).
68 Luther, H., *Vor dem Abgrund. 1930–1933. Reichsbankpräsident in Krisenzeiten* (West Berlin, 1964).
69 Meissner, O., *Staatssekretär unter Ebert–Hindenburg–Hitler* (Hamburg, 1950).
70 Noske, G., *Erlebtes aus Aufstieg und Niedergang einer Demokratie* (Offenbach, 1947).
71 Papen, F. von, *Vom Scheitern einer Demokratie 1930–1933* (Mainz, 1968).
72 Pünder, H., *Politik in der Reichskanzlei. Aufzeichnungen aus den Jahren 1929–1932*, ed. by T. Vogelsang (Stuttgart, 1961).
73 Pünder, H., *Von Preussen nach Europa. Lebenserinnerungen* (Stuttgart, 1968).
74 Radbruch, G., *Briefe*, ed. by E. Wolf (Göttingen, 1968).
75 Radbruch, G., *Der innere Weg. Aufriss meines Lebens* (Stuttgart, 1951).
76 Rathenau, W., *Hauptwerke und Gespräche*, ed. by E. Schulin (Munich and Heidelberg, 1977) (Vol 2: *Walther Rathenau – Gesamtausgabe*).
77 Rathenau, W., *Ein preussischer Europäer. Briefe*, ed. by M. von Eynern (West Berlin, 1955).

78 Rathenau, W., *Tagebuch 1907–1922*, ed. by H. Pogge von Strandmann (Düsseldorf, 1967).

*79 Schacht, H., *My First Seventy-six Years. Autobiography* (London, 1955).

80 Schmidt, P., *Statist auf diplomatischer Bühne 1923–1945* (Bonn, 1949). Abridged trans.: *Hitler's Interpreter* (London, 1951).

81 Schwerin von Krosigk, L. Graf, *Staatsbankrott. Die Geschichte der Finanzpolitik des deutschen Reiches 1920–1945* (Göttingen, 1974).

82 Severing, C., *Mein Lebensweg*, 2 vols (Cologne, 1950).

*83 Stresemann, G., *Diaries, Letters and Papers*, ed. by E. Sutton, 3 vols (London, 1935–40).

84 Treviranus, G. R., *Das Ende von Weimar. Heinrich Brüning und seine Zeit* (Düsseldorf and Vienna, 1968).

B Secondary Works

I Handbooks and General Accounts

85 Aubin, H., and Zorn, W. (eds), *Handbuch der deutschen Wirtschafts- und Sozialgeschichte*, vol. 2 (Stuttgart, 1976).

86 Bracher, K. D., *Die Auflösung der Weimarer Republik. Eine Studie zum Problem des Machtverfalls in der Demokratie* (Villingen, 1955; 6th edn, Königstein and Düsseldorf, 1978).

87 Bracher, K. D., *Die Krise Europas 1917–1975* (West Berlin, 1976).

88 Cipolla, C. M., and Borchardt, K. (eds), *Europäische Wirtschaftsgeschichte*, Vol. 5: *Die europäischen Volkswirtschaften im 20. Jahrhundert* (Stuttgart and New York, 1980).

89 Conze, W., 'Die Weimarer Republik', in P. Rassow (ed.), *Deutsche Geschichte im Überblick* (Stuttgart, 1953; 3rd edn 1973).

90 Conze, W., and Raupach, H. (eds), *Die Staats- und Wirtschaftskrise des Deutschen Reichs 1929/33* (Stuttgart, 1967).

91 Craig, G. A., *Germany 1866–1945*, Oxford History of Modern Europe, Vol. 5 (Oxford, 1978).

92 Dederke, K., *Reich und Republik. Deutschland 1917–1933*, 4th edn (Stuttgart, 1981).

93 Erdmann, K. D., 'Die Geschichte der Weimarer Republik als Problem der Wissenschaft', *VfZg*, vol. 3 (1955), pp. 1–19.

94 Erdmann, K. D., 'Die Weimarer Republik', B. Gebhardt, *Handbuch der deutschen Geschichte*, 9th edn, Vol. IV/1 (Stuttgart, 1973).

95 Erdmann, K. D., and Schulze, H. (eds), *Weimar. Selbstpreisgabe einer Demokratie* (Düsseldorf, 1980).

96 Eschenburg, T., *Die improvisierte Demokratie* (Munich, 1963).

*97 Eyck, E., *A History of the Weimar Republic*, 2 vols (Cambridge, Mass., 1962–3).

98 Friedensburg, F., *Die Weimarer Republik* (West Berlin, 1946; 2nd edn 1957).

99 Gessner, D., *Das Ende der Weimarer Republik. Fragen, Methoden und Ergebnisse interdisziplinärer Forschung* (Darmstadt, 1978).

100 Graml, H., *Europa zwischen den Kriegen*, 5th edn (Munich, 1982).

101 Heiber, H., *Die Republik von Weimar*, 15th edn (Munich, 1982).

102 Hermens, F. A., and Schieder, T. (eds), *Staat, Wirtschaft und Politik in der Weimarer Republik. Festschrift für Heinrich Brüning* (West Berlin, 1967).

103 Holborn, H., *A History of Modern Germany*, Vol. 3:*1840–1945* (New York, 1959–69).

104 Huber, E. R., *Deutsche Verfassungsgeschichte seit 1789*, Vol. 6: *Die Weimarer Ver-*

fassung (Stuttgart, 1981); Vol. 7: *Ausbau, Schutz und Untergang der Weimarer Republik* (Stuttgart, 1984); cf. no. 149.

105 Institut für Marxismus-Leninismus beim ZK der SED, *Geschichte der deutschen Arbeiterbewegung*, Vols 3 (1917–23) and 4 (1924–January 1933) (East Berlin, 1966).
106 Jasper, G. (ed.), *Von Weimar zu Hitler 1930–1933* (Cologne, 1968).
107 Jeserich, K., Pohl, H., and Unruh, G.-C. von (eds), *Deutsche Verwaltungsgeschichte*, Vol. 4: *Das Reich als Republik und in der Zeit des Nationalsozialismus* (Stuttgart, 1985).
107a Kershaw, I. (ed.), *Weimar: Why did German Democracy fail?* (London, 1990).
108 Köhler, H., *Geschichte der Weimarer Republik* (West Berlin, 1981).
109 Mann, G., *Deutsche Geschichte 1919–1945*, 15th edn (Frankfurt, 1980).
109a Mommsen, H., *Die verspielte Freiheit. Der Weg der Republik von Weimar in den Untergang 1918 bis 1933* (West Berlin, 1989).
*110 Nolte, E., *Three Faces of Fascism. Action Française, Italian Fascism, National Socialism* (London and New York, 1965–6).
111 Overesch, M., and Saal, F. W., *Chronik deutscher Zeitgeschichte*, Vol. 1: *Die Weimarer Republik* (Düsseldorf, 1982).
*112 Rosenberg, A., *A History of the German Republic* (London, 1936).
113 Ruge, W., *Deutschland von 1917 bis 1933*, 2nd edn (East Berlin, 1969).
114 Schieder, T. (ed.), *Handbuch der Europäischen Geschichte*, Vol. 7, pts 1 and 2: *Europa im Zeitalter der Weltmächte* (Stuttgart, 1979).
115 Schulz, G., *Faschismus-Nationalsozialismus. Versionen und theoretische Kontroversen 1922–1972* (Frankfurt, West Berlin and Vienna, 1974).
116 Schulz, G., *Aufstieg des Nationalsozialismus. Krise und Revolution in Deutschland* (Frankfurt, 1975).
117 Schulze, H., *Weimar. Deutschland 1917–1933* (West Berlin, 1982).
118 Schwarz, A., 'Die Weimarer Republik', in O. Brandt, A. O. Meyer and L. Just (eds), *Handbuch der deutschen Geschichte*, vol. 4/III (Constance, 1958; 2nd edn, Frankfurt, 1964).
119 Stampfer, F., *Die ersten 14 Jahre der Deutschen Republik* (Offenbach, 1947).
120 Stürmer, M. (ed.), *Die Weimarer Republik* (Königstein, 1980).
121 Tormin, W. (ed.), *Die Weimarer Republik*, 12th edn (Hanover, 1978).

II Bibliographies

112 ABC-Clio Information Services (ed.), *The Weimar Republic. A Historical Bibliography* (Santa Barbara, Calif., Denver, Colo, and Oxford, 1984).
123 Benz, W., *Quellen zur Zeitgeschichte* (= *Deutsche Geschichte seit dem Ersten Weltkrieg*, Vol. 3) (Stuttgart, 1973).
124 *Bibliographie zur Zeitgeschichte*, supplement to *Vierteljahrshefte für Zeitgeschichte* (Munich, 1953 ff.).
125 *Bibliographie zur Zeitgeschichte 1953–1980*, ed. by T. Vogelsang and H. Auerbach, Vols 1 and 2 (Munich and New York, 1982).
126 Bracher, K. D., Jacobson, H.-A., and Funke, M. (eds), *Bibliographie zur Politik in Theorie und Praxis*, rev. edn (Düsseldorf, 1976).
127 Eisfeld, G., and Koszyk, K., *Die Presse der deutschen Sozialdemokratie*, 2nd edn (Bonn, 1980).
128 Gunzenhäuser, M., *Die Pariser Friedenskonferenz 1919 und die Friedensverträge 1919–1920* (Frankfurt, 1970).
129 Hess, J. C., and Steensel van der Aa, E. van, *Bibliographie zum deutschen Liberalismus* (Göttingen, 1981).

130 *Jahresberichte für Deutsche Geschichte*, new series, ed. by Institut für Geschichte an der Deutschen Akademie der Wissenschaften (East Berlin, 1949 ff.).
131 *Jahresbibliographie der Bibliothek für Zeitgeschichte* (Frankfurt, 1960 ff.; Munich, 1973 ff.).
132 Klotzbach, K., *Bibliographie zur Geschichte der deutschen Arbeiterbewegung 1914–1945*, 3rd edn (Bonn, 1981).
133 Meyer, G. P., *Bibliographie zur deutschen Revolution 1918/19* (Göttingen, 1977).
134 Schumacher, M., *Wahlen und Abstimmungen 1918–1933* (Düsseldorf, 1976).
135 Stachura, P. D., *The Weimar Era and Hitler, 1918–1933* (Oxford, 1977).
136 Ullmann, H.-P., *Bibliographie zur Geschichte der deutschen Parteien und Interessenverbände* (Göttingen, 1978).
137 Walsdorff, M., *Bibliographie Gustav Stresemann* (Düsseldorf, 1972).

III   End of the First World War; Revolution; Reich Constitution

138 Apelt, W., *Geschichte der Weimarer Verfassung* (Munich, 1946; 2nd edn 1964).
138a Bertrand, Ch., *Revolutionary Situations in Europe 1917–1922: Germany, Italy, and Austria Hungary* (Montreal, 1976).
139 Bieber, H.-J., *Gewerkschaften in Krieg und Revolution*, 2 vols (Hamburg, 1981).
140 Bosl, K. (ed.), *Bayern im Umbruch. Die Revolution von 1918, ihre Voraussetzungen, ihr Verlauf und ihre Folgen* (Munich, 1969).
141 Carsten, F. L., *Revolution in Central Europe, 1918–1919* (London, 1972).
142 Drabkin, J. S., *Die Novemberrevolution 1918 in Deutschland* (East Berlin, 1968).
143 Ehlert, H. G., *Die wirtschaftliche Zentralbehörde des Deutschen Reiches 1914 bis 1919. Das problem der 'Gemeinwirtschaft' in Krieg und Frieden* (Wiesbaden, 1982).
114 Elben, W., *Das Problem der Kontinuität in der deutschen Revolution. Die Politik der Staatssekretäre und der militärischen Führung vom November 1918 bis February 1919* (Düsseldorf, 1965).
145 Feldman, G. D., *Army, Industry and Labor in Germany, 1914–1918* (Princeton, NJ, 1966).
146 Feldman, G. D., 'Economic and Social Problems of the German Demobilization, 1918/19', *JMH*, vol. 47 (1975), pp. 1–47.
147 Feldman, G. D., Kolb, E., and Rürup, R., 'Die Massenbewegungen der Arbeiterschaft in Deutschland am Ende des ersten Weltkrieges (1917–1920)', *PVS*, vol. 13 (1972), pp. 84–105.
148 Heinemann, U., *Die verdrängte Niederlage. Politische Öffentlichkeit und Kriegsschuldfrage in der Weimarer Republik* (Göttingen, 1983).
149 Huber, E. R., *Deutsche Verfassungsgeschichte seit 1789*, Vol. 5: *Weltkrieg, Revolution und Reichserneuerung 1914–1919* (Stuttgart, 1978).
150 Institut für Marxismus-Leninismus beim ZK der SED (ed.), *Illustrierte Geschichte der Novemberrevolution in Deutschland* (East Berlin, 1968). New edn entitled *Illustrierte Geschichte der deutschen Novemberrevolution 1918/19* (East Berlin, 1978).
151 Kluge, U., *Soldatenräte und Revolution. Studien zur Militärpolitik in Deutschland 1918/19* (Göttingen, 1975).
152 Kluge, U., *Die deutsche Revolution 1918/19* (Frankfurt, 1985).
153 Kolb, E., *Die Arbeiterräte in der deutschen Innenpolitik 1918 bis 1919* (Düsseldorf, 1962; 2nd edn, Frankfurt, Berlin and Vienna, 1978).
154 Kolb, E., (ed.), *Vom Kaiserreich zur Weimarer Republik* (Cologne, 1972).
155 Kolb, E., 'Internationale Rahmenbedingungen einer demokratischen Neuordnung in Deutschland 1918/19', in L. Albertin and W. Link (eds), *Politische Parteien auf dem Weg zur parlamentarischen Demokratie in Deutschland* (Düsseldorf, 1981), pp. 147–76.

156 Lehnert, D., *Sozialdemokratie und Novemberrevolution. Die Neuordnungsdebatte 1918/19 in der politischen Publizistik von SPD and USPD* (Frankfurt and New York, 1953).

157 Lösche, P., *Der Bolschewismus im Urteil der deutschen Sozialdemokratie* (West Berlin, 1967).

158 Materna, I., *Der Vollzugsrat der Berliner Arbeiter- und Soldatenräte 1918/19* (East Berlin, 1978).

159 Matthias, E., *Zwischen Räten und Geheimräten. Die deutsche Revolutionsregierung 1918–1919* (Düsseldorf, 1970).

160 Mehnert, G., *Evangelische Kirche und Politik 1917–1919* (Düsseldorf, 1959).

161 Miller, S., *Die Bürde der Macht. Die deutsche Sozialdemokratie 1918–1920* (Düsseldorff, 1978).

162 Mosse, W. E. (ed.), *Deutsches Judentum in Krieg und Revolution 1916–1923* (Tübingen, 1971).

163 Muth, H., 'Die Entstehung der Bauern- und Landarbeiterräte im November 1918 und die Politik des Bundes der Landwirte', *VfZg*, vol. 21 (1973), pp. 1–38.

164 Oeckel, H., *Die revolutionäre Volkswehr 1918/19* (East Berlin, 1968).

165 Oertzen, P. von, *Betriebsräte in der Novemberrevolution* (Düsseldorf, 1963; 2nd edn, Bonn, 1976).

166 Portner, E., *Die Verfassungspolitik der Liberalen 1919* (Bonn, 1973).

167 Potthoff, H., 'Das Weimarer Verfassungswerk und die deutsche Linke', *AfS*, vol. 12 (1972), pp. 433–83.

168 Rakenius, G. W., *Wilhelm Groener als Erster Generalquartiermeister. Die Politik der Obersten Heeresleitung 1918/19* (Boppard, 1977).

169 Renouvin, P., *L'Armistice de Rethondes: 11 novembre 1918* (Paris, 1968).

170 Rürup, R., *Probleme der Revolution in Deutschland 1918–19* (Wiesbaden, 1968).

171 Rürup, R. (ed.), *Arbeiter- und Soldatenräte im rheinisch-westfälischen Industriegebiet* (Wuppertal, 1975).

172 Schieck, H., *Der Kampf um die deutsche Wirtschaftspolitik nach dem Novemberumsturz 1918*, thesis (Heidelberg, 1958).

173 Schmidt, E.-H., *Heimatheer und Revolution 1918* (Stuttgart, 1981).

174 Tampke, J., *The Ruhr and Revolution. The Revolutionary Movement in the Rhenish-Westphalian Region, 1912–1919* (London, 1979).

175 Vincent, C. P., *The Politics of Hunger. The Allied Blockade of Germany, 1915–1919* (Athens, Ohio, 1985).

175a Wachs, F.C., *Das Verordnungswerk des Reichsdemobilmachungsamtes. Stabilisierender Faktor zu Beginn der Weimarer Republik* (Frankfurt, Berne, New York and Paris, 1991).

176 Winkler, H. A., *Die Sozialdemokratie und die Revolution 1918/19* (Bonn, 1979).

177 Zunkel, F., *Industrie und Staatssozialismus. Der Kampf um die Wirtschaftsordnung in Deutschland 1914–1918* (Düsseldorf, 1974).

IV   The Paris Peace Conference

178 Baumgart, W., *Vom Europäischen Konzert zum Völkerbund* (Darmstadt, 1974).

179 Birdsall, P., *Versailles Twenty Years After* (New York, 1941; repr. Hamden, Conn., 1962).

180 Bosl, K. (ed.), *Versailles-St Germain-Trianon* (Munich and Vienna; 1971).

181 Dickmann, F., *Die Kriegsschuldfrage auf der Friedenskonferenz von Paris 1919* (Munich, 1964). First published in *HZ*, vol. 197 (1963), pp. 1–101.

182 Dockrill, M. L., and Goold, J. D., *Peace without Promise. Britain and the Peace Conference 1919–23* (London, 1981).

183 Elcock, H., *Portrait of a Decision. The Council of Four and the Treaty of Versailles* (London, 1972).

184 Floto, J., *Colonel House in Paris. A Study of American Policy at the Paris Peace Conference 1919* (Princeton, NJ, 1980).

185 Gelfand, L. E., *The Inquiry. American Preparations for Peace 1917–1919* (New Haven, Conn., and London, 1963).

185a Goldstein, E., *Winning the Peace. British Diplomacy Strategy, Peace Planing, and the Paris Peace Conference 1916–1920* (Oxford, 1991).

186 Haupts, L., *Deutsche Friedenspolitik 1918–19* (Düsseldorf, 1976).

187 Helmreich, P. E., *From Paris to Sèvres. The Partition of the Ottoman Empire at the Peace Conference of 1919–1920* (Columbus, Ohio, 1974).

188 Jaffe, L. S., *The Decision to Disarm Germany. British Policy towards Postwar German Disarmament, 1914–1919* (Boston, London and Sydney, 1985).

189 Köhler, H., *Novemberrevolution und Frankreich. Die französische Deutschlandpolitik 1918–1919* (Düsseldorf, 1979).

190 Krüger, P., *Deutschland und die Reparationen 1918/19* (Stuttgart, 1973).

191 Krüger, P., 'Die Reparationen und das Scheitern einer Verständigungspolitik auf der Pariser Friedenskonferenz im Jahre 1919', *HZ*, vol. 221 (1975), pp. 326–75.

192 Low, A., *The Anschluss Movement, 1918–1919, and the Paris Peace Conference* (Philadelphia, 1974).

193 Lundgreen-Nielsen, K., *The Polish Problem at the Paris Peace Conference* (Odense, 1979).

194 Marks, S., *Innocent Abroad. Belgium at the Paris Peace Conference of 1919* (Chapel Hill, NC, 1981).

195 Mayer, A. J., *Politics and Diplomacy of Peacemaking. Containment and Counter-Revolution at Versailles 1918–1919* (London, 1967).

196 Miquel, P., *La Paix de Versailles et l'opinion publique française* (Paris, 1972).

197 Muhr, J., *Die deutsch-italienischen Beziehungen in der Ära des Ersten Weltkrieges (1914–1922)* (Göttingen, Frankfurt and Zurich, 1977).

198 Nelson, H. I., *Land and Power. British and Allied Policy on Germany's Frontiers 1916–1919* (London and Toronto, 1963).

199 Nelson, K. L., *Victors Divided. America and the Allies in Germany, 1918–1923* (Berkeley, Calif., 1975).

200 Perman, D., *The Shaping of the Czechoslovak State* (Leiden, 1961).

201 Renouvin, P., *Le Traité de Versailles* (Paris, 1969).

202 Rössler, H. (ed.), *Ideologie und Machtpolitik 1919. Plan und Werk der Pariser Friedenskonferenz 1919* (Göttingen, 1966).

203 Rothwell, V. H., *British War Aims and Peace Diplomacy 1914–1918* (Oxford, 1971).

204 Schober, R., *Die Tiroler Frage auf der Friedenskonferenz von Saint Germain* (Innsbruck, 1982).

*205 Schulz, G., *Revolutions and Peace Treaties, 1917–20* (London and New York, 1974).

*206 Schwabe, K., *Woodrow Wilson, Revolutionary Germany, and Peacemaking 1918–1919. Missionary Diplomacy and the Realities of Power* (Chapel Hill, NC, 1985).

207 Schwengler, W., *Völkerrecht, Versailler Vertrag und Auslieferungsfrage. Die Strafverfolgung wegen Kriegsverbrechen als Problem des Friedensschlusses 1919/20* (Stuttgart, 1982).

208 Steinmeyer, G., *Die Grundlagen der französischen Deutschlandpolitik 1917–1919* (Stuttgart, 1979).

209 Stevenson, D., *French War Aims against Germany 1914–1919* (Oxford, 1982).

210 Thompson, J. M., *Russia, Bolshevism and the Versailles Peace* (Princeton, NJ, 1966).

211 Tillman, S. P., *Anglo-American Relations at the Paris Peace Conference of 1919* (Princeton, NJ, 1961).

212 Ullman, R., *Anglo-Soviet Relations, 1917–1921*, 3 vols (Princeton, NJ, 1961–72).

213 Viefhaus, E., *Die Minderheitenfrage und die Entstehung der Minderheitenschutzverträge auf der Pariser Friedenskonferenz 1919* (Würzburg, 1960).

214 Walworth, A., *America's Moment: 1918. American Diplomacy at the End of World War I* (New York, 1977).

215 Wengst, U., *Graf Brockdorff-Rantzau und die aussenpolitischen Anfänge der Weimarer Republik* (Berne and Frankfurt, 1973).

216 Willis, J. F., *Prologue to Nuremberg. The Politics and Diplomacy of Punishing War Criminals of the First World War* (Westport, Conn. and London, 1982).

217 Wüest, W. E., *Der Vertrag von Versailles im Licht und Schatten der Kritik* (Zurich, 1962).

218 Živojinović, D. R., *America, Italy and the Birth of Yugoslavia (1917–1919)* (New York, 1972).

V International Relations, 1919–32

219 Bariéty, J., *Les Relations franco-allemandes après la première guerre mondiale, 10 novembre 1918–10 janvier 1925* (Paris, 1977).

220 Becker, J., and Hildebrand, K. (eds), *Internationale Beziehungen in der Weltwirtschaftskrise 1929–1933* (Munich, 1980).

221 Beitel, W., and Nötzold, J., *Deutsch-sowjetische Wirtschaftsbeziehungen in der Zeit der Weimarer Republik* (Baden-Baden, 1979).

221a Berg, M., *Gustav Stresemann und die Vereinigten Staaten von Amerika, Weltwirtschaftliche Verflechtung und Revisions-politik 1907–1929* (Baden-Baden, 1990).

222 Bournazel, R., *Rapallo, ein französisches Trauma* (Cologne, 1976).

223 Campbell, F. G., *Confrontation in Central Europe. Weimar Germany and Czechoslovakia* (Chicago, 1975).

224 Dohrmann, B., *Die englische Europapolitik in der Wirtschaftskrise 1921–1923* (Munich and Vienna, 1980).

225 Duroselle, M., *Les Relations franco-allemandes de 1914 à 1929*, 2 vols (Paris, 1969).

226 Düwell, K., *Deutschlands auswärtige Kulturpolitik, 1918–1932* (Cologne, 1976).

227 Dyck, H. L., *Weimar Germany and Soviet Russia 1926–1933* (New York, 1966).

228 Eichwede, W., *Revolution und internationale Politik. Zur kommunistischen Interpretation der kapitalistischen Welt 1921–1925* (Cologne and Vienna, 1971).

229 Enssle, M., *Stresemann's Territorial Revisionism. Germany, Belgium and the Eupen-Malmédy Question 1919–1929* (Wiesbaden, 1980).

230 Erdmann, K. D., 'Deutschland, Rapallo und der Westen', *VfZg*, vol. 11 (1963), pp. 105–65.

231 Fink, C., *The Genoa Conference, European Diplomacy, 1921–22* (Chapel Hill, NC and London, 1984).

232 Fleury, A., *La Pénétration allemande au Moyen-Orient 1919–1939. Le cas de la Turquie, de l'Iran et de l'Afghanistan* (Leiden, 1977).

233 Frommelt, R., *Paneuropa oder Mitteleuropa. Einigungsbestrebungen im Kalkül deutscher Wirtschaft und Politik 1925–1933* (Stuttgart, 1977).

234 Geyer, D. (ed.), *Osteuropa-Handbuch Sowjetunion, Aussenpolitik 1917–1955* (Cologne and Vienna, 1972).

235 Graml, H., 'Die Rapallo-Politik im Urteil der westdeutschen Forschung', *VfZg*, vol. 18 (1970), pp. 366–91.

236 Grieser, H., *Die Sowjetpresse über Deutschland in Europa 1922–1932* (Stuttgart, 1970).

237 Grundmann, K. H., *Deutschtumspolitik zur Zeit der Weimarer Republik. Eine Studie am Beispeil der deutsch-baltischen Minderheit in Estland und Lettland* (Hanover, 1977).

237a Grupp, P., *Deutsche Aussenpolitik im Schatten von Versailles 1918–1920* (Paderborn, 1988).

237b Hagspiel, H., *Verständigung zwischen Deutschland und Frankreich? Die deutsch-französische Aussenpolitik der zwanziger Jahre im innenpolitischen Kräftefeld beider Länder* (Bonn, 1987).

238 Hehn, J. von, Rimscha, H. von, and Weiss, H. (eds), *Von den Baltischen Provinzen zu den baltischen Staaten 1918–1920* (Marburg, 1977).

239 Heideking, J., *Areopag der Diplomaten. Die Pariser Botschafterkonferenz der alliierten Hauptmächte und die Probleme der europäischen Politik 1920–1931* (Husum, 1979).

240 Helbig, H., *Die Träger der Rapallo-Politik* (Göttingen, 1958).

241 Hildebrand, K., *Das Deutsche Reich und die Sowjetunion im internationalen System, 1918–1932* (Wiesbaden, 1977).

242 Hillgruber, A., *Grossmachtpolitik und Militarismus im 20. Jahrhundert* (Düsseldorf, 1974).

243 Hoepfner, H.-P., *Deutsche Südosteuropapolitik in der Weimarer Republik* (Frankfurt, 1983).

244 Holl, K., 'Europapolitik im Vorfeld der deutschen Regierungspolitik. Zur Tätigkeit proeuropäischer Organisationen in der Weimarer Republik', *HZ*, vol. 219 (1974), pp. 33–94.

245 Höltje, C., *Die Weimarer Republik und das Ostlocarno-Problem 1919–1934* (Würzburg, 1958).

246 Jacobson, J., *Locarno Diplomacy. Germany and the West, 1925–1929* (Princeton, NJ, 1972).

247 Jaworsky, R., *Vorposten oder Minderheit? Der sudetendeutsche Volkstumskampf in den Beziehungen zwischen der Weimarer Republik und der ČSR* (Stuttgart, 1977).

247a Kaiser, A., *Lord d'Abernon und die englische Deutschland-politik 1920–1926* (Frankfurt, Berne, New York and Paris, 1989).

248 Kimmich, C. M., *Germany and the League of Nations* (Chicago, 1976).

249 Krekeler, N., *Revisionsanspruch und geheime Ostpolitik der Weimarer Republik. Die Subventionierung der deutschen Minderheiten in Polen 1919–1933* (Stuttgart, 1973).

250 Krüger, P., 'Friedenssicherung und deutsche Revisionspolitik. Die deutsche Aussenpolitik und die Verhandlungen über den Kellogg-Pakt', *VfZg*, vol. 22 (1974), pp. 227–57.

251 Krüger, P., *Die Aussenpolitik der Republik von Weimar* (Darmstadt, 1985).

252 Lee, M., and Michalka, W., *German Foreign Policy, 1917–33: Continuity or Break?* (Leamington Spa, 1987).

253 Leffler, M. P., *The Elusive Quest. America's Pursuit of European Stability and French Security, 1919–1933* (Chapel Hill, NC, 1979).

254 Link, W., *Die amerikanische Stabilisierungspolitik in Deutschland 1921–1932* (Düsseldorf, 1970).

255 Link, W., 'Die Beziehungen zwischen der Weimarer Republik und den USA', in M. Knapp et al., *Die USA und Deutschland 1918–1975* (Munich, 1978), pp. 62–106.

256 Linke, H. G., *Deutsch-sowjetische Beziehungen bis Rapallo* (Cologne, 1970).

257 Luks, L., *Entstehung der kommunistischen Faschismustheorie. Die Auseinandersetzung*

der Komintern mit Faschismus und Nationalsozialismus 1921–1925 (Stuttgart, 1984).

258 McDougall, W. A., *France's Rhineland Diplomacy 1914–1924* (Princeton, NJ, 1978).

259 Maier, C., *Recasting Bourgeois Europe. Stabilization in France, Germany and Italy in the Decade after World War I* (Princeton, NJ, 1975).

260 Maxelon, M.-O., *Stresemann und Frankreich 1914–1929* (Düsseldorf, 1972).

260a Mayer, K.J., *Die Weimarer Republik und das Problem der Sicherheit in den deutsch-französischen Beziehungen, 1918–1925* (Frankfurt, Berne, New York and Paris, 1990).

261 Megerle, K., *Deutsche Aussenpolitik 1925. Ansatz zu aktivem Revisionismus* (Frankfurt, 1974).

262 Michalka, W., and Lee, M. M. (eds), *Gustav Stresemann* (Darmstadt, 1982).

262a Müller, H.J., *Auswärtige Pressepolitik und Propaganda zwischen Ruhrkampf und Locarno (1923–1925). Eine Untersuchung über die Rolle der Öffentlichkeit in der Aussenpolitik Stresemanns* (Frankfurt, 1991).

263 Nadolny, S., *Abrüstungsdiplomatie 1932/33. Deutschland auf der Genfer Konferenz im Übergang von Weimar zu Hitler* (Munich, 1978).

263a Orde, A., *British Policy and European Reconstruction after the First World War* (Cambridge, 1990).

264 Pieper, H., *Die Minderheitenfrage und das Deutsche Reich 1919–1933/34* (Hamburg, 1974).

265 Plieg, E.-A., *Das Memelland 1920–1939. Deutsche Autonomiebestrebungen im litauischen Gesamtstaat* (Würzburg, 1962).

266 Pogge von Strandmann, H., 'Grossindustrie und Rapallopolitik. Deutsch-sowjetische Handelsbeziehungen in der Weimarer Republik', *HZ*, vol. 222 (1976), pp. 265–341.

267 Pogge von Strandmann, H., 'Rapallo – Strategy in Preventive Diplomacy: New Sources and New Interpretations', in V. R. Berghahn and M. Kitchen (eds), *Germany in the Age of Total War* (London, 1981), pp. 123–46.

268 Pohl, K.-H., *Weimars Wirtschaft und die Aussenpolitik der Republik 1924–1926. Vom Dawes-Plan zum Internationalen Eisenpakt* (Düsseldorf, 1979).

269 Poidevin, R., and Bariéty, J., *Relations franco-allemandes 1815–1975* (Paris, 1977).

270 Post, G., *The Civil-Military Fabric of Weimar Foreign Policy* (Princeton, NJ, 1973).

270a Ratliff, W.G., *Faithful to the Fatherland. Julius Curtius and the Weimar Foreign Policy* (New York, 1990).

271 Recker, M.-L., *England und der Donauraum, 1919–1929. Probleme einer Europäischen Nachkriegsordnung* (Stuttgart, 1976).

272 Reikhoff, H. von, *German-Polish Relations, 1918–1933* (Baltimore, Md, 1971).

*273 Roos, H., *A History of Modern Poland* (London and New York, 1966).

273a Rosenthal, H.K., *German and Pole. National Conflict and Modern Myth* (Gainesville, Fla., 1976).

274 Rössler, H. (ed.), *Die Folgen von Versailles 1910–1924* (Göttingen, 1969).

275 Rössler, H., and Hölzle, E. (eds), *Locarno und die Weltpolitik 1924–1932* (Göttingen, 1969).

276 Schieder, T., 'Die Entstehungsgeschichte des Rapallo-Vertrags', *HZ*, vol. 204 (1967), pp. 545–609.

276a Schot, B., *Nation oder Staat? Deutschland und der Minderheitenschutz. Zur Völkerbundspolitik der Stresemann-Ära* (Marburg, 1988).

277 Schröder, H.-J., *Südosteuropa im Spannungsfeld der Grossmächte 1919–1939* (Wiesbaden, 1983).

278 Schuker, S. A., *The End of French Predominance in Europe. The Financial Crisis of 1924 and the Adoption of the Dawes Plan* (Chapel Hill, NC, 1976).

279 Stehlin, S. A., *Weimar and the Vatican 1919–1933* (Princeton, NJ, 1983).

280 Suval, S., *The Anschluss Question in the Weimar Era. A Study of Nationalism in Ger-*

many and Austria, 1918–1932 (Baltimore, Md, 1974).

281 Trachtenberg, M., *Reparation in World Politics: France and European Economic Diplomacy, 1916–1923* (New York, 1980).

282 Wagner, G., *Deutschland und der polnisch-sowjetische Krieg 1920* (Wiesbaden, 1979).

283 Walsdorff, M., *Westorientierung und Ostpolitik. Stresemanns Russlandpolitik in der Locarno-Ära* (Bremen, 1971).

284 Walters, F. P., *A History of the League of Nations*, 2 vols (1st edn, London, 1952; 2nd edn, London and New York, 1965).

285 Weidenfeld, W., *Die Englandpolitik Gustav Stresemanns* (Mainz, 1972).

286 Weingartner, T., *Stalin und der Aufstieg Hitlers. Die Deutschlandpolitik der Sowjetunion und der Kommunistischen Internationale 1929–1934* (West Berlin, 1970).

287 Wurm, C. A., *Die französische Sicherheitspolitik in der Phase der Umorientierung 1924–1926* (Frankfurt, Berne and Las Vegas, Nev., 1979).

288 Zimmermann, L., *Deutsche Aussenpolitik in der Ära der Weimarer Republik* (Göttingen, 1958).

289 Zimmermann, L., *Frankreichs Ruhrpolitik. Von Versailles bis zum Dawesplan* (Göttingen, 1971).

VI Government, Reich and Länder; Main Internal Events

290 Arns, G., *Regierungsbildung und Koalitionspolitik in der Weimarer Republik 1919–1924* (Clausthal-Zellerfeld, 1971).

291 Becker, J., 'Joseph Wirth und die Krise des Zentrums während des 4. Kabinetts Marx (1927–1928)', *Zeitschrift für die Geschichte des Oberrheins*, vol. 109 (1961), pp. 361–482.

292 Becker, J., 'Brüning, Prälat Kaas und das problem einer Regierungsbeteiligung der NSDAP 1930–1932', *HZ*, vol. 196 (1963), pp. 74–111.

293 Benz, W., *Süddeutschland in der Weimarer Republik. Ein Beitrag zur deutschen Innenpolitik 1918–1923* (West Berlin, 1970).

294 Besson, W., *Württemberg und die deutsche Staatskrise 1928–1933* (Stuttgart, 1959).

295 Biewer, L., *Reichsreformbestrebungen in der Weimarer Republik* (Frankfurt and Berne, 1980).

296 Blaich, F., *Grenzlandpolitik im Westen 1926–1936. Die 'Westhilfe' zwischen Reichspolitik und Länderinteressen* (Stuttgart, 1978).

297 Büsch, O., Wölk, M., and Wölk, W. (eds), *Wählerbewegungen in der deutschen Geschichte. Analysen und Berichte zu den Reichstagswahlen 1871–1933* (West Berlin, 1978).

298 Conze, W., 'Die Krise des Parteienstaates in Deutschland 1929/30', *HZ*, vol. 178 (1954), pp. 47–83 (also in Jasper, no. 106).

298a Doose, G., *Die separatistische Bewegung in Oberschlesien nach dem Ersten Weltkrieg (1918–1922)* (Wiesbaden, 1987).

299 Ehni, H.-P., *Bollwerk Preussen? Preussen-Regierung, Reich-Länder-Problem und Sozialdemokratie 1928–1932* (Bonn, 1975).

300 Eimers, E., *Das Verhältnis von Preussen und Reich in den ersten Jahren der Weimarer Republik (1918–1923)* (West Berlin, 1969).

301 Eliasberg, G., *Der Ruhrkrieg von 1920* (Bonn, 1974).

302 Erdmann, K. D., *Adenauer in der Rheinlandpolitik nach dem Ersten Weltkrieg* (Stuttgart, 1966).

303 Erger, J., *Der Kapp-Lüttwitz-Putsch* (Düsseldorf, 1967).

304 Falter, J., Lindenberg, T., and Schumann, S., *Wahlen und Abstimmungen in der Weimarer Republik. Materialien zum Wahlverhalten 1919–1932* (Munich, 1986).

305 Fenske, H., *Wahlrecht und Parteiensystem* (Frankfurt, 1972).

306 Graf, C., *Politische Polizei zwischen Demokratie und Diktatur. Die Entwicklung der preussischen Politischen Polizei vom Staatsschutzorgan der Weimarer Republik zum Geheimen Staatspolizeiamt des Dritten Reiches* (West Berlin, 1983).

307 Grund, H., *'Preussenschlag' und Staatsgerichtshof im Jahre 1932* (Baden-Baden, 1976).

307a Gusy, C., *Weimar – die wehrlose Republik? Verfassungsschutzrecht und Verfassungsschutz in der Weimarer Republik* (Tübingen, 1991).

308 Haungs, P., *Reichspräsident und parlamentarische Kabinettsregierung. Eine Studie zum Regierungssystem der Weimarer Republik in den Jahren 1924 bis 1929* (Cologne, 1968).

309 Hauss, H.-J., *Die erste Volkswahl des deutschen Reichspräsidenten* (Kallmünz, 1965).

310 Henschel, V., *Weimars letzte Monate* (Düsseldorf, 1978).

311 Holzer, J., *Parteien und Massen. Die politische Krise in Deutschland 1928–1930* (Wiesbaden, 1975).

312 Hörster-Philipps, U., *Konservative Politik in der Endphase der Weimarer Republik. Die Regierung Franz von Papen* (Cologne, 1982).

313 Jasper, G., *Der Schutz der Republik. Studien zur staatlichen Sicherung der Demokratie in der Weimarer Republik 1922–1930* (Tübingen, 1963).

314 Jasper, G., 'Justiz und Politik in der Weimarer Republik', *VfZg*, vol. 30 (1982), pp. 167–205.

314a Jung, O., *Direkte Demokratie in der Weimarer Zeit. Die Fälle 'Aufwertung', 'Fürstenenteignung', 'Panzerkreuzerverbot' und 'Youngplan'* (Frankfurt and New York, 1989).

315 Kirchheimer, O., *Political Justice. The Use of Legal Procedures for Political Ends* (Princeton, NJ, 1961).

316 Könnemann, E., and Krusch, H.-J., *Aktionseinheit contra Kapp-Putsch* (East Berlin, 1972).

317 Kühr, H., *Parteien und Wahlen im Stadt- und Landkreis Essen in der Zeit der Weimarer Republik* (Düsseldorf, 1973).

318 Laubach, E., *Die Politik der Kabinette Wirth 1921/22* (Lübeck, 1968).

319 Lepsius, R. M., 'From Fragmented Party Democracy to Government by Emergency Decree and National Socialist Takeover: Germany', in J. J. Linz and A. Stepan (eds), *The Breakdown of Democratic Regimes* (Baltimore, Md and London, 1978), pp. 34–79.

320 Lucas, E., *Märzrevolution 1920*, 3 vols (Frankfurt, 1970–8).

321 Ludewig, H. U., *Arbeiterbewegung und Aufstand. Eine Untersuchung zum Verhalten der Arbeiterparteien in den Aufstandsbewegungen der frühen Weimarer Republik 1920–1923* (Husum, 1973).

322 Milatz, A., *Wähler und Wahlen in der Weimarer Republik* (Neuwied, 1965).

323 Möller, H., *Parlamentarismus in Preussen 1919–1932* (Düsseldorf, 1985).

324 Mommsen, H., *Die Stellung der Beamtenschaft in Reich, Ländern und Gemeinden in der Ära Bruning', VfZg*, vol. 21 (1973), pp. 151–65.

325 Orlow, D., *Weimar Prussia 1918–1925. The Unlikely Rock of Democracy* (Pittsburgh, Pa, 1986).

325a Petersen, K., *Literatur und Justiz in der Weimarer Republik* (Stuttgart, 1988).

326 Reimer, K., *Rheinlandfrage und Rheinlandbewegung (1918–1933)* (Frankfurt, Berne and Las Vegas, Nev., 1979).

327 Rück, M., *Die freien Gewerkschaften im Ruhrkampf 1923* (Cologne, 1986).

328 Runge, W., *Politik und Beamtentum im Parteienstaat. Die Demokratisierung der politischen Beamten in Preussen zwischen 1918 und 1933* (Stuttgart, 1965).

329 Schaap, K., *Die Endphase der Weimarer Republik im Freistaat Oldenburg 1928–1933* (Düsseldorf, 1975).

330 Schanbacher, E., *Parlamentarische Wahlen und Wahlsystem in der Weimarer Republik. Wahlgesetzgebung und Wahlreform im Reich und in den Ländern* (Düsseldorf, 1982).

331 Schiffers, R., *Elemente direkter Demokratie im Weimarer Regierungssystem* (Düsseldorf, 1971).

332 Schmahl, H., *Disziplinarrecht und politische Betätigung der Beamten in der Weimarer Republik* (West Berlin, 1977).

333 Schulz, G., *Zwischen Demokratie und Diktatur. Verfassungspolitik und Reichsreform in der Weimarer Republik*, Vol. 1: *(1919–1930)* (West Berlin, 1963).

334 Schüren, U., *Der Volksentscheid zur Fürstenenteignung 1926* (Düsseldorf, 1978).

335 Steffani, W., *Die Untersuchungsausschüsse des Preussischen Landtages zur Zeit der Weimarer Republik* (Düsseldorf, 1960).

336 Stürmer, M., *Koalition und Opposition in der Weimarer Republik 1924–1928* (Düsseldorf, 1967).

336a Süss, M., *Rheinhessen unter französischer Besatzung. Vom Waffenstillstand im November 1918 bis zum Ende der Separatistenunruhen im Februar 1924* (Stuttgart, 1988).

337 Vogel, B., Nohlen, D., and Schultze, R.-O., *Wahlen in Deutschland 1848–1970* (West Berlin, 1971).

338 Witt, P.-C., *Reichsfinanzminister und Reichsfinanzverwaltung. Zum Problem des Verhältnisses von politischer Führung und bürokratischer Herrschaft in den Anfangs-jahren der Weimarer Republik 1918/19–1924.' VfZg*, vol. 23 (1975), pp. 1–16.

VII Parties, Churches, Organizations and Movements

339 Albertin, L., *Liberalismus und Demokratie am Anfang der Weimarer Republik. Eine vergleichende Analyse der Deutschen Demokratischen Partei und der Deutschen Volkspartei* (Düsseldorf, 1972).

340 Angress, W. T., *Die Kampfzeit der KPD 1921–1923* (Düsseldorf, 1973).

341 Aretz, J., *Katholische Arbeiterbewegung und Nationalsozialismus. Der Verband katholischer Arbeiter- und Knappenvereine Westdeutschlands 1923–1945* (Mainz, 1978).

342 Bahne, S., *Die KPD und das Ende von Weimar* (Frankfurt, 1976).

343 Bergsträsser, L., *Geschichte der politischen Parteien in Deutschland*, 11th edn (Munich, 1965).

344 Bock, H. M., *Syndikalismus und Linkskommunismus von 1918–1923. Zur Geschichte und Soziologie der Freien Arbeiter-Union Deutschlands (Syndikalisten), der Allge-meinen Arbeiter-Union Deutschlands und der Kommunistischen Arbeiter-Partei Deutschlands* (Meisenheim am Glan, 1969).

345 Breitman, R., *German Socialism and Weimar Democracy* (Chapel Hill, NC, 1981).

346 Dahm, K.-W., *Pfarrer und Politik. Soziale Position und Politische Mentalität des deutschen evangelischen Pfarrerstandes zwischen 1918 und 1933* (Cologne, 1965).

347 Döhn, L., *Politik und Interesse. Die Interessenstruktur der Deutschen Volkspartei* (Meisenheim am Glan, 1970).

348 Donat, H., and Holl, K. (eds), *Die Friedensbewegung. Organisierter Pazifismus in Deutschland, Österreich und der Schweiz* (Düsseldorf, 1983).

349 Drechsler, H., *Die Sozialistische Arbeiterpartei Deutschlands (SAPD)* (Meisenheim am Glan, 1965).

350 Evans, E. L., *The German Center Party, 1870–1933* (Carbondale, Ill., 1981).

351 Evans, R. J., *The Feminist Movement in Germany 1894–1933* (London, 1976).

352 Flechtheim, O. K., *Die KPD in der Weimarer Republik*, with introd. by H. Weber (Frankfurt, 1969).

353 Fowkes, B., *Communism in Germany under the Weimar Republic* (London, 1983).

354 Fricke, D. (chief ed.), *Die bürgerlichen Parteien in Deutschland*, 2 vols (Leipzig, 1968–70).

354a Frye, B.B., *Liberal Democrats in the Weimar Republic. The History of the German Democratic Party and the German State Party* (Carbondale and Edwardsville, 1985).

355 Gessner, D., *Agrarverbände in der Weimarer Republik* (Düsseldorf, 1976).

356 Geyer, D., 'Sowjetrussland und die deutsche Arbeiterbewegung 1918–1932', *VfZg*, vol. 24 (1976), pp. 2–37.

357 Giesecke, H., *Vom Wandervogel bis zur Hitlerjugend* (Munich, 1981).

358 Golombek, D., *Die politische Vorgeschichte des Preussenkonkordats (1929)* (Mainz, 1970).

359 Grathwol, R. P., *Stresemann and the DNVP* (Lawrence, Kans, 1980).

360 Greven-Aschoff, B., *Die bürgerliche Frauenbewegung in Deutschland 1894–1933* (Göttingen, 1981).

361 Hamel, I., *Völkischer Verband und nationale Gewerkschaft. Der deutschnationale Handlungsgehilfen-Verband 1893–1933* (Frankfurt, 1967).

362 Hartenstein, W., *Die Anfänge der Deutschen Volkspartei 1918–1920* (Düsseldorf, 1962).

363 Hertzman, L., *DNVP. Right-Wing Opposition in the Weimar Republic 1918–1924* (Lincoln, Nebr., 1963).

364 Hess, J. C., *'Das ganze Deutschland soll es sein'. Demokratischer Nationalismus in der Weimarer Republik am Beispiel der Deutschen Demokratischen Partei* (Stuttgart, 1978).

365 Hillgruber, A., 'Die politischen Kräfte der Mitte und die Auflösung der Weimarer Republik', in H. Bodensieck (ed.), *Preussen, Deutschland und der Westen. Festschrift O. Hauser* (Göttingen, 1980), pp. 155–75.

366 Hoepke, K. P., *Die deutsche Rechte und der italienische Faschismus* (Düsseldorf, 1968).

367 Holbach, H., *Das 'System Hugenberg'. Die Organisation bürgerlicher Sammlungspolitik vor dem Aufstieg der NSDAP 1918–1928* (Stuttgart, 1980).

368 Hömig, H., *Das preussische Zentrum in der Weimarer Republik* (Mainz, 1979).

369 Hunt, R. N., *German Social Democracy 1918–1933*, 2nd edn (Chicago, 1970).

370 Jacke, J., *Kirche zwischen Monarchie und Republik. Der preussische Protestantismus nach dem Zusammenbruch von 1918* (Hamburg, 1976).

371 Jonas, E., *Die Volkskonservativen 1928–1933* (Düsseldorf, 1965).

372 Jones, L. E., 'Sammlung oder Zersplitterung? Die Bestrebungen zur Bildung einer neuen Mittelpartei in der Endphase der Weimarer Republik', *VfZg*, vol. 25 (1977), pp. 265–304.

372a Jones, L.E., *German Liberalism and the Dissolution of the Weimar Party System, 1918–1933* (Chapel Hill, NC, and London, 1988).

373 Junker, D., *Die Deutsche Zentrumspartei und Hitler 1932/33* (Stuttgart, 1969).

374 Kaack, H., *Geschichte und Struktur des deutschen Parteiensystems* (Opladen, 1971).

374a Kaiser, J.C., *Sozialer Protestantismus im 20 Jahrhundert. Beiträge zur Geschichte der Inneren Mission 1914–1945* (Munich, 1989).

375 Kastning, A., *Die deutsche Sozialdemokratie zwischen Koalition und Opposition 1919 bis 1923* (Paderborn, 1970).

376 Kindt, W.; (ed.), *Die deutsche Jugendbewegung 1920 bis 1933. Die Bündische Zeit* (Düsseldorf, 1974).

376a Kolb, E., 'Die sozialdemokratische Strategie in der Ära des Präsidialkabinetts Brüning – Strategie ohne Alternative?', in U. Büttner (ed.), *Das Ünrechtsregime. Festschrift für W. Jochmann*, 2 vols (Hamburg, 1986), Vol. 1, pp. 157–76.

377 Krause, H., *USPD. Zur Geschichte der Unabhängigen Sozialdemokratischen Partei*

Deutschlands (Frankfurt, 1975).

378 Kruck, A., *Geschichte des Alldeutschen Verbandes 1890–1939* (Wiesbaden, 1954).
379 Laubscher, G., *Die Opposition im Allgemeinen Deutschen Gewerkschaftsbund (ADGB) 1918–1923* (Frankfurt, 1975).
380 Lepsius, R. M., 'Parteiensystem und Sozialstruktur. Zum Problem der Demokratisierung der deutschen Gesellschaft', in G. A. Ritter (ed.), *Deutsche Parteien vor 1918* (Cologne, 1973), pp. 56–80; first published in W. Abel *et al.* (eds), *Wirtschaft, Geschichte und Wirtschaftsgeschichte. Festschrift zum 65. Geburtstag von Friedrich Lütge* (Stuttgart, 1966), pp. 37–93.
381 Leuschen-Seppel, R., *Zwischen Staatsverantwortung und Klasseninteresse. Die Wirtschafts- und Finanzpolitik der SPD zur Zeit der Weimarer Republik unter besonderer Berücksichtigung der Mittelphase 1924–1928/9* (Bonn, 1981).
382 Liebe, W., *Die Deutschnationale Volkspartei 1918–1924* (Düsseldorf, 1956).
383 Lohalm, U., *Völkischer Radikalismus. Die Geschichte des Deutschvölkischen Schutz- und Trutz-Bundes 1919–1923* (Hamburg, 1970).
384 Luthardt, W. (ed.), *Sozialdemokratische Arbeiterbewegung und Weimarer Republik. Materialien zur gesellschaftlichen Entwicklung 1927–1933*, 2 vols (Frankfurt, 1978).
385 Matthias, E., and Morsey, R. (eds), *Das Ende der Parteien 1933* (Düsseldorf, 1960; 2nd edn, 1979).
386 Mommsen, H., 'Die Sozialdemokratie in der Defensive. Der Immobilismus der SPD und der Aufstieg des Nationalsozialismus', in idem (ed.), *Sozialdemokratie zwischen Klassenbewegung und Volkspartei* (Frankfurt, 1974), pp. 106–33.
387 Morgan, D. W., *The Socialist Left and the German Revolution. A History of the German Independent Socialist Democratic Party 1917–1922* (Ithaca, NY and London, 1975).
388 Morsey, R., *Die Deutsche Zentrumspartei 1917–1923* (Düsseldorf, 1966).
389 Morsey R., *Der Untergang des politischen Katholizismus. Die Zentrumspartei zwischen christlichem Selbstverständnis und 'Nationaler Erhebung' 1923/1933* (Stuttgart and Zurich, 1977).
389a Müller, W., Lohnkampf, Massenstreik, Sowjetmacht. *Ziele und Grenzen der 'Revolutionären Gewerkschafts-Opposition' (RGO) in Deutschland 1928–1933* (Cologne, 1988).
390 Neumann, S., *Die Parteien der Weimarer Republik*, 4th edn (Stuttgart, 1977); first published as *Die politischen Parteien in Deutschland* (Berlin, 1932).
391 Niewyk, D. L., *The Jews in Weimar Germany* (Manchester, 1980).
392 Nowak, K., *Evangelische Kirche und Weimarer Republik. Zum politischen Weg des deutschen Protestantismus zwischen 1918 und 1932* (Göttingen, 1981).
393 Opitz, G., *Der Christlich-soziale Volksdienst* (Düsseldorf, 1969).
393a Patch, W.L. Jr., *Christian Trade Unions in the Weimar Republic, 1918–1933* (New Haven, Conn., 1985).
394 Plum, G., *Gesellschaftsstruktur und politisches Bewusstsein in einer katholischen Region, 1928–1933. Untersuchungen am Beispiel des Regierungsbezirks Aachen* (Stuttgart, 1972).
395 Pois, R. A., *The Bourgeois Democrats of Weimar Germany* (Philadelphia, Pa, 1976).
396 Potthoff, H., *Gewerkschaften und Politik zwischen Revolution und Inflation* (Düsseldorf, 1979).
397 Priamus, H.-J., *Angestellte und Demokratie. Die nationalliberale Angestelltenbewegung in der Weimarer Republik* (Stuttgart, 1979).
397a Pyta, W., *Gegen Hitler und für die Republik. Die Auseinandersetzung der deutschen Sozialdemokratie mit der NSDAP in der Weimarer Republik* (Düsseldorf, 1989).
398 Raabe, F., *die Bündische Jugend* (Stuttgart, 1961).
399 Reisenberger, D., *Die katholische Friedensbewegung in der Weimarer Republik*

(Düsseldorf, 1976).

400 Ritter, G. A., 'Kontinuität und Umformung des deutschen Parteiensystems 1918–1920', in idem, *Arbeiterbewegung, Parteien und Parliamentarismus* (Göttingen, 1976), pp. 116–57.

401 Rosenhaft, E., *Beating the Fascists? The German Communists and Political Violence 1929–1933* (Cambridge, 1983).

401a Ruck, M., *Bollwerk gegen Hitler? Arbeiterschaft, Arbeiterbewegung und die Anfänge des Nationalsozialismus* (Cologne, 1988).

401b Ruppert, K., *Im Dienst am Staat von Weimar. Das Zentrum als regierende Partei in der Weimarer Demokratie 1923–1930* (Düsseldorf, 1992).

401c Schaefer, R., *SPD in der Ära Brüning: Tolerierung oder Mobilisierung? Handlungsspielräume und Strategien sozialdemokratischer Politik 1930–1932* (Frankfurt and New York, 1990).

402 Scheer, F.-K., *Die Deutsche Friedensgesellschaft (1892–1933)* (Frankfurt, 1981).

403 Schneider M., *Die Christlichen Gewerkschaften 1894–1933* (Bonn, 1982).

404 Schneider, W., *Die Deutsche Demokratische Partei in der Weimarer Republik 1924–1930* (Munich, 1978).

405 Sholder, K., *Die Kirchen und das Dritte Reich*, Vol. 1: *Vorgeschichte und Zeit der Illusionen 1918–1934* (Frankfurt, Berlin and Vienna, 1977).

406 Schönhoven, K., *Die Bayerische Volkspartei 1924–1932* (Düsseldorf, 1972).

407 Schönhoven, K., 'Zwischen Anpassung und Ausschaltung. Die Bayerische Volkspartei in der Endphase der Weimarer Republik 1932/33', *HZ*, vol. 224 (1977), pp. 340–878.

407a Schönhoven, K., *Reformismus und Radikalismus. Gespaltene Arbeiterbewegung im Weimarer Sozialstaat* (Munich, 1989).

408 Schumacher, M., *Mittelstandsfront und Republik. Die Wirtschaftspartei, Reichspartei des deutschen Mittelstandes 1919–1933* (Düsseldorf, 1972).

409 Schumacher, M., *Land und Politik. Eine Untersuchung über politische Parteien und agrarische Interessen 1914–1923* (Düsseldorf, 1979).

410 Schustereit, H., *Linksliberalismus und Sozialdemokratie in der Weimarer Republik. Eine vergleichende Betrachtung von DDP und SPD 1919–1930* (Düsseldorf, 1975).

411 Stoltenberg, G., *Politische Strömungen im schleswig-holsteinischen Landvolk 1918–1933* (Düsseldorf, 1962).

412 Striesow, J., *Die Deutschnationale Volkspartei und die Völkisch-Radikalen 1918–1922*, 2 vols (Frankfurt, 1981).

413 Stupperich, A., *Volksgemeinschaft oder Arbeitersolidarität. Studien zur Arbeitnehmerpolitik in der Deutschnationalen Volkspartei (1918–1933)* (Göttingen and Zurich, 1982).

414 Thimme, A., *Flucht in den Mythos. Die Deutschnationale Volkspartei und die Niederlage von 1918* (Göttingen, 1969).

415 Tjaden, K. H., *Struktur und Funktion der 'KPD-Opposition' (KPO). Eine organisationssoziologische Untersuchung zur 'Rechts'-Opposition im deutschen Kommunismus zur Zeit der Weimarer Republik* (Meisenheim am Glan, 1964).

416 Wächtler, J., *Zwischen Revolutionserwartung und Untergang. Die Vorbereitung der KPD auf die Illegalität in den Jahren 1929–1933* (Frankfurt, 1983).

417 Weber, H., *Die Wandlungen des deutschen Kommunismus. Die Stalinisierung der KPD in der Weimarer Republik*, 2 vols (Frankfurt, 1969).

418 Weber, H., *Hauptfeind Sozialdemokratie. Strategie und Taktik der KPD 1929–1933* (Düsseldorf, 1982).

419 Weber, H., *Kommunismus in Deutschland 1918–1945* (Darmstadt, 1983).

420 Wheeler, R. F., *USPD und Internationale* (Frankfurt, 1975).

421 Winkler, H. A., 'Unternehmerverbände zwischen Ständeideologie und National-

sozialismus', *VfZg*, vol. 17 (1969), pp. 341–71.

422 Winkler, H. A., 'Klassenbewegung oder Volkspartei? Zur Programmdiskussion in der Weimarer Sozialdemokratie 1920–1925', *GG*, vol. 8 (1982), pp. 9–54.

423 Winkler, H. A., *Von der Revolution zur Stabilisierung, Arbeiter und Arbeiterbewegung in der Weimarer Republik 1918 bis 1924* (Berlin and Bonn, 1984).

424 Winkler, H. A., *Der Schein der Normalität. Arbeiter und Arbeiterbewegung in der Weimarer Republik 1924 bis 1930* (Berlin and Bonn, 1985).

425 Wright, J. R. C., *'Above Parties'. The Political Attitudes of the German Protestant Church Leadership 1918–33* (London, 1974).

VIII Education, Culture and the Media; Ideologies

426 Bauer, W., *Wertrelativismus und Wertbestimmtheit in Kampf um die Weimarer Demokratie. Zur Politologie des Methodenstreites der Staatsrechtlehrer* (West Berlin, 1968).

427 Baumgartner, A., *Sehnsucht nach Gemeinschaft. Ideen und Strömungen im Sozialkatholizismus der Weimarer Republik* (Munich, 1977).

428 Becker, W., *Demokratie des sozialen Rechts. Die politische Haltung der Frankfurter Zeitung, der Vossischen Zeitung und des Berliner Tageblatts 1918–1924* (Göttingen, 1971).

429 Bergmann, K., *Agrarromantik und Grossstadtfeindschaft* (Meisenheim am Glan, 1970).

429a Bering, D., *Kampf um Namen. Bernhard Weiss gegen Joseph Goebbels* (Stuttgart, 1991).

430 Bölling, R., *Volksschullehrer und Politik. Der Deutsche Lehrerverein 1918–1933* (Göttingen, 1978).

430a Bolz, N., *'Auszug aus der entzauberten Welt.' Philosophischer Extremismus zwischen den Weltkriegen* (Munich, 1990).

431 Bosch, M., *Liberale Presse in der Krise. Die Innenpolitik der Jahre 1930 bis 1933 im Spiegel des 'Berliner Tageblatts', der 'Frankfurter Zeitung' und der 'Vossischen Zeitung'* (Frankfurt, 1976).

*432 Bracher, K. D., *The Age of Ideologies* (London and New York, 1984).

433 Breuning, K., *Die Vision des Reiches. Deutscher Katholizismus zwischen Demokratie und Diktatur (1929 bis 1934)* (Munich, 1969).

434 Bussmann, W., 'Politische Ideologien zwischen Monarchie und Weimarer Republik', *HZ*, vol. 190 (1960), pp. 55–77.

435 Campbell, J., *The German Werkbund. The Politics of Reform in the Applied Arts* (Princeton, NJ, 1978).

436 Döring, H., *Der Weimarer Kreis. Studien zum politischen Bewusstsein verfassungstreuer Hochschullehrer in der Weimarer Republik* (Meisenheim am Glan, 1975).

437 Dupeux, L., *'Nationalbolschewismus' in Deutschland 1919–1933* (Munich, 1985).

438 Faulenbach, B., *Ideologie des deutschen Weges. Die deutsche Geschichte in der Historiographie zwischen Kaiserreich und Nationalsozialismus* (Munich, 1980).

439 Fijalkowski, J., *Die Wendung zum Führerstaat. Ideologische Komponenten der politischen Philosophie Carl Schmitts* (Cologne, 1958).

440 Führ, C., *Zur Schulpolitik der Weimarer Republik. Die Zusammenarbeit von Reich und Ländern im Reichsschulausschuss (1919–1923) und im Ausschuss für Unterrichtswesen (1924–1933)* (Weinheim, 1970).

441 Gay, P., *Weimar Culture. The Outsider as Insider* (London, 1969).

442 Gollbach, M., *Die Wiederkehr des Weltkrieges in der Literatur. Zu den Frontromanen der späten zwanziger Jahre* (Kronberg am Taunus, 1978).

443 Grünthal, G., *Reichsschulgesetz und Zentrumspartei in der Weimarer Republik* (Düsseldorf, 1968).

443a Guttsman, W.L., *Workers' Culture in Weimar Germany between Tradition and Commitment* (New York, Oxford and Munich, 1990).

444 Hermand, J., and Trommler, F., *Die Kultur der Weimarer Republik* (Munich, 1978).

445 Holl, K., and Wette, W. (eds), *Pazifismus in der Weimarer Republik* (Paderborn, 1981).

446 Kater, M. H., *Studentenschaft und Rechtsradikalismus in Deutschland 1918–1933* (Hamburg, 1975).

447 Knütter, H.-H., *Die Juden und die deutsche Linke in der Weimarer Republik 1918–1933* (Düsseldorf, 1971).

448 Koerner, T. (ed.), *Weimars Ende. Prognosen und Diagnosen in der deutschen Literatur und politischen Publizistik 1930–1933* (Frankfurt, 1982).

449 Koszyk, K., *Deutsche Presse 1914–1945* (West Berlin, 1972).

450 Lane, B. M., *Architecture and Politics in Germany 1918–1945* (Cambridge, Mass., 1968).

450a Langewiesche, D. and Tenorth, H.-E. (eds), *Handbuch der deutschen Bildungsgeschichte, Vol. V, 1918–1945: Die Weimarer Republik und die nationalsozialistische Diktatur* (Munich, 1989).

451 Laqueur, W., *Weimar. A Cultural History, 1918–1933* (London and New York, 1974).

452 Lebovics, H., *Social Conservatism and the Middle Classes in Germany, 1914–1933* (Princeton, NJ, 1969).

453 Lepsius, R. M., *Extremer Nationalismus. Strukturbedingungen vor der nationalsozialistischen Machtergreifung* (Stuttgart, 1966).

454 Lerg, W. B., *Rundfunkpolitik in der Weimarer Republik* (Munich, 1980).

455 Lutzhöft, H.-J., *Der nordische Gedanke in Deutschland 1920–1940* (Stuttgart, 1971).

456 Meinck, J., *Weimarer Staatslehre und Nationalsozialismus* (Frankfurt, 1978).

457 Mohler, A., *Die konservative Revolution in Deutschland 1918–1932*, 2nd edn (Darmstadt, 1972).

458 Mosse, W. E., and Paucker, A. (eds), *Entscheidungsjahr 1932. Zur Judenfrage in der Endphase der Weimarer Republik* (Tübingen, 1965).

459 Müller, S. F., *Die Höhere Schule Preussens in der Weimarer Republik* (Weinheim, 1977).

459a Nachmansoh, D., and Schmid R., *Die grosse Ära der Wissenschaft in Deutschland 1900 bis 1933. Jüdische und nichtjüdische Pioniere in der Atomphysik, Chemie und Biochemie* (Stuttgart, 1988).

460 Paucker, A., *Der jüdische Abwehrkampf gegen Antisemitismus und Nationalsozialismus in den letzten Jahren der Weimarer Republik* (Hamburg, 1968).

460a Petro, P., *Joyless Streets. Women and Melodramatic Representation in Weimar Germany* (Princeton, NJ, 1989).

461 Petzold, J., *Wegbereiter des deutschen Faschismus. Die Jungkonservativen in der Weimarer Republik* (Cologne, 1978).

462 Prümm, K., *Die Literatur des soldatischen Nationalismus der 20er Jahre, 1918–1933*, 2 vols (Kronberg, 1974).

463 Ringer, F. K., *Die Gelehrten. Der Niedergang der deutschen Mandarine 1890–1933* (Stuttgart, 1983).

464 Schleier, H., *Die Bürgerliche deutsche Geschichtsschreibung der Weimarer Republik*, 2 vols (East Berlin, 1975).

465 Schluchter, W., *Entscheidung für den sozialen Rechtsstaat. Hermann Heller und die staatstheoretische Diskussion in der Weimarer Republik* (Cologne, 1968).

466 Schüddekopf, O.-E., *Linke Leute von Rechts. Die nationalrevolutionären Minderheiten und der Kommunismus in der Weimarer Republik* (Stuttgart, 1960).
466a Schürgers, N.J., *Politische Philosophie in der Weimarer Republik* (Stuttgart, 1989).
467 Schwarz, H.-P., *Der konservative Anarchist. Politik und Zeitkritik Ernst Jüngers* (Freiburg, 1962).
468 Schwierskott, H.-J., *Arthur Moeller van den Bruck und der revolutionäre Nationalismus in der Weimarer Republik* (Göttingen, 1962).
469 Sontheimer, K., *Antidemokratisches Denken in der Weimarer Republik. Die politischen Ideen des deutschen Nationalismus zwischen 1918 und 1933* (Munich, 1962; 2nd edn, 1968).
470 Sösemann, B., *Das Ende der Weimarer Republik in der Kritik demokratischer Publizisten. Th. Wolff, E. Feder, J. Elbau und L. Schwarzschild* (West Berlin, 1976).
471 Stern, F., *The Politics of Cultural Despair. A Study in the Rise of the Germanic Ideology* (Berkeley and Los Angeles, Calif., 1961).
472 Struve, W., *Elites against Democracy. Leadership Ideals in Bourgeois Political Thought in Germany, 1890–1933* (Princeton, NJ, 1973).
472a Vierhaus, R. and vom Brocke, B. (eds), *Forschung im Spannungsfeld von Politik und Gesellschaft. Geschichte und Struktur der Kaiser-Wilhelm-/Max-Planck-Gesellschaft* (Stuttgart, 1990).
472b Weindling, P., *Health, Race and German Politics between National Unification and Nazism, 1870–1945* (Cambridge, 1989).
472c Weinstein, J., *The End of Expressionism. Art and the November Revolution in Germany, 1918–19* (Chicago and London, 1990).
473 Wippermann, K. W., *Politische Propaganda und Staatsbürgerliche Bildung. Die Reichszentrale für Heimatdienst in der Weimarer Republik* (Bonn, 1976).
474 Wittwer, W., *Die Sozialdemokratische Schulpolitik in der Weimarer Republik* (West Berlin, 1980).

IX Economic and Social Matters

475 Abraham, D., *The Collapse of the Weimar Republic. Political Economy and Crisis* (Princeton, NJ, 1981).
475 Abraham, D., *The Collapse of the Weimar Republic. Political Economy and Crisis* (2nd edn, New York, 1986).
476 Aldcroft, D. H., *Die zwanziger Jahre. Von Versailles zur Wall Street 1919–1929* (Munich, 1978).
476a Bähr, J., *Staatliche Schlichtung in der Weimarer Republik. Tarifpolitik, Korporatismus und industrieller Konflikt zwischen Inflation und Deflation 1919–1932* (West Berlin, 1989).
476b Becker, H., *Handlungsspielräume der Agrarpolitik in der Weimarer Republik zwischen 1923 und 1929* (Stuttgart, 1990).
477 Blaich, F., *Die Wirtschaftskrise 1925/26 und die Reichsregierung. Von der Erwerbslosenfürsorge zur Konjunkturpolitik* (Kallmünz, 1977).
478 Böhret, C., *Aktionen gegen die 'kalte Sozialisierung' 1926–1930. Ein Beitrag zum Wirken ökonomischer Einflussverbände in der Weimarer Republik* (West Berlin, 1966).
479 Borchardt, K., *Wachstum, Krisen, Handlungsspielräume der Wirtschaftspolitik* (Göttingen, 1982).
480 Born, K. E., *Die deutsche Bankenkrise 1931* (Munich, 1967).
481 Bry, G., *Wages in Germany 1871–1945* (Princeton, NJ, 1960).
482 Bundesbank, Deutsche (ed.), *Währung und Wirtschaft in Deutschland 1876–1975* (Frankfurt, 1976).

483 Büsch, O., and Feldman, G. D. (eds), *Historische Prozesse der deutschen Inflation 1914–1924* (West Berlin, 1978).

484 Büttner, U., *Hamburg in der Staats- und Wirtschaftskrise 1928–1931* (Hamburg, 1982).

484a Büttner, U., 'Politische Alternativen zum Brüningschen Deflationskurs. Ein Beitrag zur Diskussion über "ökonomische Zwangslagen" in der Endphase von Weimar', *VfZg*, vol. 37 (1989), pp. 209–51.

484b Evans, R.J. (ed.), *The German Working Class 1888–1933* (London, 1982).

485 Feldman, G. D., *Iron and Steel in the German Inflation 1916–1923* (Princeton, NJ, 1977).

486 Feldman, G. D., *Vom Weltkrieg zur Wirtschaftskrise. Studien zur deutschen Wirtschafts- und Sozialgeschichte 1914–1932* (Göttingen, 1984).

487 Feldman, G. D., and Homburg, H., *Industrie und Inflation. Studien und Dokumente zur Politik der deutschen Unternehmer 1916–1923* (Hamburg, 1977).

488 Feldman, G. D., and Steinisch, I., 'Die Weimarer Republik zwischen Sozial- und Wirtschaftsstaat. Die Entscheidung gegen den Achtstundentag', *AfS*, vol. 18 (1978), pp. 353–439.

489 Feldman, G. D., and Steinisch, I., *Industrie und Gewerkschaften 1918–1924. Die überforderte Zentralarbeitsgemeinschaft* (Stuttgart, 1985).

489 Feldman, G. D., and Steinisch, I., *Industrie und Gewerkschaften 1918–1924. Die überforderte Zentralarbeitsgemeinschaft* (Stuttgart, 1985).

490 Feldman, G. D., Holtfrerich, C.-L., Ritter, G. A., and Witt, C. (eds), *Die deutsche Inflation* (Berlin and New York, 1982).

490a Feldman, G.D., Holtfrerich, C.-L., Ritter, G.A., and Witt, P.-C. (eds), *Konsequenzen der Inflation* (West Berlin, 1989).

491 Felix, D., *Walther Rathenau and the Weimar Republic. The Politics of Reparations* (Baltimore, Md, 1971).

492 Fischer, W., *Deutsche Wirtschaftspolitik 1918–1945*, 3rd edn (Opladen, 1968).

493 Flemming, J., *Landwirtschaftliche Interessen und Demokratie. Ländliche Gesellschaft, Agrarverbände und Staat 1890–1925* (Bonn, 1978).

494 Fraenkel, E., 'Der Ruhreisenstreit 1928–1929 in historisch-politischer Sicht', in Hermans and Schieder, no. 102.

494a Führer, K.C., *Arbeitslosigkeit und die Entstehung der Arbeitslosenversicherung in Deutschland 1902–1927* (West Berlin, 1990).

495 Geiger, T., *Die soziale Schichtung des deutschen Volkes* (Stuttgart, 1932; 2nd edn, Darmstadt, 1967).

496 Gessner, D., *Agrardepression und Präsidialregierungen in Deutschland 1930 bis 1933. Probleme des Agrarprotektionismus am Ende der Weimarer Republik* (Düsseldorf, 1977).

497 Glashagen, W., *Die Reparationspolitik Heinrich Brünings 1930–1931*, thesis (Bonn, 1980).

498 Gossweiler, K., *Grossbanken, Industriemonopole, Staat, Ökonomie und Politik des staatsmonopolistischen Kapitalismus in Deutschland 1914–1932* (East Berlin, 1971).

499 Grotkopp, W., *Die grose Krise. Lehren aus der Überwindung der Weltwirtschaftskrise 1929–1932* (Düsseldorf, 1954).

500 Grübler, M., *Die Spitzenverbände der Wirtschaft und das erste Kabinett Brüning* (Düsseldorf, 1982).

501 Habedank, H., *Die Reichsbank in der Weimarer Republik* (East Berlin, 1981).

501a Hagemann, K., *Frauenalltag und Männerpolitik. Alltagsleben und gesellschaftspolitisches Handeln von Arbeiterfrauen in der Weimarer Republik* (Bonn, 1990).

502 Hardach, G., *Weltmarktorientierung und relative Stagnation. Währungspolitik in Deutschland 1924–1931* (West Berlin, 1976).

503 Hartwich, H.-H., *Arbeitsmarkt, Verbände und Staat 1918–1933. Die öffentliche Bindung unternehmerischer Funktionen in der Weimarer Republik* (West Berlin, 1967).

504 Helbich, W. J., *Die Reparationen in der Ära Brüning* (West Berlin, 1962).

505 Hertz-Eichenrode, D., *Politik und Landwirtschaft in Ostpreussen 1919–1930* (Cologne, 1969).

506 Hertz-Eichenrode, D., *Wirtschaftskrise und Arbeitsbeschaffung. Konjunkturpolitik 1925/26 und die Grundlagen der Krisenpolitik Brünings* (Frankfurt, 1982).

507 Holl, K. (ed.), *Wirtschaftskrise und liberale Demokratie* (Göttingen, 1978).

*508 Holtfrerich, C.-L., *The German Inflation 1914–1923. Causes and Effects in International Perspective* (West Berlin and New York, 1986).

509 Holtfrerich, C.-L., 'Alternativen zu Brünings Wirtschaftspolitik in der Weltwirtschaftskrise?', *HZ*, vol. 235 (1982), pp. 605–31.

510 Holz, K. A., *Die Diskussion um den Dawes- und Young-Plan in der deutschen Presse*, 2 vols (Frankfurt, 1977).

510a Hughes, M.L., *Paying for the German Inflation* (Chapel Hill, NC, and London, 1988).

511 James, H., *The Reichsbank and Public Finance in Germany 1924–1933* (Frankfurt, 1985).

512 James, H., *The German Slump. Politics and Economics 1924–1936* (Oxford, 1986).

513 Jochmann, W., 'Brünings Deflationspolitik und der Untergang der Weimarer Republik', in D. Stegmann, B.-J. Wendt and P.-C. Witt (eds), *Industrielle Gesellschaft und politisches System* (Bonn, 1978), pp. 97–112.

513a Kent, B., *The Spoils of War. The Politics, Economics, and Diplomacy of Reparations 1918–1932* (Oxford, 1989).

514 Kindleberger, C. P., *The World in Depression, 1929–1939* (New York, 1973).

515 Krohn, C.-D., *Stabilisierung und ökonomische Interessen. Die Finanzpolitik des Deutschen Reiches 1923–1927* (Düsseldorf, 1974).

516 Kroll, G., *Von der Weltwirtschaftskrise zur Staatskonjunktur* (West Berlin, 1958).

516a Kruedener, J. Baron von (ed.), *Economic Crisis and Political Collapse. The Weimar Republic 1924–1933* (New York, Oxford and Munich, 1990).

517 Kunz, A., *Civil Servants and the Politics of Inflation in Germany 1914–1924* (West Berlin, 1986).

518 Lederer, E., *Kapitalismus, Klassenstruktur und Probleme der Demokratie in Deutschland 1910–1940* (Göttingen, 1979).

518a Lee, W.R. and Rosenhaft, E. (eds), *The State and Social Change in Germany, 1880–1890* (New York, Oxford and Munich, 1990).

518b McNeil, W.C., *American Money and the Weimar Republic. Economics and Politics on the Eve of the Great Depression* (New York, 1986).

519 Marcon, H., *Arbeitsbeschaffungspolitik der Regierungen Papen und Schleicher* (Berne and Frankfurt, 1974).

520 Maurer, I., *Reichsfinanzen und Grosse Koalition. Zur Geschichte des Reichskabinetts Müllen (1928–1930)* (Berne and Frankfurt, 1973).

521 Moeller, R., *Peasants, Politics and Pressure Groups in War and Inflation. A Study of the Rhineland and Westphalia, 1914–1924* (Chapel Hill, NC, 1986).

522 Mommsen, H., *Klassenkampf oder Mitbestimmung. Zum Problem der Kontrolle wirtschaftlicher Macht in der Weimarer Republik* (Cologne, 1978).

523 Mommsen, H., Petzina, D., and Weisbrod, B. (eds), *Industrielles System und politische Entwicklung in der Weimarer Republik* (Düsseldorf, 1974; 2nd edn, 2 vols, Kronberg and Düsseldorf, 1977).

523a Mosse, W.E., *Jews in the German Economy. The German–Jewish Economic Élite, 1820–1935* (Oxford, 1987).

523b Mosse, W.E., *The German Jewish Economic Élite 1820–1935* (Oxford, 1989).

523c Mühlberger, D. (ed.), *The Social Basis of European Fascist Movements* (London, New

York and Sydney, 1987).

524 Müller, H., *Die Zentralbank, eine Nebenregierung. Reichsbankpräsident Hjalmar Schacht als Politiker der Weimarer Republik* (Opladen, 1973).

525 Neebe, R., *Grossindustrie, Staat und NSDAP 1930–1933. Paul Silverberg und der Reichsverband der Deutschen Industrie in der Krise der Weimarer Republik* (Göttingen, 1981).

526 Niehuss, M., *Arbeiterschaft in Krieg und Inflation. Soziale Schichtung und Lage der Arbeiter in Augsburg und Linz 1910 bis 1925* (Berlin and New York, 1985).

527 Nussbaum, M., *Wirtschaft und Staat in Deutschland während der Weimarer Republik* (East Berlin, 1978).

528 Panzer, A., *Das Ringen um die deutsche Agrarpolitik von der Währungsstabilisierung bis zur Agrardebatte im Reichstag im Dezember 1928* (Kiel, 1970).

529 Petzina, D., *Die deutsche Wirtschaft in der Zwischenkriegszeit* (Wiesbaden, 1977).

530 Petzina, D., Abelshauser, W., and Faust, A., *Sozialgeschichtliches Arbeitsbuch*, Vol. 3: *Materialien zur Statistik des Deutschen Reiches 1914–1945* (Munich, 1978).

530a Plumpe, G., *Die I.G. Farbenindustrie AG. Wirtschaft, Technik und Politik 1904–1945* (West Berlin, 1990).

531 Preller, L., *Sozialpolitik in der Weimarer Republik* (Stuttgart, 1949; 2nd edn, Düsseldorf, 1978).

532 Rebentisch, D., 'Kommunalpolitik, Konjunktur und Arbeitsmarkt in der Endphase der Weimarer Republik', in R. Morsey (ed.), *Verwaltungsgeschichte* (West Berlin, 1977), pp. 107–57.

533 Ritter, G. A., *Staat, Arbeiterschaft und Arbeiterbewegung in Deutschland* (West Berlin and Bonn, 1980).

534 Rupieper, H. J., *The Cuno Government and Reparations 1922–1923, Politics and Economics* (The Hague, 1979).

534a Sachsse, C./Tennstedt, F., *Geschichte der Armenfürsorge in Deutschland. Vol. 2: Fürsorge und Wohlfahrtspflege 1871–1929* (Stuttgart *et al.*, 1988).

535 Sanmann, H., 'Daten und Alternativen der deutschen Wirtschafts- und Finanzpolitik in der Ära Brüning', *Hamburger Jahrbuch für Wirtschafts- und Gesellschaftspolitik*, vol. 10 (1965), pp. 109–40.

535a Schildt, A. and Sywottek, A. (eds), *Massenwohnung und Eigenheim. Wohnungsbau und Wohnen in der Grossstadt seit dem Ersten Weltkrieg* (Frankfurt and New York, 1988).

536 Schneider, M., *Das Arbeitsbeschaffungsprogramm des ADGB. Zur gewerkschaftlichen Politik in der Endphase der Weimarer Republik* (Bonn, 1975).

537 Schneider, M., *Unternehmer und Demokratie. Die freien Gewerkschaften in der unternehmerischen Ideologie der Jahre 1918 bis 1933* (Bonn, 1975).

537a Schötz, H.O., *Der Kampf um die Mark 1923/24, Die deutsche Währungsstabilisierung unter dem Einfluss der nationalen Interessen Frankreichs, Grossbritanniens und der USA* (West Berlin and New York, 1987).

537b Schröter, V., *Die deutsche Industrie auf dem Weltmarkt 1929–1933* (Frankfurt, Berne, New York and Nancy, 1984).

538 Speier, H., *Die Angestellten vor dem Nationalsozialismus* (Göttingen, 1977).

538a Tenfelde, K. (ed.), *Arbeiter im 20. Jahrhundert* (Stuttgart, 1991).

539 Timm, H., *Die deutsche Sozialpolitik und Bruch der grossen Koalition im März 1930* (Düsseldorf, 1952; 2nd edn, 1982).

540 Trumpp, T., and Köhne, R. (eds), *Archivbestände zur Wirtschafts- und Sozialgeschichte der Weimarer Republik. Übersicht über Quellen in Archiven der Bundesrepublik Deutschland* (Boppard, 1979).

541 Tschirbs, R., *Tarifpolitik im Ruhrbergbau 1918–1933* (West Berlin and New York, 1986).

541a Unterstell, R., *Mittelstand in der Weimarer Republik* (Frankfurt, 1989).

542 Vetter, H. O. (ed.), *Vom Sozialistengesetz zur Mitbestimmung. Zum 100. Geburtstag von Hans Böckler* (Cologne, 1975).

543 Wee, H. van der (ed.), *The Great Depression Revisited* (The Hague, 1972).

544 Weisbrod, B., *Die Schwerindustrie in der Weimarer Republik* (Wuppertal, 1978).

545 Whalen, R. W., *Bitter Wounds. German Victims of the Great War, 1914–1939* (Ithaca, NY, 1984).

545a Wiedenhoeft, R., *Berlin's Housing Revolution. German Reform in the 1920s* (Ann Arbor, Mich., 1985).

546 Winkler, H. A., *Mittelstand, Demokratie und Nationalsozialismus. Die politische Entwicklung von Handwerk und Kleinhandel in der Weimarer Republik* (Cologne, 1972).

547 Winkler, H.-J., *Preussen als Unternehmer 1923–1932. Staatliche Erwerbsunternehmen im Spannungsfeld der Politik am Beispiel der Preussag, Hibernia und Veba* (Berlin, 1965).

548 Witt, P.-C., 'Finanzpolitik als Verfassungs- und Gesellschaftspolitik', *GG*, vol. 8 (1982), pp. 386–414.

549 Witt, P.-C., 'Inflation, Wohnungszwangswirtschaft und Hauszinssteuer', in L. Niethammer (ed.), *Wohnen im Wandel* (Wuppertal, 1979), pp. 385–407.

550 Wolffsohn, M., *Industrie und Handwerk im Konflikt mit staatlicher Wirtschaftspolitik? Studien zur Politik der Arbeitsbeschaffung in Deutschland 1930–1934* (West Berlin, 1977).

550a Woycke, J., *Birth Control in Germany 1871–1933* (London and New York, 1988).

551 Wulf, P., *Die politische Haltung des schleswig-holsteinischen Handwerks 1928–1932* (Cologne, 1969).

552 Zollitsch, W., 'Einzelgewerkschaften und Arbeitsbeschaffung: Zum Handlungsspielraum der Arbeiterbewegung in der Spätphase der Weimarer Republik', *GG*, vol. 8 (1982), pp. 87–115.

552a Zollitsch, W., *Arbeiter zwischen Weltwirtschaftskrise und Nationalsozialismus* (Göttingen, 1990).

X   The Reichswehr, Military Policy, Paramilitary Organizations, and Police

553 Bennett, E. W., *German Rearmament and the West, 1932/33* (Princeton, NJ, 1979).

554 Berghahn, V., *Der Stahlhelm. Bund der Frontsoldaten 1918–1935* (Düsseldorf, 1966).

555 Bird, K. W., *Weimar, the German Naval Officer Corps and the Rise of National Socialism* (Amsterdam, 1977).

556 Bucher, P., *Der Reichswehrprozess. Der Hochverrat der Ulmer Reichswehroffiziere 1929/30* (Boppard, 1967).

* 557 Carsten, F. L., *The Reichswehr and Politics, 1918 to 1933* (Oxford, 1966).

558 Deist, W., Messerschmidt, M., Volkmann, H.-E., and Wette, W., *Ursachen und Voraussetzungen der deutschen Kriegspolitik* (Vol. 1 of *Das Deutsche Reich und der Zweite Weltkrieg* (Stuttgart, 1979; translation in preparation).

559 Diehl, J. M., *Paramilitary Politics in Weimar Germany* (Bloomington, Ind., 1977).

560 Dülffer, J., *Weimar, Hitler und die Marine. Reichspolitik und Flottenbau 1920–1939* (Düsseldorf, 1973).

561 Flemming, J., 'Die Bewaffnung des "Landvolks". Ländliche Schutzwehren und agrarischer Konservatismus in der Anfangsphase der Weimarer Republik', *MGM*, vol. 26 (1979), pp. 7–36.

562 Geyer, M., *Aufrüstung oder Sicherheit. Die Reichswehr in der Krise der Machtpolitik 1924–1936* (Wiesbaden, 1980).

563 Gordon, H. J., *The Reichswehr and the German Republic 1919–26* (Princeton, NJ, 1957).

564 Guske, C., *Das politische Denken des Generals von Seeckt* (Lübeck, 1971).
565 Hansen, E. W., *Reichswehr und Industrie. Rüstungswirtschaftliche Zusammenarbeit und wirtschaftliche Mobilmachungsvorbereitungen 1923–1932* (Boppard, 1978).
566 Hornung, K., *Der Jungdeutsche Orden* (Düsseldorf, 1958).
567 Könnemann, E., *Einwohnerwehren und Zeitfreiwilligenverbände* (East Berlin, 1971).
568 Krüger, G., *Die Brigade Ehrhardt* (Hamburg, 1971).
568a Lessmann, P., *Die preussische Schutzpolizei in der Weimarer Republik* (Düsseldorf, 1989).
569 Mauch, H. J., *Nationalistische Wehrorganisationen in der Weimarer Republik. Zur Entwicklung und Ideologie des 'Paramilitarismus'* (Frankfurt and Berne, 1982).
570 Müller, K. H., and Opitz, E. (eds), *Militär und Militarismus in der Weimarer Republik* (Düsseldorf, 1978).
571 Nuss, K., *Militär und Aufrüstung in der Weimarer Republik* (East Berlin, 1977).
572 Rahn, W., *Reichsmarine und Landesverteidigung 1919–1928* (Munich, 1976).
573 Rohe, K., *Das Reichsbanner Schwarz Rot Gold* (Düsseldorf, 1966).
574 Salewski, M., *Entwaffnung und Militärkontrolle in Deutschland 1919–1927* (Munich, 1966).
575 Schildt, A., *Militärdiktatur mit Massenbasis? Die Querfrontkonzeption der Reichswehrführung um General von Schleicher am Ende der Weimarer Republik* (Frankfurt, 1981).
576 Schmädeke, J., *Militärische Kommandogewalt und parlamentarische Demokratie. Zum Problem der Verantwortlichkeit des Reichswehrministers in der Weimarer Republik* (Lübeck, 1967).
577 Schulze, H., *Freikorps und Republik 1918–1920* (Boppard, 1969).
578 Schuster, K. G. P., *Der Rote Frontkämpferbund 1924–1929* (Düsseldorf, 1975).
579 Vogelsang, T., *Reichswehr, Staat und NSDAP 1930–1932* (Stuttgart, 1962).
580 Wohlfeil, R., and Matuschka, E. Graf von, *Reichswehr und Republik 1918–1933* (Vol. III, section 6 of *Handbuch zur deutschen Militärgeschichte 1648–1939* (Frankfurt, 1970).

XI The National Socialist Movement before 1933

581 Allen, W.S., *The Nazi Seizure of Power: The Experience of a single German Town, 1922–1945* (2nd edn, New York, Toronto and Sydney, 1984).
582 Bessel, R., *Political Violence and the Rise of Nazism. The Storm Troopers in Eastern Germany 1925–1934* (New Haven, Conn. and London, 1984).
583 Böhnke, W., *Die NSDAP im Ruhrgebiet 1920–1933* (Bonn, 1974).
*584 Broszat, M., *The Hitler State. The Foundation and Development of the Internal Structure of the Third Reich* (London and New York, 1981).
585 Broszat, M., 'Soziale Motivation und Führerbindung des Nationalsozialismus', *VfZg*, vol. 18 (1970), pp. 392–409.
586 Broszat, M., 'Zur Struktur des NS-Massenbewegung', *VfZg*, vol. 31 (1983), pp. 52–76.
587 Broszat, M., *Die Machtergreifung. Der Aufstieg der NSDAP und die Zerstörung der Weimarer Republik* (Munich, 1984).
588 Childers, T., *The Nazi Voter. The Social Foundations of Fascism in Germany, 1919–1933* (Chapel Hill, NC, 1983).
589 Falter, J. W., 'Wer verhalf der NSDAP zum Sieg?', *Aus Politik und Zeitgeschichte*, B 28–29/79, 14 July 1979, pp. 3–21.
589a Falter, J.W., *Hitlers Wähler* (Munich, 1991).

590 Faust, A., *Der Nationalsozialistische Deutsche Studentenbund*, 2 vols (Düsseldorf, 1973).

591 Fischer, C., *Stormtroopers. A Social, Economic and Ideological Analysis, 1929–35* (London, 1983).

592 Franz-Willing, G., *Die Hitlerbewegung. Der Ursprung 1919 bis 1922* (Hamburg, 1962; 2nd edn, Preussisch Oldendorf, 1974).

593 Franz-Willing, G., *Krisenjahr der Hitlerbewegung, 1923* (Preussisch Oldendorf, 1975).

594 Franz-Willing, G., *Putsch und Verbotszeit der Hitlerbewegung. November 1923 bis Februar 1925* (Preussisch Oldendorf, 1977).

594a Fritzsche, P., *Rehearsals for Fascism. Populism and Political Mobilization in Weimar Germany* (New York and Oxford, 1990).

595 Gies, H., 'NSDAP und landwirtschaftliche Organisationen in der Endphase der Weimarer Republik', *VfZg*, vol. 15 (1967), pp. 341–76.

596 Giles, G. J., *Students and National Socialism in Germany* (Princeton, NJ, 1985).

597 Gordon, H. J., *Hitler and the Beer Hall Putsch* (Princeton, NJ, 1972).

598 Gordon, S., *Hitler, Germans, and the 'Jewish question'* (Princeton, NJ, 1984).

599 Gossweiler, K., *Kapital, Reichswehr und NSDAP 1919–1924* (Cologne, 1982).

600 Granzow, B., *A Mirror of Nazism. British Opinion and the Emergence of Hitler, 1929–1933* (London, 1964).

601 Grieswelle, D., *Propaganda der Friedlosigkeit. Eine Studie zu Hitlers Rhetorik 1920–1933* (Stuttgart, 1972).

602 Hambrecht, R., *Der Aufstieg der NSDAP in Mittel- und Oberfranken 1925–1933* (Nuremberg, 1976).

603 Hamilton, R. F., *Who Voted for Hitler?* (Princeton, NJ, 1982).

604 Herberle, R., *Landbevölkerung und Nationalsozialismus. Eine soziologische Untersuchung zur politischen Willensibildung in Schleswig-Holstein 1918–1932* (Stuttgart, 1963).

605 Hofmann, H. H., *Der Hitlerputsch. Krisenjahre deutscher Geschichte, 1920–1924* (Munich, 1961).

606 Horn, W., *Führerideologie und Parteiorganisation in der NSDAP, 1919–1933* (Düsseldorf, 1972; repr. under the title *Der Marsch zur Machtergreifung. Die NSDAP bis 1933*, Königstein/Düsseldorf, 1980).

607 Hüttenberger, P., *Die Gauleiter. Studie zum Wandel des Machtgefüges in der NSDAP* (Stuttgart, 1969).

*608 Jäckel, E., *Hitler's World View* (Cambridge, Mass., 1981).

609 Jamin, M., *Zwischen den Klassen. Zur Sozialstruktur der SA-Führerschaft* (Wuppertal, 1984).

610 Kater, M. H., *The Nazi Party. A Social Profile of Members and Leaders 1919–1945* (Oxford, 1983).

611 Kele, M. H., *Nazis and Workers. National Socialist Appeals to German Labor, 1919–1933* (Chapel Hill, NC, 1972).

*612 Kershaw, I., *Popular Opinion and Political Dissent in the Third Reich: Bavaria 1933–1945* (Oxford, 1983).

613 Kissenkoetter, U., *Gregor Strasser und die NSDAP* (Stuttgart, 1978).

614 Kocka, J., 'Ursachen des Nationalsozialismus', *Aus Politik und Zeitgeschichte*, B 25/80, 21 June 1980, pp. 3–15.

615 Koehl, R. L., *The Black Corps. The Structure and Power Struggles of the Nazi SS* (London, 1983).

616 Kuhn, A., *Hitlers aussenpolitisches Programm. Entstehung und Entwicklung 1919–1939* (Stuttgart, 1970).

617 Kühnl, R., *Die Nationalsozialistische Linke 1925–1930* (Meisenheim am Glan, 1966).

617a Longerich, P., *Die braunen Bataillone. Geschichte der SA* (Munich, 1989).

618 Maser, W., _Der Sturm auf die Republik. Frühgeschichte der NSDAP_, 2nd edn (Stuttgart, 1973).

619 Matzerath, H., and Turner, H. A., 'Die Selbstfinanzierung der NSDAP 1930–1932', _GG_, vol. 3 (1977), pp. 59–92.

620 Merkl, P., _Political Violence under the Swastika. 581 Early Nazis_ (Princeton, NJ, 1975).

620a Merkl, P., The Making of a Stormtrooper (Princeton, NJ, 1980).

620b Mühlberger, D., _Hitler's Followers. Studies in the Sociology of the Nazi Movement_ (London and New York, 1991).

621 Noakes, J., _The Nazi Party in Lower Saxony, 1921–1933_ (London, 1971).

622 Nyomarkay, J., _Charisma and Factionalism in the Nazi Party_ (Minneapolis, Minn., 1967).

623 Orlow, D., _The History of the Nazi Party_, Vol. 1: _1919–1933_ (Pittsburgh, Pa, 1969).

623a Paul, G., _Aufstand der Bilder – Die NS-Propaganda vor 1933_ (Bonn, 1990).

623b Reiche, E.G., _The Development of the SA in Nuremberg, 1922–1934_ (Cambridge, 1986).

624 Rhodes, J. M., _The Hitler Movement. A Modern Millenarian Revolution_ (Stanford, Calif., 1980).

625 Rietzler, R., _'Kampf in der Nordmark'. Das Aufkommen des Nationalsozialismus in Schleswig-Holstein (1919–1928)_ (Neumünster, 1982).

626 Rogowski, R., 'The Gauleiter and the Social Origins of Fascism', _Comparative Studies in Society and History_, vol. 19 (1977), pp. 399–430.

627 Schreiber, G., _Hitler. Interpretationen 1923–1983. Ergebnisse, Methoden und Probleme der Forschung_ (Darmstadt, 1984).

628 Stachura, P. D., _Nazi Youth in the Weimar Republic_ (Santa Barbara, Calif., 1975).

629 Stachura, P. D., 'Der kritische Wendepunkt? Die NSDAP und die Reichstagswahlen vom 20. Mai 1928', _VfZg_, vol. 26 (1978), pp. 68–99.

630 Stachura, P. D., _Gregor Strasser and the Rise of Nazism_ (London, 1983).

631 Stachura, P. D. (ed.), _The Nazi Machtergreifung_ (London, 1983).

632 Stegmann, D., _Zum Verhältnis von Grossindustrie und Nationalsozialismus 1930–1933'_, _AfS_, vol. 13 (1973), pp. 399–482.

633 Thamer, H.-U., _Verführung und Gewalt. Deutschland 1933–1945_ (West Berlin, 1986), pp. 9–228.

634 Turner, H. A., _Faschismus und Kapitalismus in Deutschland. Studien zum Verhältnis zwischen Nationalsozialismus und Wirtschaft_ (Göttingen, 1972).

635 Turner, H. A., 'Grossunternehmertum und Nationalsozialismus 1930–1933. Kritisches und Ergänzendes zu zwei neuen Forschungsbeiträgen', _HZ_, vol. 221 (1975), pp. 18–68.

636 Turner, H. A., _German Big Business and the Rise of Hitler_ (New York and Oxford, 1985).

637 Tyrell, A., _Vom 'Trommler' zum 'Führer'. Der Wandel von Hitlers Selbstverständnis zwischen 1919 und 1924 und die Entwicklung der NSDAP_ (Munich, 1975).

638 Werner, A., _SA und NSDAP. 'Wehrverband', 'Parteigruppe' oder 'Revolutionsarmee'? Studien zur Geschichte der SA und der NSDAP 1920–1933_, thesis (Erlangen/Nuremberg, 1964).

639 Wiesemann, F., _Die Vorgeschichte der nationalsozialistischen Machtübernahme in Bayern 1932/33_ (Munich, 1975).

640 Winkler, H. A., 'Mittelstandsbewegung oder Volkspartei? Zur Sozialen Basis der NSDAP', in W. Schieder (ed.), _Faschismus als soziale Bewegung_ (Hamburg, 1976), pp. 97–118.

XII Biographies

ADENAUER

641 Stehkämper, H. (ed.), *Konrad Adenauer, Oberbürgermeister von Köln* (Cologne, 1976).

BOLZ

642 Miller, M., *Eugen Bolz* (Stuttgart, 1951).

BÖSS

643 Engeli, C., *Gustav Böss. Oberbürgermeister von Berlin 1921–1930* (Stuttgart, 1971).

BRAUN

644 Schulze, H., *Otto Braun oder Preussens demokratische Sendung* (Frankfurt, 1977).

BRAUNS

645 Mockenhaupt, H., *Weg und Wirken des geistlichen Sozialpolitikers Heinrich Brauns* (Paderborn, 1977).

DIETRICH

646 Saldern, A. von, *Hermann Dietrich. Ein Staatsmann der Weimarer Republik* (Boppard, 1966).

EBERT

647 Witt, P.-C., *Friedrich Ebert. Parteiführer, Reichskanzler, Volksbeauftragter, Reichspräsident* (Bonn, 1982).

EISNER

648 Eisner, F., *Kurt Eisner. Die Politik des libertären Sozialismus* (Frankfurt, 1979).

ERZBERGER

649 Epstein, K., *Matthias Erzberger and the Dilemma of German Democracy* (Princeton, NJ, 1959).

HAASE

650 Calkins, K. R., *Hugo Haase. Democrat and Revolutionary* (Durham, NC, 1979).

HELFFERICH

651 Williamson, J. G., *Karl Helfferich, 1872–1924. Economist, Financier, Politician* (Princeton, NJ, 1971).

HEUSS

652 Hess, J. C., *Theodor Heuss vor 1933* (Stuttgart, 1973).

HINDENBURG

653 Dorpalen, A., *Hindenburg and the Weimar Republic* (Princeton, NJ, 1964).

654 Wheeler-Bennett, J., *Hindenburg. The Wooden Titan* (London and New York, 1967).

HITLER

655 Bullock, A., *Hitler. A Study in Tyranny* (London, 1964).
*656 Fest, J. C., *Hitler* (London and New York, 1974).

HUGENBERG
657 Leopold, J. A., *Alfred Hugenberg. The Radical Nationalist Campaign against the Weimar Republic* (New Heaven, Conn. and London, 1977).

JOSS
658 Wachtling, O., *Joseph Joos. Journalist, Arbeiterführer, Zentrumspolitiker* (Mainz, 1974).

KOCH-WESER
658a Papke, G., *Der liberale Politiker Erich Koch-Weser in der Weimarer Republik* (Baden-Baden, 1989).

LUPPE
659 Hanschel, H., *Oberbürgermeister Luppe. Nürnberger Kommunalpolitiker in der Weimarer Republik* (Nuremberg, 1977).

OSSIETZKY
660 Grossmann, K. R., *Ossietzky* (Munich, 1963).

PAPEN
661 Bach, J. A., *Franz von Papen in der Weimarer Republik. Aktivitäten in Politik und Presse. 1918–1932* (Düsseldorf, 1977).

RATHENAU
662 Berglar, P., *Walther Rathenau* (Bremen, 1970).
*663 Kessler, Count H., *Walther Rathenau* (London, 1929).
663a Schulin, E., *Walter Rathenau, Repräsentant, Kritiker und Opfer seiner Zeit* (Göttingen, 1979).

SCHACHT
664 Pentzlin, H., *Hjalmar Schacht. Leben und Wirken einer umstrittenen Persönlichkeit* (Berlin, Frankfurt and Vienna, 1980).
665 Simpson, A. E., *Hjalmar Schacht in Perspective* (The Hague, 1969).

SCHÄFFER
666 Wandel, E., *Hans Schäffer, Steuermann in wirtschaftlichen und politischen Krisen* (Stuttgart, 1974).

SCHLEICHER
666a Vogelsang, T., *Kurt von Schleicher. Ein General als Politiker* (Göttingen, Frankfurt and Zürich, 1965).

SEECKT
667 Meier-Welcker, H., *Seeckt* (Frankfurt, 1967).

SIMONS
668 Gründer, H., *Walter Simons als Staatsmann, Jurist und Kirchenpolitiker* (Neustadt an der Aisch, 1975).

STEGERWALD
669 Schorr, H. J., *Adam Stegerwald. Gewerkschaftler und Politiker der ersten deutsche Republik* (Recklinghausen, 1966).

STINNES

670 Wulf, P., *Hugo Stinnes. Wirtschaft und Politik 1918–1924* (Stuttgart, 1979).

STRESEMANN

671 Hirsch, F., *Stresemann* (Göttingen, 1978).
671a Koszyk, K., *Gustav Stresemann. Der kaisertreue Demokrat* (Cologne, 1989).
672 Thimme, A., *Gustav Stresemann* (Frankfurt, 1957).
673 Turner, H. A., *Stresemann and the Politics of the Weimar Republic* (Princeton, NJ, 1963).

WEBER

674 Mommsen, W. J., *Max Weber und die deutsche Politik 1890–1920* (Tübingen, 1959; 2nd edn, 1974).

WELS

675 Adolph, H. J. L., *Otto Wels und die Politik der deutschen Sozialdemokratie 1894–1939* (West Berlin, 1971).
676 Benz, W. and Graml, H. (eds), *Biographisches Lexikon zur Weimarer Republik* (Munich, 1988).
677 Morsey, R. (ed.), *Zeitgeschichte in Lebensbildern*, Vol. 1 (Mainz, 1973), including, among others, Erzberger, Porsch, Fehrenbach, Brauns, Wirth, Marx, Stegerwald, Held, Joos, Brüning and Kaas; Vol. 2 (Mainz, 1975) includes Papen; Vol. 3 (Mainz, 1979) includes J. Hess; Vol. 6 (Mainz, 1984) includes Gröber, Hermes and F. Schäffer.

Index